Haynes

Guitar
Playing
Manual

Contents

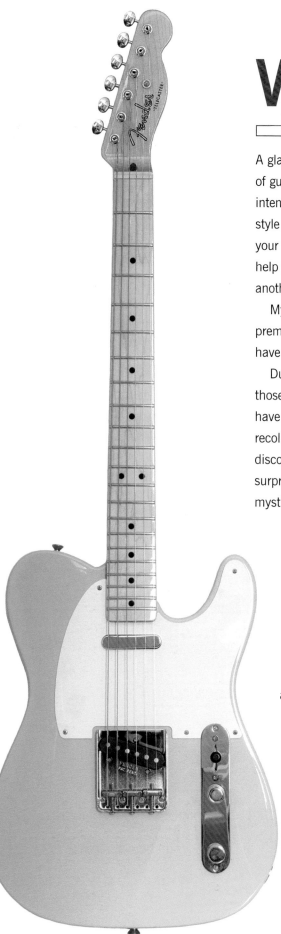

Why this book?

A glance around the shelves of any music store reveals no shortage of guitar instruction books. Some are very basic, and some are more intended for the advanced guitar student. Some specialise in a specific style of music or artist, whilst others are more general. Depending upon your requirements and preferences, there's certain to be something to help you along the way. So, why this book? Does the world really need another guitar manual?

My decision to compile this work was based upon one basic premise. To put it simply, it was designed to be the book I'd like to have had available when I was a beginner.

During my research the task was to recall my own problems from those early days and provide you with the answers, some of which have taken many years and frustrations to resolve. Added to these recollections were conversations with other guitarists in order to discover what their own stumbling blocks had been. Perhaps not too surprisingly many common factors began to emerge, and with the same mystified comment: 'Why does no one ever tell you about that?'

Well, the answers to your questions (even the ones you haven't learned enough to ask yet) are within these pages, all presented in a non-technical, easy-to-understand style.

In addition you'll find comprehensive instruction on how to keep your guitar in first class playing condition at all times, and how to put things right when they go wrong.

You'll learn why different types of guitar sound the way they do, and how simple variations in playing technique can radically alter the sound produced. Also included is information on guitar accessories such as tuners, effects units, transmitters, capos and, most basic but essential of all, the modest plectrum.

There's a comprehensive guide to chords, rhythm and lead guitar playing, and, if it isn't too terrifying to contemplate, how you can easily learn to read music.

There are tips on how to work out guitar parts from your favourite recordings, and when you're ready, how to get a position playing in a band.

Left: Fender Telecaster

How to get the most from this book

This book is designed to be read from start to finish, providing maximum benefit to the guitar student. However, depending upon your present level of ability you may prefer to read in a more selective manner. For instance, if you already play another instrument the section on reading music may be less applicable to you. Or, if you play guitar to some degree already, the beginners' section will probably be unnecessary, but you may wish to learn more about general guitar maintenance and perhaps explore some new playing techniques.

   Therefore, each chapter is not only a logical progression from the one which precedes it, but can also be read as a self-contained instructional in its own right.

   As you read through these pages you'll frequently encounter cross-references to other pages. These occur where a description or picture of a component may be of informative value. An example of this can be found almost immediately on the first page of Chapter 1, where the subject under discussion is the guitar pickup – the reference to **pages 184–89** tells you where more information on this subject can be located if required.

   Whatever your current level of proficiency or requirements, I'm confident that you'll find this to be an interesting, educational and entertaining read. So, let's get started.

Right: Fender Stratocaster

Getting started

Before becoming a guitar hero, the first thing you need to do is get yourself properly equipped for the job, and your ascent to superstardom will be somewhat easier if you get this right straight from the beginning. In this section of the book you will find all the necessary information to help you to avoid the pitfalls of wasting money on unsuitable or excessive musical equipment, or even just buying something which isn't right for your own intended musical style and the type of sound you wish to create.

At this stage of the game your equipment requirements will probably be limited. But, even so, it's much wiser, and entirely feasible, to purchase, for a modest financial outlay, guitar equipment of a sufficiently professional standard to ensure that it will continue to be of use for many years to come.

Buying a guitar

In purchasing a guitar it's important to ask yourself what you intend using it for. Do you want to sound like a wild heavy metal rocker? Do you prefer old style rock and roll? Perhaps you wonder how Hank Marvin produces that crystal clear distinctive tone. Or perhaps you enjoy many types of music and simply want a good quality, general-purpose instrument.

Broadly speaking, electric guitars fall into two basic categories: solid-body guitars and semi-acoustics. Of these, the solid-body is by far the most commonly used in rock music, its name deriving from the fact that its body contains no resonant cavities but instead relies entirely upon the pickup (see **pages 184–89** to produce its sound. On the other hand, the semi-acoustic is, as the name implies, a combination of both electric and acoustic guitar, which is clearly audible, if not at great volume, without amplification.

Solid-body guitars are extremely resistant to feedback (see **pages 164–65**) and therefore most advantageous if you intend playing at any serious volume levels. For this, and other, reasons (all-round versatility, convenience etc), I'd generally be inclined to recommend this type of guitar as the preferred option. However, since my requirements may not coincide with yours, here's a brief list of some well-known users of this type of guitar, which should help to give some idea of what I'm talking about.

Jimi Hendrix (Fender Stratocaster)

Eric Clapton (Fender Stratocaster)

Jimmy Page (Gibson Les Paul)

James Burton (Fender Telecaster)

John Lennon (Rickenbacker 325)

Albert Lee (Fender Telecaster)

Hank Marvin (Fender Stratocaster)

Single-coil (Fender Stratocaster) pickups

On the other hand, semi-acoustics have proved popular with:

George Harrison (Gretsch Country Gentleman)

Larry Carlton (Gibson ES 335)

Chuck Berry (Gibson 330 series)

B.B. King (Gibson ES 335)

Duane Eddy (Gretsch Chet Atkins)

Brian Setzer (Gretsch 6120)

Eddie Cochran (Gretsch 6120)

Twin-coil (Gibson Les Paul) pickups

Another important consideration is the choice between single-coil pickups or twin-coil (humbucker) pickups (see pictures above). To put it simply, single coils have a more biting, twangy sound, whilst twin coils have a heavier sound. In truth, both types have a fairly wide versatility; but if you mainly prefer to play heavy rock music, a guitar fitted with twin-coil pickups would likely be the preferred choice. Conversely, those who mainly play with a clean sound (Mark Knopfler, Hank Marvin etc) generally opt for the single coil.

When buying a first guitar, your knowledge of the subject is probably limited. This is why buying second-hand is not recommended, unless you can take an expert with you to check it out. Problems such as fret buzz or even a twisted neck (see **page 175**) could be overlooked by a novice, and might leave you stuck with an unusable instrument.

When buying new there are two choices: High Street stores or the Internet. The advantage of the latter option is obviously a potential saving on price. The disadvantages are that you cannot try out the instrument before buying, and it will be inconvenient if something goes wrong and you need to pursue their after-sales service, which may be hundreds of miles away.

Most High Street guitar retailers are generally reliable and, of course, convenient. Their sales staff are usually musicians themselves and will be happy to demonstrate the instrument in which you're interested.

The question of how much you wish to spend is likely to be an important consideration. Guitars can vary widely in price, with some being fairly inexpensive (£100) whilst others may be well over £1,000.

The more outrageous price tags don't necessarily denote vastly superior sound quality as compared to a decent mid-priced instrument (£450–£500). Sometimes you really are paying too much for a prestigious name.

So let's assume that you're a beginner with a modest budget, but naturally want a guitar that's well made and will be well up to gigging (playing in public) standard. Here are some good brands, these being companies which really don't make any rubbish guitars: Fender, Aria, Epiphone, Yamaha, and Washburn. I haven't mentioned certain other quality makes such as Gibson or Rickenbacker simply because they tend to be rather expensive.

Yamaha in particular have several lower-priced models of very good quality indeed, which are well up to a professional standard whilst often not exceeding the £200 mark. The same can be said of the Fender company, which produces the excellent Squier range of Stratocasters and Telecasters. It is probably unwise, in terms of quality, to consider anything much lower than the £150 price range. With so many guitars available, and more appearing all the time, this is obviously not an absolute statement, but it should help to steer the inexperienced buyer away from anything too doubtful.

However, if you really are on a tight budget there are several points to watch for in cheaper instruments, which require no specialist knowledge or prior experience:

1 Ensure that the machine heads (see pages 174 and 195) are smooth to operate, with no undue slack in the mechanism.

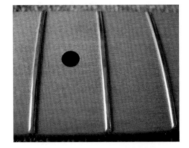

2 Check that there are no rough edges to the frets (see page 181).

3 Be sure that the bridge saddles (see pages 177 and 180) are well machined and have no loose-fitting screws.

4 If the action (see pages 175–79) is too high or too low for comfort and freedom from fret buzz, check that there's plenty of room for adjustment at the bridge.

5 Some cheaper pickups can be microphonic (see page 189). This isn't a desirable attribute.

Some of these can be corrected, but it's best not to start with any problems which may require specialist knowledge to put right.

All of this information may sound a bit daunting to the beginner, but it should be said that most guitars are very well constructed nowadays. So, when buying from a reputable dealer it's much easier to go right than wrong.

You'll notice that most guitars have more than one pickup, two or three being the norm depending upon the type of instrument. Humbucker (twin-coil) pickups are usually in pairs, whilst single-coil pickups are in sets of two or three. A Fender Stratocaster, for example, has three. This offers a wide range of sound options and tonal possibilities.

It's not that the three pickups are constructed differently from each other (exceptions apply), but rather it's where they're placed along the length of the string that is responsible for the variation in tone. A pickup placed near the bridge will produce a clear, cutting tone, whereas the pickup nearest to the neck will have a mellow, softer sound. A middle pickup, of course, will sound somewhere between these two extremes. There will also be a tone adjustment control to modify these options further.

Another interesting sound possibility is the fact that many guitars are fitted with a so-called 'tremolo' arm (see **pages 74, 182–83 and 203**). This is a spring-loaded pitch-bending mechanism, which many guitarists have featured as an integral part of their playing style, two notable examples being Hank Marvin and Jimi Hendrix. These devices, whilst useful, also have their shortcomings, and some players 'lock off' the mechanism (see **page 183–84**), with no intention of using it.

If you're naturally left-handed (see **page 225**) there's another point to be considered: do you decide to play a conventional right-handed guitar, whereby the right hand does the strumming and the left hand plays the fretboard, or will you require a guitar made for left-handed playing, whereby the left hand does the strumming and the right hand plays the fretboard? This may sound like a stupid question, but whilst there are left-handed people who do indeed play guitar left-handed (Paul McCartney, Tony Iommi), it's also true that there are lefties who play right-handed guitar (Mark Knopfler, B.B. King, Wilko Johnson, Noel Gallagher). So, bearing in mind that right-handed instruments are the more readily available, and often cheaper, of the two options, which would be the best approach?

In an attempt to resolve this question I recently attempted, as a right-handed player, to teach myself to play left-handed. I found that it was, in fact, no more difficult than when I first learned to play right-handed all those years ago, and, given the comparatively limited time involved, I progressed at a fairly normal rate of learning, and quickly built up a good repertoire of chords, riffs etc.

The fact is, since both hands must learn previously unaccustomed skills it probably doesn't matter which hand does what. But, against this, there are left-handed guitarists who claim that they simply couldn't learn to play right-handed. So this may be a very individual thing, or it may be all in the mind. Perhaps you can only decide by holding the instrument and seeing which feels most comfortable and natural to you.

One final consideration when trying out an electric guitar is to remember that whichever amplifier is being used for the demonstration will have a substantial effect upon the sound

Buying an acoustic guitar

If you're interested in buying an acoustic guitar, many of the same points apply as when choosing an electric. I refer to a fully acoustic instrument as opposed to the aforementioned semi-acoustic. Whereas a semi-acoustic is basically an electric guitar with some acoustic properties, the opposite is true of a traditional steel string acoustic instrument. This is primarily intended for use with no amplification other than its own soundbox. That said there are various ways of increasing its volume output whilst retaining the distinctive acoustic tone (see pages 187–88).

When purchasing this type of guitar, much of the same advice applies as with an electric. Obviously pickups aren't an issue, and the question of tonal quality is best decided by simply listening to the sound and volume which the instrument is capable of producing.

The more expensive acoustic guitars have soundboards (the part facing the strings with the large hole in it) made of book-matched timber, whereas models in the lower price range tend to have laminated soundboards. Still, these often have good tone quality and volume projection. Again, the best advice is simply to listen, and bear in mind most of the aforementioned advice regarding electrics (machine heads, fretwork, action etc).

quality produced, as will the playing skill of the person who may be demonstrating the instrument for you. If you hear the guitar through a £2,000 Mesa Boogie amplifier, then don't expect the sound to be quite so dynamic when played through a 10W practice amp.

Buying an amplifier

In the early stages of learning to play, it's quite possible to manage without any amplification at all. Even a solid-body guitar produces enough resonance to hear yourself playing at home. Indeed, many players practise this way most of the time. However, at some point in the near future you'll want to plug in and make some noise. So what should you buy and what will it cost?

The main controversy surrounding guitar amplification is the dispute over the varying merits of valve amps versus transistor amps. The long running story behind it goes like this.

Long, long ago, when Elvis was upsetting adults everywhere and the Beatles were still suffering from acne, all amps were powered by valves. At the time this was a bit of a nuisance, because valves break down from time to time and, being glass tubes, are susceptible to impact damage if not handled with reasonable care. Still, they did the job, and having no other option everyone accepted it. Eventually, however, technology moved on, and the transistorised circuit began to rule the world. Guitarists found this convenient and durable, and so gradually moved over to transistorised amplification, with the traditional valve amps taking something of a back seat for a number of years.

Guitarists, however, tend to be traditionalists in many ways, and steadily, as time passed, an appreciation for the 'old' sound began to grow. Musicians seeking to replicate the sound of early rockabilly, or perhaps the authentic Beatles or Hendrix guitar tones, realised that the old amps and other equipment had much to commend them after all. The search was on. Items such as the legendary Vox AC30 amp, or a Wem copycat tape echo (see **page 196–97**) became highly desirable equipment. If, on top of that, you could get hold of a genuine 1950s Fender Telecaster, or maybe a Gibson Les Paul from that era, you practically became an overnight legend on your local music scene.

Much of the preference and status accorded to valve amps was based upon their ability to supposedly produce a superior distortion sound. This gradually became the accepted wisdom, and any guitarist who valued his credibility dare not say otherwise.

So, how much truth is there in all of this? How much is fact and how much is myth?

I have, over the years, used both transistor and valve amplification and, laying myself open to the wrath and ridicule of 'serious musicians' everywhere, I have to say that I can't see much in it either way. A good quality guitar amp is going to produce an excellent sound, on clean tone and distortion, be it valve-powered or transistorised. Add to that

the more recent trend toward various 'amp simulation' (see **page 202**) alternatives and you will realise that the valve/transistor controversy has become generally less relevant anyway.

Another thing to bear in mind is that nowadays there are many pre-amp devices (see **page 196**) that can also create a first class overdrive/distortion sound. Many players, myself included, prefer to use these, and simply leave the amp itself on a clean (non-distorted) setting.

Try out a few different amplifiers, using your own guitar if possible, to see if you have any preference in the great valve/transistor debate, and then make your decision based upon what you hear, and not on what the salesman tries to promote.

Another important question is one of power, which essentially means how much volume are you going to need? Obviously this will depend upon where you're likely to be playing. It might also depend upon how the band you might join utilise their sound system (see **page 166**).

At home a small 10W practice amp, such as the model pictured here, is really more than enough. These small but useful amp/speaker units are often included as part of the deal when you purchase certain instruments in the lower price range. This type of amplifier, although of limited versatility and sound quality, will probably offer the usual choice of clean or distorted channels, and give you the opportunity to experience the feel of dynamics and tone of an amplified sound.

But let's say you're playing in a small to medium-sized club. In this environment a 50W combo-type amp should suffice. The term 'combo' (an abbreviation of the word 'combination') refers to a single unit combining the amplifier and loudspeaker(s) in one piece, as in the case of the Fender amp pictured here. In any larger room or medium-sized hall 100W should be entirely adequate for the job.

Although there's an understandable temptation to buy the biggest, most powerful amplifier you can afford, this isn't necessarily of any particular advantage. For one thing, there's simply no point in wasting money on more than you sensibly require; and there's also the additional burden of having to physically transport equipment which is often bigger, and therefore heavier, than is strictly necessary. When you've carried your gear in and out of various clubs, pubs etc a few times, believe me, you'll know what I'm talking about.

These examples regarding the range of power (volume) likely to be required assume that your guitar will be amplified only by its own amp/speaker unit. When you get to the level of playing large concert halls or outdoor arenas you'll be well past the point of worrying about amp size, as such places will doubtless have their own sound system.

Apart from combo amps there are also setups that feature the amplifier and speaker as separate units. However, the trend among most players is to opt for the convenience of a unit that combines the two.

What about price? Well, as with guitars, prices can range from reasonable (£250–£500) to ridiculous. Laney, Fender, Peavey, Marshall, and Line6 are all excellent makes, along with others – there are plenty to choose from. Don't rush things. Take your time and try some out. Remember that most places will discount for cash, and even more so if you should happen to buy your guitar and amp as a combined purchase.

Other essential equipment

Guitar tuner

There's one small, but absolutely priceless, unit which I would recommend very highly indeed. An electronic guitar tuner. These inexpensive items (£10–£20) are so useful for reliable pitch accuracy that no guitarist should ever be without one. This will be set to provide a tuning reference known as 'concert pitch', which is an agreed standard to which all fixed pitch instruments are tuned. It should be mentioned that although they're frequently an addition to multi-effect units, it's still very handy to own a small separate tuner for general use.

Plectrum(s)

The plural is actually 'plectra', but why quibble. Also known, perhaps more descriptively, as a guitar pick, the plectrum is a small, usually triangular piece of plastic (or occasionally other materials) used for strumming the strings. Although some guitarists prefer to use their fingers, there are certain styles for which a plectrum is more or less essential. They vary in thickness, but if you start out with a medium gauge (0.70mm approx), this will prove generally satisfactory. I suggest that you buy several, because you'll certainly lose them from time to time. Incidentally, if you play an acoustic guitar the lost plectrums often disappear into the sound hole. So when you don't see the missing pick on the floor, give the guitar a good shake. If it rattles you've found the missing plectrum.

Leads

Almost too obvious to mention, but it's no good having your new guitar and amp all ready to go, only to find that you've no cable to connect one to the other. Make certain they throw in a couple of leads when you buy the guitar.

Strap

Quite probably this will be included as part of the package when you acquire the guitar. If not you'll need to get one, unless you intend to always play whilst sitting down.

The basics – and much more

Okay, now you're ready to rock & roll, and this is where the fun (and the work) begins. It is always best to develop good habits and avoid bad ones early on. So this is where we discover the real musical essentials, such as accurate tuning and razor sharp timing, along with learning a substantial collection of chords and interesting rhythms. You will quickly and easily learn how to read chord charts, while understanding why some chords just naturally sound good together, and in this context we introduce the legendary 12- bar blues. You will have heard it many times on hundreds of classic recordings, and now you'll see how it's done.

In addition to all of this, we will be taking an introductory look at the significance of minor chords, and we'll delve into the mysteries of key transposition – soon to be a mystery no longer.

Tuning

Before attempting to play anything at all you must put your guitar in tune. So for this, and general reference purposes, you'll need to know how the strings are numbered, and how guitar strings produce their pitch.

Obviously they're numbered from one to six. But, contrary to what you might expect, number one is the thinnest string and number six is the thickest. So when you're holding your guitar in normal playing position, looking down, number six string is nearest and the first string farthest away. Guitar strings are traditionally tuned according to these notes: sixth string = E, fifth string = A, fourth string = D, third string = G, second string = B, first string = E. Although both the sixth and first strings are E notes, they're considerably different in pitch. This is because they're set two octaves apart (see **page 30**).

The pitch of a note produced by any string depends upon three factors: its length, its thickness, and its tension. Since all six strings are the same length that leaves only two variables; and when two different strings are placed under the same tension, the thicker of the two will produce the lower pitched note. As each string varies from the next in gauge (thickness) the principle of accurate tuning is simply to apply the correct amount of tension to each one. This is the purpose of the machine (tuning) heads (see **page 195**).

There are several methods by which the guitar can be tuned. By far the easiest and most accurate is to use an electronic guitar tuner (see **page 11**). Different makes vary slightly in operation, so refer to the instructions specific to your model. If you haven't yet acquired a tuner, my advice is to make this your next purchase. They're a considerable asset in every way, being a fast, reliable and efficient system. Truly one of the great guitar accessories.

An important point here, whatever your method of tuning: as you adjust the tension of any string it will begin to exert a greater or lesser force on the neck of the guitar – greater if you tune up, lesser if you tune down. And as this force changes it will slightly alter the tension, and therefore the pitch, of all the other strings. So if your guitar is significantly out of tune, you may need to adjust the respective string tensions to a notable degree. The result of this will be that whichever string you adjust first, by the time you've tuned the other five strings the one that you started with is likely to have altered its pitch to an undesirable margin of inaccuracy. The same applies to the others in varying degrees.

The remedy to this problem is to tune the strings gradually. For example, begin by tuning all strings slightly lower than the precise reference pitch. Then steadily, one by

one, tune them up to correct pitch. This minimises the effect of any tension changes on the guitar neck, and will result in perfect pitch accuracy for all six strings.

Notice that I refer to tuning strings 'up' to pitch, and never down. This is significant because it ensures that an even string tension is constantly maintained, whereas if you tune 'down' to pitch a certain degree of slack can occur, which will result in a slight drop in pitch accuracy when you apply normal playing pressure to the strings. So always begin by tuning each string a bit lower than required, and then tune up.

If you have no tuning reference handy – that is, no electronic tuner and no other tuning guide – you'll have to resort to another method. This is the system of relative tuning, by which your guitar will at least be in tune with itself, if not necessarily at perfect concert pitch (see **page 11**).

Along its entire length the guitar neck is divided into approximately 21 divisions by narrow steel bars called frets (see **page 195**). When playing, it is these frets that define the pitch of notes. And, like the strings, these frets are referred to by number (1st fret, 2nd fret etc). The 1st fret is nearest to the end with the tuning heads, all others being counted upward from there until you reach the highest number fret, nearest the body of the instrument.

When a string is sounded along its entire length – that is, not pressed down to the fretboard anywhere – this is called playing an 'open' string. This will be the lowest note that particular string can produce. However, when you press the string down to the fretboard at any point, this effectively shortens the available vibrating length of that string, causing it to sound a higher note.

Any guitar instruction, when describing how to play a certain note, will tend to phrase it by telling you to play 'at' a given fret number – for example, 'pressing down the fifth string at the 3rd fret will produce the note of **C**'. What this actually means is that you should apply the pressure just behind the fret (ie the side nearest the headstock), and not (as might easily be misunderstood by a novice) directly on top of the fret. So apply the pressure as illustrated on the next page, keeping close to the fret to ensure maximum efficiency with minimum effort.

Now, having established this information, we can return to the subject of tuning the guitar to relative pitch, without using a guitar tuner or other guide.

When tuning by this method you would select a 'reference' string from which to tune the other five. This reference string would be the one that you believe to be nearest to accurate pitch. If, for instance, two strings already

Apply pressure as shown here

And NOT as shown here

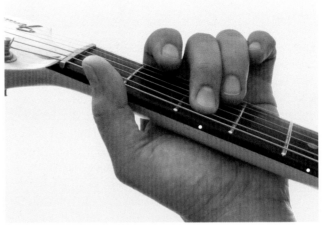

Using a plectrum

Handling a plectrum (pick) is relatively straightforward, but in order to prevent developing any bad habits that could hinder your progress later on, there are some points to be noted.

The plectrum is held between the thumb and index finger of your strumming hand, which we'll assume to be your right hand. If you're a left-handed player the opposite is obviously the case. Don't grip the plectrum too tightly as this can impair ease of movement, and possibly cause muscular aggravation over a period of time.

When you start strumming the guitar strings you'll find that this action tends to dislodge the plectrum from your fingers, causing you to drop it; and although this can be irritating, you mustn't be tempted to counter by increasing the strength of your grip. For one thing, it doesn't really solve the problem anyway, and it will prevent the plectrum from flowing smoothly across the strings. Holding a plectrum correctly is as much a question of balance as of grip, and don't worry, you'll soon get the feel of it.

happened to be more or less in tune with each other (from a previous tuning) this would suggest that they're likely to be fairly true to pitch. In this case either of these would be a good tuning reference guide.

You'll soon understand how to work from any string, but for ease of description we'll assume that your starting point is the lowest string, number six.

Press down the sixth string at the 5th fret. Now play this string, and at the same time play the fifth string 'open'. These two notes should be identical. If they're not, you must adjust the open fifth string until you've corrected the difference. Don't adjust the sixth string, remember, because this is your reference pitch.

OK, now repeat this procedure on the next-highest string. Press down the fifth string at the 5th fret, and then match the open fourth string to this note, by adjusting accordingly.

Next string please. Press the fourth string at the 5th fret and adjust the open third string to match.

So far so good. But there's a small difference on the next move. Play the third string at the 4th fret (yes, that's right, the 4th fret, not the 5th on this occasion) and match the open second string to this.

And now it's back to normal for the final move. So, play the second string at the 5th fret and match the open first string to this.

Tuning a guitar by ear can be tricky at first, but will improve with practice. And bear in mind that a small inaccuracy at any stage can become a cumulative error over the six strings, so take your time and proceed with careful diligence. Or, better still, invest in an electronic guitar tuner. You'll be glad you did.

There are sometimes reasons why a guitar may be more than usually difficult to tune. Problems are mostly caused by the instrument being badly 'set up' (poorly adjusted in some way). If you think this may apply to your guitar, don't panic; the subject is covered extensively later on in this book (see Chapter 9).

Some basic chords

A chord is the name given to a minimum of three notes when they're sounded together. And since a guitar has six strings this usually results in some notes being doubled or even tripled. A basic open position 'A' major chord, for example, consists of two A notes, one C# (pronounced 'C sharp') note, and three E notes.

At this stage, however, it isn't necessary to understand too much detail about chord construction. Much more important is to learn how to play some basic chords, and to know them by name.

Chord diagrams are pictured as below. (Left-handed players see **page 225**.)

Chord diagram (enlarged version)

D (D major)

'O' indicates a string to be played 'open'

Markers indicate where to place your fingers. The numbers recommend which finger to place in each position

'X' indicates a string not to be sounded in this chord

1   2   3   4

This assumes that you're looking over the neck of your guitar, with the headstock – where the tuners are – off to the left, but not pictured (to save space). So in a photograph this is what the above actually looks like. (For left-handed picture version, see **page 225**.)

Chords form the background to all forms of popular music. For this reason a sound knowledge of chords is essential for the aspiring guitarist. And the ability to change smoothly and effortlessly from one chord to another should be your first goal. So, let's consider three chords: A major, D major and E major, generally referred to as simply A, D and E.

There are numerous songs which can be played with just these three chords, including many of the classic early rock and roll recordings, which makes this a pretty good place to begin. (Left-handed illustrations of these chords are on **page 232**.)

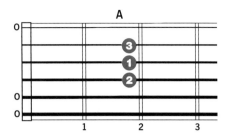

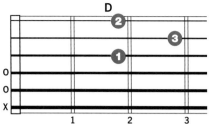

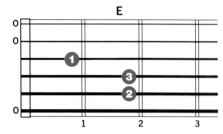

Practise the finger positions of each chord carefully. Be certain to place each finger at the position suggested in the diagram. This fingering is designed to permit the most efficient use of economical movement, and therefore make your chord changes as fluent as possible. To illustrate this point, you'll notice that the index (first) finger always remains in contact with the third string. Only the other two fingers move over to different strings when you change chords in this sequence. This might seem trivial, but it's a helpful point when you need to change between chords quickly.

As you begin to get the feel of each chord it's important to ensure that each note is sounding clearly and without obstruction. For instance, if you don't press a string down firmly enough on to the fretboard it won't sound with clarity. Also, be careful to avoid any finger accidentally touching strings you aren't intending it to touch, as this will mute (silence) a note which should be heard.

There are, however, certain situations in which muting can be used to your advantage. The D chord provides us with an example of this. In this chord you'll notice that the lowest string is marked with an 'X', indicating that it shouldn't be played as part of the chord. If it were played, this open string would sound an E note, which doesn't belong in a D major chord. Put simply, it would sound wrong. So you have to prevent this lowest string from being sounded whenever you're playing this particular chord. Obviously it wouldn't be possible to avoid striking this one note every time the plectrum sweeps across the strings, so there has to be another way. The answer is string muting.

As you hold down the strings to create the D chord, your hand will be wrapped around the guitar neck with your thumb resting along the top edge of the fingerboard (see photograph on **page 15**). All you have to do is to bring your thumb lightly into contact with the open E string in order to effect a muting (silencing) action to that particular note. Be careful not to apply any pressure on to this string or you could create a different unwanted sound. You only need make the slightest contact between thumb and E string to successfully prevent that string from vibrating. Then, no matter how enthusiastically you may be strumming, the string will be quite unable to produce any audible sound whatever.

When you're satisfied that you can play each chord correctly, the next step is to practise moving from one chord to another. This will be quite difficult at first, but you must persist in this until you can change between these three chords in any given order.

Take it slowly and acquire speed naturally as your fingers become familiar with the different chord 'shapes'. My advice is to repeat one chord change movement over and over again – A to D, A to D, A to D etc. Do this until you don't even need to think about it.

Around this time you'll notice your fingertips becoming sore from contact with the strings. When this happens it's best to give it a rest until tomorrow. This won't be a problem for very long. If you practise every day your fingers will toughen up in about two weeks.

Playing the chords

Now that you've begun to train your left hand in chord changes, it's time to pay some attention to what the right hand should be doing.

It's best to begin training your picking/strumming hand with some simple downward strokes of the plectrum. Play all the strings in one sweeping motion, and continue to repeat this action to a count of four – '1–2–3–4, 1–2–3–4,' and so on. Do this at a leisurely pace, and try to keep the count even. This will be harder to do when changing chords, and for this reason it's useful to work to some kind of timing device. In playing music, timing is an essential skill that must be acquired. This basically means playing a piece of music through from beginning to end without altering the tempo (speed) at any point. And if left to your own devices, this would most likely occur sooner rather than later, which is why the metronome was invented.

Timing

A metronome in its basic form is a clockwork device that produces a clear ticking sound at a regular pace. The speed at which it does this is widely adjustable, making it a valuable asset to any musician.

There are other, more elaborate timing devices that can be used for the same purpose, but a relatively inexpensive clockwork metronome is usually quite sufficient for practice at home. However, if you intend to practise at much beyond acoustic volume you'll need a timing device capable of being amplified. You may also need to move to a completely detached home far away from any irate neighbours.
So keep it fairly quiet and buy yourself a metronome. It's cheaper than a new house.

In order to communicate musical ideas it's necessary to understand some form of written language, so this is where we introduce the basic chord chart.

The diagram below presents a simplified version of written music, which will enable you to easily read any chord sequence in this book.

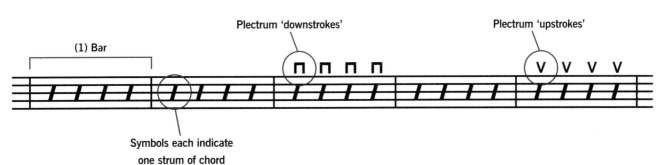

If written music were one long string of notes from start to finish, it would be almost unreadable. Therefore it is divided up into convenient little sections called 'bars', which make it much easier to understand. The number of 'beats' (counts) per bar can vary from one song to another. In most popular music the number of beats is usually four. These can be divided or joined in various ways, as you'll learn, in order to make for an interesting rhythmic pattern. But let's start here by playing a straight four beats to the bar, using the three chords with which you're presently familiar.

Study the following chord diagram, and play each chord in its turn as written above the bars. In this particular sequence all chords are played as 'downstrokes' of the plectrum.

Chord chart 1

This chord chart tells you exactly *what* to play, the metronome tells you *when* to play it. Set your metronome (or other timing device) to 100 beats per minute (bpm). If you find this too fast, slow down until you get the hang of it. Alternately, when you're confident playing at this tempo feel free to speed up as you wish, always aiming to keep in steady time by playing one downstroke for each click.

Although this is a fairly simple eight-bar piece, there are several things requiring your attention, such as keeping up an even plectrum stroke without dropping the pick; changing chords smoothly (and quickly) with precise fingering; and also staying in time with your metronome, if you're using one.

From time to time it's a good idea to check that your left hand is holding down the chord properly. Do this by sounding each string individually, to ensure a clear tone. If, despite your best efforts, you find that excessive finger pressure is required to hold down any (or all) of the strings, then your guitar may have a very high 'action'. To correct this, refer to **pages 175–79**.

OK, now that you've mastered your first basic sequence, let's make that rhythm a bit more interesting. Look at the next chord chart. Yes, the chord sequence and number of bars are the same as above, but what we've changed is the way the chords are played, by simply adding some upstrokes.

Notice here that a new symbol has been added. This indicates that two chord strokes should be played, where previously you played only one. So, although the tempo is the same these extra strokes create a more lively rhythm.

1 quarter note chord stroke
(4 per bar)

2 eighth note chord strokes
(8 per bar)

Chord chart 2

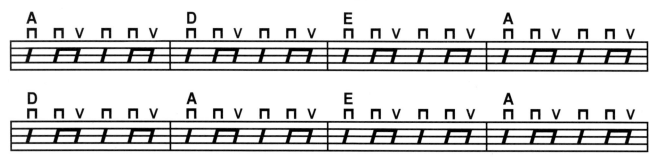

Instead of the plectrum playing four downstrokes to each bar, what we have now is a pattern that includes some alternating strokes, playing literally 'down, down-up, down, down-up'. This doesn't change the actual time required to play each beat of the bar, because beats two and four still only occupy one click of the metronome, as in the previous exercise. The difference is that when you play these beats, and make ready for the next downstroke, you simply bring the plectrum

into contact with the strings on the way back up again.

This may seem tricky at first, but you'll soon get the hang of it. And notice how that small adjustment makes the sound a lot more interesting.

Although I've again written only eight bars in this sequence, there's no need for you to stop or pause at the end. Continue to repeat this as many times as you wish, until you feel fully conversant with this new rhythm.

Twelve-bar blues

Probably the most famous chord sequence ever is the so-called '12-bar blues' format. Derived from a much earlier music source, this became the foundation of early rock and roll. Indeed, many of the major hit songs from that era were based entirely upon the 12-bar blues formula. Elvis, Buddy Holly, Chuck Berry and many others used this format extensively in their recordings, and no self-respecting guitar player's arsenal is complete without at least a reasonable familiarity with this style.

Before we get into this, let's look at an important variation on the basic major chord, namely the 'seventh' chord. So far we've been playing the E chord as a straight major chord; but very often, and especially when used in a sequence centred upon the key of A, the E will be played in what is known as an E7 chord. The way to change an E chord into an E7 chord is simplicity itself, as can be seen from the diagram opposite. (For left-handed version see page 232.)

E7

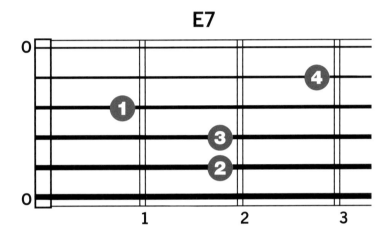

All that's changing here is the addition of your fourth (little) finger on to the second string at the 3rd fret. This is called E7 (pronounced 'E seventh'), because you're adding a D note into the chord, which is the (flatted) seventh note of the E major scale. More on scales later on, but for now just listen to the subtle but significant change in the sound.

If you find it difficult to make the stretch necessary for adding on your little finger, try this: instead of holding the guitar neck with your hand wrapped around it, just lower your grip position so that most of the pressure is maintained by the thumb. This will enable a wider finger spread and make things much easier for you.

Try this

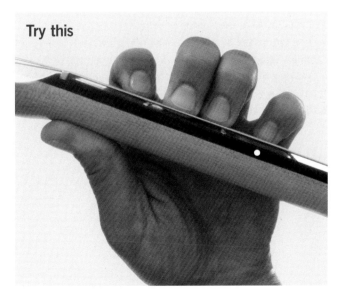

Instead of this

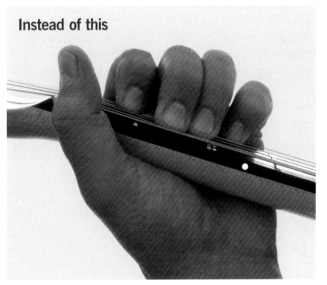

So let's make a big step here. A new chord sequence, a variation on the E chord, and even another new rhythm has been added. Pay careful attention and practise as slowly as you like until it all comes together. And don't forget to learn the correct pattern of up and down strokes.

If you should still be experiencing any difficulty with the actual chord changes, then just back up a little and take your time. You won't learn any faster by rushing things beyond your natural pace.

Chord chart 3

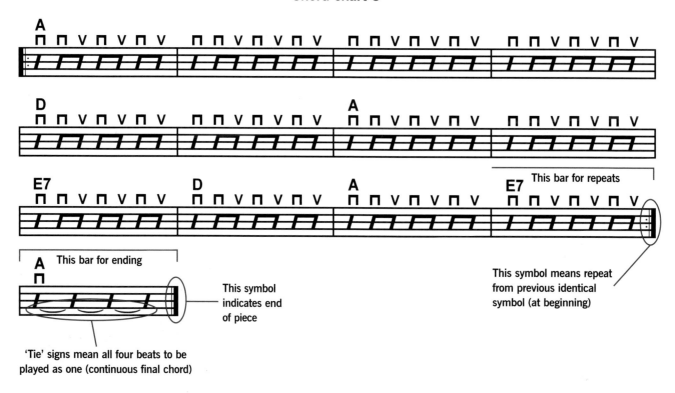

You can be certain that the 12-bar sequence would be played many times in any song, and this is why the 12th bar is an E7 chord, because it gives the feeling of leading into another verse. The A chord ending is used for the absolute end of the piece. It has a final, conclusive sound that would likely be played with one stroke and then left to fade into silence.

You'll notice that three new symbols have been added in this chord diagram. At the very beginning and after the final E7 chord is a double line mark with two small dots on the inner side. This is a standard musical repeat indicator, designed to prevent the need for writing the same thing over and over again. Then, at the very end of the piece, after the final A chord, is a similar symbol, but without the two dots. This signifies the conclusion of the entire song.

The third of the new symbols are the so-called 'tie' signs. As the name suggests, a tie sign connects one note with another. This simply means that you only need actually play the first chord, but it is left to sound for (in this case) four times as long, because it's 'tied' to three others of the same duration.

Some new chords

By now you're probably keen to play something in a different key (different pitch) other than **A**. So let's take a look at a traditional type of chord sequence in the key of **C**. For this you'll need to learn three new chords: **C**, **F** and **G7**. (Left-handed illustrations see **page 232**.)

Again, take careful note of which fingers go where, and be sure that each string is clearly sounding. Also, remember when you learnt how to mute the lowest string in order to silence it from the **D** chord? Use the same technique here when playing the **F** chord.

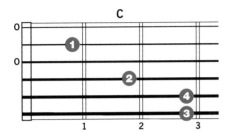
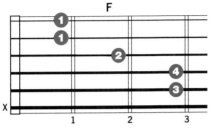
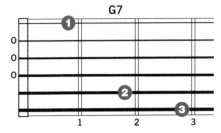

Your main difficulty in this case is likely to be holding down two strings with one finger. The trick here is to flatten your finger across these two strings, instead of pressing with the fingertips as usual. Most players recall this as one of their early problems, but they all overcame it quickly enough, and so will you.

A reminder, as you wrestle with the chord changes, to stay as relaxed as possible. Don't grip the plectrum too tightly, or tense your neck and shoulder muscles. Sometimes, because you'll be concentrating hard, these things can occur.

Here's a little warm-up exercise to get you started on these three chords. You'll be relieved to see that only the chords are new, and that you already know the rhythm pattern and other symbols from your previous work. Indeed, whilst you're learning the actual chord changes it's not always necessary to keep on strumming non-stop. Feel free to give your plectrum hand a rest for a while, and just go silently through the chord movements until they become easier.

In this photograph of an F chord you can see how the index (first) finger holds down two strings at the same time. Take special care to ensure that both strings (first and second) are held firmly on to the fretboard and that neither string is permitted to rattle against the frets due to insufficient grip.

Chord chart 4

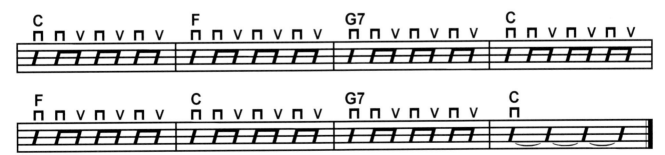

Remember, there's no absolute rule in these exercises with regard to the speed at which they should be played. Start out as slowly as you like. Get things right at a comfortable tempo and the speed will come naturally with improved confidence and experience.

It is, of course, understandable that you'll want to progress

quickly. No doubt you've been listening to your favourite guitar players and want to create that kind of sound yourself. But those musicians have been playing for many years (or decades), and didn't get to be that good by accident – they've all put in hours, days, weeks etc, of practise.

Transposing

To 'transpose' a song simply means to play it in a different key from the one in which it's presently written or recorded. As briefly mentioned earlier the word 'key' in musical terms refers to the pitch at which the music is performed.

There are a few reasons for changing the key of any given piece of music, but the most common of all is because people vary in their vocal range. And in order for a vocalist to give his or her best performance, the appropriate key must first be ascertained.

You already know the 12-bar chord sequence in the key of A, and as a first step toward understanding transposition let's suppose that your vocalist finds this too low for his voice. He might ask you to play it in another key. 'Let's try it in C,' he asks. A reasonable enough request, but what exactly does this require?

In basic chord terms this isn't too difficult to achieve, for just as A, D and E7 are the three chords required in the key of A, so too are C, F and G7 the chords necessary to do the same job in the key of C.

It's really a question of 'relative pitch'. For example, A has the same relationship to D as C and F have to each other. And the same applies regarding A and E7 which,

when transposed, would become C and G7. It's actually a case of moving all the notes in a song up or down by the same degree. But, due to the way in which chord shapes are formed on the neck of a guitar, this isn't always immediately apparent.

When you become familiar with all the notes along the guitar neck (page 30 – it's easier than you think), the mysteries of key transposition will be a mystery no longer. But as far as chords are concerned there's one rule you can learn right now: any chord, when transposed, always retains its harmonic integrity. This means that any major chord will always transpose into another major chord; a minor chord will always be a minor chord; a seventh chord will always be a seventh chord, and so on. In other words, the *type* of chord remains constant.

With all of this in mind, we return to our original goal – to transpose the 12-bar chord sequence into the key of C. And in doing this we can simply say that, for the purpose of conversion, the chord of A becomes C, whilst D becomes F, and E7 becomes G7. So now we can see our 12-bar sequence, essentially similar, but with a change of chords.

Chord chart 5

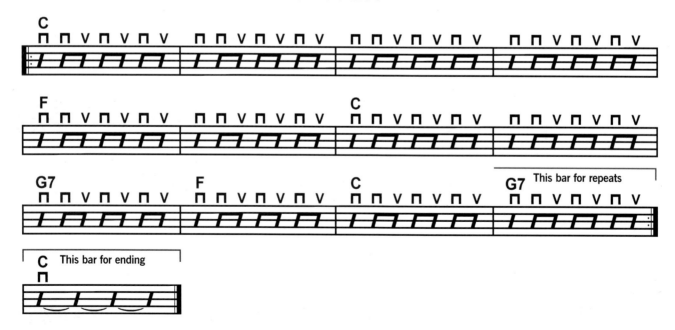

Minor chords

The number of songs based upon just three chords is truly immense. Certain styles of music, such as rock and roll, country, blues and heavy rock, depend largely upon a simplistic approach for their characteristic sound. But even for Buddy Holly, The Rolling Stones and Status Quo, there comes a time when a change of tonality is unavoidable.

Welcome to the world of minor chords. Where would a heartbroken ballad be without them? For, whilst major chords have a strong dynamic quality, the minor chord creates a rather more plaintive mood. And, although they add a new level of musical sophistication to your repertoire, they're no more difficult to learn than any major chord. In fact, your first minor chord will be the easiest lesson so far, and here's why.

Study the following two chord diagrams carefully – the **E** major chord with which you're already familiar, and your new chord **A** minor (written 'Am'). (For left hand, see **page 233**.)

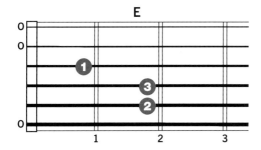
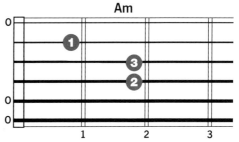

At a glance they almost appear to be the same chord. But closer examination reveals the crucial difference. In the **E** chord you hold down notes on the third, fourth and fifth strings, whereas in the **Am** chord you hold down notes on the second, third and fourth strings. So, your fingers are forming exactly the same 'shape', but that shape has simply been moved across by one string movement. It's almost like learning a new chord with no extra effort.

The chord of **Am** is most commonly used in the key of **C**, and is referred to as the 'relative minor' of that chord. So if you play it with the three chords you already know in that key sequence (**C**, **F**, **G7**), you'll hear how naturally it fits in with them.

The following chord pattern also includes a new rhythm that's played entirely as eight strokes to the bar. And watch out for the double downstrokes on the second beat of each bar.

Chord chart 6

With this type of chord sequence one verse just naturally leads into the other, and it feels as if you could continue endlessly. And, as with the 12-bar blues format, this four-chord repetition format has formed the basis of many songs. Often it's used as a two chords per bar pattern as below.

Chord chart 7

The only difference here is the quicker changing of chords required, so don't attempt it too fast at first. Steady but accurate is much better than fast and messy. Only you can monitor your own rate of progress, so make certain that you practise this to the point where it becomes effortless before moving on.

Some more open chords

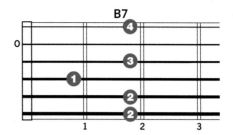

An interesting thing about chord knowledge is the fact that some of the chords learnt for one key sequence can also form part of the same pattern in a completely different key. What I mean is this: having learnt the chords of A, D and E (for example), you can play the 12-bar blues formula in the key of A. But in order to play that same chord sequence in the key of E you only need to learn one extra chord, which in this case is B7.

Also helpful to your progress is the fact that some new chords are no more than a slight variation on those that you already know, as you discovered when converting the E chord into an E7. So, having learnt only eight chords your knowledge is already becoming cumulative. As a useful example let's now learn the chord of B7, which will enable you to play the three-chord format in the key of E.

The difficult bit here is to hold down both the fifth and sixth strings with one finger. There's no particular technique involved in doing this, other than to flatten the fingertip slightly across the two strings. It's really just a question of practice and getting the feel of it. But if you really do find this too difficult, it's perfectly acceptable to leave out the lowest string completely by muting it, and playing

the B7 as a five-string chord. (For left hand see page 232.) When you've learnt this chord try using it by playing the 12-bar blues sequence in the key of E. I won't write this out for you because you know enough by now to experiment with various rhythms, and at whatever tempo you prefer. For the correct transposition sequence see below and compare to the previous keys.

Key	Chords
A	A – D – E7
C	C – F – G7
E	E – A – B7

Two more chords that can be learnt very easily are Em (E minor) and A7. This is because they're very close in fingering to the E and A chords. In both cases all you need do is to remove one finger from those two familiar chords and you've learnt two new ones. (For left hand see pages 232–33.)

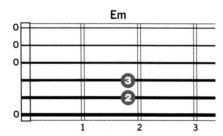

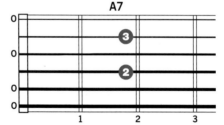

As you can see, these chords are formed by simply lifting away your first finger from its position on E and A respectively.

Your last three chords in this chapter are a bit more challenging, or perhaps more interesting, depending upon your point of view. (For left hand see pages 232–33.)

The challenge here is mainly with the G chord, and having

to reach across the full width of the guitar neck between your second and third fingers. When you're getting used to the actual fingering of this chord, practise moving back and forward between G and D7, remembering that your third finger stays on the first string in both chords. Don't make more work for yourself by lifting it away from the string; just slide it up and down.

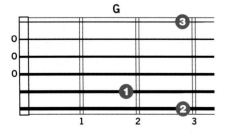

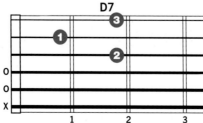

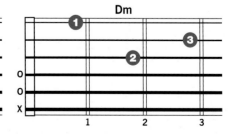

Where are we now?

You now have a working knowledge of 13 chord shapes, which is a very useful range to have at your command. With these chords it's possible to play basic versions of hundreds of popular songs.

But they're by no means just 'beginners' chords. They'll continue to be an important part of your musical repertoire. Below are some chord sequences that can be used to practise your chord range.

Chord chart 8

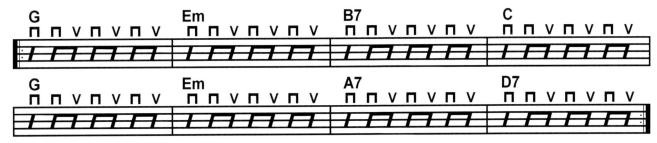

Chord chart 9

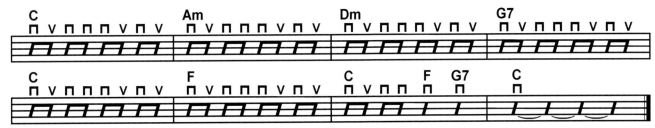

Let's round off this chapter with an interesting new rhythm, somewhat different to anything you've done so far. This looks complicated but is actually quite straightforward. As you see, there are three chord strokes together, and four of these will be played in each bar. Start by setting your metronome to approximately 60bpm (beats per minute, remember); or if you have no such timing device, try tapping a foot in time with the second hand of a clock. In other words, a fairly slow tempo. For every beat you should play three evenly spaced chord strokes: '1, 2, 3 – 1, 2,

3 – 1, 2, 3,' etc. This type of rhythm is known as a 'triplet', and the numeral '3' under the notes means that three notes (or chord strokes) are to be played in the space usually occupied by two. As seen below, this means three 'eighth' notes in place of two, but would also apply to notes of any other duration.

The triplet is an attractive and extremely useful rhythm that's most often (but not always) played at a slow tempo.

3 triplet time chord strokes (12 per bar)

Chord chart 10

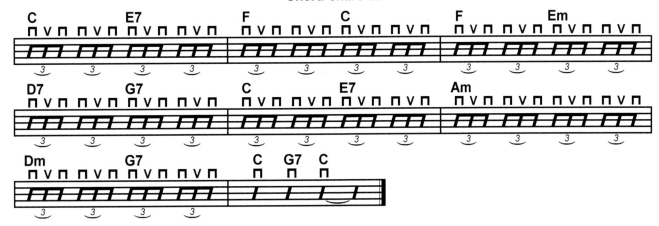

Adding to the essentials

Up to this point we have concentrated mainly upon the invaluable qualities of the guitar as a rhythm instrument, and building up an impressive repertoire of open chords. This is where we start to bring out the melodic characteristics of the instrument with the introduction of arpeggios. We will also learn some exciting new ways to apply an extra touch of musical magic, by simply understanding the importance of silence – that's the quiet bits in between all that frantic strumming – while continuing to add to your ever-growing list of new chords. It's also where you will learn the secrets of 'bar' chords, and every time you learn one of those you get another eleven chords thrown in for free. If that sounds too good to be true, just read on.

Arpeggios

An arpeggio is the term used to describe a chord when played as a succession of individual notes, as opposed to strumming all the strings together. This technique is used in various ways on countless songs, and in many different rhythmic patterns. Even the simplest arpeggio can enhance the backing to a considerable degree, by creating melody from straightforward chord playing.

In order to introduce you to the basics of this style we can begin by playing some open chords, using rhythm timing with which you already have some experience. The difference in reading these chord charts lies in the fact that the rhythm display is lighter, indicating single strings instead of full chords, and under each pick stroke you'll see a number. That number represents which string to play. In the **C** chord, for example, you start by playing the fifth string, followed by the fourth string, then the third, and so on.

Don't overcomplicate your approach to this. Simply draw the plectrum steadily across each string in turn, with downstrokes, and then back again with upstrokes as indicated on the diagram. Take care to keep your timing steady, and be sure that each note sounds clearly, with none being unintentionally muffled by inaccurate left-hand technique.

Chord chart 11

As played here, the arpeggio in each case begins on the 'root' (name) note of the chord. This simply means that the **C** chord arpeggio starts with the note of **C**, whilst the **Am** chord begins with an **A** note, and so on through to the **F** and **G7**. An arpeggio doesn't actually have to start on a root note in all cases, but this often does tend to sound musically appropriate.

A special point to notice occurs on the **G7** chord. This starts on the sixth string but doesn't continue, as might be expected, on to the fifth string. Instead, you skip over to the fourth string and continue the run of notes from there, leading back neatly into the **C** chord, for as many repetitions as you care to play.

Picking accuracy

Although this isn't a complicated exercise in some ways, it will become immediately apparent that the skill level requirements of the picking hand are far more demanding than for basic chord strumming. When playing a full chord it's hard to hit a wrong note, but when aiming for individual strings it's all too easy.

Needless to say, the only real answer to this problem is practice and persistence. But, having said that, there are some important points to consider which will ease the struggle somewhat.

First let's think about the coordination and stability of your forearm, wrist and hand, because basically there are three ways of driving the plectrum: forearm movement (from the elbow), wrist movement (rotation of the wrist), and finger and thumb movement.

Taking the last one first, finger and thumb action feels natural enough when fingerpicking (more on that subject later), but is rather movement limiting when using a plectrum. And alternately, full forearm motion, as when strumming from the elbow, has all the opposite effects – too much movement. This can work for chord rhythm playing, but with individual string picking it's hard to be accurate.

For the above reasons I recommend movement generated by the wrist, which affords both accuracy and flexibility. So, resting your forearm and wrist lightly across the body and bridge (see **page 195**) of your guitar, play the strings with light but definite movements of the wrist.

At first this may feel a bit difficult; but do resist the temptation of looking down at your picking hand to assist accuracy, as this would not be a helpful habit to get into. Instead, just do it by feel, until you begin to get the hang of it naturally. It does take a while for your brain to learn where the various strings are in relation to each other, but with constant repetition and diligence the message will soon get through.

Triplet arpeggios

An arpeggio can be fitted into any rhythmic pattern, and played in many different ways. Consider, for instance, how the exercise on the previous page might be played as a triplet rhythm. And in order to allow room for the string number under the picking sequence, and also to avoid any numbering confusion, I have, on this occasion, omitted the '3' symbol which would usually be shown to indicate a triplet, as seen on **page 25**.

Chord chart 12

It is important to take notice of the recommended up and down picking instructions, mainly for reasons of playing convenience. There's a tendency for relative beginners to feel more comfortable playing downstrokes than upstrokes. Presumably the laws of gravity have something to do with this.

When strumming a chord there's a difference in the sound produced by playing either down or up. A downstroke will accent the lower notes in a chord, whereas an upstroke does the opposite. But when playing single strings, as in arpeggios, the note will sound the same either way, so it makes sense to play in the direction of greater convenience and ease of approach. As you gain experience these up and down directions will become largely unnecessary, and you'll instinctively know what to do without really having to think about it.

A useful variation of this style is to create a pattern combining both single notes and chord strokes. The following is one of the most widely used of all rhythms, especially in country and folk music:

Chord chart 13

Simple but effective – an alternating bass note chord strum. But the real key to this lies in the playing of the second and fourth beats of each bar, where the chord occurs. The secret is to strum only the higher notes of the chord instead of all five (or six) strings, as would be usual. So, play the specified single string first, followed by the top three strings of that chord. This gives a crisper, more effective sound, and so adds an extra touch of professionalism to your playing. When you get the hang of this, so that it feels comfortable and easy to play, try the following variation on the above, wherein the second beat of every bar is played as a chord strum, and all the other notes as arpeggio.

Chord chart 14

Although these chord sequences are only four bars long, they can be repeated or varied in any way that you choose. They're really just samples to give you a start in arpeggio styles of playing. You can, once you understand the principle of these picking/strumming patterns, adapt them to any of the chord charts you've previously learned, or perhaps make up some of your own. Also consider playing them at different tempi (that's the posh plural of 'tempo'), or maybe varying the number of bars per chord. Whatever you do will be all in the name of good experience.

We'll explore arpeggios in greater detail later on, particularly in the context of fingerpicking styles, of which somewhat more complex arpeggios form a central part. Meanwhile, let's move onward and upward.

The guitar fretboard

Up to this point your musical adventures haven't taken you past the 3rd fret. In order to progress in a satisfactory manner beyond this, it's desirable that you begin to understand the positions of notes along the fretboard. Doing so will greatly increase your comprehension of all things musical, and inform you as to exactly what it is that you're playing. It's possible to learn something just by imitation and repetition, but it makes a lot more sense to understand why.

When you first consider the guitar neck it can seem a daunting task. Six strings and a range of more than 20 frets for each one adds up to a lot of notes to be learned, doesn't it?

Well, no, actually, it doesn't. You'll be pleased to know that there are only 12 notes to demand your attention. The entire range of western popular music consists of the following:

A - A♯ - B - C - C♯ - D - D♯ - E - F - F♯ - G - G♯

Every song you've ever heard is made up of a combination of these notes. The sign that looks like a hash mark (♯) is the sign meaning 'sharp' (ie F♯ is pronounced 'F sharp'). Conversely, there's also a sign that looks like a small letter B (♭), which is the sign meaning 'flat' (ie B♭ is pronounced 'B flat'). The sharp of any given note is also the flat of the next highest note (ie C♯ is the same as D♭). They are merely two ways of saying the same thing. So the range of notes above could also be written as below:

A - B♭ - B - C - D♭ - D - E♭ - E - F - G♭ - G - A♭

The reason for this apparently odd situation, of writing the same thing in two different ways, is to provide a certain convenience in written music, which will become clear later on. At the moment it's only important to be aware of this, or confusion would quickly arise when studying the guitar neck chart detailed overleaf. (Left-handed players see **page 225** for chart.) You'll also observe that the notes of **B** and **C**, along with the notes of **E** and **F**, have no sharps (or flats) between them. This is perfectly correct and not an oversight on my part.

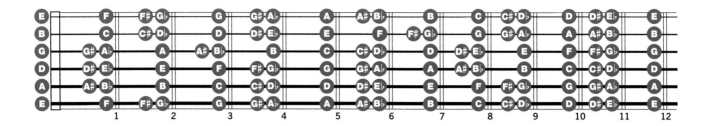

You should spend some time comparing this chart to the notes as they appear on your guitar so that you come to understand what it means. Always keep in mind that, in these illustrations, you're looking over your guitar neck, so the lowest (and thickest) string is nearest your viewpoint, and consequently at the bottom of the picture above. However, it isn't really necessary to make a deliberate effort to memorise all of these note positions before moving on, as this would be both confusing and extremely boring. This chart serves more as a continuing source of reference for your progress from here onward, and in this way you'll find that you acquire your fretboard knowledge quite naturally, without having to make a tedious effort to do so.

On the guitar fretboard you'll see that there are markers at certain points along the neck, at specific fret positions. Often simple 'dot' markers (see **page 195**), but sometimes more decorative pearl-type inlays, they all serve the same purpose – to distinguish certain fret positions from the many others. Without them it would be very easy to lose your way amid so many identical-looking frets. The marks are placed at frets 3, 5, 7, 9, 12, and so on, past the octave point. They're invaluable in their way, and will make it much easier to learn your way around the notes.

Although your guitar has a neck consisting of approximately 21 frets, this chart only goes up as far as fret number 12. This isn't only because there's no more width to the page. The real reason is that the entire range of named note positions only goes up to fret 12, after which they begin to repeat themselves at fret number 13. In fact, you can see that the notes across fret 12 are exactly the same as the strings when played 'open'. So in note-name terms fret number 13 is the same as fret number 1, which is to say that both will produce the (sixth string) note of **F**. This situation continues in a like manner as you move on up the neck. So fret 14 has the same name as fret 2 (**F#**), fret 15 is the same as fret 3 (**G**), and so on.

You may be wondering why, if it's the same note as fret 1, does fret 13 sound so much higher in pitch? This is due to a natural musical phenomenon known as an 'octave'.

Any two notes that have the same name, but are different in pitch, will have the same tonal characteristics but different frequencies. This is why the open first string is tuned to an **E**, and the open sixth string, sounding much lower, is also tuned to **E**. They're both **E** notes but are separated by (in this case) two complete octaves.

Moveable chords

A moveable chord is a chord shape that can be used at any position on the fretboard, without the necessity of any alteration to its basic finger positioning. This differentiates them from open chords, which are limited to one position per shape. And to make this all quite clear I want you to try a quick experiment.

First, play an open **C** chord in the usual way. It sounds fine, doesn't it? But now, still holding that same chord shape, just slide your left hand up the neck by one fret. And when you play the chord now it will sound awful.

You could try the same thing with all the other chords learned so far and the result would be the same. All the other chords, that is, except one – the **F** chord, which will sound fine at any fret position.

The **F** chord shape differs from all the others in one crucial respect: it contains no open strings, so all its notes maintain the same harmonic relationship to each other at all times, at whichever position on the neck it may be played. This is simply because all notes move up the neck together, whereas in the **C** chord shape (for instance) only four of the notes move up together, whilst the two open string notes stay right where they are. So, as the fretted string notes move up one position and become a **C#** chord, the open string notes still belong to the **C** chord. In effect a clash of two different chords is taking place, and it doesn't sound good. Moveable chords solve this problem by moving all strings together by the same degree, thereby maintaining the correct musical 'distance' between notes at all times.

Bar chords

A bar chord is so called because it depends upon one finger (usually the index) to hold down several strings at once, by forming a 'bar' across the fretboard. In doing this you can transform what was an open chord shape into one that can be played at any position on the guitar neck. This is good news for several reasons: first of all, because there are no open strings your left hand has greater control over the notes; secondly, because you can move it up the neck one chord shape learnt means 12 new chords (one for each fret); and thirdly, it gives you a choice of several ways in which any given chord can be played, creating different sound options.

The less attractive feature of bar chords is the fact that they do tend to be a bit more difficult to learn than open chords. But this is only a temporary disadvantage, and once you overcome this hurdle bar chords represent a major step in your musical development.

Here is how it works. Look again at an open **E** chord and consider the three strings held down on the fifth, fourth and third strings. You've already moved these notes up one fret to form an **F** chord, by adjusting the fingering and using your index finger to secure the first and second strings. This is a very useful five-string chord, but how would you manage to play it as a six-string chord, without actually growing an extra finger? Simply by using your index finger to also hold down the sixth string, as shown in the picture below. (Left-hand illustration is on **page 226**.)

Due to the difficulty most bar chord beginners experience in keeping the bar itself secured (from fret rattle or unintentionally muffled notes, etc), it's important to counterbalance the fingering pressure with correct thumb positioning. The appropriate placing of the thumb is lower than for playing most open chords, and is indicated in the picture shown here. (For left hand see **page 226**.)

Because of the unaccustomed stress this places upon your thumb, and to some extent the wrist as well, don't over-practise this to the point of causing muscular strain. And remember that the bar in this case isn't actually responsible for pressure on all six strings, but only on the three not being held down by the other fingers.

An F major bar chord. Careful observation of this picture reveals that it's simply the open E chord, moved up one fret. The change of finger positions is necessary to free the index (first) finger in order to form the bar across the entire fretboard. Although the principle applied is simple enough, in practice some care must be taken to apply sufficient pressure to hold down the bar, or else the chord won't sound clearly.

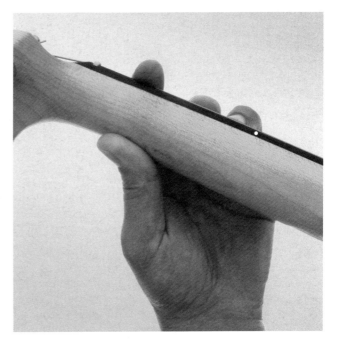

This type of thumb position is achieved by a somewhat greater curvature of the wrist than would usually be required for open chords. Initially this can be demanding for the novice, but within a fairly short time increased flexibility and hand strength will develop, enabling bar chords to be played with ease.

Bar chord diagram (enlarged version)

F (F major)

With regard to the bar itself, you'll notice that the index finger numbers are only displayed on the strings not secured elsewhere, but the fact that a bar goes completely across the fretboard is indicated by the joining line connecting the barred notes.

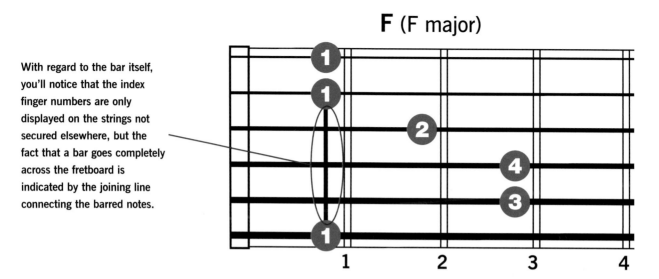

Since bar chords will often be used in conjunction with open chords, it's also necessary to get used to the change between, say, an open **C** chord and an **F** bar chord. Don't worry, don't hurry, it will soon become easy.

In terms of chord diagrams bar chords are shown as above. (Left-handed players see **page 226**.)

The pitch name of this particular chord shape is determined by the note found on the sixth string. So if you were to play it one fret higher it would be an **F#** chord. Move it up once again and it becomes a **G** chord, and so on. Check out the fretboard notation chart on **page 30**, and experiment with some of the many new major chords offered by this one shape.

The versatility of a bar chord such as this one is easily demonstrated if we refer back to the classic format of the 12-bar blues. Initially, in order to play this in the key of **A**, you had to learn three different chords, **A**, **D** and **E** (or **E7**). Then later, in order to transpose it into the key of **C**, it was

necessary to learn another three chord shapes. In fact, for every different key there were new chords to be learnt. And for some keys it would be impossible to play at all with open chords. But now, with just this one bar chord, you could play the 12-bar blues in absolutely any key there is. And the formula for doing so could hardly be easier.

Suppose you're required to play this chord sequence in the key of **F**. Then obviously the first chord is going to be **F** (bar chord 1st fret as above). The next chord you need is five frets higher (**B♭**), and the final chord required will be two frets higher again (**C**). So the format compares to **A**, **D** and **E**, by becoming **F**, **B♭** and **C**.

It works this way for every key. Name the first chord, add five frets for the next chord, and two more frets for the other one. If, as in some keys, you find yourself impractically high on the neck beyond the 12th fret, just play the necessary chord an octave lower, and it will sound just fine there too.

Rhythm dynamics

All the rhythms up to now have been based upon continuous chord strumming. But sometimes a different approach is required, because on many occasions what you don't play is as crucial to the rhythm as what you do play. And when it comes to creating some exciting rhythmic tension, nothing is quite as helpful as a bar chord. This is because they're very controllable.

Try playing an open **G** chord. No problem, just strum once and a nice clear chord keeps ringing out until the sound dies away. But what if you don't want that, and would prefer a quick chord stab followed by immediate silence – what then? How do you 'stop' the sound? The easiest way is to use a bar chord.

Now, instead of that open **G** chord let's try a bar chord **G** at the 3rd fret. It's the same shape fingering as the **F** chord in the diagram, but played two frets higher. And as I said earlier, these types of chords are much easier to control than open chords because your fingers are in contact with all of the strings. If you maintain left-hand pressure the notes keep ringing, so if you release pressure somewhat, the notes stop ringing.

When using this technique the degree of left-hand pressure is the key to getting it right. You don't release the strings completely; just make sure it's enough so that none of the strings are still in contact with the frets.

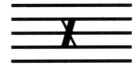

Quarter note percussion chord stroke

Take a look at the next exercise, which includes a new rhythmic device, the percussive stroke. The first and third beats of the bar are quite straightforward, but the second and fourth beats introduce a new symbol.

All this indicates is to play a chord stroke whilst the pressure is away from the frets. This will produce a percussive-sounding click, as the plectrum contacts the muted strings. And, bearing in mind that these chords are all played in bar versions, this places **G** at the 3rd fret, **B♭** at the 6th fret, **C** at the 8th fret and **D** at the 10th fret.

Chord chart 15

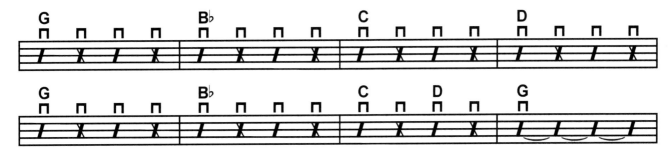

So the first stroke sounds the chord as normal. Then you immediately release hand pressure and play the next stroke. It will take a short time to get the hang of this, but shouldn't prove too difficult. The important thing is that all notes should sound clearly on first and third, and all notes should be muted on second and fourth. Choose a tempo that feels comfortable and vary it as you gain confidence. Now that you've taken the trouble to learn your first bar chord (and I know it wasn't easy), here are an extra 24 chords you can add to your list for hardly any extra effort – all of the minor chords and all of the seventh chords, simply by slight variations on your original major bar chord. (For left hand see **pages 238–39**).

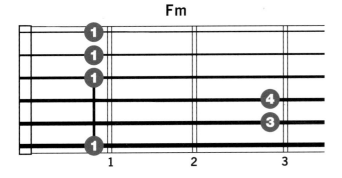

Fm

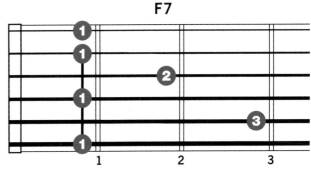

F7

You can tell at a glance that this could hardly be easier. In order to convert the **F** (F major) chord into an **Fm** (F minor) chord, all you do is lift your second finger away from the fretboard. And, to play the **F7** (F seventh) chord, just remove your fourth finger away, and there it is.

As with any bar chord shape this immediately gives you 12 new chords, one for each position on the neck. So now, with this simple expedient, you can play any major, minor or seventh chord in the known universe. As a reminder, the name of the chord is defined by the note held down on the sixth string, which in these examples is **F**. If you want a **Gm** or a **G7** perhaps, just move the appropriate shape up two frets and there it is. Remember, of course, to keep the bar held firmly on the notes not fingered elsewhere, and you can't go wrong.

Armed with access to all these new chords, your horizons are considerably broadened as to what you can play, and indeed where you can play it. Take, for example, the idea of adding some percussive strokes to the old C–Am–F–G7 pattern. You can give it an entirely new approach with this technique.

The **C** chord is at the 8th fret, followed by the **Am** at the 5th fret. Then it's F at the 1st fret, rounded off with G7 at the 3rd. This requires some moving up and down the neck, but with a bit of practice it's surprising how quickly you'll be able to get around the fretboard. Always remember to take the path of least resistance, maintaining a light touch contact with the strings even when changing chords, and just slide up and down, only applying thumb pressure when you reach the next chord.

Chord chart 16

There are obviously many ways in which these type of percussion strokes can be utilised, and feel free to devise some of your own as you gain experience with the stop-go feel of your left-hand pressure against the strings. In the meantime here are a couple of other ideas to play with. The first is a variation on exercise 15, consisting of a straight four to the bar. The significant difference lies in the fact that beats two and four are played with plectrum upstrokes. Play these upstrokes with a slight accent (louder), which gives a sharper 'chop' to the rhythm.

Another useful tip is to strum nearer the bridge than the neck. This will help those percussive downstrokes cut through, which is particularly important when playing with other instruments in a band.

Chord chart 17

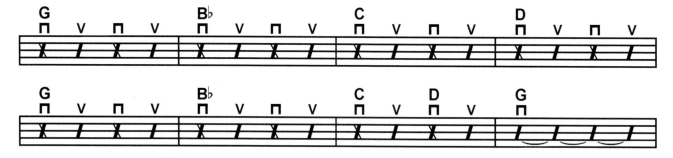

Chord chart 18

This exercise will sharpen up your fret-hand action, but take it steady until you get into the flow of the rhythm.

Remember, every now and then it can be a good idea just to run through each chord note by note, as if playing an arpeggio, to check that you're holding down all the strings firmly on to the fretboard, without any loose string buzzing or muffled notes.

More majors, minors and sevenths

Now that you've learned bar chord versions of every major, minor and seventh, the obvious question is, why learn any others? The answer is convenience. I realise that learning more bar chords may not strike you as a very convenient thing to have to do, but when you've actually done so a whole new range of options become available.

It's probably already occurred to you that moving one basic bar chord up and down the neck isn't without its shortcomings. For one thing, as you go up past the 9th or 10th fret some of the chord notes are perhaps a bit too high for some occasions. Also the closeness of the frets themselves can be a bit constricting. But the really big nuisance is the lack of a quick-change option between chords, as is sometimes required. Take, for example, changing from a **G** chord (bar 3rd fret) to a **C** chord (bar 8th fret). It's not too difficult to make the five-fret jump every bar (music bar, not bar chord) or two. But what if you had to make this move every couple of beats (half bar), or even on every beat of certain bars. That's four quick chord changes per bar, so it doesn't bear thinking about as a realistic option. But fortunately (you guessed it) there is an alternative.

Somewhat less fortunate is the rather difficult finger positions required to play this new major chord shape. If you thought the first bar chord was a difficult exercise, then this new one is really going to ruin your weekend.

Whereas the other one is based upon the open **E** chord shape, as explained earlier, this next one is based upon the open **A** chord, and therefore takes its name from the note found on the fifth string. And again, in order to free your first finger to make the bar you'll need to reposition your fingers for holding down strings two, three and four. There are two possible ways of doing this, as illustrated in the pictures above right. (Left-handed players see **page 226**.)

The first picture demonstrates a method of fingering which requires a considerable stretch between the bar finger and the others. This is a perfectly credible way of forming this chord, but it does have some notable limitations, the most obvious one being that it's almost impossible to use higher up the neck, due to the frets being too close together to allow space for the fingers.

The other method of fingering is preferable in almost every way.

No awkward finger stretch is required, and it's workable from very low to very high on the neck. This is really a case of a 'double bar' chord (my description only). One bar is formed, as usual, by your index finger, and goes right across the neck, while the other is a partial bar, formed by your third finger, covering strings two, three and four.

In chord diagrams these are your two options. (Left-handed players see **page 238**.)

The problem experienced by everyone learning this second option concerns the small bar across three strings. It's almost impossible to avoid touching the first string as well, which is not at all helpful and must be overcome.

B♭

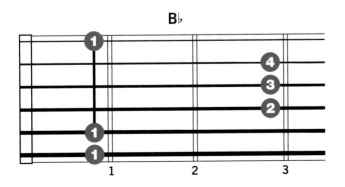

B♭

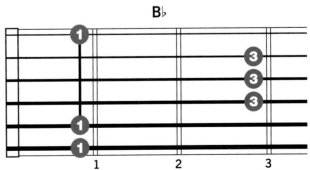

Quite frankly it's at this point that many aspiring guitarists fall by the wayside, and this is certainly a chord that separates the men from the boys. But if you're diligent and dedicated your perseverance will pay off, and pretty soon you'll be using this chord shape without a second thought.

My advice is not to worry too much if you do accidentally muffle the first string (if you don't, go straight to the head of the class). Instead, just get the overall feel of the chord

by changing to it from your other major bar chord shape, and it'll gradually sort itself out as you incorporate it into your playing.

A useful place to begin practising this chord is around the 5th fret. It will be somewhat easier in this position, where the frets are closer together, than it would be at the 1st fret. And in this position just practice moving from the usual **A** bar chord to your new **D** chord shape, as in the exercise below.

Chord chart 19

When you start getting competent with this, have a go at the next exercise, which is basically similar but just slightly more demanding.

Chord chart 20

Whilst you're still struggling to master this new chord you may be somewhat encouraged to learn that, from a chord standpoint, this is about as annoying as it gets. I can't think of any chord in general use that will seem difficult after this. And, as if to underline that statement, here are the minor and seventh variations of this particular

chord shape. You'll see that the minor shape is just the **Am** chord moved up a fret and barred, and of course the same rule applies to the seventh shape. As before, both take their names from the note found on the fifth string, so don't forget to refer to the fret notes diagram on **page 30** to find out where you are.

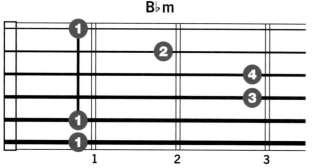

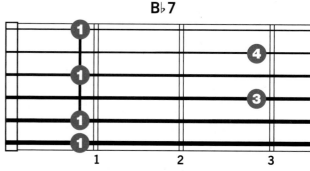

Take your time over these chord shapes (left-handed versions are on **pages 238–39**), because it's a lot to learn in one lesson. Concentrate on accuracy rather than speed. The choice of tempo is your decision, so set a realistic pace at which you can achieve results at a steady rate of progress.

I know that learning these bar chords has made for a tough session (or two), but take heart from the fact that you've already come a very long way, and achieved a great deal. You now have command of literally dozens of the most commonly used chords in popular music, which gives you the ability to play the chord patterns from many hundreds of songs.

Take a rest

As you've already discovered, bar chords are very easy to silence, by simply easing the left-hand pressure. You've used this to create percussive effects, but now we'll try something slightly different by creating periods of complete silence. This can be seen as a variation on the percussion approach, except that instead of playing on muted strings you simply play nothing at all where indicated.

Although it sounds contradictory, silence is an important part of playing music, which is why there are ways of indicating pauses that can be easily understood on any chord chart. And because pauses, like musical notes, have different durations, there are several symbols that make clear exactly how long any moment of silence should last. These symbols are called 'rests'. Let's begin with one beat of silence, for which the appropriate symbol is displayed here.

When you see this, simply refrain from strumming any strings for a period of one beat. An easy way to keep in steady time and not lose your rhythmic flow whilst doing

1 beat rest

this is to continue with the same up and down strumming motion, but simply 'miss' the strings on the silent beats.

The following exercise requires the use of several new bar chord versions in order to achieve maximum effect. And, although there are a number of possibilities, I would recommend the following arrangement: E at the 7th fret, C#m at the 4th fret, A at the 5th fret, and then B7 at the 7th fret. As always, remember to practise with your metronome (or other timepiece), because this really does make a big difference to accuracy, and exerts a necessary discipline on your practice sessions.

Chord chart 21

Another approach to playing chords whilst making good use of 'space' can be to use all downstrokes whilst playing only on the lower strings. This gives a powerful, heavier sound that can be made even more dynamic by adding a touch of distortion (see **page 196**) to your amp sound.

When playing in this style try to ensure that the root (name) note of the chord is the lowest note sounded. Obviously this is easy when the root note is on the sixth string, but rather more difficult when it happens to be on the fifth string, as in your second major bar chord. The answer to this problem is illustrated in the picture seen here:

At first glance this may appear identical to the lower picture on page 35. But here, instead of barring all six strings you bar only the first five, leaving the tip of your index finger just touching the sixth string, thereby muting it to avoid sounding. This takes practise to do accurately at playing speed, but, when mastered, provides a failsafe method of avoiding unwanted sixth string sound.

Try the next exercise as explained, playing only on the two or three lowest notes of your bar chords. But before you start, there are a couple of useful tips you should know about. First of all, it's usually best to use the bridge pickup (the one farthest away from the neck) in this kind of style. This is because the more mellow tones of the other position pickups don't tend to provide such an aggressive and powerful sound. The second point is to keep the guitar volume knob turned up to its maximum setting. This helps to 'drive' the amplifier, making it much easier to create a nice touch of distortion.

You can control the overall volume setting (and avoid scaring the neighbours) from the amp itself. For advice on amplifier settings, refer to **page 196**.

Chord chart 22

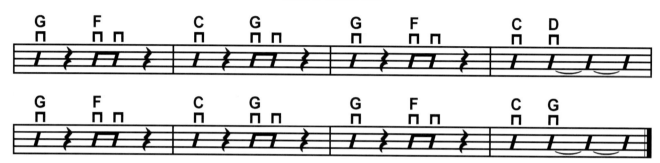

Having now acquired some experience with rests of one-beat duration, let's take a look at a half-beat (eighth note) rest, which will expand your musical possibilities considerably. As you're already familiar with the practice of playing eighth notes in pairs, as represented in numerous rhythms so far, just think of this new symbol as being half of such a pair. Of course, in order to rest on half a beat and then play on the other half, you'll also need to learn the symbol for a single eighth note chord strum. Both symbols are pictured below:

1 eighth note (half beat)
rest (8 per bar)

1 eighth note (half beat)
chord stroke (8 per bar)

Although this may appear complicated, it's really just a slightly different way of looking at an extremely familiar rhythmic timing sequence. The illustrations below will demonstrate this point.

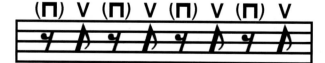

Strictly from a timing point of view the two are identical. Of course, the diagram above left would present no problem to you. And the diagram above right is essentially similar, except that where the downstroke would be, as shown in brackets, you 'play' nothing but silence. In an actual chord sequence diagram a rest symbol doesn't have any down or upstroke marker above it, because no string contact occurs. This is shown here just to give you an idea of the timing principle underlying this type of rhythmic structure.

This next rhythm is extremely versatile, and for best effect concentrate mainly on the upper strings. Playing a full six-string chord can, in some cases, reduce the impact and somewhat clutter the sound. Think brisk and snappy for this exercise and aim for a medium to lively tempo once you're at ease with the feel of the rhythm.

Chord chart 23

Another interesting variation can be to create a rhythm which is played over two bars, instead of the more usual one. This is simply two slightly different rhythms played in a sequence that repeats itself every other bar. The following example demonstrates this approach, with the two alternating bars having a similarity to each other that's complementary rather than sounding in any way inappropriate.

Note that once again all the actual string contact is with upstrokes, to give that sharp, clear sound. And although you can vary according to requirements, I would recommend a fairly clean (not distorted) amplifier sound.

Chord chart 24

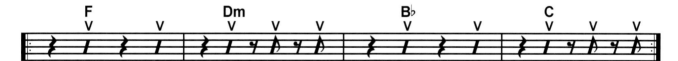

In playing a guitar part such as this, it's obviously essential to have full control of the chords with regard to left-hand pressure. This is, as we've established, one of the advantages of a bar chord over an open chord. But when you're really just playing on the top few strings only, a full bar across the neck isn't always necessary. It's a perfectly acceptable method, of course, but it isn't the only way.

Consider the previous exercise, and imagine playing this for several minutes over the duration of an entire song. It's okay at first, but after a while the constant thumb pressure begins to cause difficulties, and muscular ache becomes problematic. So, bearing in mind that only a few upper strings are in use on this rhythm, let's try some different fingering options.

I'll assume that your choice of chords might be as follows: F chord, bar at the 8th fret; Dm chord, bar at the 5th fret; B♭ chord, bar at the 6th fret; C chord, bar at the 8th fret. This is a good choice of chord positions, for sound quality, smooth changes and general pitch symmetry. So in order to adjust the fingering, you still play the same fret position for the same type of sound, but you simply abbreviate them by leaving out some of the notes that aren't being used in this instance. The comparative chord diagrams shown overleaf illustrate how easily this can be done. On the left are the regular bar chord versions, and to the right of these are abbreviated three-string versions of the same chord shape and at the same fret position. (For left-handed comparison see **page 226**.)

F (8th fret)

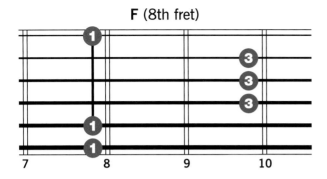

F (8th fret)

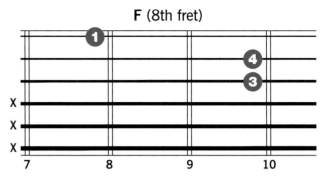

Notice that these aren't 1st fret positions as would be normally shown, but in this case are higher up the neck as applies to this particular exercise. As usual the X marks any strings not being played. It's unlikely that you would be in any danger of accidentally striking them because you're playing upstrokes throughout. But to avoid any chance of sounding the fourth string (the only likely culprit), it's easily muted by touching that string with the edge of your nearest available (fretting hand) digit, which in this case would be the third finger.

These types of chords are very useful at times, as they can be played with your hand wrapped around the neck, in the manner of an open chord, and thereby avoiding the dreaded thumb-cramping sensation which is pretty much unavoidable when playing an unremitting sequence of bar chords.

OK, that's the F chord taken care of, so now let's take a look at the diagram below for a stress-free version of the 5th fret position Dm. (Left-handed players see **page 226**.)

Dm (5th fret)

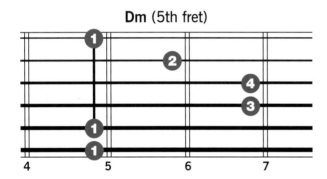

Dm (5th fret)

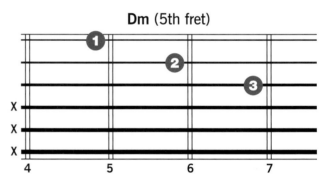

Again this is an obvious alternative. Therefore it isn't too difficult to guess what the abbreviated version of B♭ will look like, as shown below. (Left-handed version is on **page 226**.)

B♭ (6th fret)

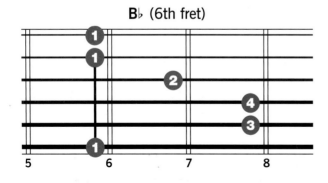

B♭ (6th fret)

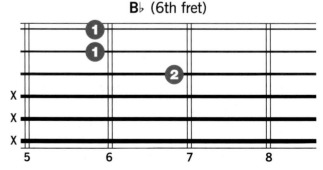

Needless to say, the C chord is the same thing moved up two frets, which completes this particular chord sequence. However, keep in mind that there will be many times when you need play only certain notes of a chord and, depending on the practicalities of finger positioning, it will often be possible to make things easier by playing only partial chord structures.

The classic rock rhythm

There's a rhythm pattern that has featured on hundreds of recordings over the years, from rock and roll to heavy metal. Indeed, one band has used it so much that it's often casually referred to as the 'Status Quo' rhythm. Having said that, I'm sure you'll know what I'm talking about.

This rhythmic 'riff' (a riff is a repetitive pattern forming the basis of a song) is mostly played on the two or three lower strings, and is only applicable when used for major chords. In fact, the easiest way to understand this is to think of it as being a variation on your first major bar chord, which you have, to some extent, explored in exercise 22 on **page 38**. However, the interesting difference here lies in an alternating movement played by your fourth finger. The two diagrams below will show you what this is all about. (Left-handed players see **page 227**.)

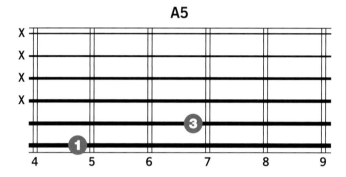

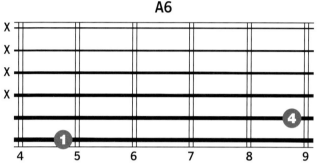

Above left is a partial chord, which is commonly referred to as an **A5**. Although this sounds more like a major road than a major chord, there's a good reason behind it. This isn't quite the place for too much theory so I'll try to make it brief. Basically, as mentioned earlier, a major chord always comprises a minimum of three notes. These are notes derived from an eight-note scale (more about scales on **page 49**). They're the 1st note, the 3rd note and the 5th note. As long as these three notes are present the combined result will be a major chord. But if one of these notes were omitted, then the chord could not be, by strict musical definition, a true major chord.

That said, sometimes musicians do play these 'part chords', and leave out one of the traditionally essential chord notes. And, as it happens, the note most often avoided turns out to be the 3rd note of the scale. This leaves a partial chord form consisting of the 1st note (which in this example is **A**) and the 5th note (**E**), and in recent times this has become known as an **A5** chord. It's very easy to play, and much used, mainly due to the fact that a 1st and 5th played together sound extremely effective when used with distorted guitar tones. But if you played a 1st and 3rd combination, on the other hand, you'd find that it isn't very attractive at all.

So, now study the diagram to the right of the **A5** chord, described here for convenience as an 'A6' chord, although again it's only a partial version, and you can see that the fifth string is now being played two frets higher at fret 9. So basically there's an alternating movement covering a span of two frets, created by the placing on of your little finger. But whilst doing this, try to keep your third finger in its original position at fret 7, which might appear a bit pointless at first consideration. However, this particular rhythm requires a constant repetition of this on/off little finger action, which can be much more effectively done (and a lot easier too) if the third finger remains constantly in place.

The diagram below demonstrates how this works in practice whilst playing a familiar eighth note rhythm pattern. The double note combination as played is clearly shown underneath, though this is purely for the purpose of this demonstration, and won't normally be displayed in any chord diagram. Note that it's played with all downstrokes, which is a common approach with this type of rhythm, although this can vary according to the situation. And although this may look complicated, remember that it's only a case of moving one finger to and from the fretboard.

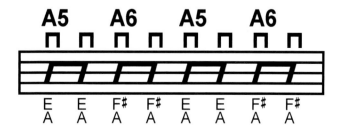

Position your hand and wrist as if you were playing a bar chord, which will permit maximum finger stretch. Naturally this is easier to play as you go higher up the neck where the frets are closer together. However, it's perfectly playable even in the 1st fret (**F** chord) position, where the widest possible finger stretch is required. Also, be aware that this riff can be played in open chord position, as in the key of **E**, by changing your finger placing. Both positions are pictured above. (Left-handed players see **page 227**.)

As with any bar chord, the only difference between this moveable riff and its open position counterpart is that your index finger isn't required to hold down certain strings (in this case the **E** string) on the latter version.

And because of this you're free to play the alternating fifth string movement with your first and third fingers as pictured above, which, because of the wide fret spacing, is somewhat easier to do. It's really just common sense and, with a bit of practise, shouldn't present any problems.

If you play this riff on the lowest two strings it will sound good at any position on the neck, and some players just move up and down the fretboard as the chord changes require. But if you prefer to take things nice and easy, and not have to move around the neck quite so much, why not also learn to play it on the next two strings across, as shown below? (Left-handed players see **page 227**.)

D5

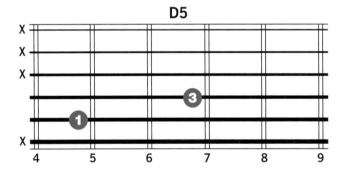

D6

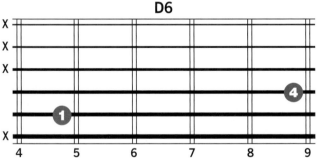

It's really no different than when you learnt a second major bar chord, in order to facilitate smoother changes and not have to move around so much. And again, this means that the name note of this chord riff has now moved over to the fifth string when you play it on these two higher strings. Need I add that any sixth string muting can easily be done with the tip of your index finger, as you learned on **page 37** And when you play it in open position (**A**), use your thumb for this purpose.

As an exercise try playing the 12-bar blues with this riff. Play it in several different keys, making use of both open and bar chord (moveable) positions as applicable. Experiment as much as you wish, trying both clean and distortion amp sounds. Remember, this can be applied to chord sequences involving major chords, but not minor; so make up some of your own variations if you wish. You may be surprised at how much variety you can get out of this one simple rhythm.

Palm muting

An additional effect can be easily created with a technique known as 'palm muting', or 'damping', which works extremely well with the riff played above. All you need do is to rest the palm of your strumming hand on the strings at the point where they meet the bridge. This creates a semi-muted sound that is much used and sounds very dynamic. The photograph seen here illustrates the correct hand position for best effect.

This is a fairly simple technique, and the only requirement is to ensure that the right-hand palm is placed with some accuracy across the bridge. Too far forward will muffle the strings excessively, whereas too far back toward the bridge lacks the desired effect. It's not strictly necessary to dampen all strings, which may inhibit hand movement, but only those being played.

It's worth noting that there are two additional versions, or variations, on this popular riff. In the first (and most commonly employed of them all) it's often played by lifting away the little finger (or third finger in open position) exactly one half-beat sooner than usual, as seen below left. This is easy enough to do once you get the feel of it. The second variation, lower right, is slightly more difficult because it involves a wide (five-fret) stretch for your fourth finger, which is used in forming both the A6 and A7 positions. This can be seen as a partial seventh chord involving the low A note and the higher G note. Due to this tricky movement it's easiest played in the higher fret (or open) chord positions.

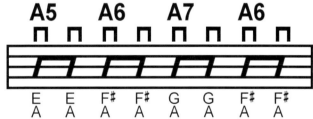

It's likely that you will, at some point, encounter all three of these riff variations, so it's worth being at least familiar with what's required. But you can take some comfort in the fact that the first of these illustrated variations (above left) is certainly the one most often used. The more difficult version three can be mastered with a little extra effort, and, once acquired, will present no obvious complications. But unless you have reasonably large hands it's somewhat impractical to play this any lower than the 3rd fret position. The solution to this dilemma, if encountered, is to either use a capo (see **pages 143–45**), whereby it can be played as an open version, or simply play it an octave higher where the frets are closer together.

Sixteenth notes

Dividing one bar up into 16 parts does sound rather complicated and confusing, so instead consider it as each beat played in groups of four. The rhythm diagram seen here demonstrates this in comparison to the now familiar 8th note chord symbol.

2 eighth note chord strokes
(8 strokes per bar)

4 sixteenth note chord strokes
(16 strokes per bar)

In practice, rhythms don't necessarily consist of an unremitting sequence of 16th chord strokes. What's rather more common is a combination rhythm of 8th note and 16th note rhythms together in any one bar. A typical example might be the following exercise:

Chord chart 25

As a simple repetitive chord sequence this leads smoothly back into itself, with the fast 16th beat adding a touch of variety. Try it quite slowly at first, or you'll probably trip up and lose your timing. But be careful not to try too hard, because it's a common mistake to play the 16th part of the rhythm too fast with a natural tendency toward overcompensating for the change in rhythm strokes. Listen first to the metronome tempo without actually playing, and learn it in your head before you go strumming away at high speed.

Another useful way of employing 16th note strumming is to incorporate it into the 8th strums. This means that you effectively combine 8ths and 16ths within the same beat. Actually this sounds more confusing than it really is. The easiest way to get this into perspective is to compare it directly with a straight 8th rhythm. Study the diagrams below, where the familiar 8th rhythm strokes are displayed alongside the combination 8th/16th rhythm. If you count the down-up 8th rhythm as shown, by saying '1 & 2 & 3 & 4 &', this won't be a problem. Then, looking at the combination rhythm below, you count in the same even way, but for every 'and' you play two strokes of the pick. So, instead of 'down-up, down-up' etc, you will be playing 'down – down-up, down – down-up' etc.

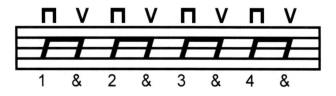

Another way of understanding this rhythm, purely for learning purposes, would be to view it as two separate beats played in the space of one. This can be demonstrated by comparing an 8th/16th (far right) with a straight quarter/eighth beat. If you were to play either of these without reference to any timing device, they'd be exactly the same. The real difference becomes apparent when you play along to your metronome, because then you would play the first example as two separate beats, whereas the second example is played within the time of only one beat. In other words, it's the same thing played twice as fast. But this difference is crucial because it affects the overall rhythmic structure of the piece of music

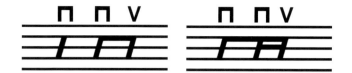

in conjunction with other instruments and vocals.

An ideal way to begin learning this type of thing is to once again combine both types of strumming patterns within the same bar.

Consider the following example carefully before playing. Remember that despite the seeming complexity of the structure, we're still only dealing with four beats to the bar.

Chord chart 26

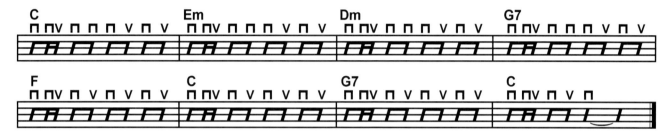

Another interesting variation is to place a 'tie' sign at a suitable place within each bar, as opposed to just using it for an ending chord as we've done so far. In the next example you'll see this sign in the middle of the bar, which simply means that your upstroke at this point is not immediately followed by the usual downstroke. Instead, you 'miss'

that downstroke, allowing the previous chord stroke to sustain for another half beat, when it's followed by another upstroke. Simple though this is, it's a widely used technique in rhythm playing, and can of course be used in many rhythms, as decided by your discretion and the requirements of the song in question.

Chord chart 27

An additional technique which you may care to try is to accent (play louder) the tied stroke. In other words, the second upstroke of each bar is slightly emphasised for added rhythmic effect. This is purely optional and left to your own judgement as to what sounds attractive in any particular case.

As you familiarise yourself with the many rhythmic choices available, using 8ths, 16ths, triplets, rests, ties and combinations of these, it becomes clear that an immense range of options presents itself to the guitar player. This may cause you to question which rhythm is best for any particular song you choose to play. Dreary as it sounds to say

it again, time and experience will provide the answer. For instance, if you're playing a familiar song, listen carefully to the recording and try to work out what's being played. Sometimes this is obvious, but it may be more difficult if the guitar part isn't very prominent. But remember that there may be several suitable alternatives, so always experiment until you feel satisfied that you have something fitting to the vocal and drum patterns of the music in question. This is actually not too difficult with a bit of practice, and the more you do so the better your 'feel' for rhythm will become.

CHAPTER 4

Reading Music

This is the moment when half of you race for the exit door and the others hide, whimpering, under the table. Don't worry, it isn't that scary. My approach here is based upon the 'If I can do it, how tough can it be?' principle. The basics behind understanding music notation really are simple, so just humour me and give it a try, okay? I promise that by the time you have read a couple of pages you will be keen to learn even more.

Reading music

Being rather more serious for a moment, it really is amazing how many people seem to believe that reading music is some strange and incomprehensible ability that can be mastered by very few people. I've actually heard many times, from otherwise sane people, something to the effect of 'I want to learn guitar, but only if I don't have to read music.' And this odd phobia is so widespread that many guitar instructors avoid the subject entirely, presumably for fear of scaring away potential students.

Let's cut out all the nonsense and get straight to the point. The ability to understand basic music notation is something that can be easily acquired by anyone of average intelligence. There's no arcane mystery involved in this. It's a perfectly straightforward and logical medium of communication, through which musical ideas and information can be exchanged in a clear and comprehensive manner. Contrary to popular opinion, reading music doesn't complicate matters at all. In fact the opposite is true. It actually simplifies everything, by permitting me to communicate things to you that would otherwise require long and detailed explanations, accompanied by several diagrams.

To illustrate this point, consider the information detailed on **pages 41–42**. All of this can be conveyed in written music with the notation below.

As you see, it saves a lot of room on the page when written in music notation. But what does it mean, and how should you understand it? Well, as far as this riff is concerned it really is easy. The notes, as you see, are set in pairs. The lower notes represent the **A** note, whilst the upper row is the movement between the notes of **E** and **F♯**. They're written in pairs because, on this occasion, that's how they're played. So it's all quite logical really, and very shortly all of this will become clear to you.

The basics

Music is written along five parallel lines, which are referred to as the 'staff' or 'staves'. This is more or less identical in appearance to that which we've used in our chord charts. The music staff is pictured here, along with the basic symbols which accompany it:

The symbol at the far left is called a 'treble clef'. This indicates that the notes following it are written for those instruments (including guitar) that are of medium to upper range in pitch. This is opposed to lower pitch instruments covered by the bass clef range, such as a bass guitar for example.

The symbol next to this, which is called the 'time signature', indicates how many beats to the bar will occur in this piece of music. In this case it's in 4/4 time (pronounced 'four-four' time), which means four beats to every bar, as you're accustomed to from your rhythm charts. Frequently this symbol may be substituted by the letter 'C', as shown next along the staff. This is an abbreviation of 'common time', which also means four beats to the bar. So 4/4 time and common time are just two different ways of saying the same thing – they are both shown

here for demonstration purposes only, and in practice only one symbol or the other will be present.

The actual notes that will follow along the staff are defined by two things: pitch and duration. Simply stated, the higher on the staff line any note is placed, the higher its pitch will be. Any notes that are too high or too low to have a position on the staff, which has only five lines, will be placed upon small lines of their own, above or below the staff itself; these are called 'leger lines'.

Note duration (how long a note sounds for) is defined in two ways: by the 'tail' attached to it, and/or whether it's solid black or hollow. Any note has no 'absolute' duration other than that as defined by the tempo. So for example, a quarter note played at a slow tempo would last longer than a quarter note played at a fast tempo.

Whole note
(1 per bar)

Half note
(2 per bar)

Quarter note
(4 per bar)

Eighth note
(8 per bar)

Sixteenth note
(16 per bar)

You'll notice that the notes are described here by their literal terms, such as half note, quarter note, etc. This is the non-technical, but increasingly common, terminology in current use. More traditionally they have other names, which reading left to right would be semibreve, minim, crotchet, quaver and semi-quaver. However, this book will continue to use the more descriptive (and frankly more logical) terms, in the interests of clarity and general learning efficiency.

So let's get down to business. By this time you should be acquiring a reasonable familiarity with the names of various notes along the fretboard, from referring to the chart on **page 30**. You'll have noticed that notes on the guitar, apart from the five lowest and five highest, can be played in more than one position. The low **A** note, for example, can be played at the sixth string 5th fret, or on the open fifth string. And the **D** note, found on the open fourth string, can also be played on the fifth string 5th fret position, or the low **E** string 10th fret position. These are just two examples. Some notes have even more available options. But the point I'm making is that written music indicates which note (pitch) should be played, but it doesn't refer to any specific fret position. So where you choose to play any given note is entirely your decision.

The notation chart below shows how each note is written along the stave, working upward from the lowest **E** note which is, of course, played on the open sixth string. In this diagram I haven't divided the notes into bars (as would usually be the case), in order to save space across the page.

This chart demonstrates only the placing of notes on the stave. If you begin playing these notes as written, you would play the sixth string open, followed by the sixth string 1st fret, then the sixth string 3rd fret. At this point you have a choice between sixth string 5th fret, and so on up the neck, or change over to the fifth string open and continue from there. This choice, which occurs on each string at some point, is generally based upon the convenience of finger positioning,

although tone differences can be a consideration also. The same pitch note on a guitar does have differing sound characteristics when played upon different strings.

But what about those in-between notes, at the 2nd fret or the 4th fret for example? Well, these are the sharps and flats as we discussed on **page 29**. So in order to represent these notes on a stave we need only to place the appropriate sharp or flat symbol in front of the written note.

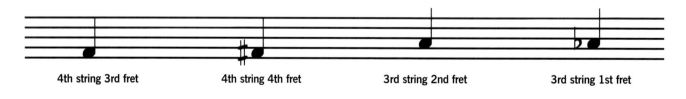

4th string 3rd fret

4th string 4th fret

3rd string 2nd fret

3rd string 1st fret

As you see, it could hardly be easier. A sharp symbol raises any note by one fret, whereas a flat symbol lowers any note by one fret. When seen in this way it's very obvious that a note has been sharpened or flattened because the appropriate symbol is

right next to it. But this isn't always the most convenient way of doing things. Suppose, for instance, that a melody has a great many of its notes sharp or flat. In that case it could get messy, with sharp or flat symbols cluttering up all the staves.

It happens that, in certain keys, a great many sharps or flats do indeed occur. The key of **C** major is straightforward enough, as it essentially contains only natural (not sharp or flat) notes, but other keys are less accommodating. In **G** major you'll find that every **F** note is sharpened. Alternately, in the key of **F** major every **B** note is flattened. Other keys tend to be even more inclined

in these ways. **D** major has two sharps (**F♯** and **C♯**), whilst **B♭** major contains two flats (**B♭** and **E♭**). And so it continues, in various keys, with more sharps or flats added all the time. So the question remains of how to avoid a lot of sharps and flat signs everywhere. The solution is to include them all in one place, right at the beginning of the stave, as in the example seen here:

This method is known as the 'key signature', which tells you which key the music is in – which in this case is the key of **A** major, and it's telling you that every **C**, **F** and **G** note is to be played sharp.

All of this might sound complicated, and on some other instruments it could be. But due to the construction and nature of their instrument, guitarists tend to think in terms of fretboard positions, which, as you'll learn, does simplify things a great deal. As an example of this point, consider a **G** bar chord at

the 3rd fret. Reading from lowest string to highest you find the following notes: **G–D–G–B–D–G**. No problem and no sharps or flats. But if you move that chord up one fret, where it becomes an **A♭** chord, reading again from low to high it now consists of the notes **A♭–E♭–A♭–C–E♭–A♭**. Now that sounds more complex because of all the flats involved, but all you've actually done is to move up one fretboard position. And a similar situation applies to individual notes, just as it does to chords. When you get the feel of your fretboard positions everything will become clear.

The C major scale

A scale is the name given to a series of notes covering the musical distance between any note and its octave. In the case of **C** this could be from the note found on the 3rd fret of the fifth string, to the note at the 5th fret of the third string. So written on a stave the **C** major scale appears as below left.

OK, so it's a **C** major scale, but what exactly does this mean to you, and what's it for? Well, let's think of it as the series of notes which can be used to compose (and therefore play) a melody in the key of **C**. It may not seem much, having just these few notes to work with, but as they can be arranged in any order and time phrasing the possibilities are immense. Of course, you can add to these the next octave upward (or, to some extent on a guitar, downward), thereby extending the melodic opportunities still further. With this in mind, the diagram below right is also a **C** major scale:

So you get the idea. Any combination of the notes **C–D–E–F–G–A–B**, at whatever pitch, could legitimately be used to form a composition in the key of **C** major.

As a starter let's try running up and down each of these scale positions. It's always important to use the most convenient fingering, and as a guide to this be sure to study the charts overleaf. (Left-handed versions are on **page 227**.) On the left is the **C** scale in the lower octave, and at right is shown the correct fingering for the upper octave. Notice that this one begins at the 5th fret. As in the chord diagrams, the number in a circle indicates which finger of your left hand to use for each note – it does not refer to the order in which the notes should be played. That information is shown in the notation charts seen below. Sound each note clearly and at your own speed, playing the scale in both ascending and descending order.

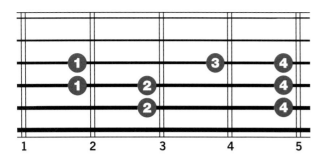

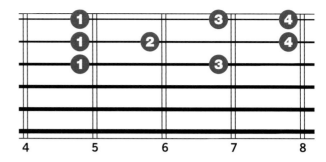

This isn't the first time I've used the phrase about 'sounding the notes clearly', and it's an important point, because it's a common mistake for aspiring guitarists to concentrate on speed, at the expense of accuracy. It doesn't matter how slowly you learn to play something, as long as you play it well. Greater dexterity is a natural by-product of consistent practice. It is, however, a good idea to keep to a steady sense of rhythm, at whatever pace you choose to play. Set a comfortable tempo and play these scales at one note per beat.

You may have realised that these note sequences can be played in several different fretboard positions, some of which might include open strings. But I've suggested these specific fingerings for very good reasons. For one thing, this enables you to play a complete run of notes without changing your hand position at all. This is far more practical (and a lot less effort) than leaping about all over the fretboard. And also, it makes the scales (like bar chords) moveable. Without having to think about changing your relative finger movements at all, you can now play the scale of any major key just by starting from a new note. I'll give you an example of this by comparing the scale of **C** major with the scale of **D** major:

Looking at these two scales as notes on a page they're obviously very different. But when you consider them as fingering positions on the fretboard the differences are less readily apparent. In fact, at a casual glance you might think that you're looking at the same thing twice. (Left-handed guitarists see **page 227**.)

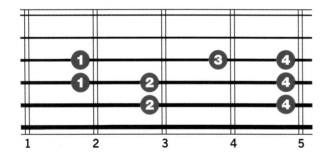

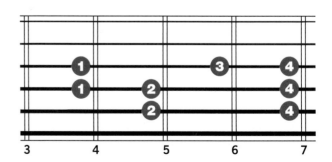

Of course, a closer look reveals that the fret numbers aren't identical. So whereas the key of **C** scale starts its run of notes at the 3rd fret, the **D** scale begins two frets higher at the 5th fret. But it shows how, when you think in terms of fretboard positions, it's easy to play a scale in any key, because the relative fingering remains the same. And it works that way right up the neck. Whatever key you might wish to play a scale in, just start on the note which defines that scale and keep to the relative fingering pattern as shown.

Note-reading practice

The following exercises are intended not as melodic phrases, but simply to familiarise you with which note on the staff represents which note along the guitar neck. At this stage you will find the note name (C, E, G etc) written below each note as it occurs. This will help you to find your way, although you'll be surprised at how quickly the notes start to look familiar. Again I remind you that the note name positions on the neck can be found on page 30 if you haven't learned them yet. This first exercise is in the key of C, so there are no sharps or flats to think about, and the timing is a straightforward four beats to the bar.

Exercise 1

I think you'll agree that wasn't too difficult to comprehend, but practise it as many times as you wish before moving on. Get thoroughly comfortable with the relationship between written notes and their respective fretboard positions, and then take a look at the next exercise. Again it's four notes per bar, but with a few more note changes this time around.

Exercise 2

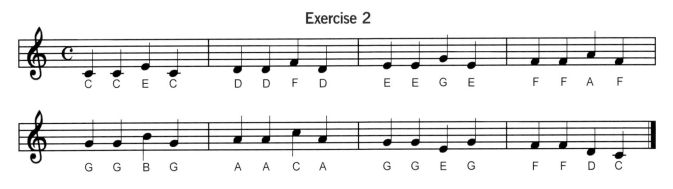

It doesn't exactly tax the brain, does it? So for those of you who thought you could never learn to read music, well, that's just what you *are* doing. When it comes to basic music-reading skills the fundamentals really are as easy as this. It's simply the ability to recognise which notes on the page correspond to which strings/frets on the guitar. Add to that a timing pattern (just like in the chord rhythms), and there you have it. And, for most guitarists' requirements, it usually isn't necessary to be able to read and play straight from the page. You can take your time in studying the piece and learn it at leisure. Music reading is, like most skills, something you can develop as much or as little as you wish. It all depends upon your needs and interests. The aim of this book is to provide the essentials, from which you can then progress to your own limits.

So let's take another step here and include some eighth notes. Remember that eight notes, when played together, can be stated singly or joined at the top of the stem, as demonstrated in the two examples below:

On this next exercise let's try something based around a familiar chord sequence. This will make things more interesting, and also give you an idea of how certain chords tend to fit well with particular notes. Keep in mind that this is primarily note-reading practice, as opposed to being a dexterity exercise, so take your time learning the piece, and choose the easiest fingering option available. You can play this in one position (2nd–5th fret), so there's no need to go leaping around the neck making things difficult for yourself.

If you have some type of recording device available, you might record the rhythm guitar chord sequence (with metronome, of course), and then play the notes in time with that. This is just a suggestion for a bit of added interest, and is by no means essential at this stage. As long as you keep steady time and play each note accurately, it'll sound good either way.

Exercise 3

Notice that this doesn't end on a final sounding note, and also that there are repeat signs before and after the notes. You will, of course, recognise these from chord chart work. This indicates that you could play it over as many times as you like. When you do wish to end, just play a **C** chord (and note) after the last bar of **G7**.

Up to this point you've been working within a range of one octave. This next piece steps outside of this somewhat, by adding a couple of extra notes on top. It's basically a simple riff, constructed around the familiar 12-bar blues format, again in the key of **C**.

The first part, played over the **C** chord, is a repetitive pattern that combines quarter notes and eighth notes over a two-bar structure. However, when this is transposed to the **F** chord, although it's the same riff, the choice of fingering needs to be given

some consideration. If you wish to maintain the same relative finger movements, then you'll need to play the pattern on the same three strings (third, fourth and fifth), but move the whole thing five frets higher. On the other hand, if you prefer to stay within the same fret position, but move over to the next three highest strings (second, third and fourth), then you'll have to alter the relative fingering on the fourth beat of every bar. A study of the neck chart on **page 30** (**page 225** for left-handed players) will clarify why this is so. Either way it doesn't present any problem, but you need to be aware of this to decide upon your preferred option. Bear in mind these same considerations when playing over the **G7** chord also, which will be the same fingering pattern as **F** but two frets higher again.

Exercise 4

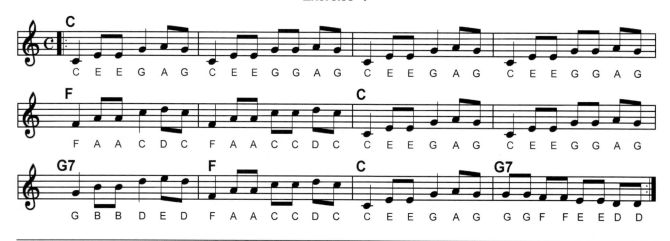

Since I keep referring to the importance of position playing, let's consider what happens when a change of fret position is required partway through a particular melodic phrase. Remember that economy of movement is best, whenever possible, to ensure smooth sounding note runs.

Our next exercise takes us mainly into the upper **C** octave

range, the best fingering for which has already been displayed on **page 50**. So the first finger is at the 5th fret and the fourth finger reaches easily up to the 8th fret. Now, this will cover most of the notes for the next piece until we reach the final bar, which contains a **B** note. This falls just below the fret fingering position as described, because it's located at fret 4 of the third string. So the trick is to shift your positioning without making hard work for yourself or breaking the natural-sounding flow of notes. Although there's more than one place where this could be done, my own preferred choice would be as follows: begin the third bar playing in your established position, but when you play the

final note (**A**) of that bar, don't secure it with your third finger, as would be usual, but fret it with your fourth finger instead. In doing this simple action you'll have instantly changed positions to one fret lower, leaving the remaining notes in comfortable playing order.

Exercise 5

No doubt the notes of the **C** major scale are starting to look familiar to you by this point, so I'll stop pampering you by writing the note names below the stave, and give you the chance to consider the next exercise all by yourself. But before we get to that, let's revisit the humble (but essential) 'rest'.

As with rhythm guitar charts, the rest sign is an essential feature of any music notation. And, by happy coincidence, these rest signs are no different to those (partially) introduced in chord chart work. To remind you of these, and present a few more, take a look at the range of rest symbols shown below:

This little collection isn't entirely comprehensive, but it certainly illustrates the ones in most common use. Any others, such as dotted rests (see **page 61**), are basically variations or extensions of those seen here.

OK, fun time again. Exercise 6 is a fairly simple riff, the educational value of which is enhanced by some strategically placed rests. And, as the purpose of any rest is silence, don't forget to effectively mute whichever note immediately precedes it.

As with a chord, the simplest way to silence any note is to play it fretted (as opposed to playing an open string) and then release the pressure on that string, whilst maintaining light contact to prevent any unwanted residual sound. Due to the sparse notation involved, this can be played at a brisk tempo without undue difficulty. Think in terms of a lively rockabilly style, and aim for at least 180bpm on the tempo. When you get the hang of it feel free to pick up the speed even more, to suit your own discretion.

Exercise 6

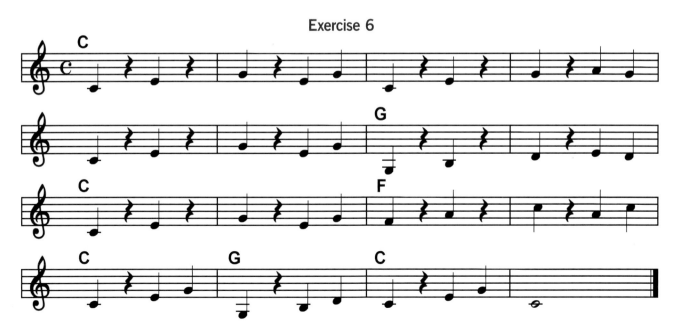

Due to the 'riffy' nature of this piece, the use of rests quickly becomes a familiar pattern. This is in common with rhythm guitar work, whereby learning the rhythmic structure of one or two bars generally gives you the basis of the entire song. In music of a less repetitive nature this wouldn't be the case, and the rests, along with the notes, assume a more random format. Obviously this presents a greater musical challenge, but it needn't be seen as a problem. It's surprising how quickly a melody becomes a familiar rhythmic pattern in your head, including all of the rests contained within its musical structure. And since it's highly unlikely at this stage that you'll need to play a piece 'straight off the page', just peruse it at your leisure until you can play it in time.

So, welcome to exercise number 7. This contains some twists and turns for your edification, but I've kept it brief so that it shouldn't be too demanding overall. It may surprise you to see that the piece actually begins with a pair of rests. After all, you may wonder, what's the point in resting before you've even played anything? Well, that's true if you're playing the only instrument involved in the performance, but may not be when other instruments are involved.

For example, what if a composition begins with a run of notes from the bass guitar or piano? They'd be playing during the couple of beats before the guitar begins, so we need to leave some 'space' for them to do so. This is why you sometimes need to be aware of a pause before your playing begins. And in this case what you do is to start your metronome (or other device) to get the tempo (try 100bpm), then, when you feel ready to begin, mentally count '1 & 2 & 3 & 4 &', etc. The first note will be played on the third '&'. This is because there's a combination of rests precisely equal to the time value of two and a half beats. The remaining one and a half beats of this four-beat bar will be occupied by your guitar notes, all mathematically and musically correct. To make this entirely clear I've written the count directly below each note as it occurs, which should assist you in working this through.

Exercise 7

I know it might look a bit complicated at first, so the thing to do is learn it one bar at a time. The bars without any rests at all should be straightforward, and elsewhere the rests that do occur are all on the first beats of their respective bars. At the end there's a neat turnaround leading back into the beginning – although you can, of course, just end it by letting the final **C** note and chord ring on

instead of resorting to the **G7** chord lead-in again. It'll help you get the feel of the piece if you consider the first bar as an intro to the musical phrase that properly begins at bar two. This is a common device that occurs in musical composition, which you'll encounter frequently in your guitar playing. The same applies to the last bar, which serves the same purpose, being of identical construction to bar one.

A change of key

Before you start thinking that all songs must be in the key of **C** major, we're now about to try something slightly different, and bravely venture into the key of **A** major. This should make for an interesting change of fretboard scenery, and give you the chance to wrestle with a few sharps, as defined by the key signature.

The key of **A** major is what guitarists like to refer to as a 'guitar friendly' key. But what does this term, accurate though it is, really mean? Well, basically it comes down to the fact that some keys are just easier to play in than others. And this, in turn, is mainly due to the availability of open string notes that generally occur in those keys. A side-effect of all this is that because of the frequency with which any guitar player uses a 'guitar friendly' key such as A major, he or she attains considerable familiarity with the fretboard layout of notes in that key. Give any guitarist a choice between performing a song in G# or A, and I can pretty well guarantee that the preferred choice will be the latter. Of course, A isn't the only

friendly key, but it's certainly in the top five, the others being E, G, C and D. This situation relates only to unmodified standard tuning. Other keys can have their 'friendliness' enhanced by the use of a capo (see pages 143–45), but that's another story for another chapter. For now let's just keep to the point and take a look at the A major scale.

As you see, these diagrams cover a range of two octaves, which is basically just two A major scales placed together. So we're looking at notes ranging from the 5th fret of the sixth string up to the 5th fret of the first string. Notice that all the C, F and G notes are sharpened, as you would expect for this key. So, the fretboard positions for each octave are as follows (left-handed players see page 227):

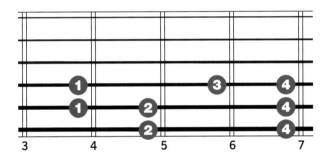

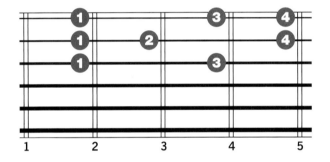

Comparing this to the finger placing of the C major scale, as seen on page 50, you'll observe that the first diagram has been moved across so that it begins on the sixth string instead of the fifth. This is to allow for the fact that we start on the A note as opposed to the C note. But the actual fingering is (relatively speaking) exactly the same, and from that starting point you can play the scale with comfortable familiarity. There are always alternative fingering options on a guitar fretboard,

but the above illustrations provide a good starting point.

So, this is perfectly OK as far as playing the scale itself is concerned, but it can place limits on the virtues of A major as being a 'guitar friendly' key. This is because it contains no open string notes, which more or less negates the points I made earlier. So we have to do something about it, and the answer is to establish a new fingering pattern. No sooner said than done:

In this diagram the letters 'O' are the recommended open string positions. These notes of A–D–B–E are also shown in black at their fretted positions, as this can be optional.

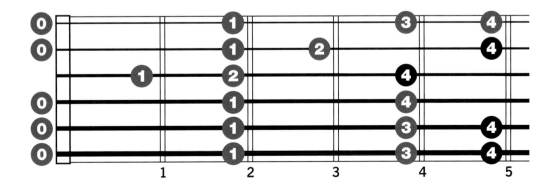

Both octaves are included in this diagram, along with the additional notes (E, F♯ and G♯) on the low sixth string, as they're available for use in this key. (Left-handed players see **page 227**.)

Working in this open position at the lower end of the neck presents you with a wider range of fingering options than fretted notes alone would allow. And, with this additional choice, there are more decisions to be made. For instance, should you play a D note on the open fourth string, or at the 5th fret position of the fifth string? And why play the open second string for a B note, as opposed to the 4th fret of the third string? These decisions will be based upon three principle factors: *feasibility*, *convenience* and *tone*. So let's consider these three points, one at a time. *Feasibility* means that something intended (composed) for playing with the inclusion of some open string notes may be impossible (or impracticably difficult) to play using all fretted notes. *Convenience* is the logical decision to achieve a satisfactory musical result in the easiest way; it's usually best to keep things simple whenever possible, although this decision will be partly influenced by point three. *Tone* is obviously important, because you'll find that any fretted note has a different sound quality compared to the open-string version of that same pitch. The musical value of these influential factors may be slightly lost on you at the moment, but will become clearer as we progress.

One of the principle assets of open strings is simply the fact that they can be played and, whilst still sounding, additional notes can be added using other strings, without having to deal with the limitations of movement which a sustained fretted note would impose. Consider the simple but effective riff shown here:

Let ring------------------------------------|

When you've played the first note of this bar, it's perfectly possible to let it continue sounding whilst the following notes are being played. Allowing a note to sustain can provide a musical foundation for those above (or below) it, which adds to the effect of your music.

Strictly speaking this is notationally inaccurate, because the first note is written as a quarter note. Therefore it should logically be silenced after one beat, as the following note begins. So, literally speaking, it should be written as two separate lines of notes sharing the same stave. The diagram shown here illustrates this principle accurately, whereby the first note is shown as a whole note underlying the others, which would begin after a one-beat rest.

However, for reasons of simplicity this type of approach is often avoided in modern guitar transcriptions, being replaced with the instruction 'let ring' written beneath the sustained note. Often even this is omitted, and it becomes a question of sensible interpretation on your part, in order to achieve the most pleasing result. A case in point would be the arpeggios you learned earlier (see **page 27**). Although these would be written as eighth notes along their stave, in actual playing terms each note is permitted to sustain until it fades naturally or is struck again by the plectrum.

OK, now that I've cleared up that ambiguity let's get back to that open-string riff, and apply it to the three main chords in the key of **A**.

Exercise 8

Let ring-----------------------------------|

These pictures clearly illustrate the chordal (based around chords) nature of riff playing. Above left is essentially an A major chord as held by the index finger. Above right is the D major version as used here.

As always it's important to consider your finger positioning when learning a new piece. After a while this will become second nature to you, but at this stage it's worthy of some deliberation. Let's take a look at some important points in this regard, as demonstrated in the pictures above.

As you see, the most effective way of playing a riff like this is to position your first (index) finger as a partial bar across the third and fourth strings at the 2nd fret, but be sure to avoid touching the open fifth string. This covers the action for most of the required notes (A, E and A), then you can easily play the additional F♯ note with your third finger as necessary. When playing the D chord riff, just hold down the second and third strings with your second and first fingers respectively, and use your free third finger for the B note. You can, of course, play the E chord part in the same manner as the A riff, but one string lower. It's just a case of minimum effort to achieve maximum effect, which is what good fretboard positioning is all about.

Open position playing is also very helpful when you might wish to elaborate upon a basic chord sequence. This can be

achieved by adding some notes as passing tones, in order to connect one chord to the next in its sequence. To understand this, it's necessary to look at how a chord might be written as notes on a stave. The example chord given here is A major. This might look a bit demanding, but all you're looking at here is an open A chord in notational form with the notes reading, from low to high, E–A–E–A–C♯–E. And, precisely because this is a bit long-winded, it's usually easier all round to just write an 'A' above the stave, and leave it at that.

On occasion, however, it may be necessary to present a chord (or, more often, a partial chord) in notation form. This is usually done when that chord forms part of a more elaborate musical pattern, consisting of chords and single notes. And, by an amazing coincidence, that's exactly what we have in our next lesson.

Exercise 9

As you practise playing this, remember that all C, F and G notes are sharpened. It's easy to forget this after playing for a while in the key of C major, which, of course, contains no such distractions. But even so, there are occasions when certain notes can occur which aren't included in the key signature,

and which might not appear to be usual for that particular key, based purely upon its basic scale notes. We deal with this situation by giving such notes individual attention in that regard, and a familiarity with this approach will expand your musical repertoire considerably.

Sharps, flats and naturals

To explain how sharps and flats work, within the context of notes on a stave, is something we introduced briefly on **page 48**. But it's  also essential to understand how we cancel out the effect of either symbol, when an altered (sharpened or flattened) note is returned to its basic pitch. The symbol used for this instruction is called a 'natural' and is shown above.

This natural indicates that the note which immediately follows it on the stave, which in this example would be an **A**, is neither sharp nor flat. The effect of this natural lasts only for the duration of the bar in which it appears, after which all notes revert back to the instruction as defined by the original key signature. To see how all of this works in practical terms, here's an example in the key of **C** major. As you're aware, **C** major is a key in which you might not usually expect to encounter any sharps or flats. In fact it's the only key of which this would be true. But sometimes they become melodically desirable. There's no technical musical reason for this occurrence, other than the fact that it just sounds right within the requirements of a particular song or riff.

In the example seen here you're looking at a sequence of notes which proceed in an ascending and then descending pattern and, apart from the first (**C**) note, are all one semitone (one fret) apart from each other in pitch. And because both the **F** note and the **F♯** note are used in this sequence as it goes up and then down again, we have to differentiate between the two in an unmistakable way. So, reading along the stave, this is what happens. The first **F** note is played in its natural form simply because the key signature of **C** major would not suggest otherwise. But the next thing you see is the 'sharp' sign, which clearly tells you to raise the following note by one fret and play it as an **F♯**. Then, after playing a normal **G** note, there's another note in the **F** position on the stave, which still falls under the effect of that earlier sharp sign, and is therefore also played as an **F♯**. The next note, however, is preceded by the natural sign, which automatically cancels out the sharp sign, and is therefore played as a normal **F** note once again.

You should be aware that a natural sign means only that you must play a note that is neither a sharp nor a flat. It doesn't mean 'revert to original key signature' or anything of that nature. This rule applies no matter what key you're in, or what that particular key signature might normally suggest. So, if a key signature such as **A** major is being used it would be the usual thing to play every **F** in its sharpened form, as you've already experienced; and if a natural (non-sharpened) **F** were used in that key, it would be preceded by a natural sign. An example of such a situation is seen here:

Reading through the notes you see that the natural sign appears before the first **F** note. This is because we're playing in the key of **A** major, wherein the key signature tells you to play every **F** as a sharp. So, in order to play it unsharpened we need the natural sign to cancel out the key signature. The next **F** note we encounter is preceded by a sharp sign, which brings it back up to **F♯** once again. This is necessary or else, despite the key signature, this note would still fall under the influence of that natural sign. The final **F** note is again given a natural symbol, in order to cancel out the previous sharp sign, and so tells you to play the unsharpened **F** once again.

There are some basic principles that can simplify and therefore help you to remember all of this:

1 When sharps or flats are in the *key signature* they apply to all specified notes along the stave, unless contradicted by individual symbols, as in the examples above.

2 Individual sharp, flat and natural signs are referred to as 'accidentals', and they apply *only* to notes within the particular bar in which they appear. As soon as you reach the next bar all notes are once again determined by the key signature.

3 Any sharp, flat or natural accidental symbol applies to *all* specified notes within that bar, unless it's contradicted (and thereby cancelled out) by another accidental, as shown in the examples above.

Return of the 'tie' sign

It's time to give some more attention to the tie sign, as last seen on **page 45**. The principle of employing a tie sign on a music stave is exactly the same as in a chord chart, except that instead of extending the duration of a chord it extends the duration of a single note or notes. The reasons for using a tie sign to make a note longer, instead of just using a different note symbol (of longer duration), can vary with the requirements of musical circumstances. Consider the two illustrations below:

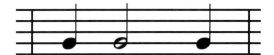

On the left is one bar of music notation consisting of four quarter notes, the middle two of which are 'tied' together to give them the time value of one half note, whereas on the right is a bar consisting of one quarter note, one half note and another quarter note. In other words, they both tell you to play exactly the same thing. In this case, although it's musically correct if you wish to do so, there's little point in using a tie sign.

The following example is entirely different. This presents us with two bars of music in which the final note of bar one is carried over into the adjacent bar, where it continues uninterrupted for the first beat of bar two. In this situation a tie sign is essential, as it's the only way of continuing the duration of a note beyond the bar in which it is first sounded.

Another use for a tie sign might be to combine note time values, which, although connected within the same bar, couldn't be represented in any other way. The next diagram gives us a fairly basic example of this type of situation, but of course the range of tie combinations can vary widely in complexity.

All of these examples, intricate as they might appear to be, are still just four beats to each bar. These beats may be (notationally) joined or divided in various ways, but if you examine them carefully you'll see that they all add up to four in their total time value.

Anyway, the real point here is to clarify the need for tie signs in various musical circumstances. We'll experiment with some of these in our next exercise, along with the occasional accidental thrown in just for the fun of it. And, as if that wasn't enough to keep you awake, we're going to do this all in the new key of **G** major. But before we get to that, let's just have a quick look at the **G** major scale.

As before, this covers a range of two octaves, which in this case is from the 3rd fret on the sixth string up to the 3rd fret on the first string. Notice that the **G** major key signature indicates every **F** should be played sharp, unless instructed otherwise by any accidentals on the music you may be playing. You know enough by now to work out your own finger positions, so I'm not including any fretboard diagrams here. The choice of fretted or open strings for certain notes is optional, depending upon the relative convenience of what you may be required to play.

Exercise 10

(musical notation: G, G7, C, C7 / D, D7, G, F, F#, G)

As an exercise in **G** major you might expect most, if not all, of the **F** notes to be played sharp. In this case, however, two of them are played natural, and one of the **B** notes is flattened too. This might seem to be overdoing it a little, but the number of accidentals in this piece are essential in maintaining the basic structure of the main riff. For instance, just try playing that **B♭** note as a normal **B** instead. Your ears will instantly tell you that something is wrong. To put it simply, it just sounds better the other way – which must always be the determining factor in any piece of music. These accidental notes don't in any way contradict the fact that **G** major is the essential key centre to this piece. A good indication of key centre is usually the last note played. This final **G** note gives the sound a satisfactory conclusion, whereas any other note would leave the music sounding 'unresolved'.

The tie signs here aren't too difficult to follow, as they form a repetitive rhythmic pattern. But do go over this exercise (and any others) as many times as necessary, in order to ensure that you understand what's going on here. It's really quite straightforward, but try to avoid impatience, which might hinder your progress later on.

A situation which can occur with tie signs, and which therefore you need to be aware of, is when notes are played in pairs and a tie sign is shown which applies to only one note of that pair. This is best illustrated by an example, as seen here in its basic form:

This tie sign could be easily misunderstood, simply because the notes are set in pairs. This could be taken to mean that the tie sign applies to both notes of that pair. This isn't the case, and in fact it only relates to the lower (**D**) note of that pair, whilst the upper (**A**) note remains unaffected. In playing terms this means that the A note is struck (by the plectrum) five times, and the D note is played only four times. If the upper line of notes were also 'tied' at the same point the written example would look somewhat different, as in the second example pictured here:

As you see, a distinctly different picture is created by the addition of that extra tie sign, which permits all notes in this bar to maintain their rhythmic uniformity.

Dotted notes

Whilst note duration can be extended by tying, there's another method which, although less versatile than the tie, is commonly used to increase the time of any note by half its usual duration. This is the dotted note, examples of which are pictured below in comparison with tied notes.

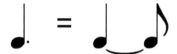 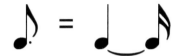

As you see, a dotted half note (minim) is increased in time value as if it were tied to a quarter note. Next in line is a dotted quarter note (crotchet), which equals the time value as if tied to an eighth note. And finally we see a dotted eighth note (quaver), which is as if tied to a 16th note. This rule applies to a note or rest of any time value, whereby you simply add half as much time on to the standard duration value of that note.

There will obviously be situations where tied notes are employed instead of an equally timed dotted note, and indeed the opposite is true, whereby a dotted note is used, although tied notes would do the same job. There's no fixed rule about which of these two options should be used in a particular situation. It usually depends upon which is visually most convenient, and helps the musician to read a phrase more easily. And bearing all these interesting little details in mind we now look at another exercise in the key of **G** major, which features both dotted notes and ties on both single and double-note (harmony) phrases.

In this exercise there are no accidentals to demand your attention, so all the **F** notes are actually **F** sharp, and all other notes are played natural. But don't worry, you'll have plenty to think about anyway, so it shouldn't get too boring.

Exercise 11

The large number of ties and notes of varying duration makes this a tricky piece to learn. However, in order to assist you in understanding where the beats fall in relation to each note, I've again (as in exercise 7) placed the counts directly below each note. The choice of where to play each note on the fretboard is obviously your decision, but here are a few suggestions that may be helpful to you for ease of fingering convenience.

1 The first two bars can be played mostly in the 3rd fret position, but then shift to an open position on that final (**E**) note of bar two.

2 On the third bar, played over an **Em** chord, use open strings whenever possible.

3 In bar four (**Bm**), watch out for that tie sign, because it only applies to the lower (**B**) note. So that note is a continuation of the preceding note and is allowed to sustain as the note above it (**D**) is played.

4 The **C** and **D7** bars are straightforward enough, and again use open strings as necessary.

5 Bar number seven, played over the **G** chord, is probably the one that requires most careful attention, as it contains three ties, one of which carries over into the following bar. It may help if you learn the actual note sequence of this bar first, in order to then give full attention to the rhythmic feel of where the notes fall in relation to the count of beats.

6 Bars nine and eleven have phrases which bear timing similarities to the previously mentioned bar seven. Make use of this fact in getting the feel of these bars.

Now that you understand how dotted notes work, this opens up your versatility to one of the most widely used of all rhythmic patterns. This is a timing phrase used commonly in both rhythm and lead playing, which, in its notational form (shown with equivalent individual notes), appears like this:

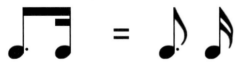

What you see is a dotted eighth note followed by a 16th note. In other words, the first note has a combined time value of three 16th notes, and this is immediately followed by a single 16th note. And, because four 16ths add up to one quarter, you would need four such pairs to make

up a full bar. How this looks and sounds in timing terms is displayed, with plectrum strokes and beats counts for added clarification, pictured in the following diagram.

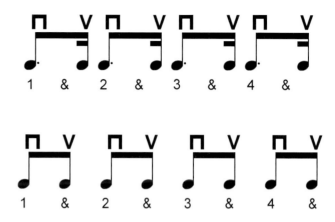

To assist you in understanding the timing of this, just think of it as a rhythm pattern instead of worrying about any particular note pitch. And, in this context, try comparing it with the straight eighth note rhythm as also illustrated.

Pay careful attention to the relationship between the notes and the count numbers under the notes. In the basic familiar eighth rhythm, the notes are directly above the count of '1 & 2 & 3 & 4 &', giving a very steady timing pace. However, when you study the dotted eighth/sixteenth rhythm, the situation is somewhat different. Although the *first* of each note pairing is directly in line with the timing count (1, 2, 3, 4) the second of these note pairs does not appear immediately above the '&' symbol. So, when you count evenly along with your metronome, each upstroke note is slightly behind the '&' count. To be precise, the second note of each pair occurs exactly halfway between the '&' and the following number, making this a very exaggerated type of rhythm, with a long downstroke and a very quick upstroke.

In order for you to get the feel of this, I'd recommend strumming a chord (any chord will do) to this rhythmic pattern. This will help to familiarise you with the basic idea of the timing before we attempt anything more complicated. Set a tempo of around 100bpm. Anything significantly faster will be too frantic to start with, and much slower would make it very difficult to get into the correct feel of things.

Shuffling along

When this type of timing is used in rhythm playing it's generally referred to as a 'shuffle rhythm'. Status Quo wouldn't want to be without it, and once you get the hang of it neither will you. It comes up everywhere in its various forms, including rock and roll, country music, blues, 'heavy' rock, and really any other popular music you care to name. The most immediate example that comes to mind is the good old rock and roll rhythm from way back on **pages 41–43**. All you need do in order to bring an entirely different feel to this riff is play it with this new type of timing. Look at the example below to see what I mean when played over a **G** major chord, first in straight eighths and then in shuffle rhythm.

Shuffle rhythms are frequently written and played in a somewhat modified, less exaggerated way. This next form is based upon a triplet style as will be familiar to you from chord chart 10 (**page 25**). But in this case it's usually played in a somewhat 'heavier' manner, often using the good old rock and blues riff as shown above, and with the rhythm played in a 'broken' style for added effect. The following examples will demonstrate exactly how this works:

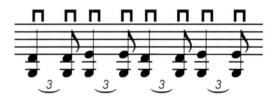

Although these two examples (above left and right) appear quite different, they're actually variations of the same thing. The first one, as seen on the left, is a familiar triplet rhythm played over the classic rock riff based on a **G** chord – with a limited amount of study you'd be able to play this with no difficulty – whereas the other diagram, above right, looks rather unfamiliar and complicated. But all it is, in fact, is the same thing as the triplet riff, played without the upstrokes. So instead of counting '1–2–3, 1–2–3,' etc, you'd be thinking more like '1 & 3, 1 & 3,' etc, and 'missing' the strings on each upstroke of the triplet where the '&' count occurs.

All of this is perfectly fine and very useable in many situations, but it isn't the end of the story. Ask yourself what happens if, instead of allowing each 'missed' stroke to sustain until the next note(s) occurs, you decide to silence those particular strokes by slightly relaxing your left-hand pressure on the strings. In that case you'd be looking at something like the next diagram. Again we have a triplet rhythm, but with the middle notes of that rhythm silenced, instead of sustaining until the next plectrum downstroke.

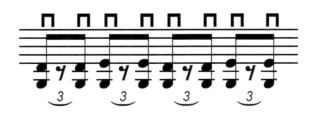

With timing phrases such as these the notation can make a simple riff look rather more complicated than it actually is. And when you familiarise yourself with the way it sounds, and indeed feels, to play this type of notation, it will quickly lose its mystery and then be easily understood on future occasions. To help you get into this type of shuffle rhythm, the next exercise is mainly a basic rock and roll riff, with just a few connecting notes along the way. This also introduces you to the key of **D** major, so let's have a look at the **D** scale before we begin.

As usual this scale covers two octaves, for general demonstration purposes, but any other notes above or below these pitches will apply in the same way. In other words, all **F**s and **C**s are sharpened in the key or **D** major unless any accidentals (remember them?) indicate otherwise.

The only part of this next piece that requires any special mention is the very last bar. This begins with a brief strum of the **D** chord, followed by an **A7** chord for the remainder of the bar. Although it's written in notation form, that's all this actually is: an **A7** bar chord at the 5th fret. I recommend playing this final bar with alternate up and down strokes of the plectrum, whereas the rest of the piece should preferably be played with just downstrokes.

Exercise 12

Start out by keeping to a fairly slow tempo, in order to make space for the rest parts of the rhythm. Begin at a pace of around 80–90bpm, and when you're completely at ease playing this rhythm aim to gradually pick up to something like 112–120bpm. This isn't really the type of thing which can be played very fast anyway, because of the staccato (with distinct breaks between notes) nature of the rhythm.

The effect of these rests is to make the rhythm a lot more dynamic, and this can be exaggerated still further by damping the strings slightly with the palm of your strumming hand. In this situation it doesn't do any harm to add a nice touch of overdrive/distortion to your amp sound, which I'm sure you'll find very effective indeed.

Onward and upward

Much of what we've done so far has been played, or at least is playable (there are always alternatives), in the lower part of the fretboard, but this still leaves about half of the neck unexplored. Before we venture in that upward direction, have a look at the following diagram, which is simply the notes E, F,

G and A as might be played on the first and second strings around frets 5–8, and then one octave higher around frets 17–20.

When you look at these two examples, it probably occurs to you that the written version of the upper octave doesn't exactly fit comfortably on to the stave. In fact it's so far above the stave that it could almost seem to be written on the stave above it! Any notes higher than this on a stave would represent a hazard to low-flying aircraft, so it's just as well that we have an alternative. And here it is – the 'octave' sign.

When you see this written above the stave it means that all the notes 'covered' by the dotted line are to be played exactly one octave higher. This can cover several bars, or alternately only part of a bar. So it's not 'bar specific' in the way that something such as an accidental would be.

If we now revisit the previous example, but with the octave sign added, the situation has changed. Now both apparently different pitch notations would be played exactly the same, around frets 17–20. This octave sign isn't particularly limited only to the notes beyond the 12th fret, but it would serve little purpose applied to anything much lower, simply because they're able to be placed comfortably on the stave without getting too high for practical use. You'll also find that it makes things just a lot more readable this way because, quite frankly, it's very easy to get lost among endlessly ascending rows of leger lines.

As an example of how this looks on a stave within a piece of music, exercise 13 makes use of this octave sign on a nifty little riff, again in the key of D major.

Exercise 13

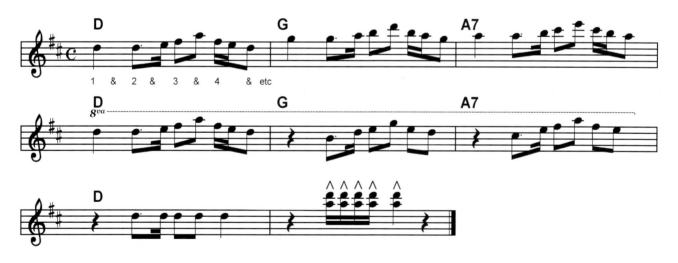

The counts below the notes in bar one will help you get into the rhythmic feel of this piece. So get the first bar right and then the others will more easily fall into place. As you observe in bar three, the notes are climbing high enough above the stave that you wouldn't want to keep heading in that upward direction, leading us logically toward the use of the octave sign over the next bar. But

notice that this applies only to the three bars 'covered' by the dotted line, and so it's back to normal pitch for the last two bars.

The final bar notes all have a strange arrow sign (∧) above them, which you haven't encountered before. This is an easy one to learn. It's an 'accent' sign, a commonly used symbol in written music, and all it tells you is to play those notes slightly louder than the others.

Time for a waltz

Without a doubt 4/4 (common) time is by far the most widely used time signature in popular music, but of course it isn't the only one. In fact it's likely that you'll encounter several different time signatures as you progress with your musical career. But having said that, apart from common time the next most essential for you to learn is 3/4 time, which contains only three beats to the bar. Also referred to as waltz time, I'm sure you'll have heard it on a great many occasions, even if you didn't recognise it as such. It most often occurs in more genteel types of music such as (you guessed it) waltzes.

I realise that the idea of playing a waltz may not be high on your list of musical priorities at the moment, but this isn't a time signature that went out of use somewhere in the 19th century. It really does continue to show up in popular songs right up to and including the present day. Unquestionably, your musical education will be seriously incomplete if you don't become familiar with 3/4 time.

Without this in your repertoire you will, sooner or later, be trying to learn some piece of music and wondering why you can't fit four beats into every bar. So let's start with a few sample bars, to give you the idea of how this looks with regard to notes of various time values.

There's nothing especially complicated about this situation. As you see, each bar is made up of notes with a combined maximum time value of three beats, or quarter notes. This could equally apply to rest symbols, as the situation may require. Notice the dotted half note (minim) occupying the entire last bar, because 3/4 time doesn't permit a whole note to be used as in 4/4 time.

When you play in waltz time the emphasis tends to fall on the first beat of the bar, giving that characteristic lilting rhythm. Try counting '1–2–3, 1–2–3,' etc, as you strum along

to any chord sequence. The pattern shown below should get you into the correct feel to get you started in 3/4 time.

If you're playing in time with the basic click from a metronome, just set the tempo as usual (about 120bpm). However, if your timing device is more elaborate – such as a drum rhythm machine, for instance – you'll need to adjust its settings from 4/4 time into 3/4 time. Otherwise you'll end up in a rhythmic mess, with the accents in all the wrong places. The instruction manual for your particular timepiece will explain how to make the necessary adjustments.

Exercise 14

You'll notice that this bears strong similarities to exercise 9 (page 57) in terms of the bass note/chord strum rhythm style. It's simply adapted for waltz time, with three beats instead of four per bar. And that basically is what we're looking at here – one beat less than you're accustomed to

in every bar. So we aren't dealing with anything particularly confusing, it's just a question of being aware of the requirements of a particular musical situation, and knowing how to apply the correct rhythmic feel to your playing.

Clear, clean and accurate

It's worth adding a timely reminder at this point about the importance of accuracy in your playing, as was mentioned briefly on **page 27**. This is one of those things that is often given little emphasis when learning to play the guitar, but is actually something which separates the amateur from the more professional player. Guitarists are generally obsessed with playing faster and flashier than all the rest, but this is a bit pointless without precision of timing and general playing sensitivity. When you practise, albeit with a timepiece for guidance, the occasional error (sometimes fairly slight) can easily go unnoticed. So I recommend that from time to time

you should record yourself performing these exercises. It doesn't need to be an expensive hi-tech multi-track recording unit for this purpose. Anything functional will suffice. Then listen carefully to the playback, for any discrepancies of timing (compared to the metronome), or interruption in the smooth flow of notes. You may be surprised to discover than there's room for improvement in even the simplest piece. This kind of self-imposed discipline may initially be a little discouraging, but will pay off in the long run when you're the one band member who doesn't need 50 takes in the studio before it comes out right.

Arpeggio in waltz time

To help fix this new time signature in your mind, the following exercise is a waltz time arpeggio. This time we'll be playing in

the key of **E** major, and so a new key signature applies, which features sharpened notes on every **F**, **G**, **C** and **D**.

Exercise 15

Occasionally you will encounter a piece of music in which more than one time signature is employed. The written music for such a composition would make this quite clear by introducing a new time signature at the appropriate point along the stave. So, for example, the song begins in 4/4 time but

then changes into 3/4 time (or vice versa), and quite possibly later changes back into 4/4 time again. This type of situation in popular music is relatively uncommon, but not remarkably so. The Beatles were fond of using this device in some of their later work, two examples being *All You Need is Love* and *Lucy in the Sky with Diamonds* (which also, incidentally, features a key change – as explained below).

Another time signature that's often encountered in this context is 2/4 time, which is essentially the same as 4/4 time but of only half the duration. Because of this, 2/4 time is useful to a composer if he or she feels that, say, two bars of 4/4 time is too much for a certain musical situation, but one bar would be too little. So the answer would logically be that one and a half bars feel just about right. The solution is to add a bar of 2/4 time next to the bar of 4/4 time. A well-known example of this would be the Roy Orbison classic, *Pretty Woman*. In either listening or playing terms, none of these things are really problematic, but you need to be aware of them in order to understand a seemingly unusual rhythmic structure whenever it may occur. Study the examples below, keeping a steady but changing count as you practise.

Example 1: Time signature change between common time (4/4) and waltz time (3/4)

Example 2: Time signature change from 4/4 time into 2/4 time

In a related context, it's also true that key changes can occur within the same song. Again a similar situation applies, in that the new key signature with its appropriate sharps or flats would be introduced at some relevant point on the stave. I need hardly add that this can be reversed at any time by reintroduction of the original key signature, or for that matter any other key signature which the composition may require.

In the following example a piece of music changes from the key of E major into the key of F major. As you've not yet encountered this key signature, I need only tell you that F major is a key in which all B notes are played flat, and therefore its signature is as shown in brief here. For a more complete reference to this, and other key signatures, please refer to **page 104**.

In our key change example, as seen here, there are initially two bars of E notation, and before the key change can occur all of the E major signature sharps must be cancelled out by the appropriate series of naturals. This is so that the introduction of the B♭ following isn't mistaken as simply being an accidental. Then the new key signature is introduced, effectively shifting everything up one step in pitch into F major.

Obviously these are only a few demonstration bars, and in reality it isn't likely that a key change would occur so immediately in any piece of genuine composition. Again, it's all simple enough to understand, and isn't something you'll encounter very often. But without this option of completely changing key when required, a composer would have to resort to using a comprehensive and confusing clutter of accidentals to achieve the same musical effect.

Other instructional signs and symbols

Apart from those that you've already learned, there are a number of other musical directions that you will, to some degree, commonly encounter in almost any piece of written music. And if we all spoke fluent Italian this would make things a lot easier. Unfortunately this isn't the case, so it becomes a situation whereby we must commit to memory a number of words and phrases, some of which are accompanied rather helpfully by visual symbols that act as cues for our attention at crucial points in the music.

Nowadays it's likely that you'll be familiar with the overall sound and format of much of the music you wish to play, because you'll have heard a recording of it. But it must be remembered that written music predates recorded sound by a substantial margin of time, and it was therefore necessary that it should act as a complete self-contained language of the most comprehensive kind, requiring no additional instruction in order to convey the intention of the composer to a high degree of accuracy. Implicit to this intent would be dynamic directions involving volume and phrasing, which is where we begin. Occasionally you'll find that the English word is used instead of the Italian, but it's as well to be familiar with both options.

Symbol	Italian word	English meaning
ff	Fortissimo	Very loud
f	Forte	Loud
mf	Mezzo forte	Moderately loud
mp	Mezzo piano	Moderately soft (quiet)
p	Piano	Soft
pp	Pianissimo	Very soft

In addition to these dynamic directions, another commonly seen instruction – usually found at the beginning of the music – would be that involving tempo, or the approximate speed at which the music should ideally be played. These are necessarily generalised and are sometimes replaced with the more specific and somewhat more satisfactory designation of actual beats per minute. But the traditional Italian words describing music speed are within the tempo range as shown here.

Italian word	English meaning	Beats per minute
Presto	Very fast	168–200
Allegro	Fast	120–168
Moderato	Moderate speed	108–120
Andante	Brisk walking pace	76–108
Adagio	Slow	66–76
Largo	Very slow	40–60

Also worth noting are those symbols which give regard to volume changes. These are the *crescendo* (increase volume gradually) and *diminuendo* (decrease volume gradually) symbols, which add to the expressive feel of the music. These are as displayed here (although the actual words wouldn't normally appear below the stave, as in this demonstration).

Crescendo

Diminuendo

Certain other directions occur with regard to the format of the music – that is to say, which verse follows the first, and then where to go after that, and so on. This information is conveyed with the *segno* and *coda* signs, which work in an interactive sort of way and are pictured here.

Segno   **Coda**

Bearing in mind that most pieces of music have numerous verse and chorus structures, it would be very long-winded to write a piece of music in its entirety when much of it is basically repetitions of what's gone before. You'll be aware that the melody of the second verse of any popular song is almost certainly identical to that of the first verse. So to avoid using up ten pages of manuscript where two or three would suffice we resort to these symbols, in order to clarify the order in which these repetitions should be played. An example of how they might appear is seen below.

Exercise 16

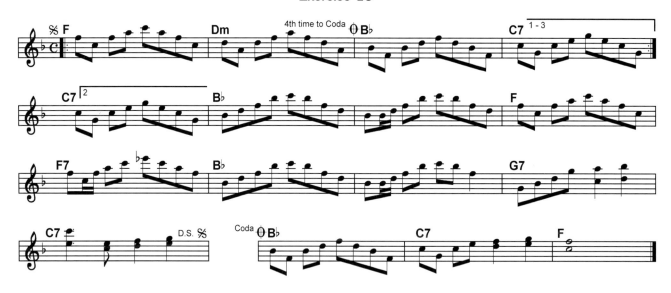

A piece of music written in this way provides you with all the necessary instructions as to the direction it should take, and where any repeats (and how many) should occur. This is in fact an efficient form of shorthand, and can be easily understood with a modicum of care and attention. For a detailed explanation of this piece and its symbols see below.

Exercise 16 should be interpreted as follows. Play the first four bars until you arrive at the repeat symbols (see **page 20**). The instruction above the bar at this point informs you that this bar is to be played on the first and (later) third run-through, but not on the second and fourth. Then begin again, playing from bars one to three, where you then continue at bar five. Note the instruction over this bar, which confirms it as the correct direction to proceed on the second occasion. Continue up until the end of bar 13 where you encounter the DS and segno symbol. This literally means Dal Segno or 'from the sign'. So you return to the segno sign above the very first bar. Continue until the repeat signs and then play bars one and two again where you encounter the *coda* (literally 'to the

tail') symbol. This tells you to skip to the ending part as marked by the *coda* symbol. At this point you follow through to the end.

Admittedly it seems a bit cluttered in this instance, but that's because it's a brief example. On an actual full-length composition the symbols and instructions will be less crowded. At this time it will be useful (if you haven't already done so) to acquire some sheet music of your choice, and apply what you've learnt to a realistic situation. No doubt you will, to a substantial degree, be guided by the familiarity of music you've heard many times in recorded form. This isn't necessarily a bad thing, and it will help you to see how your studies so far have paid off when you're able to interpret sheet music in a practical way.

Reading tab

An abbreviation of the word 'tablature', tab is simply an alternative system of written music for stringed and fretted instruments. Although, contrary to popular belief, it's been around for several centuries, the use of tablature has greatly increased in popularity over recent years. It's important that you acquire an understanding of this system because you're likely to encounter it at least as often as standard music notation.

You'll be happy to know that because it's specific to string/

fretted instruments, tab is relatively easy to understand. So the obvious question is, why have I devoted this entire chapter thus far to learning traditional notation, which is rather more complicated and (in the case of guitar music) no more widely used than tab? The answer is that both systems have something going for them that the other doesn't. But before I get too far into explaining these comparative virtues, I'll demonstrate exactly how tab works. Take a look at the example diagram below:

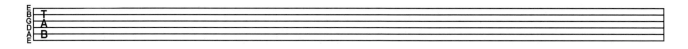

Although this initially resembles the conventional music staff, a closer examination reveals the difference. Whereas the music staff consists of five horizontal lines, tab music uses six. Each of these lines represents one of the strings on your guitar, and bears no relationship to the lines on a traditional music staff. Reading from the bottom line upward these 'strings' are, as you might expect, E–A–D–G–B–E.

Any sequence of notes can be indicated by placing a fret number along the appropriate 'string' line, so a basic C major scale could be written as shown above right.

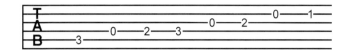

Reading along the tab, you see how simple this is. Begin with the fifth string 3rd fret, then play the fourth string open, followed by the fourth string 2nd fret; fourth string 3rd fret; third string open; third string 2nd fret; second string open, and finally the second string 1st fret.

When you encounter guitar tab in music books it's often used in conjunction with standard notation. This provides you with the benefits of both systems at once, and, as an example, would be written as seen above.

Tabby timing

With this tab system of numbers written along the 'string' lines, it's obviously necessary to indicate note duration when no other system is employed alongside the tab. This, for a note reader such as you are now, is simplicity itself, as the diagram below illustrates:

This is identical to the example above, except that it isn't paired with notation which would inform you as to timing of the notes. So the tab itself has timing strokes, which in this case is a combination of quarter notes and eighth notes. If longer note duration is required then a tie sign will be used to indicate this. But most tab will be used along with standard notation, and will then not employ rhythmic strokes under (or over) the numbers.

An important point to remember is that because this system relates directly to strings and fret positions, there's never a need for key signatures of any kind. All tab lines therefore, whatever the key, appear identical in this regard. And, because tab is usually written in conjunction with

standard notation, the tab line won't have any time signature either.

Whilst traditional music notation tells you which note to play, tab also specifies exactly where (on the guitar fretboard) that note should ideally be played. This can be handy, because a guitar offers a range of positions for many notes. Sometimes your choice of position can improve the playability or indeed the tonal quality of a riff or sequence of notes, and tab usually provides you with the best option.

The disadvantage of the tab system is that all too often it assumes your familiarity with a song, and omits certain crucial information such as timing, format or dynamic directions. This problem is particularly common on the Internet, where many music websites provide tab and chords in a rather basic form, with no regard for the finer points of musical detail.

Mindful of these pros and cons for each system you now have the advantage of both options, by having taken the time to learn traditional music notation and standard guitar tab.

Tips, tricks and techniques

When you play any note on the guitar, there are several ways in which your left (fretboard) or right (picking) hand can vary and enhance the basic sound produced by the string. The various techniques described in this chapter are essential in creating a professional and distinctive sound in your lead (melody) guitar work. And almost any guitar solo you've ever heard will incorporate some, and occasionally all, of these features.

String bending

This is a technique in which any fretted note, when sounded, is raised in pitch by pushing (bending) the string across the neck, thereby increasing its tension, causing pitch change to occur. So the degree of pitch change depends upon exactly how far you bend the string. Typically a bent note will be raised between a semitone (one fret higher in pitch) and a tone and a half (three frets higher). It's possible to bend more than this, but you'd need considerable finger strength and very light gauge strings (see **page 169**).

To give you the general idea of what a 'bent' string looks like, refer to the picture below.

As you see in this photograph, the thumb is hooked over the guitar neck. This helps by providing stability and increasing the leverage between the thumb and whichever finger (in this example the third) is creating the bend. As you push on the bent string you will collide with adjacent strings, which can create unwanted noise. The answer is to use any available fret hand finger (any not actually doing the bending) to mute other strings as may be necessary.

The obvious questions that you may be asking are: does bending tend to put the strings out of tune, and does it cause strings to break very often? The answers are: if the machine heads (tuners) are in good order and the strings have been properly stretched (see **page 172**) they'll maintain good tuning stability, and if you change your strings at sensible intervals (see **page 173**) they're in little danger of breaking.

Be aware that if the action (see **page 175**) on your guitar is too low it becomes difficult to get a decent grip on the string, and your fingers will tend to slip over them. Low action may be convenient for holding down chords, but it does create its own problems, so adjust accordingly.

A good way to begin is with a simple one semitone (one fret) bend, and the strongest finger to begin with is your third. So, press down the second string at the 4th fret and play the D♯ note. Then, whilst it's still sounding, bend the string upward until the pitch reaches the note of **E**. You don't actually play the string again on the **E** note; it just reaches that pitch from the original pick stroke. The trick is to apply just enough pressure to reach the higher note, but without overdoing it. The reason I've suggested this particular movement is that when your ear tells you that you've bent up accurately, you

Example 1

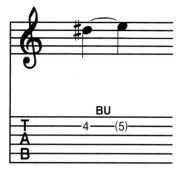

can compare the bent second string against the pitch of the open first string. This (assuming your guitar is correctly in tune) will be an accurate **E** note.

The written notation and tab for what you're playing are shown here, with the letters 'BU' as an abbreviation of 'bend up'. The tab note you're bending up to is shown in brackets, indicating the fret pitch created by that bend. In other words, bending up from the 4th fret (accurately) results in a pitch identical to that which you would hear from a note *played* at the 5th fret.

When you feel comfortable with the semitone bend at this position on the neck, feel free to try it at other fret positions. As you play it elsewhere on the neck it will require different degrees of pressure. The higher up you go, the easier it becomes to bend. But lower down, especially nearer the nut, it's generally harder to string bend. Wherever you play, your ear should tell you when accurate pitch has been achieved.

The next logical move is to try a whole tone (two fret) bend – and this time we'll move across to the third string at the 7th fret, and begin on the **D** note. Secure this firmly with your third finger as before, and bend it up until it reaches the note of **E**. Again this is convenient for checking your pitch accuracy against the open first string; and see how this reads on the written (note and tab) music seen at right.

A special mention here if your guitar is equipped with a so-called 'tremolo (vibrato) arm', such as that fitted to a Fender Stratocaster. When you bend any string, it increases the tension on the springs of this device (see **page 183**). This pulls the bridge unit forward slightly, the same as if

Example 2

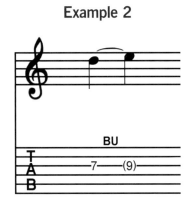

you were operating the tremolo bar, thereby lowering the pitch of all strings. And exactly how severely it does this depends not only upon the amount of bend, but also on how the tremolo springs are tensioned. To reduce this situation to a manageable compromise you may need to refer to Chapter 9 (**pages 182–84**), and make adjustments as necessary.

Grace notes

What we've done so far is to play a note and then bend it up into the following note. So it's two distinctly separate notes from one pick stroke. But very often a bend occurs immediately upon playing the note, and effectively this means that as the plectrum strikes the string, bending is already taking place. And because this has to be somehow indicated in written music we refer to something known as a 'grace note'.

A grace note, which looks like a miniature version of a normal note, has no actual time value of its own. Instead it becomes part of the note to which it is tied, and therefore exists only (in this case) to indicate where the bend starts. So from a timing perspective you should consider that the grace note is instantaneously played into its accompanying

note. Example 3 shows you what this is all about, in that you bend up as you play the note instead of just afterwards, as in the previous examples.

When you bend notes with the third finger, as you've done so far, there's the tendency to support the bend with the other fingers as well. This is OK, and is something pretty much everyone does. But it might deceive you as to the greater effort required when you try bending with other fingers. The index finger, as an example, is a lot harder to bend with, and the second finger can be tricky too. These fingers have minimal, if any, support from others, and also the angle of the thumb against the neck affords less leverage. Nevertheless, there are many occasions when those fingers must be used for bending, usually because of where you approach from (notationally speaking), or where your next move is going to be. So practise with these fingers also, to build up strength and get the feel of their use as 'benders'.

You should find that a semitone bend isn't too difficult with the index finger, particularly higher up the neck, but a two-fret bend is hard work, and pretty well impossible lower down. As usual it's just a question of practice and experience for you to become aware of your limits, and how best to deal with them in terms of neck positioning and fret choice. Also important is the gauge of the strings on your guitar (see **page 169**). Light gauge strings are obviously easier to bend than heavy ones simply because they have less tension when tuned to correct pitch.

Example 3

Bending in harmony

An attractive use of string bending is to pair the bent note with another string that remains unbent. This provides a harmony (note of sympathetic pitch) to the bend, which can be very effective in the appropriate context. So, what we're doing is playing two strings together, but with only one actually doing any bending. Of course, it's important to pair notes which are mutually appropriate to the chord against which they're being played. To begin with a typical example, let's suppose the chord being played is E major, and two notes which would certainly belong with this chord are G# and B.

The B note should be held steady (with your fourth finger, I suggest) on the first string (7th fret), and the second string note is bent up (with your third finger) from F# into the G#. This is a typical phrase that has a country guitar style to it, but would work well in many musical situations.

At first you'll find it tricky to hold the first string steady whilst bending the lower string, but it won't take long to get over this. So look at the note/tab in example 4 and practise until you get it right.

Example 4

The advantage of playing two notes together, where one is bent and the other isn't, can be the fact that despite (in this case) not being of unison pitch, the unbent note tends to act as a pitch guide to the bent note. So you can tell if your bend is slightly inaccurate because it will sound out of tune with the steady note.

A variation on this theme is to add yet another harmony note above the bend. This is basically a case of bending one note within a chord, creating a sound like that of a pedal steel guitar. The legendary country rock and session guitarist James Burton had this type of effect in mind when he helped to develop this style in the 1950s, and was one of the first to use very light-gauge strings for the purpose of easier bending. Back then the gauge range of 'off-the-shelf' guitar strings was rather limited in comparison with that of today, so he rather imaginatively used banjo strings wherever necessary to achieve his purpose.

Try the next exercise (example 5), which is bending into a D major chord. I've placed it in this neck position to make it easier to play, but as your fingers get stronger you'll be able to play it lower down also. The principle here is quite straightforward. Your fourth finger should hold down the notes of D and A on the first

Example 5

and second strings respectively, whilst your third finger on the third string bends the E note up into an F#. So, with D, F# and A together you're actually playing a D major triad (three-note chord).

Another cute little trick made possible by string bending is to play the same (unison) pitch note on two different strings. Now obviously this can be done quite easily without bending, on any of the open strings, but elsewhere on the guitar fretboard it would require a four or five-fret stretch. So unless you happen to have exceptionally long fingers it isn't a very practical thing to do. The next couple of examples will introduce you to the possibilities of this approach. Both involve the same two strings (first and second) and fret positions (5 and 8). The difference lies either in bending immediately as you play both strings together or, alternately, bending up the second string and then holding the bend whilst playing the first string to match it.

Hold the first string, 5th fret, with the index finger, and hold the second string, 8th fret, with your little finger. Then, as in the example at upper right, play both strings together, bending as you play. In the other example, at lower right, secure the strings in the same way and then play only the second string. Bend the string upward into the higher note and then play the first string to achieve the unison pitch.

Example 6

Example 7

Although string bending is most often done on the higher strings, in actuality any of the six strings can be bent, in accordance with your musical taste and melodic requirements. It's just that because the lower three strings are wound (see pages 169–70), they're harder to manipulate in this way. It's unlikely that you'd be able to bend the low strings much more than a couple of frets in pitch, although this will vary somewhat, depending upon your position on the fretboard.

An additional hazard in playing lower string bends is that the low **E** and **A** strings (and sometimes the **D**) will have a tendency to slip over the edge of the guitar neck if they're bent upward in the usual way.

The way to avoid this embarrassing and noisy situation is to bend them in the opposite direction, pulling the string downward instead of pushing up. The picture below illustrates this in action.

This type of approach is an obvious necessity when attempting low string bends, and isn't really difficult to do. But, not having the weight and strength of your hand behind the bend, you'll be relying on finger strength alone. Ensure that you secure the string firmly against the fretboard so that slippage doesn't occur, and don't be over-ambitious with the extent of pitch bend you wish to achieve.

Bending over backwards: pre-bends

Of special note is the technique of bending a string before it's actually sounded. This might seem a little weird, but the object here is to play a string that's already in bent position, and then release hand/finger pressure in order to return that string to its unbent condition. This creates the somewhat different sound of a note that's gracefully (we hope) descending in pitch. This is referred to as a 'pre-bend', and requires the additional skill of bending the string to an accurate degree, without first having heard any sound to act as pitch guidance.

In ordinary string bending you play the note first and then bend upward. You know when to stop bending because your ear tells you that correct pitch has been reached. But in a pre-bend situation, you hear no sound until after the string has been bent and played. So how do you know how much bend pressure to apply? The boring answer is, of course, experience. And, by way of additional advice, always use strings of a familiar gauge, so that the hand/finger pressure required at least remains constant.

A basic example of a pre-bend is seen here, of a note descending from **A** into **G#**, as might be played over an **E** major chord. And considering that you already know the letters BU to mean 'bend up', I'm sure you can guess that BD is an abbreviation of 'bend down'.

Example 8

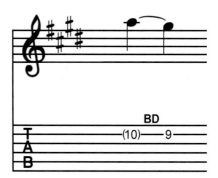

Obviously, bends of varying degrees (of pitch) will require varying degrees of pressure, but keep in mind that different fretboard positions also affect the amount of effort needed to achieve an accurate bend. This is quite enough to handle with ordinary upward bends, but that much more difficult to calculate with precision in a pre-bend situation. But don't drive yourself crazy striving for 100% accuracy in every fret position at this stage. It works out much better, and easier, to just gradually incorporate the occasional pre-bend into your solos as you naturally progress. You'll find that your feel for this kind of thing will develop without any real problems if you approach it in this way.

There are any number of ways in which string bending can be employed within a guitar solo or phrase, and you should consider the ideas given here as merely a starting point for your own creativity. The following are examples of a few more general bend phrases and ideas for you to practice and vary as you see fit. Of these bends, the only one that may prove problematic is example 9, because it involves bending two strings together. Slightly different degrees of finger pressure will be required for each of the strings. Again, this example has a steady (unbent) string that can serve as a reference for the other two, so take advantage of that as a guide to accurate pitching of your bends. Later in this chapter we'll include some of these ideas into the more substantial context of a longer guitar solo. Meanwhile practise each of them in several positions (and therefore different keys), which will help familiarise you with the varying string tensions around the neck of your guitar.

Example 9

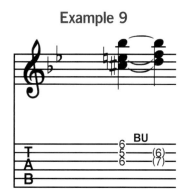

Based on B♭ chord (Note the key signature), this is a tricky one. Sustain the upper note whilst accurately bending the two lower notes.

Example 10

Played against a C major chord, this phrase has a blues feel to it.

Example 11

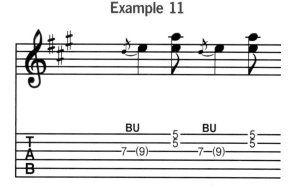

Played over an A chord, this is a classic rock and roll type of phrase. Hold down the upper notes with your 1st fingers as you play the bends on the lower (3rd) string.

Example 12

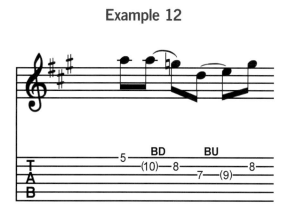

Again with an A major chord. Be careful to get that pre-bend ready, with your 4th finger on the 2nd string, whilst you are actually playing the first note.

Example 13

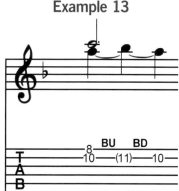

Play the two notes together, then bend the lower note up and down whilst sustaining the upper note. (Chord, F major).

Example 14

A variation on exercise 13. But this time based upon the C major chord, and with an extra upper sustaining note.

Bending behind the nut

The most obvious limitation of string bending, as practised so far, is that it's limited to fretted notes only. Generally this isn't too much of a problem, because most of the notes you play will fall into this category; and indeed, any note on a guitar (with one exception being the low open E string) can, if required, be played at a fretted position. Nevertheless, there may be occasions when you'll wish to bend an open string, or its harmonic (see **pages 93–95**), and this is where the technique of bending behind the nut will come in handy.

This particular guitar skill is actually extremely simple to understand, and not particularly difficult to achieve. The name itself more or less tells you what's required, which is to place an available left-hand finger behind the nut (see below) and apply pressure to the string you wish to bend. (Left-handed players see **page 228**.)

Some types of guitar will lend themselves to this technique more readily than others, simply because of the design of the headstock and how the machine heads (tuners) are placed. Fender designs such as the Telecaster or Stratocaster are particularly good in this regard due to the fact that there's a decent amount of clearance between string and headstock, thereby permitting you to press down (bend) any string behind the nut, as much as is sensibly required. Also, of course, these instruments have all six machine heads on the upper edge, as opposed to the three-a-side design generally favoured by Gibson, Rickenbacker and numerous others. This, as illustrated below, gives you plenty of 'hand room', without any danger of accidentally touching these tuners and possibly de-tuning your upper E string. That said, this type of bending can, to a reasonable extent, be practised on most guitars, with an awareness of any inherent design limitations.

Pressure for creating the bend can be applied in either a downward or (as would apply in standard string bending) a sideways movement. Either method can be effective, but if the string grooves in your guitar nut are rather shallow, sideways movement can dislodge the bent string from its groove. When attempting to master this type of bending technique it will become apparent that the main area of stress is on your fingertips, as the lack of fretboard support causes the string to cut in rather forcefully.

Obviously any string can be bent upward in this manner, but it may be easier to start out by experimenting with the upper strings, simply because they're closer to where your fret hand fingers can easily reach. And a good starter for getting the feel of this technique is a basic up and down bend of the second string.

Being familiar with the general requirements of string bending, this exercise could hardly be simpler. Play the open second string whilst holding the index finger of your left (fretting) hand in position over that string, and behind the nut, as seen in the photograph below left. Whilst the string is sounding, apply sufficient downward pressure to raise the pitch of the note up one semitone, and then release pressure to return the note to its original pitch, as in example 15, below.

Example 15

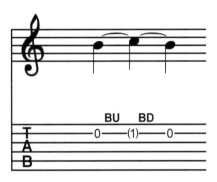

It's unlikely that you'll experience any difficulties in this, except perhaps in getting the hang of what is sufficient pressure for the correct degree of pitch bend. In order to make things as easy as possible on your fingertips, you'll find that less effort will be required if you apply the pressure as far back behind the nut as is practical. And, as always, some diligent practise will get you into the right feel for this after a few attempts.

What we've considered so far is a very definite bend of the string, and therefore a noticeable and specific change in pitch. However, you can also utilise this technique when you wish to apply vibrato (see **pages 92–93**) to an open string. Achieving this is a relatively straightforward procedure, whereby you play any open string and apply a rapid pressure and release to that string behind the nut.

Generally speaking, my own personal preference for behind the nut bending is to apply downward pressure, as opposed to sideways movement of the string. Depending upon various factors, such as the design of whatever guitar you may be playing, and obviously whichever approach you personally may happen to prefer, these types of bends can be applied either way. However, when it comes to the vibrato style you'll probably find that it's easier to use the downward movement instead of bending sideways.

Another useful trick in this particular style is bending strings within a chord. In example 16, for instance, a three-string **A** major chord can be altered by bending the **C#** note, raising it by a semitone, and then releasing it back again, creating an attractive country rock feel. This is, in effect, similar to the previous example shown, in that we're bending the second string up and down by one semitone, but because of the chord in which it's played this will require careful positioning of the left (fretting) hand fingers. The obvious choice is to hold down the third string with your third finger; hold the second string with your fourth finger, playing the first string open; which leaves your index finger free to effect the bend.

Although we've already experimented with the technique of bending one string within a chord, this situation is somewhat unusual in that the bend is applied to the 'middle' string of those being sounded. This particular type of bend wouldn't be practicable with the usual method of bending, without inevitably colliding with one of the other strings during the bending process. The sound

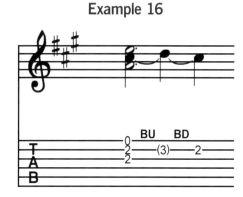

Example 16

created in this exercise is essentially similar to exercises 13 and 14, as it's a case of bending from a standard major chord into a suspended fourth chord and back again. This isn't the only behind the nut bend where this is feasible. It can also be applied to the chords of **E** major, **C** major and **G** major, exercises 17, 18 and 19.

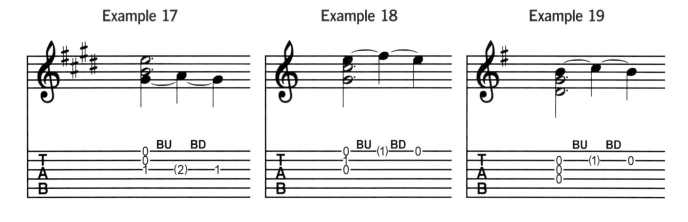

Example 17   Example 18   Example 19

This approach of bending one string within a chord can be effected in numerous ways, albeit limited by a necessarily close proximity to the nut in these types of bend. A slightly different example, as illustrated below left (example 20), would be a straightforward instance of bending into a **C** chord by simply playing the three upper strings open, and then bending the open second (**B**) string upward.

A bend such as this could, for instance, be usefully employed as a variation on a more standard **C** chord ending, perhaps adding a touch of vibrato as the chord sustains. As usual, it depends upon your imagination as to the variations available on any particular theme.

The technique of pre-bending (see **pages 76–77**) can also be applied to behind the nut bends, and example 21 utilises this approach to create a variation on the previous example. As

with the more usual string bending style, this pre-bending obviously depends upon your ability to correctly estimate the necessary pressure required for attaining the desired note pitch before striking the string. In this context it should be remembered that the 'necessary' pressure required varies, not only from one string to another, but also dependant upon how far back behind the nut you apply pressure.

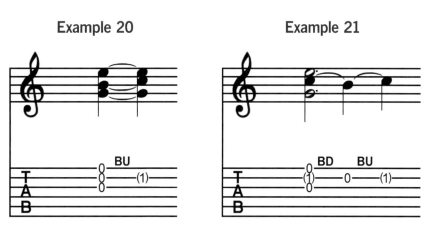

Example 20   Example 21

Example 22

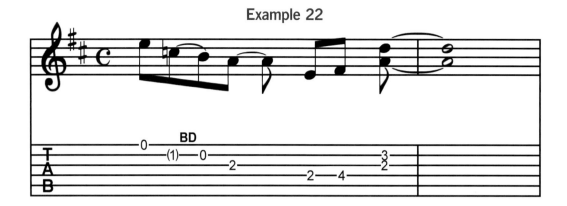

Let's try a simple ending riff which makes use of behind the nut pre-bending. Exercise 22 is based around a **D** major chord ending phrase, which might be useful in a blues or country rock context.

You'll have noticed by now that your finger positioning is always particularly crucial in applying these behind the nut bends. In any type of guitar playing it makes thing easier if you give some consideration to this aspect of your technique. This is just basic common sense really, but because you are, to some extent, locked into a very close proximity to the nut in these examples it just becomes that bit more important than it usually would be. In the above example, for instance, it's likely that your first fretted note (the **A** note) will be played with the fourth finger, followed by a position change on to the fourth string with the second finger (for the **E** note), followed by the fourth finger playing the **F#**, as fingers one and two are freed from

their bending position behind the nut to secure the two strings playing the final harmonised notes.

All of the behind the nut bends practised so far have been limited to one semitone (one fret in pitch), and whilst it's true that this style does tend to impose greater limitations in this regard than conventional string bending, it's sometimes possible – depending upon guitar design and finger strength – to extend this to whole tone (two fret) bending. So let's round things off with something a little more ambitious in exercise 23, as notated and tabbed below.

The whole tone bend into the **Em** chord requires considerable leverage and therefore greater finger pressure, so it's as well to take advantage of whatever room is available by exerting pressure as far back from the nut as is practical for the occasion. An additional point to remember is that these bent notes should be held for the duration of each bar whilst the other arpeggio notes are being played.

Example 23

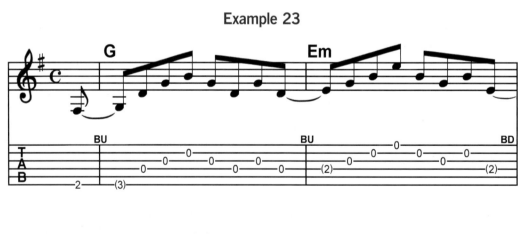

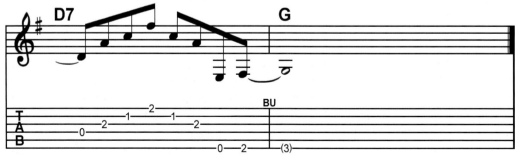

Hammer-ons, pull-offs and trills

These three techniques are all basically variations of the same theme, which is the sounding of notes without actually picking the string. Apart from its value as a sound variant, this also allows you to clearly play phrases at high speed, without the usual difficulty of having to coordinate left and right-hand movement, to the same extent as required with traditional picking.

The idea behind the 'hammering-on' technique is quite straightforward. First of all you play a note with a normal plectrum stroke, and then, whilst it's still ringing, sound a higher note on the same string by simply 'hammering' down with an available left-hand finger, a fret or two further up the neck. The new note is created by a combination of the fact that the string is still vibrating, and the forceful impact of your finger against that string. It's really easy to get the basics of this, so let's try an example as written in the notation and tab seen here.

Example 24

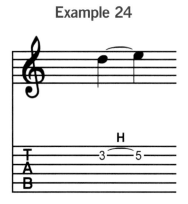

In order to play this simple hammer-on, secure the first note (second string, 3rd fret) with your index finger and play as normal. Then, very quickly and with some degree of force, bring down your third finger at the 5th fret. The new note (E) should ring out clearly, and with sufficient volume as if it had been picked with the plectrum.

The success of this manoeuvre will depend upon the speed and force with which your finger makes contact with the string and fretboard. As I said, it isn't too hard to do this, but you might need a bit of practice just to (literally) get into the swing of things. Be sure to hit the string with the tip of your finger for a nice clean and rapid contact, and mind you don't accidentally whack any adjacent strings and produce discordant sound.

The opposite of a hammer-on is a pull-off, so it's a good idea to learn them together, as they're frequently – although by no means always – played together as a complete musical movement.

So, starting with both fingers in place, as from the previous example, pick the string then briskly pull your third finger away from the string at a downward (toward the floor) angle. When executed correctly this movement effectively plucks at the string as it's moved quickly away from the fretboard. Since you are, in this case, pulling off from the second string it's likely that you'll brush against the first string whilst so doing. In order to avoid sounding this adjacent string, keep your index finger lightly in contact with it whilst still fretting the second string.

Example 25

The pull-off does tend to be slightly more difficult to master than the hammer-on, but as usual persistence will sort things out. In written form, as in practice, this appears similar to the hammer-on, although instead of 'H' for hammer-on, there is obviously 'PO' for pull-off, and this is shown here for your information.

Although tab is pretty much a standardised formula wherever it's used, there are occasionally slight variations in the way it's presented. For instance, the helpful abbreviations used here, such as 'BU' for bend-up and 'PO' for pull-off etc, are occasionally not included with some transcriptions. This is another of those things with which you'll need to be flexible in your common-sense approach to musical interpretation. I've seen several minor variations with regard to the tab situation, but it never really presents a problem. Indeed, music books often have a section dedicated to clarifying their tab layout so that it won't be confusing to the reader.

So, now on to the delightfully named 'trill'. This is really a combination of the hammer-on, pull-off technique, applied with speed and repetition. It's like playing the two previous examples together several times over, very quickly. So it's 'hammer-on/pull-off, hammer-on/pull-off, hammer-on/pull-off,' etc What causes it to be thought of as a separate technique, and written accordingly, is simply the speed and number of times it occurs. As a written comparison, consider the two examples overleaf:

Example 26

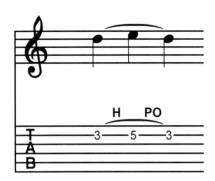

Both of these are examples of the 'hammer-on/pull-off' technique played over the duration of three quarter notes. But example 26 is played as three separate notes of one quarter each (pick, hammer-on, pull-off), whereas example 27 is a constant and rapid hammering on and off, covering the same duration of musical time.

Example 27

So, the difference between these two is that with a trill we're talking about essentially one note (which in this case is **D**), enhanced by a flurry of grace notes, the time value of which is incorporated into that of the main **D** note. And the speed at which these are played is really left to your own discretion, although the overall tempo of the music will tend to influence you in this regard.

So far these hammer-ons and pull-offs have been limited to the musical distance between a couple of notes. It's been a case of pick the string, hammer-on, and then maybe pull-off again. This is OK, and is very often the way in which you'll use this technique. But it's also possible to play several different notes in succession, with only one pick stroke. And as a starter on this type of playing let's look at the example shown here:

I would advise you to practise this phrase for a while, until it feels comfortable for you to play. As with much else in this book there's little point in impatiently dashing ahead to the next bit without having attained at least a reasonable familiarity with each lesson or example as it appears. In this case the hard work will probably be in achieving an effective hammer-on with the fourth finger, as will be required to play the third note of each string sequence.

Having played six notes from only two pick strokes, the next logical move would be to expand upon this principle and try for a couple more. And as it happens that's exactly what we're about to do. Not just seven notes, in fact, but a complete sequence of eight notes is played in this next example.

Example 28

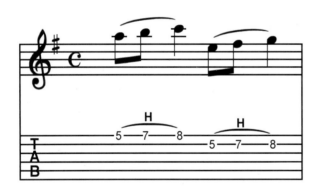

This is one complete bar of music containing six notes, but only two of them (the first and fourth) are sounded by the plectrum. The other four are the result of successive hammering-on by the left hand. In this case it only becomes necessary to pick the string again when you move from the first string over to the second string.

Example 29

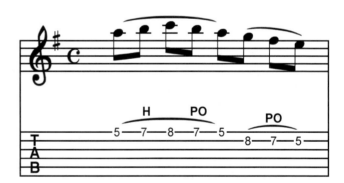

The 'H' and 'PO' symbols clearly indicate where the changeover from hammer-on to pull-off occurs; and, of course, the two actual picking strokes are on the first note played on each string. Actually, it's possible, with a forceful left-hand action, to begin playing on another string by hammer-on only, with no need of a plectrum stroke, but the picking action does lend fresh impetus and clarity when moving across to another string.

This technique, known as 'legato', was a big favourite with Jimi Hendrix. He would sometimes play long sequences of hammer-ons and pull-offs, occasionally whilst holding the guitar up near his mouth. This gave rise to the (still) widely believed myth that he could play the strings with his teeth. That's just an old rock and roll legend now, but it does illustrate how effective this technique can be in clearly sounding notes with just the left (or in Jimi's case, the right) hand.

I mentioned earlier that one of the really useful things about these techniques is the fact that they enable you to play fast-moving phrases with greater ease than might otherwise be the case. This makes them very popular with the heavy metal players, who sometimes have a thing about cramming as many notes as possible into a bar. You've probably listened with some wonder at these lightning fast guitar players and wondered how it could ever be possible to play like that. The fact is that some people seem to possess greater dexterity than others, and if you add to that many years of practise it gradually becomes attainable. But the good news for ordinary mortals is that it's possible to (dare I say it) cheat a bit too, and as you work on playing a few trills you'll realise that it's not too difficult to do so at a very impressive speed. But, because any trill is a continuous repetition of the same two notes over and over again it obviously has a limited value in this regard before it becomes a bit monotonous. Nevertheless, there's a wide variety of ways in which hammer-ons, pull-offs, bends, slides (see **pages 86–91**) and trills can be employed to enhance your high-speed manoeuvres. Don't misunderstand me here, because I'm not saying that speed is the ultimate reason for these techniques, or that speed is, in itself, a virtue.

Your aim as a musician should always be to play what's most appropriate for the song. But we both know that there will be times when you'll want to show off with a few flashy licks, if only to impress other guitar players who may be within earshot. So, musical integrity aside, take a look at the next example.

This is a lively little lick that would make an attractive ending phrase played over an **F** major chord. But if you were to play it at even a moderate sort of tempo, say around 132bpm, you'd find that the hammer-ons and pull-offs make it a lot easier to manage than if it were played by individually picking each note. Try it both ways and you'll see what I mean. In fact, once you've mastered these techniques properly you'll be amazed at how they enhance your playing at speed. Of course, you shouldn't neglect the need to practise faster picking in the usual way, but it's quite handy to have the occasional short cut available when needed.

Example 30

Fret tapping

I've included the so-called fret tapping technique in this section because it's basically an extension of the hammer-on, pull-off principle. This style gained widespread popularity in the '80s and is usually credited to Eddie Van Halen, although some say it's been known of much longer. And although this technique still seems to be surrounded by a degree of confusion and misunderstanding by some, the actual principle behind it is really very easy to understand.

When you hammer-on or pull-off you'll realise that the range over which you can do this will be between four and six frets, depending on whereabouts on the neck you're playing. The limiting factor beyond this will obviously be the width of your finger spread. So holding down a note at the 5th fret and then hammering-on to a note at the 12th fret would clearly be impossible. However, with the fret tapping technique the apparently impossible becomes possible by applying the technique of hammering and pulling with the right (picking) hand as well as the more usual left (fretting) hand. It's one of those remarkably simple ideas that, once you become aware of it, you'll wonder why it never occurred to you in the first place.

This picture illustrates the fret tapping principle, as played by the right hand at (in this case) the 12th fret, whilst the left hand secures the string elsewhere for the following note. The note clarity depends upon the rapid and forceful attack of the finger hitting the string and neck. This is generally done using the first finger, although sometimes the second finger is used when the player is still holding the plectrum.

If you consider the two following examples you'll see that they're notationally identical. But example 31 is written as a normal hammer-on pull-off phrase, whilst example 32 is played as a right-hand fret tapping piece. Study and understand these comparative examples first, in order to get the idea of what this is all about.

We begin by playing this as a normal hammer-on/pull-off phrase. So basically you pick the string whilst holding down at the 8th fret, and then pull-off to the 5th fret, then

Example 31

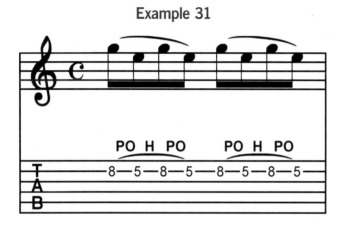

Example 32

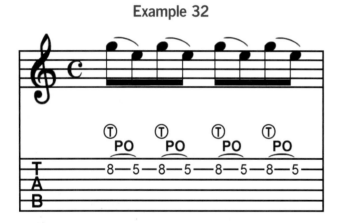

Example 33

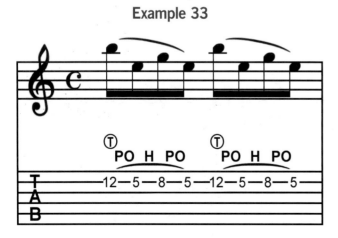

hammer back on to the 8th fret and so on, in accordance with the musical instructions. It's just two notes repeated over the one full bar, although for practice purposes you can obviously continue for as many bars as you wish.

Now, turn your attention to the right-hand tapping method as shown in example 32. What you do here is to hold down the 5th fret note as normal and, using the index finger of your right hand, sound the 8th fret note by hammering down firmly (the 'T' stands for tap) at the 8th fret. In effect you're playing the first note (**G**) of each pair by hammer-on, instead of by picking. The following note is, of course, sounded by pulling-off from the first note. This is best done by (the right hand) pulling upward and away, instead of downward and away, as would be the case with a traditional left-hand pull-off.

Remember, this is just a demonstration to clarify your understanding of how fret tapping actually works. In reality there'd be no need for right-hand fret tapping between the 5th and 8th frets, because they're close enough together for the more usual left hand to take care of the hammer-ons and pull-offs. So this technique really comes into effect over longer fret distances. And, needless to say, this is precisely what we're looking at next.

Example 33 is a typical fret tapping phrase, in which the right hand fret taps at the 12th fret, pulls-off to the 5th fret, followed by a traditional left-hand hammer-on and pull-off between frets 8 and 5. Take this slowly at first, to ensure clear definition between notes.

I'm assuming that you're still using your metronome or other timepiece to achieve accuracy, and if not then you certainly should be, or else any habitual timing errors will eventually return to haunt you. So having lectured you once again on that point, I'll suggest a tempo of around 120bpm as a good starting point. Gradually speed up only when you're comfortably into the rhythm of these moves. And if you should be playing through an amplifier, then adding a touch of overdrive/distortion would tend to enhance this type of playing.

After doing this for a while you'll realise that it's not difficult to pick up the tempo without too much extra effort, simply because the interaction of both hands playing alternately requires less work than if only one hand were picking each note. At this point you'll find that eighth notes are rather limiting for this type of riff at any speed, without the metronome clicking away at a rather excessive pace. So the thing to do is convert the whole thing into 16th notes. In this way the tempo of the beat need not increase whilst the speed of this same riff actually doubles. So welcome to exercise 34, where we're playing a similar lick but with four notes per beat and, for added interest, a slight variation between bars.

Example 34

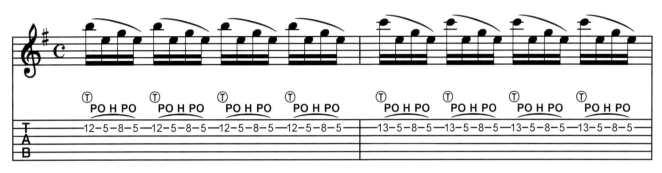

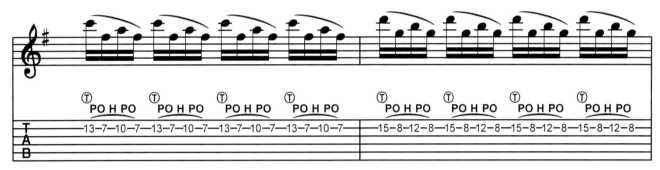

At first glance I know this looks extremely complicated, but it's really just a variation on the previous example. Although each bar consists of 16 notes only the first four of each bar need attention because there are several repetitions per bar, which makes it a lot easier to learn.

Bar one is easy because it's exactly the same as in example 33, except in 16th notes instead of eighths. So, no real problem there. Bar two varies only slightly because the 'tapped' note (the first of each group of four) is played one fret higher, but all other notes are unchanged. Bar three keeps the tapped note in place, whilst raising your left-hand action a couple of frets higher. Only bar four is slightly tricky, where you move both tapped and fretted notes up at the same time. Incidentally, if you want to play some chords for this sequence, it goes like this: first bar **Em**, second bar **C**, third bar **D7**, fourth bar **G**. In fact if you care to examine the notes being played you'll realise that this is basically an arpeggio (see **page 27**), albeit played in a rather fancy way.

Whenever you see a piece of music that looks incredibly complicated (and therefore difficult), always remember to break it down into separate bars for learning. This way it's considerably easier to assimilate, and a lot less scary to contemplate.

Now, before we move on to something different let's go for one more nifty little fret tapping lick. Well, after all, it's something to impress your friends with if nothing else.

This is based around a **G** major chord, and would make a lively ending riff, when played at a fast tempo. And although you can obviously play anything at whatever speed you choose, these fret tapping licks do tend to rely more upon fast playing than slow for their characteristic sound. When you really get the hang of this technique try playing these riffs (and make up a few of your own) at different positions on the neck, and on various strings. Certain possibilities occur higher up than are really feasible lower down, because of the narrower fret spacing, and other strings obviously have a different feel and offer a wider range of pitch.

Example 35

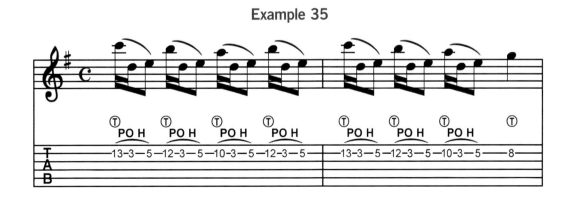

Slides

A slide (or 'glissando' if you're posh) is one of the easier manoeuvres to learn on a guitar, and is precisely what the name suggests. Your left hand literally slides up or down the neck, thereby moving from one note to another with no additional picking involved. It's not much harder to learn than it is to understand, with the only essential skills being the ability to maintain finger pressure during the slide and then stop in the right place.

The difference between, say, a hammer-on and a slide is that hammering takes you instantly from one note to another, whereas a slide includes all other notes along the way. This gives a somewhat different effect, and also helps you to move around the neck more smoothly than just making a quick fretboard jump, so to speak.

When you slide from one note to another it's necessary to release hand grip pressure on the neck whilst also keeping the string firmly against the fretboard. When your slide has reached the note required, a slight increase in grip acts as a brake, ensuring that (with a little practise) you stop in the right place. You must learn to avoid stopping short, or overshooting the correct fret position. The necessary accuracy involved isn't usually a problem with a slide of just a few frets, but can be harder to achieve over greater neck distances.

As always it's best to start simple, so our first example of a slide is a one-fret movement on the fourth string, as detailed below.

Example 36

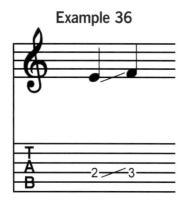

Try this starting with the first finger at fret 2, and briskly slide up to fret 3 in one quick move. You'll probably be OK on this as long as firm finger contact is maintained, which prevents a loss of volume as you reach the 'slid' note of F. Also, don't dawdle over this move, or your finger could drag on the fret instead of slipping easily over it. If you should accidentally overshoot the target just moderate the force of your wrist action, which should quickly solve the problem.

With a slide over a limited distance of just one fret hardly any arm movement will be required, and just a small movement of your wrist should suffice. As slide distances increase it becomes necessary to effect forearm movement instead. This becomes apparent even from a slide of as little as two frets. Try exercise 37 as an example of this. Again, the secret is economy of effort, and don't try too hard lest you should overdo it.

Example 37

When you make individual slide movements like this, it doesn't make too much difference which fingers you use. Unlike string bending, slides aren't necessarily any more difficult with the first finger than they are with the third finger. However, when slides are played in the more realistic context of an actual piece of music, consideration must be given as to where your next note will be after the slide is completed. For instance, if you play the slide shown here, moving from fret 3 up to fret 5, and intend to play a following note at fret 7, it would be impractical to slide with your third or (even worse) fourth finger. Try it and you'll see what I mean. It makes the move extremely impractical, to say the least. So put some common-sense thought into your slide moves before you get boxed into an awkward spot. Look at the next example and apply this principle, moving upward through a sequence of picked and slide notes.

Example 38

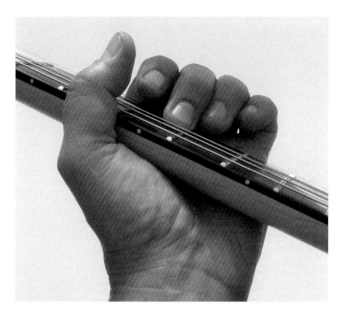
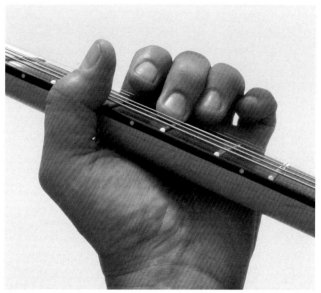

As slide movements go, this is easy enough. But, unlike exercise 37, a lot more movement from your forearm will be required for a smooth transition between all the notes. The correct approach goes like this: start with your first finger (string four, 2nd fret) and slide up one fret. Then apply your fourth finger (string four, 5th fret) and slide up two frets. Finally, your first finger again (string three, 4th fret) to complete the sequence by sliding up one fret to the ending note.

If you should have any difficulty in playing this phrase smoothly (and that's the key word here), it's probably because you're still gripping the neck too tightly, as if locked in one position. Nor is this a problem that occurs only in sliding. Several people have told me that they have no problem playing individual note sequences, but can't move around the neck in an orderly way. The pictures above give an idea of what the appropriate degree of grip looks like, when making smooth moves on your slide manoeuvres.

As you see by comparing these two illustrations, the left picture shows a firm palm pressure against the guitar neck, as might apply to fixed position playing, whereas the right picture shows a rather more relaxed grip, as would be required when sliding. This change in grip is only slight, but it's critical. And, because the difference isn't dramatic, it's easy to do. It just isn't necessary to grip excessively in order to maintain an effective hold against the neck. However, if you do feel the need to apply considerable force against the strings to avoid fret buzz (which may be caused by strings being held too lightly against the fret), then the action (see **page 175**) on your guitar is probably in need of adjustment. Refer to **pages 175–79** for the remedy to this irritating problem.

Slides can be applied in many ways, and also over several strings at once. It's certainly possible to slide an entire chord if required, although some chord shapes lend themselves to this more than others. Obviously, open chords aren't amenable to this, and equally obviously bar chords are. Often it's only certain notes of a chord, rather than all six strings, which will be played in this way. A natural place to begin would be your first basic major bar chord as learned on **pages 31–32**. A typical approach to sliding effectively with a chord such as this would be to slide the lower two or three strings only.

It will be easier if you regard this as a partial chord than as individual notes – basically an **F#** major at the 2nd fret, sliding up to the **G** major at the 3rd fret. And, because only the lower three strings are sounded, there's no need to firmly hold down all six strings. That would be a waste of effort and unnecessarily harder to play.

Example 39

This is typical of the so-called 'power chord' approach used in the heavy metal style. Try a little amp overdrive or other distortion effect to give yourself an idea of what I mean. Maybe try playing a 12-bar blues sequence, with a one-fret slide into each chord change. Although rather basic in a technical sense, these things are fun to play, generally useful to be aware of, and sound really good too.

Up or down strokes

You will have noticed that, in terms of music notation, no reference has been made to either upstrokes or downstrokes. Generally this type of decision is a matter for your own judgement, and in the case of single notes it doesn't make a difference to the sound anyway. For some reason guitar players seem to have a preference for downstrokes whenever possible, but there are no set rules. However, a fast run of notes will inevitably be possible only if you alternate between up and down movements of the pick.

When playing two or more notes together, the question of up or down becomes more significant. It depends upon which of the two (or more) notes you wish to emphasise. In exercise 39 it would be logical to use downstrokes for best effect, but if – for your own reasons – you decided to try a different approach then that would be OK too. The point is, be aware of the variance in sound created by the choice of pick stroke, and make your own decision accordingly. In this next exercise the choice of up or down is less clear, and either, or a combination of both, would be acceptable. Again, the speed at which it's played will help to make the choice for you.

In order to introduce you to a new key signature, we see here the key of **B** major. This is a key that guitarists tend not to use very often, mainly for the reasons explained on **pages 54–55**, but in this example its lack of 'guitar-friendliness' won't make any difference to the slide as illustrated.

What we have here is a double note slide from fret 6 up to fret 7. A small index finger bar across the two strings will take care of that. This is fairly typical of a rock and roll phrase, suitable for playing over a **B** major chord, where you actually slide into the first note(s) of each bar from the final eighth note of the previous bar. Pay attention to the 'natural' which converts the **F#** (as defined by the key signature) into an **F**. But don't forget that the key signature sharp regarding this note regains effect immediately afterwards, when the next bar begins. Also, be aware that the **A** note is, because of the key signature, actually an **A#**. But if you're also reading the tab, as is useful for best choice of string and fret positioning etc, this will be made clear.

Example 40

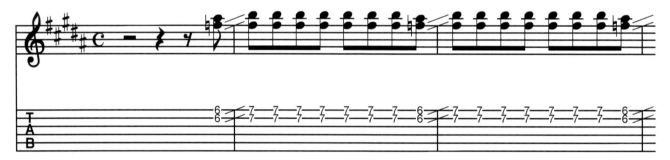

Sliding down

As with string bending and hammer-ons, sliding is something that can also be done in reverse. Although not really difficult, it requires slightly more skill to slide down than to slide up. Partly this is because an ascending (upward) slide tends to maintain its volume more easily than a descending (downward) slide, and also because moving upward increases the stability of the arm against your body. This helps maintain finger pressure against the string and neck. When moving downward, however, the opposites inevitably apply.

To begin with, just try playing a few familiar slides in reverse. Then, when you've acquired the feel of this, try a basic up and down slide, as illustrated here. And remember, it's always, worth practising this in different string and neck positions for added experience.

Example 41

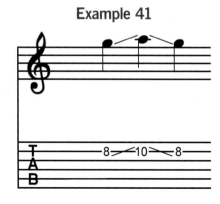

Slightly more difficult is the double note up and down, where the demand is increased by having to maintain pressure on both strings. The next two exercises explore this in slightly different ways. This first one is reasonably straightforward, wherein two strings are slid up and down by equal degrees of two frets each. But the other example is somewhat more demanding, because each of the two strings moves independently of the other. Take a look at both of these examples and give some consideration as to what's required of your left hand co-ordination.

Example 42

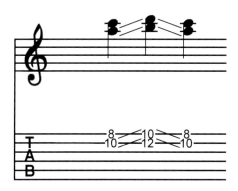

In both examples here use your first and third fingers, on strings one and two respectively. This is easy enough in exercise 42, but in exercise 43 your third finger (on the second string) must move a distance of two frets, up and back, whilst your first finger (on the first string) must only move one fret up and back.

Example 43

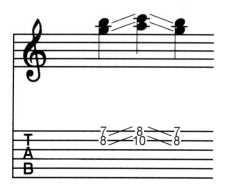

The way to get into this business of sliding adjacent strings by differing degrees is to initially practise sliding up only, and worry about the skill of sliding back down later, after you're OK with the up slide. Your actual finger positioning for this example should look like the pictures below. (Left-handed players see **page 228**.)

Your finger positioning for the first picture may look a little awkward because of using fingers one and three, despite the fact that the fretted notes are separated by only one fret. But the payoff comes when you make your move into the slide. As you do so it's necessary to move the fingers away from each other as your hand slides upward. This automatically positions your hand correctly for the notes as played in the second picture. Practise this a few times and the moves will soon flow easily from one into the other.

This is simply a 'before and after' illustration. Begin with your first finger on the first string at fret 7 and your third finger on the second string at fret 8. Slide the first finger up to the next (8th) fret, whilst sliding the third finger up by two fret positions to the 10th fret. It may be easier if you concentrate mainly on this two-fret slide, as the other finger movement is then inclined to naturally end up in the right place. When you're comfortable with this upward slide action you can work on reversing the movement, which will be a completion of the process as seen in example 43.

These continuous slide manoeuvres can be extended into whole sequences of cascading notes. Check out the next exercise, for instance – an attractive melodic phrase running from high to low, which is an interesting challenge to learn, and sounds classy too.

Take your time over this, and be certain you have the correct sequence of notes. It's all too easy, when looking at a lot of notes and tab on the page, to get something wrong on the fretboard. Remember the rule: always learn it bit by bit, and play it very slowly until you're fully at ease with what you're doing.

When you're completely conversant with this piece, it wouldn't be a bad idea to try playing it in reverse. It's all in the name of good practice and experience, which can only be a good thing.

Example 44

Sliding to (and from) nowhere

There are a couple of slide actions which deserve special mention – not because they're especially difficult to play, but so that you'll know what they are when you see and hear them. This is when a slide doesn't begin from a specific note having a relevance of its own but, as with a grace note, is incorporated into the note to which it slides. And indeed the reverse applies also, wherein a note begins from a specific pitch point and slides away into nowhere. It'll make a lot more sense to you if I present a couple of examples. These are played in the key of E♭, which means that all E, B and A notes are flattened. And in the case of example 46, pay attention to the octave sign above the stave. If you need reminding about this, refer to **page 65**.

Example 45

Starting from a lower point on the third string, slide very quickly upward into the G note. Only this note, along with the follow-up E♭ note, has any specific time value, or any pitch impression on the ear. The other example is playing a B♭ note, then immediately and very rapidly sliding down to any given point where finger pressure is released and thereby silences the sound.

Example 46

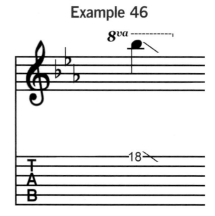

Despite having respectively no definite starting or ending point, this type of thing works precisely because of the speed at which the slide is played. And, although there's no rule about it, generally speaking it's true to say that the longer the slide (upward or downward), the better it sounds, creating more of a definite 'effect' and increasing the feel of musical excitement in your playing. Now, try out the various slides on the next page, remembering to take note of key signatures, accidentals etc. Any potential errors or confusion in this department can be avoided by referring to the tab.

Example 47

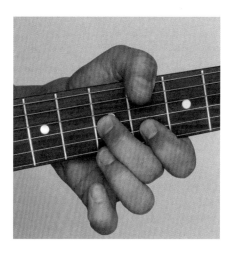

The trick in playing this B♭ chord riff is to secure the bass (6th) string with your thumb, as seen in the picture opposite. This simple technique leaves your fingers free to play the slide notes on the upper strings.

Example 48

In the key of D and played over a D major chord, this example is interesting for the alternating movement between strings. So pay careful attention to the tab instructions as to where each note should most conveniently be played.

Example 49

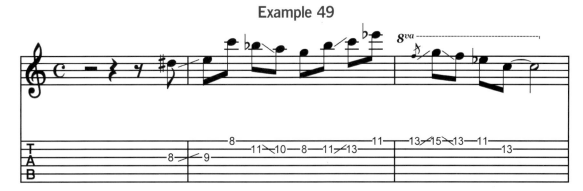

Essentially a blues style phrase in the key of C. This would go well with your R & R riff (see pages 41–43), as based around the C major chord. And don't overlook the 'octave' sign above the 3rd bar, covering the very high notes toward the end.

Example 50

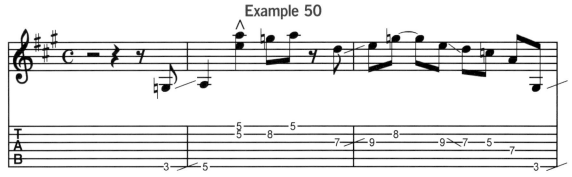

Applying the technique learned in example 47, slide your thumb from the low G note up to the A. Regarding this as a repetitive riff, what appears to be the final note is actually starting over again.

Vibrato

The term vibrato refers to changes in pitch around a given note. In the context considered here, these pitch changes are small but significant, and are created by movement of your left (fretting) hand fingers along or across the neck of your guitar. The reason for applying vibrato to any string is simply that it tends to enhance the sound of notes, by adding sustain and generally improving the tonal quality of the sound.

Applying vibrato to a note doesn't involve moving outside the confines of its fret position, but instead depends upon finger movement within that area. This movement can be either parallel to the neck length or perpendicular to it, as illustrated in the pictures on this page.

The method shown immediately below is the one most commonly used by rock guitarists. It's essentially a case of string bending/unbending over a very limited range. The note doesn't actually reach another pitch, but instead it quivers around its own pitch, usually at a very rapid rate. (Left-handed players see **page 228**.)

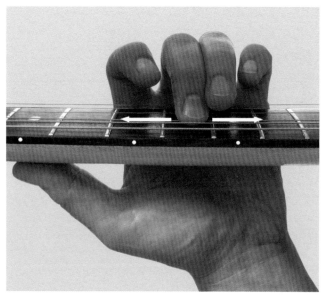

This approach is generally achieved with the thumb over the guitar neck (as illustrated), acting as a pivot point for the necessary movement. A rapid tremor generated by the wrist movement is very effective on single notes, or on several played together when you wish to apply vibrato to all notes simultaneously. However, if you only intend to apply vibrato to one of these multiple notes, a different approach is needed; and in such cases the vibrato action must be generated by individual finger action alone. This is a bit more difficult but is definitely worth learning for such occasions.

An alternative way of applying vibrato is illustrated in the photograph shown bottom left. The movement here is parallel to the string length, and is most effectively achieved by easing thumb pressure from the guitar neck. This action, as seen from above, is pictured above, where the necessary vibrato movement is generated by the forearm. This is the more traditional type of vibrato, as employed by classical guitarists and, indeed, other string players such as violinists. The motion isn't discernible as an actual slide back and forth along the string, as might be easily misunderstood, but is defined more by a rapid quiver of the forearm and wrist, and therefore of the finger against the string. It doesn't depend upon bending the string at all, but instead creates small pressure changes of your finger against the string, with the resulting fluctuation in pitch. You'll probably incline toward one of these methods more than the other, but again it's as well to become reasonably familiar with both techniques because each has its benefits according to various circumstances.

Example 51

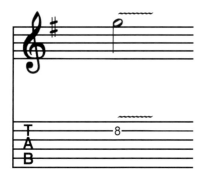

On the left is the symbol for vibrato as applied to a single note, and on the right the vibrato is shown in context, when applied to the last note of a musical phrase. The first three notes are played without vibrato.

Example 52

Unlike other techniques described in this chapter, the application of vibrato is frequently left to the player's own discretion and sense of taste, and isn't always specified by instruction in the notation or tab. However, there is a symbol for it, which is used wherever the vibrato is more or less essential to the character of the music as written. This is as shown above, alongside a demonstration of how it might appear with other notes.

Although it's a bit more difficult to master, vibrato is especially effective when applied to 'bent' notes. This means that you bend the string upward and, holding the bend in position, apply vibrato to the higher note. The inconvenient inclination here is to release pressure on the bend, rather than adding the subtle tremor necessary for a good vibrato. So it takes finger strength, a good ear for pitch, and plenty of practise to get this right. A simple example is written here, although you can obviously make up many of your own once you get the hang of it.

It's in the nature of playing vibrato that only notes of sustained duration tend to use this technique. It isn't really possible to play a fast run of notes and apply vibrato to all (or indeed any) of them. There's probably someone out

there who'll be inclined to contradict that statement, but generally speaking vibrato is for enhancing the natural sustain qualities of the guitar, or other string instrument. This doesn't mean that you must inevitably apply vibrato whenever a note is held for a second or two, because it's always a question of the most appropriate sound for each situation, and good taste should be your guide. So practise this technique in the various ways described and use it as the occasion requires.

Example 53

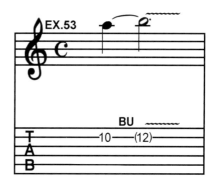

Harmonics

Although there are other implications to the word, in this case we're talking about a clear bell-tone which is quite unlike the normal sound of an electric guitar; and the easiest way to understand what this is will be to produce that sound yourself. If you're playing a solid-body instrument (see **page 7**), I suggest that you plug into the amp for this one, and select the bridge pickup for a clear sound. You won't need too much volume, but enough to clearly hear what you're doing will be especially helpful on this occasion.

So if you're all set, let's take it one step at a time.

1 Using any left-hand finger, lightly touch the sixth string directly over the 12th fret (see picture overleaf). Don't press it down to the fretboard – merely ensure light finger contact with the string.

2 Firmly pick the string with your plectrum, and then immediately remove your finger contact from the string. This should produce a clear harmonic of **E** pitch.

If you failed to create the harmonic sound, this is very probably for one of two reasons: either your finger wasn't accurately positioned precisely over the 12th fret, or your finger contact was too heavy.

This close-up view gives a clear indication of the left-hand finger barely touching the string above the 12th fret. In playing any harmonic, the accuracy of your finger being directly above the fret in question is crucial to the clarity of sound produced. Too far one way or the other and the note will be muted.

Some players make the mistake of touching the string just behind the fret, because that's the usual fretting technique, but producing harmonics is a different situation and requires a different approach. So try again and you'll soon get it right. Incidentally, this doesn't work at just any fret position. I specified the 12th fret for a reason, so don't randomly attempt this elsewhere because it may not work if you do. (If you're left-handed see page 228.)

All six strings will produce harmonics at the 12th fret, with all of them being of identical pitch to the fretted note in that position, so try playing each one before moving on.

For those of you who like to understand the technical details, these harmonic tones are created by placing your finger at the mid-point on the guitar string. This creates a point where the string doesn't vibrate at all, thereby changing the normal vibration pattern of the string. On either side of this point the string is divided into two equal parts that vibrate out of phase (basically in opposing directions) with each other, and create the unique sound of the harmonic. Now, if that's all perfectly clear, let's move on.

Harmonics can be created at various positions on the open strings, each one located at a point where the string can be theoretically divided into equal parts. These harmonic points, which always apply to all six strings, are as follows:

1 Fret 4: At this fret, where the string is at one-fifth of its length, the harmonic note is the same as the fretted note but two octaves higher.
2 Fret 5: At this fret the string is at one-quarter of its length; the note at this point is that of the open string but two octaves higher.
3 Fret 7: At this fret position, one-third of its string length, the harmonic produced is equal to the fretted note at that position but one octave higher.
4 Fret 9: Two-fifths along the string length. Same pitch as the fret 4 harmonic.

5 Fret 12: As specified previously. Identical pitch to fretted note.
6 Fret 16: Three-fifths along the string length. Same pitch as frets 4 and 9 harmonics.
7 Fret 19: Two-thirds along the string length. Same pitch as fret 7 harmonic.
8 Fret 24: If your guitar neck is long enough to have 24 frets, this is three-quarters of the string length. The harmonic pitch is identical to that of the fret 5 harmonic.

A special point to mention with regard to the last one in the list is that since harmonics don't require actual fretting, this can be played on any length fretboard. It's just a question of finding the right spot, slightly beyond the end of the fretboard. On a Fender Stratocaster, for instance, the theoretical fret 24 is located just over the pole pieces (see page 185) of the neck pickup. You can locate this harmonic on any guitar with very little effort, and memorise its position, usually relative to some identifiable part of the guitar's anatomy.

Having mastered the light touch required for harmonics at fret 12, the next easiest to play are those at frets 5 and 7, and their corresponding counterparts at frets 24 and 19. But on the other hand, you'll find it quite a bit harder to produce the harmonics found at fret 4 (along with frets 9 and 16). These will require a very delicate touch over the fret positions concerned, so it's best to begin here on the sixth string, where the sound generated by the heavy bass string is a lot stronger than on the thin upper strings.

The use of harmonics is something that, if you find the sound attractive, you may wish to experiment with in your own creative efforts. At the very least you'll be able to recognise and play what you hear on recordings where this is used. Either way it's good to have at least a general familiarity with this technique, as another addition to your guitar-playing repertoire. So let's see how this might be employed in the basic example shown here on the right. And don't let the diamond-shaped notes confuse you. I haven't just invented a new form of musical notation – this is the traditional way of showing harmonics in music transcription. Playing with a suitably light touch you should have very little difficulty playing this ascending arpeggio, using the fret 12 and fret 5 positions. Imagine this as the ending phrase of any slow piece in the key of **G** major and you'll see how effective this would be.

Example 54

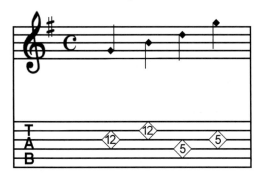

Example 55

Take it slowly, sounding each harmonic with clarity and precision, letting each note ring on in typical arpeggio style. Note that the harmonic pitch is actually an octave higher than written, although not specified here for convenience. And incidentally, this is a situation where the tab accompaniment is really indispensable in explaining where to find each harmonic for accurate effect.

The next exercise (above) is slightly more difficult, and begins with a harmonic (Em) chord. This one also requires a bit more jumping around with your fretting hand over the neck, so get the hang of positioning and accuracy of touch before worrying too much about the timing of the piece. And remember, dead slow at first until you know where each note is located; only then should you attempt to play any faster.

The choice of which finger to use for any given note is really your decision. But, as usual, you know that I'm about to offer my

opinion, based as ever on economy of movement for best effect.

Begin by playing the three-note chord with your third finger lightly covering all notes together. Then, whilst they're sustaining, move that same finger over to play the next (F♯ harmonic) note, which places you in position for your index finger to cover the G note, and back again to the F♯ on your third finger. Then continue in this manner, always planning ahead for fluidity of movement and ease of playing. Whenever two consecutive harmonics occur at the same fret, as in the beginning of bar two, cover them with one finger at the same time.

Another trick you can use with harmonics is to play them in combination with normal fretted (or open string) notes. The following exercise gives you an idea of how this can be done. As always, take your time learning it, letting the harmonic notes sustain wherever possible, and also giving some attention to the vibrato instructions over the longer notes.

Example 56

This takes a bit of getting used to, and for best effect depends upon getting the volume balance about right between these different techniques, because the normally played notes will tend to be disproportionately loud if your harmonic playing isn't quite

up to it. Take note of the octave sign covering the last part of this phrase. Although this isn't going to make any difference to your reading of the tab instructions, it is nonetheless pitch-relevant to the music notation.

Artificial harmonics

The harmonics used in the previous examples have all been playable on open strings. This is very convenient because it makes for easy playing, but as usual in this life there's a trade-off for such luxury. In other words, a disadvantage. Specifically, there's a limitation to the range of available harmonic notes on open strings, for whilst you can play harmonics for all the open string notes, plus a few others, there are certain harmonics which cannot be played by the use of open strings alone. A couple of obvious ones would be **C** and **F**. Add to that those harmonics which, although available, are often too high to be suitable for many requirements, and you'll realise that an alternative is definitely desirable. Happily there is such an alternative, but unhappily it's somewhat harder to master. This requires utilising the right hand for both touching and plucking the string at the same time. It might sound awkward or even impossible, but the picture below will put this into perspective for you. (Left-handed players see **page 228**.)

In this photograph the left hand is holding down a (C) note at the 5th fret in the usual manner. The right hand is both lightly touching the same string over the 17th fret, and simultaneously picking that string with the plectrum. This requires an adaptation to your plectrum technique, as it's necessary to handle the pick between the thumb and second finger, leaving your first finger free to touch the harmonic point over the appropriate fret.

If you fret any string, anywhere on the guitar neck, and then touch the harmonic over the position which is 12 frets higher, you'll create the harmonic of that same note, albeit one octave higher. This makes it very easy (once you've mastered the right hand technique) to produce any harmonic you require without having to search all over the place for it. A good way to utilise this advantage might be to play a basic arpeggio with harmonic tones. This is demonstrated here with a **Gm** chord over a triplet timing.

So all you have to do is to hold down the usual **Gm** chord shape at the 3rd fret, and then play the harmonic of each note shown, at one octave position above the chord. The information shown between the staves is very easy to understand, whereby 'AH' stands for artificial harmonic, and the following numbers are indicative of the fret where the harmonic of each note is located.

With this style of playing harmonics it's possible to play any melodic phrase you can imagine. Obviously there are speed limitations created by the method itself, but with practice you can develop a pretty useful technique for general purposes. Try this with a range of chord arpeggios, bearing

Example 57

AH 17 15 15 15 15 15 17 15 15 15 15 15

Example 58

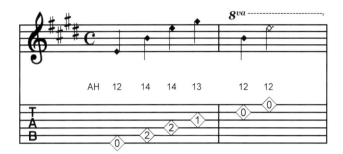

Example 59

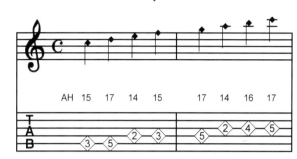

in mind that all you have to do is count up 12 frets from the note you're holding with your left (fretting) hand and you have its octave harmonic. With regard to open chords, this means that the open string chord notes will have their harmonic point at the 12th fret itself. This is demonstrated here with an open **E** chord.

One virtue about using chords for this type of technique is simply that your left hand can remain fixed in its chord shape, whilst the picking hand is free to concentrate on the tricky bit of selecting and playing the notes. So it becomes a bit harder when your left hand is playing a sequence of notes and you also must watch where your right hand is going at the same time. As a sample of this, try picking out a basic scale on harmonics, which will give you the opportunity to

work on the independent coordination necessary for this task.

Playing this **C** major scale is easiest if you first establish your left-hand positioning in such a way that you don't need to look at where your fingers are going. This way you can concentrate most of your attention on the picking hand movements. So, begin with your (left hand) second finger at the 3rd fret of the fifth string, and you can play the whole scale without having to move from that basic position.

When you're happy with your ability to play this without difficulty, try playing the same scale pattern in some of the other major key positions, gradually progressing higher up the neck. For additional experience, also practise other fixed position major scales covering the upper octave (see **pages 49–50** if you've forgotten what this is).

Pinched harmonics

Some people will pinch anything given the opportunity, and this certainly applies in the case of harmonics – never more so than with the heavy metal players, who just love this technique. With the help of a bit of distortion (well,

quite a lot actually), this is how they produce those high-pitched squealing sounds. So if this is your type of thing, let's see how it's done. (See **page 228** for the left hand.)

The trick here is getting just the right grip on the plectrum, holding it close to the playing edge so that the tip protrudes beyond your thumb just slightly. When striking the string, ensure that your thumb is touching an appropriate harmonic point. Both pick and thumb should hit the string, more or less simultaneously, in order to create the required harmonic sound.

The best results for this style are often obtained by picking between the bridge and the end of the neck, as opposed to the more usual (over a specific fret) position. This places higher harmonics within range and gives a more dynamic impact to this particular style. But, having no fret reference, you have to gauge for yourself where the correct point of contact would actually be. And when, by trial and error, you've located the appropriate place for the desired result, you'll find it relatively easy to achieve on future occasions.

Example 60 indicates how these pinched harmonics are displayed in both notation and tab form. Played, in this case, on the 2nd string, the harmonic is produced by picking as described, precisely halfway between the fretted note position and the bridge.

A useful variation of this technique is the so-called 'tapped' harmonic, which is generally easier to master. This is simply a case of playing any note and, whilst it's still sounding, lightly tapping the string at a suitable harmonic point, such as 24 frets higher than that fretted, to produce the harmonic sound.

Remember, because the actual frets get closer together as you move higher up the neck, so will the 'theoretical' frets become ever closer as you progress beyond the end of the neck in search of the correct harmonic points for various higher notes. So, having played the harmonic **C** note shown above, the next harmonic point of contact, for a **C#** note, would not be much further along the string.

Example 60

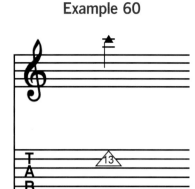

A useful point to keep in mind is that most harmonic tones can be located in more than one place. Consider, for instance, a **D** note harmonic, secured at the fourth string 12th fret, and so played halfway between that fret and the bridge. This could also be played on the fifth string secured at the 17th fret, and so played halfway from that point to the bridge. But this shortens the available vibrating length of the string, making the harmonic tone significantly more difficult to play in this position. So if you're having trouble playing a very high-position harmonic, try playing it on another string at a lower fret, which should make things somewhat easier for you.

Chicken pickin'

Certain guitar techniques tend to be characteristic of a particular type of music, and perhaps none more so than this. So-called because of its sputtering semi-staccato sound, chicken pickin' is mainly associated with country rock, and even more specifically with one player. James Burton is the man for whom this is practically the trademark sound, and who is most often credited with inventing it.

For some reason, the correct way to play the chicken pickin' style tends to be somewhat misunderstood. It's usually explained as being either an entirely percussive technique, or else played by intermittently releasing left-hand pressure from the fretboard. And whilst it's possible to achieve a facsimile of the style in this manner, there are also limitations inherent in this approach.

Hold the plectrum very close to the tip, in a manner similar to that of the pinched harmonic technique. The difference here is in the way that the string is struck by the pick and then immediately silenced by the thumb or index finger. This creates the required staccato sound,

but without having to release left-hand pressure from the string. This is an important point, because it enables you to produce the chicken pickin' sound even when string bending, which obviously wouldn't be possible with the more typical left-hand style of muting. If you play finger style, or pick and finger (or indeed fingerpick – see **page 133**) style, good results can also be obtained by alternating index finger and thumb (or finger and plectrum) picking, thereby effectively silencing each note immediately after sounding, by contact with the opposing finger or thumb.

Try this first by playing a few up and down strokes on the second string. This technique is most effective when played at a fairly brisk tempo, so begin around 160bpm. This is actually quite a modest pace for eighth notes in this style, but it's a reasonable place to start.

The best results, when amplified, will be obtained by using a bright, lively tone on your guitar, so I'd recommend using the bridge pickup with a fair amount of treble. Country guitar pickers traditionally favour the Fender Telecaster as their weapon of choice and, believe me,

Example 61

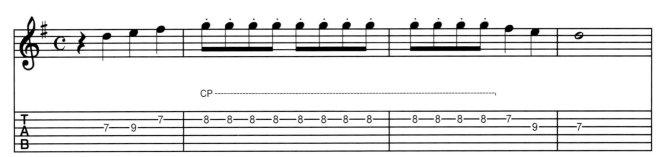

The dots above each note are traditional music notation indicating a staccato sound. As regards the tab, it seems hardly necessary to explain what 'CP' stands for, with the dotted line covering the notes so played.

The key to playing this correctly comes down to your grip on the plectrum. If too much of the pick is allowed to remain clear of your fingers, the staccato stuttering sound won't be obtained. Conversely, if no plectrum at all is protruding from your grip all you'll get will be a dull, muted tone. You'll know when you've got the hang of it because, quite simply, the sound will live up to its colourful name.

Having secured the plectrum just about right and managed to produce the appropriate sound is part of the story, but it's unlikely that you'll be playing an entire guitar solo as a chicken pickin' exercise. So you need to develop the ability to switch immediately from normal playing and back again. Example 62 provides a brief idea of what might typically be required.

guitars don't get much more twangy than that. But whatever your instrument, the chicken pickin' sound does tend to be enhanced by a sharper tone, which brings out the percussive feel required for maximum effect.

Example 62

This quick change from one type of picking to the other will be difficult unless you adopt the right approach. It's hopeless attempting to hold a plectrum in the usual manner with a reasonable bit of the tip showing, and then somehow shifting it quickly to a close grip for chicken pickin' technique. In real playing terms there just isn't the time for such pick-shuffling, so you'll need to hold the plectrum in such a way as to enable instant alternation between these two styles.

Start by gripping the plectrum lightly, fairly close to the tip – not so close that 'normal' picking is impeded, but somewhat closer than you've probably done so far, and certainly closer than you would if strumming chords. After a bit of practise you'll find that it's quite easy to produce clear, clean notes in the usual way. When you want to switch instantly over to chicken pickin' playing, all you need do is to 'pinch' the end (the picking edge) of your plectrum nearer the tips of your finger and thumb, by

simply bending the finger/thumb joints slightly. This has the effect of drawing it into your fingers just that little bit extra, thereby enabling you to apply the chicken pickin' sound.

It does take a little bit of practise to get the feel of this, but it's not the most difficult thing to master, and as a generalisation I'd recommend a medium gauge plectrum rather than a heavy one for this type of work. It makes 'close picking' playing easier to manage, and is likely to create a sharper, more percussive sound.

This style of playing is great for creating an extra bit of excitement in traditional rock and roll, and is also very useful when playing laid-back bluesy licks. The next piece of music (exercise 63) is a typical example of the classic James Burton style, and also serves as an introduction to a new time signature. The 12/8 time featured in this piece isn't as complicated as it sounds, and is easily understood when you compare it to some notes written as a triplet in common (4/4) time.

As you see, these two samples are identical in all but the triplet signs on the version at left – these are necessary in order to 'condense' three eighth notes into the theoretical time value of two. If you weren't paying attention in Chapter 2, I refer you back to **page 25** (and also **page 63**) for a refresher course in triplets. However, when you consider the version previous page right, which is in 12/8 time, the triplet sign becomes unnecessary. This is simply because 12/8 basically means that each bar contains 12 eighth notes (or the equivalent) as opposed to the usual eight when playing in 4/4 time. So in order to make it easy on yourself to learn this new time signature, just imagine you're playing with the triplet

'feel' and the rest will come naturally. Refer to this demo if in need of guidance, as it contains all the essential time phrases in the next piece of music.

This exercise will be good practice on several counts – partly because it contains several chicken pickin' phrases, but also because many other techniques learned in this chapter are included, such as sliding, string bending and vibrato. Work through it carefully, aiming for a steady tempo of around 88bpm for a country/blues feel. If a heavier sound is more to your taste, a touch of overdrive/distortion would give it an entirely different perspective. It's up to you to decide upon that, but either way, keep your timing steady and practise until you get it right.

Example 63

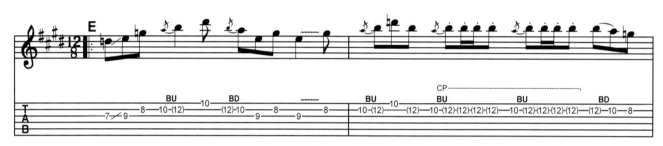

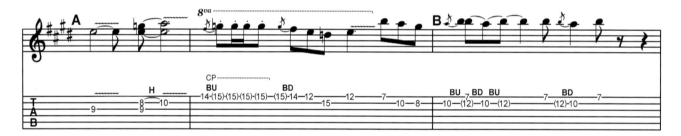

This is all quite self-explanatory from the notation and tab point of view. It's basically eight-bar blues, with the final chord leading (if you're so inclined) right back to the beginning again. Obviously, when you wish to end the piece it would be on an **E** note and chord.

A point worth mentioning here is the plentiful supply of 'naturals' in this music, effectively cancelling out some of the sharps in the **E** major key signature. This is very typical of the blues, and it's entirely characteristic of the style to play certain

notes flatted. Traditionally this would be the third and seventh notes of what is normally the major scale. More of that in Chapter 6, but I mention it here in the context of this piece so as to avoid any confusion in your mind.

If you're mostly inclined to follow the notation alone you could miss out on the effectiveness of playing some notes with open strings, as in bars six and seven. Although these notes could be played fretted, you'll find that the use of open strings here not only makes it easier to play but also improves the sound.

Tremolo picking

For some reason the word 'tremolo' seems to be a multipurpose term, with several entirely different meanings for guitarists. For instance, there's 'tremolo effect' (variation in volume), 'tremolo arm' (as attached to the Fender Stratocaster and many other guitars) and 'tremolo picking'; and because each of these applications is unrelated to the other two, the context in which the word is used will obviously be the determining factor, and must be clearly understood. Tremolo effect and tremolo arm will be dealt with later (see **pages 199 and 203** respectively), so for now let's keep to the point and establish what is meant by tremolo picking.

When you play any note on your guitar you'll understand that it occupies a certain space of time, and this can be written as a certain and specific type of note, such as a whole note (semibreve), half note (minim), quarter note (crotchet) and so on, with each successive note being of precisely half the duration of the previous one; and it's possible (depending on the overall tempo of the music) to write repeated notes of very brief duration, and therefore played at a very rapid speed. But there are occasions when one note is repeatedly played so fast that it becomes either impossible or impractical to write (or read) these repetitions as separate notes. This is where tremolo picking comes into effect, because that's the term used to describe notes played in this manner.

The principle involved in this is very easy to understand, and is typically written as shown in example 64.

In the process of moving from one note to the next there would be no discernible pause between the two, as the rapid picking of your right hand should continue without hesitation. This is easiest when the notes are on the same string as you see here, but is

obviously a bit trickier when you need to move across to another string for the following note. The thing to do is to ensure that your pick action is heading in the direction of the string toward which you intend to move. So, if you're rapidly picking on the third string and wish to move across to the second (whilst continuing to tremolo pick), it would be unwise to play your last note on string three as an upstroke. This would make it further for you to go in order to get back to string two. But if your last note (on string three) is played as a downstroke then you're already halfway there, simply because of the direction in which your plectrum plays that final third-string note. And then it's equally logical to begin playing on the next string with a continuation of that same downstroke, thereby adding to your advantage. It's just a question of common sense, really, but if you try this in slow motion you'll immediately see what I mean.

When you first attempt this tremolo picking technique it's likely that you'll experience some difficulty in attaining the very high speed necessary for the right effect. But there are a couple of useful tips that will ease this situation somewhat. First, hold your plectrum very close to the tip, almost as you did in the chicken pickin' technique. This removes any 'play' in the pick itself, which will immediately make things much easier. Also, if you were to 'dig in' too far with the plectrum this would tend to inhibit the smooth flow of its movement across the strings. So you don't want to apply any more force than is strictly necessary to sound the notes. Next, don't 'waste' any unnecessary plectrum movement. This means that when you move the pick up and down, be careful not to go any further up or down than is absolutely necessary to pick the string. Try thinking of the pick action as if you were just 'tickling' the string.

Practise at first on the three upper strings which, being of lighter gauge (see **page 169**) than the lower ones, will create less resistance against the plectrum. And do try to get the feel of moving around between notes on the same string, as in the above example, before attempting to jump around too much between alternating strings.

Example 64

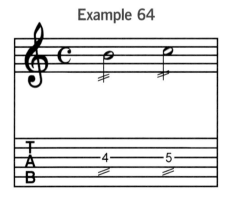

When you see notes written in this way it means that you should play them at such a rapid speed that they have no real identity as individual notes, instead becoming more a collective blur of sound over the duration as defined by the note itself. So, in this example, you'd pick the first (B) note at high speed for two beats of the bar, and then play the following (C) note for the remaining two beats of that same bar.

Summary

This covers all the main guitar techniques in general use, and to some extent your own personal preferences and music taste will determine which ones you use most. If, for instance, you're a laid-back country rocker your interest in chicken pickin' is likely to be greater than your need for pinched harmonics and fret tapping. On the other hand, if you're a heavy metal addict the exact opposite is most probably true. However, the guitar 'basics' such as string bending, slides, hammer-ons/pull-offs and vibrato are common to most styles.

CHAPTER 6

More about chords

It's entirely possible to learn and play a wide range of chords simply by copying the diagrams, as you've already discovered back in Chapter 2. Indeed, many guitarists are happy with this approach and never seek to understand chords beyond this point. This attitude is fine up to a basic level of guitar playing, and a chord won't sound any better no matter how intimate your understanding of it may be. But in music, chords are at the centre of everything, and without at least some understanding of their structure you will be placing unnecessary restrictions upon your freedom of musical expression.

Basic chord construction

Any chord is based upon certain notes of the scale that bears its name. So a **C** major chord is built from notes of the **C** major scale, and an **Am** chord is built upon notes from the 'A minor' scale, and so on. For every major scale there is what's known as a 'relative minor' scale, which has the same key signature and contains the same notes as the major scale – the essential difference is the order in which these notes are considered, and deemed to be of significance to that particular scale. You already have a certain familiarity with scales from Chapter 4. This will stand you in good stead here as we begin to elaborate upon the subject and understand their role in the structure of chords.

If you consider the notes of a **C** major scale in order of their usual ascending sequence, you have **C–D–E–F–G–A–B**; and if you then give each note a number, based on that order, **C** is 1st, **D** is 2nd, **E** is 3rd, **F** is 4th, **G** is 5th, **A** is 6th, **B** is 7th, and then back to the octave point of **C**. This numbering system is significant, because the number accompanying each note determines how chord construction is described and understood.

Any major chord is comprised of the 1st, 3rd and 5th notes of its scale. So the **C** major chord consists entirely of **C**s, **E**s and **G**s. No matter what 'shape' it may be, or whereabouts on the fretboard you play it, you'll find that this rule applies every time. And the same thing is true of the **Am** chord, of which the **A** minor scale notes are **A–B–C–D–E–F–G**. Again the chord is made up of the 1st (**A**), 3rd (**C**) and 5th (**E**). And because the **C** major scale and the **A** minor scale consist of exactly the same notes, the order in which they're placed is the only defining factor determining which notes are 1st, 3rd and 5th, making this apparently small difference a very important consideration.

An alternative (and more usual) way of considering the minor chord structure is to base it upon the major scale and simply flatten every 3rd. So an **Am** chord (based upon the **A** major scale of **A–B–C#–D–E–F#–G#**) consists of the 1st (**A**), *flatted* 3rd (**C**) and 5th (**E**).

These rules apply to every major chord and every minor chord. Every time it's a case of the 1st, 3rd (or ♭3rd) and 5th notes of the appropriate scale. But always remember to take into account the key signature of that scale, or you'll soon be in a musical mess. This might sound too obvious to mention, but it's a mistake made by musicians new to this theory. For example, if you consider an **E** major chord, don't just automatically start counting up – **E** as 1st, **F** as 2nd, **G** as 3rd and so on – thereby completely forgetting about the necessary sharps and flats of the (in this example) **E** major key signature. And if you refer to **page 104** you'll be reminded that every **F**, **G**, **C** and **D** should be sharpened, and therefore the **E** major scale should read **E–F#–G#–A–B–C#–D#**, making the chord notes **E** (1st), **G#** (3rd) and **B** (5th). A number of key signatures were introduced in Chapter 4, but a comprehensive list is shown on the next page for convenient reference within this chapter.

Most of these scales are straightforward and, to some extent, familiar to you, but there are a few points here requiring special mention. There are the 'in-between' scales, for instance – those which are sharp or flat of natural pitch. And if you think about it, you'll realise that these scales can be regarded in two different ways: the **D♭** scale could also be written as a **C#** scale, in which case each flat note would instead be described as the sharp of the next lower note – that is to say, **D♭** would be termed **C#**, **E♭** would be **D#** and so on. And also, of course, the same applies to the **G♭** scale, which is alternately known as **F#**, with all the corresponding changes of notes where applicable from sharps into flats. I've written these 'in-between' scales here, in the way in which they most often appear. If you do encounter the other versions of these scales it won't be any problem, as the key signature will speak for itself.

Another interesting detail to be explained in the **G♭** scale is where the key signature contains a flat symbol for the **C** notes. As you're aware (from **page 29**), if played flat (one fret lower) the **C** note is actually a **B** note; but occasionally this device is used in written music for reasons of convenience. Otherwise confusion would arise in differentiating the **B** (if it were not written as **C♭**) from the **B♭** note, which is also common to this scale, and would then require excessive use of 'naturals' to explain that distinction. If you play the **G♭** scale you'll quickly understand what I mean. And incidentally, a similarly odd situation occurs sometimes with a note being referred to as 'double flatted' (ie two semitones lower, written ♭♭).

Due to the extreme partiality guitarists have for 'guitar-friendly' (open) keys, you aren't likely to encounter these types of idiosyncrasies too often, but it will happen sooner or later so you must be aware of such details. Vocalists, particularly those who don't play an instrument, are inclined to choose the most natural key for their comfortable pitch range. This can result in you being handed a music sheet written in some inconvenient key (at least from a guitar point of view), which you're then expected to transpose, along with having to first identify which actual key the vocalist in question is warbling in at the time. Such fun things do happen from time to time, and you'll want to be fully equipped for these situations.

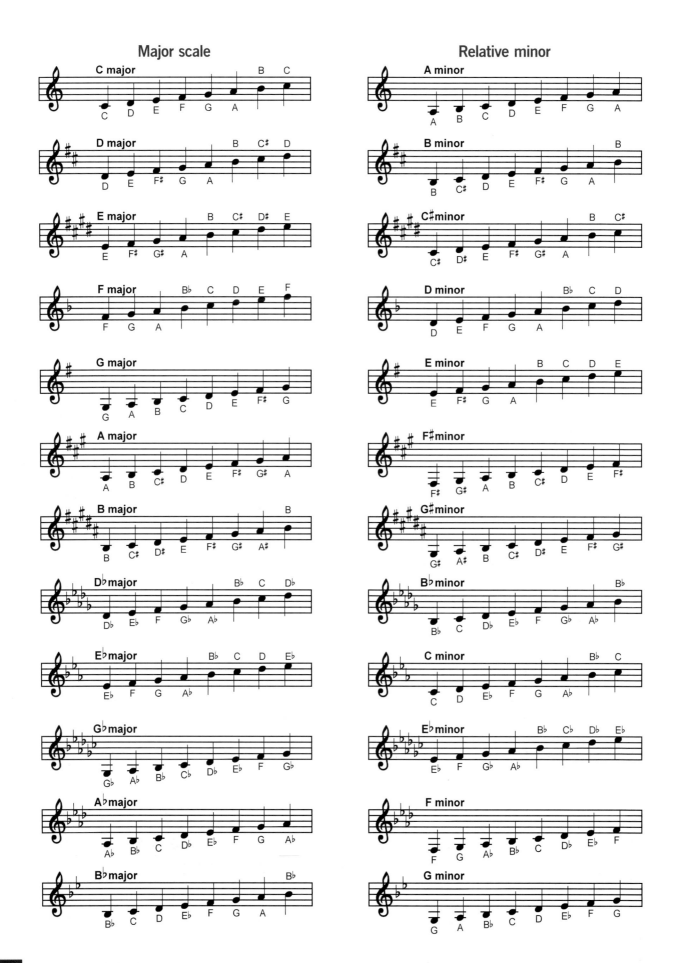

Major scale

Relative minor

Building on the basics

Any major key has three chords that are fundamental to that key. These are technically known as the tonic, the sub-dominant, and the dominant. These are major chords based upon respectively the 1st, 4th and 5th notes of the major scale. Don't misunderstand this. I'm not saying that they're built *with* those three notes, in the way that a major chord is made up of the 1st, 3rd and 5th. I'm just saying that they take those notes as their starting point – their 'name note', so to speak. So in the key of **C** these would be **C** major, **F** major and **G** major. Each of these chords, in turn, has a relative minor chord, also commonly used in that (**C**) key; and if you check on the previous page you'll realise that these will be **Am**, **Dm** and **Em**. These six chords will be the ones most likely to occur, in various combinations, in the key of **C**. This is because all of the notes used in these chords are natural to the **C** major scale, and so there's nothing which would sound 'out of place', musically speaking. Any other chords using only notes found in the **C** scale are all basically variations on these six chords, and will be introduced later in this chapter. Although we're referring here to the key of **C** major, this type of information applies equally to any major key. It's just easier to learn the basics in **C**, because there are no sharps or flats to negotiate.

It's important to understand which chords are most often used in any given key, because it will simplify things later on. Suppose you needed to play a song, but have no sheet music or chord pattern available. As soon as you establish which key the recording is in (see **page 155**), your search for the appropriate chords will be narrowed considerably by knowing the most probable chords to try out in the song. Obviously it isn't failsafe, because other chords do occur, but it does give you a substantial starting point. Experience and ear training will do the rest.

Basic chords such as majors and minors can be altered in various ways, by adding extra scale tones to the usual fundamentals. They still remain essentially major or minor chords, because the 1st, 3rd (or ♭3rd) and 5th are present, but the sound is given a different quality that is sometimes desirable, and occasionally essential, due to the melodic and harmonic structure of the music.

The most commonplace addition to a major chord is one with which you're already familiar, namely the seventh chord – although, as a first example of adding scale tones, this one is a bit of an oddity, because that extra note is actually a flatted seventh. So on top of a basic **C** major triad (three-note chord) of **C**, **E** and **G**, there's also a **B♭** note; and because of this additional note being not natural to the **C** major chord signature, the **C7** chord is more likely to be found in chord sequences from the key of **F** major (a scale in which **B** notes are flatted) rather than that of **C** (a scale in which they aren't).

In any key, the chord most likely to be played as a seventh isn't the tonic, but the dominant major. In other words, in **C** major the **G** chord is very often played as a **G7**. This works well because it maintains that comfortable sound of only using **C** scale notes of **G**, **B**, **D** and **F**, despite being a **G**-scale based chord. If you care to examine the (**G** major) scale from which this chord is constructed, you'll see that these notes are indeed the 1st (**G**), 3rd (**B**), 5th (**D**) and ♭7th (**F**).

The dominant seventh chord is present in most songs, and is characterised by its tonal quality of 'non-resolution'. By this I mean that it doesn't have the sound of finality about it, and is therefore ideal as the penultimate (next to last) chord. But don't take my word for it – just check out any chord sequence you like. The song, along with usually all the verses within it, will end on the tonic chord, whilst the chord immediately before that will most likely be the dominant seventh.

The seventh chord structure is also particularly interesting in another way, because it acts as the basis for other chord extensions. These are primarily the ninth, eleventh and thirteenth chords. They're generally used less often in popular music, and occur more commonly in jazz, where complicating matters is normal procedure, and chord variations can happen several times per bar.

But how can such chords even exist when there are only seven scale notes available? This would seem to make a ninth extension (never mind an eleventh or thirteenth) something of a contradiction in logic. Well, in an effort to complicate our lives still further, the scale theory below presents the answer to this question:

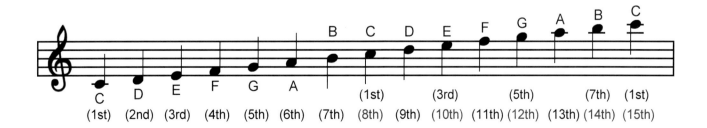

As you see, when considering seventh chord extensions a two-octave scale is employed, in which you reach the usual octave point and then simply continue counting upward. Obviously there's nothing actually different about these upper notes in terms of their tonality – the C is still a C, and the D is still just a D, and so on. This is simply a convenient way of counting above the usual seven notes, in order to describe more complex chord variations. The notes in blue are theoretical numbers to make this clear, because in music there isn't really any such thing as an 8th or a 10th etc. So the 1st, 3rd, 5th and 7th simply retain their original musical identity in factual terms, whilst the 9th, 11th and 13th are those with which we're concerned.

When you regard the scale in this way it becomes clear that a C9 chord would consist of the following notes: C (1st), E (3rd), G (5th), B♭ (♭7th) and D (9th). Note that although the chord is named C9 it does also contain the flatted seventh, because it's still fundamentally an elaboration of the basic seventh chord structure. And if you're just dying to know what a ninth chord would look like, refer to the two examples below. Left-handed versions of these chords can be found on **page 241**.

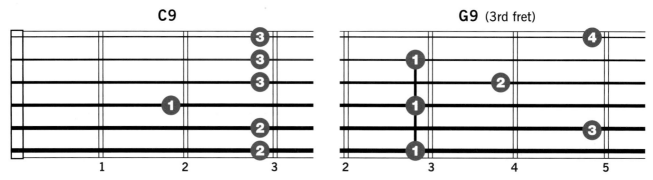

The easier (to learn) of these two chord shapes is the one on the right. This is nothing more than a G7 bar chord with an extra upper note added, and should present you with no real difficulties as regards the finger positions. The C9 shape (named from the fifth string note) is another story. You'll have to work on this one in order to master the awkward fingering necessary to secure the mini-bar across the top three strings. It may also prove difficult holding down the fifth and sixth strings with one finger, and it's perfectly acceptable to leave out the lowest note and play this as a five-string chord. Since no open strings are involved, both chords are fully moveable up (or down) the neck.

Of the seventh chord extensions, the ninth chord is one that you'll certainly encounter from time to time, far more than either the eleventh or thirteenth chords. It's sometimes used as a sophisticated ending chord in rock and roll songs. A good example of this would be the final chord in the Beatles' classic Twist and Shout, which ends on a resounding D9 chord, as played at the 5th fret.

When you do get into playing eleventh and thirteenth chords a curious situation will become apparent, due to the number of different notes in these chords. An 11th chord has, strictly speaking, six different tones for a complete chord. These are 1st, 3rd, 5th, ♭7th, 9th and 11th. The thirteenth chord has all of these plus one more: 1st, 3rd, 5th, ♭7th, 9th, 11th and 13th. And because a guitarist can only play a maximum of six notes together, the 11th is occasionally impractical (for suitable finger positions) and the 13th is impossible, so the answer has to be a compromise – which is to leave out certain notes. (Left-handed versions are on **page 242**.)

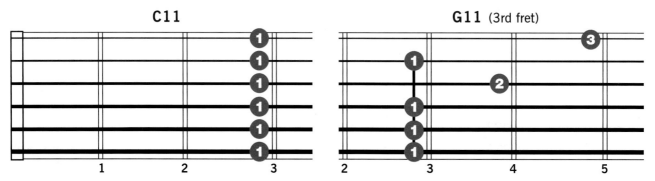

Comparing these chords to the C9 and G9 chords on the previous page, it's clear that they're built upon those shapes. However, whilst the G11 chord, above right, contains all the relevant notes (1st, 3rd, 5th, ♭7th, 9th and 11th) the C11, shown above left, doesn't have a 3rd, and may be considered something of a compromise for reasons of practicality.

There's nothing wrong with leaving out certain notes in this manner, and it's commonly done with these types of extended chords. There are alternate versions of these chords (see **page 215, or 242** if you're left-handed), which leave out certain other notes than the 3rd which is absent from the **C11** shape shown here. Which version you choose to play in any given situation will depend upon the melody and harmony concerned, and perhaps also upon which of the 'missing' notes is being covered by other musicians in your band. A keyboard or bass player might be filling in the notes absent from the guitar chord, and in this regard it can be helpful to be aware of the role each note plays in establishing the musical identity of a chord. For example, the 3rd is necessary if you need to clearly define a chord as being either major or minor, and without

this note the chord is, strictly speaking, neither. This isn't always a problem, depending upon your musical intention, but it is something to keep in mind.

The flatted seventh is a very important note within the structure of these types of chord, as it's essential in defining a chord as being a ninth, eleventh, or thirteenth. If there's no ♭7th what remains of these chords would have other names (but more of that later), and would sound substantially different. However, the 9th or 11th could be absent from respectively the eleventh or thirteenth chord with no seriously adverse effect. And, perhaps surprisingly, the 1st and 5th notes aren't really indispensable either. But don't get in too much of a tangle over all of this: learn a selection of the relevant chord shapes and apply them according to your judgement of what sounds best for the occasion.

C13

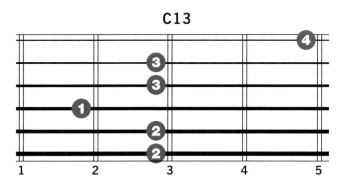

G13 (3rd fret)

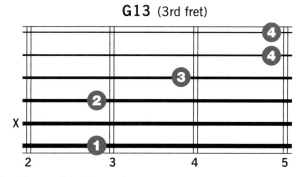

The C13 fingering requires a bit of a stretch, although it obviously gets easier when used for thirteenth chords higher up the neck. The G13 is somewhat easier, and will present little difficulty in fingering accuracy. As usual, left-handed players can refer to the chord dictionary for easier reading (see page 242).

Major seventh chords

Unlike an eleventh or thirteenth chord, it's not at all uncommon to encounter the major seventh; but what is it, and how is it different from any other seventh chord? Well, there's certainly room for confusion here, but the answer lies in the way it's described. The chord you've been studying so far would be written 'C7', as you know, and this new chord would be 'Cmaj7'. But since they're both major

chords anyway, what does this mean to you? The essential difference is to be found, as usual, in the scale. Whereas the usual **C7** would consist of 1st, 3rd, 5th and ♭7th, a **Cmaj7** chord would be 1st, 3rd, 5th and 7th. In other words, the 7th isn't played as a flatted (B♭) note, but as a natural (B) note. This is easier to understand visually, as in the chord diagrams below:

C7 (3rd fret)

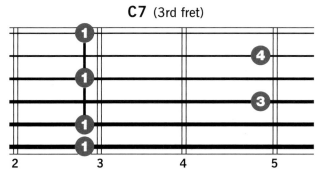

Cmaj7 (3rd fret)

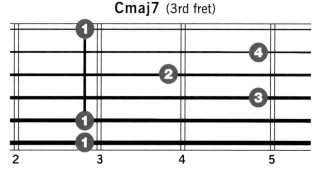

When comparing the finger positioning of these two chords the difference is clear. A small change made by adding your second finger on to the third string, and thereby raising the 7th back to its 'natural' position, makes for a big difference in sound characteristics.

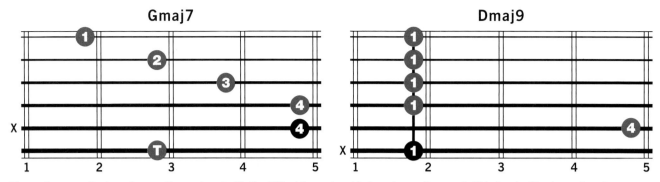

Gmaj7   Dmaj9

The major seventh above is sometimes played with the fifth string note added, and sometimes not. This is why it's shown here in black as an optional note. It can be tricky to fret the two notes with your fourth finger unless you have fairly large hands, so it's commonly played as a five-string chord with the thumb holding down the bass string (this technique is pictured on page 91) at the name note of G, and also silencing the fifth string. The Dmaj9 chord (above right) is easy enough, remembering to mute the lower string if you prefer not to include it, with the name note (D) located on the fifth string.

A logical extension on the **maj7** chord is, as you may have already anticipated, the **maj9** chord. Again, not one you'll meet every day in the pop/rock style of music, but definitely worth including in your repertoire for a musical rainy day. An example is shown above right, alongside another version of the **maj7** chord.

The chord shapes illustrated in this chapter are usually not the only available versions of each chord type. A more comprehensive range of chords can be seen on **pages 205–24**. Remember that, if required, left-handed illustrations of all the chords in this book can be found on **pages 232–51**.

An incidental, but important, point to keep in mind with all moveable chord shapes is the string on which the name note is located. The versions here are shown in one position as an example, but move a **Dmaj9** up a couple of frets and you have an **Emaj9**, and so on. Get yourself accustomed to different positions, so that when you need, for example, an E♭**maj7** you go straight to the 6th fret position (of the first shape, as seen on the previous page) without even having to think about it.

Other variations

You will have realised by now that just about any alternative or combination of scale notes can be added to a basic major chord in order to create interesting variations on the basic theme. This is pretty much the truth of the matter, although some are in common use whilst others are so rare that you'll encounter them only very infrequently.

Two chords you'll certainly need from time to time are the sixth and the suspended fourth. The sixth is exactly what you'd assume, being formed by the addition of a sixth note from the major scale on to a basic major chord. The two most common forms of this chord are seen here, being based on the two standard bar chord majors, illustrated here at the 3rd fret.

I'm fully aware that certain chord fingerings can appear to be almost impossible at first, but remember that you don't need to learn them all in one go. Take your time over these chords, and as you master each difficult finger positioning it tends to make your fingers more flexible, and other awkward fingerings will prove easier as a result.

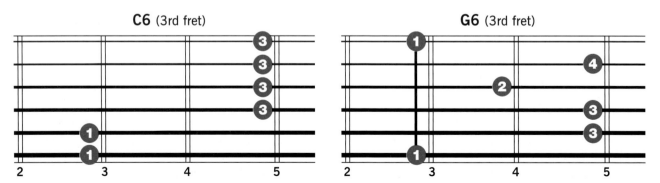

C6 (3rd fret)   G6 (3rd fret)

A couple of tricky manoeuvres here. Holding the C6 bar down with your third finger might feel awkward at first but shouldn't prove too difficult after a bit of practice. The G6 shape is more of a challenge, because of holding two strings with your third finger whilst also trying not to touch any other strings.

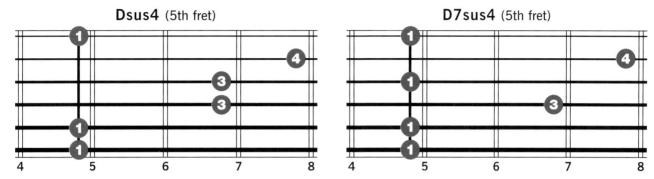

Dsus4 (5th fret) D7sus4 (5th fret)

These examples at the 5th fret show the Dsus4 and the slight variation of this chord, the D7sus4. The latter of the two is likely to be easier to learn, because there's less chance of accidentally silencing the top string with the edge of your (fourth) finger.

The suspended fourth is slightly less predictable in its construction, because the 3rd is missing from what would otherwise be a straightforward major or minor chord, and the 4th scale note is in its place. The suspended fourth chord can also be played as a seventh chord, although again it has no 3rd. Study the two examples above and you'll quickly get the idea.

Unlike the ninth, eleventh and thirteenth, these chords are of relatively simple construction, consisting of few notes. This generally makes them easier to play in their entirety (without having to omit notes), and gives them a smooth, satisfying sound. Other versions, including the very useful open **sus4** shape, can be found on pages 209 and 216 (pages 236 and 243 for the left-handed).

Another chord that falls into this category is the **add9**, formed by the simple addition of a ninth scale tone. This differs from the familiar ninth chord in that it doesn't contain a flatted seventh note as well. So whereas a **C9** chord would consist of C–E–G–B♭–D, a **Cadd9** chord has only C–E–G–D, giving it a distinctly different sound. Two versions of this chord are illustrated here. On the right is a moveable version, which is obviously the more versatile of the two. The other is an open string version, included here because this shape is so widely used that you need to be aware of it. Despite its open string limitations, use of a capo (see **pages 143–45**) enables its appearance in many keys other than the **C** chord version shown here.

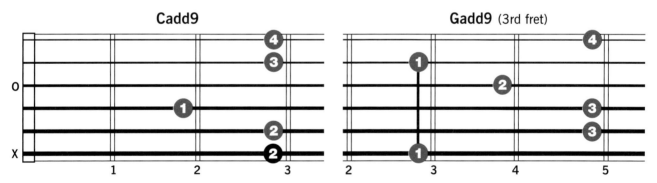

Cadd9 Gadd9 (3rd fret)

As you see, the use of six strings is entirely optional in the open chord version. It will sound good either way, and some prefer to keep the root note as the lowest string for musical (as opposed to easier fingering) reasons. The second, moveable, version has the name note on the lowest string anyway. With a similar fingering to the G6 chord, which you've (presumably) already mastered, the tricky third finger covering two strings should also be straightforward.

Augmented and diminished chords

There are two chord forms that, regardless of their unusual structure, are in reasonably general use. These are the interestingly named 'augmented' and 'diminished' chords. Despite being two completely different chord types, they do share one unusual feature – the useful fact that any note in the chord can be considered as the root, or name note. Taking things one at a time, let's first consider the structure of a diminished chord.

The diminished chord consists of a 1st, ♭3rd, ♭5th and ♭♭7th. In the case of a **Cdim** chord (instead of the word diminished, or dim, an alternate symbol is often used – example C°) this would obviously be C, E♭, G♭ and A. But bearing in mind that any of these notes can be the name note, a **Cdim** chord is also an

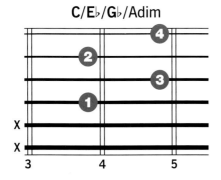

C/E♭/G♭/Adim

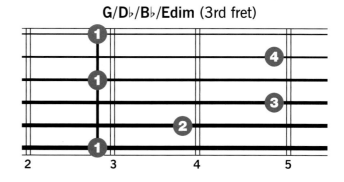

G/D♭/B♭/Edim (3rd fret)

In the four-string example at left it's clear that the diminished chord has four different root (name) notes. These are C, E♭, G♭ and A. In accordance with this there's also a ♭3rd, ♭5th and ♭♭7th for each of these. Cdim is C (1st) E♭ (♭3rd) G♭ (♭5th) and A (♭♭7th); E♭dim is E♭ (1st) G♭ (♭3rd) A (♭5th) and C (♭♭7th); G♭dim is G♭ (1st) A (♭3rd) C (♭5th) and E♭ (♭♭7th); and finally Adim is A (1st) C (♭3rd) E♭ (♭5th) and G♭ (♭♭7th). In effect this is four chords in one.

E♭dim chord, a G♭dim chord and an **Adim** chord. This peculiar state of affairs is clearly apparent if you observe the scale note sequence of all four of these major keys, although it's perhaps easier to visualise when you study a diminished chord formation as seen above.

A similar situation exists in regard to the augmented chord, except that it contains only three notes within its structure. An augmented is therefore three chords in one, instead of four. It's sometimes written (for example in C) as **Caug**, and also sometimes as **C+**. The most common form of this chord structure is illustrated in the diagram seen on the right:

So long as the unnecessary strings aren't sounded, any chord can be considered fully moveable up and down the neck. This is obviously essential, as certain chords simply aren't playable as bar chord or six-string versions. As usual there are additional versions of both diminished and augmented chords, which can be found on **pages 210, 218 and 219** (left-handed versions are on **pages 237, 245 and 246**.)

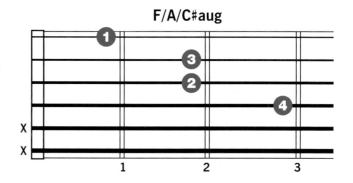

F/A/C♯aug

The augmented chord consists of a 1st, 3rd and ♯5th. Here we see an Faug – F (1st), A (3rd) and C♯ (♯5th); Aaug – A (1st), C♯ (3rd) and F (♯5th); and C♯aug – C♯ (1st), F (3rd) and A (♯5th). This enables you to cover all of the augmented chords within a span of four fret movements. The fifth string should be muted (silenced) with the edge of your fourth finger, and the sixth string with your thumb.

Minor chords

Most of the information relating to major chord extensions is also true of minor chords. In other words it's just a case of counting up to the appropriate scale note and then adding it to the basic minor chord structure. So if you take any of the major chord structures and simply flatten the 3rd you instantly have the minor version of that particular chord type. Incidentally, you might have noticed that the diminished chord actually falls into the minor category, because of the ♭3rd in its structure. Indeed, since it also contains the ♭♭7th (the technically correct name here for what's effectively a 6th) you may, on occasion, see it described as a diminished seventh chord. For the purpose of this chapter, however, I've placed it alongside the augmented chord because of their common multi-root composition.

Minor chords tend to have fewer commonly used variations than their major counterparts, although it's true to say that most of the same variations can apply if required. Again, the frequency with which you're likely to encounter some of these will depend upon the type of music you choose to play. Country, blues and rock guitarists generally won't be able to remember the last time (if ever) they needed a minor ninth, never mind a minor eleventh or minor thirteenth, whereas for jazz players it would be a very different story.

The simplest extension of any minor chord is the seventh, so basically we're talking about a series of chord shapes which differ from their major counterparts by only one note. This makes them relatively easy to learn, and very easy to remember.

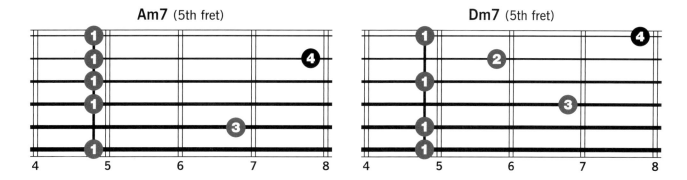

Am7 (5th fret)　　　　　　　　　　**Dm7** (5th fret)

Each of these chord shapes has an optional note, which you may include or leave out at your discretion. In both cases this optional note is an additional 7th, which would strengthen that aspect of the chord sound if appropriate to the occasion. The Am7 shape is named from the sixth string note, whilst the Dm7 shape has its name note from the fifth string.

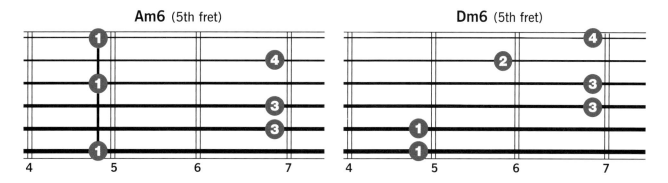

Am6 (5th fret)　　　　　　　　　　**Dm6** (5th fret)

By this time you should be experiencing very little difficulty with chord fingering positions, as they're only slight variations from previously learned chord shapes. However, some people do have ongoing problems with these third-finger bars covering two strings, and in this case it's permissible to mute the higher of the two strings and play a five-string chord instead.

The next most likely minor extension you'll encounter is the minor sixth. This is predictable enough, in that it's similar to the major sixth version, but with that one small change which converts it into a minor chord.

In describing chords, you'll sometimes hear the term 'inversion' being used. This is the way of specifying which is the lowest note sounding in any chord, and applies equally to both major and minor chords. The chords pictured above present clear examples of two different types of inversion. The **Am6** chord having the name note (**A**) as its lowest note is described as being in the root position. When any note other than the root is the lowest, then the chord is said to be inverted. If the 3rd (or ♭3rd) is lowest, then the chord is said to be in the 1st inversion. When the 5th is the lower note, the chord is in the 2nd inversion. So the **Dm6** shape, as pictured above, is an example of a chord in the 2nd inversion.

Whatever the inversion, the chord is still described in the same way, but its sound characteristics will change. An example of this is seen here on the right, where a **G**

major chord is played with different inversions, creating an ascending movement and having an harmonically pleasing effect in this regard.

This use of inversions is really a simple melody line, consisting of the upper notes G–B–D–G, supported and reinforced by their chord harmonies. Another, similar, example can be effected using several different chords,

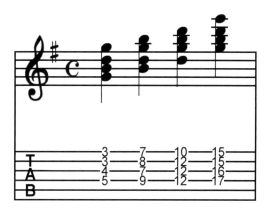

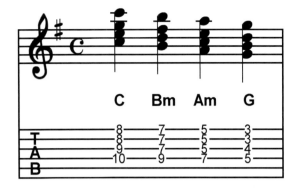

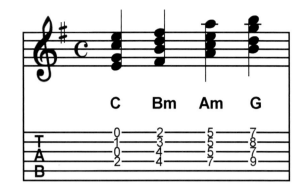

leading melodically downward to a natural **G** major conclusion. But this example is illustrated in two different ways. On the left is a choice of inversions that gives a natural and satisfying sound conclusion pleasing to the ear, whilst the alternative set of inversions is altogether less musically attractive. So, bearing in mind that these two alternatives are of exactly the same sequence of chords (**C, Bm, Am, G**), the only difference is in the choice of inversions.

These simple examples illustrate how the appropriate versions of a chord can dramatically alter the musical effect. This isn't to say that the second option is actually wrong by definition – in the right context it would doubtless suit the situation. So your choice of chord inversion depends upon what you wish to achieve.

Experienced players don't generally spend a lot of time worrying over which inversion to use in any given circumstance – not because they don't care, but simply because they instinctively know the various options, and the tonal results of any particular choice. So in this regard your sense of harmony will develop, and become a natural extension of your playing.

The inversion examples illustrated are chosen to create a melodic effect, as is sometimes the way with chord sequences. But the other, and more common, use of chords is to support a melody line, vocal or otherwise, and in this situation your choice of chord version is likely to be determined by proximity. This means that when you play the first chord in a song, your next chord will most likely be the nearest version available.

Which position, and therefore inversion, you play will depend upon several factors. If you wish to learn the guitar part from a recording your choice is simplified by copying, as accurately as possible, what you hear on that particular piece of music. This can be deceptive, however, because what you might regard as the sound of one guitar is very likely several guitars playing at different inversions, and in various ways, for best musical effect. And then there's the problem of hearing the rhythm guitar clearly, when there may be several other instruments and vocals obscuring

the sound you're trying to hear. So because of this and other considerations you'll need some basic guidelines to work with.

By now you'll have discovered that playing chords at various positions on the neck will produce widely differing sounds. If you want to create a rich resonant chord sound it's usually best to play lower down, using lots of open chords whenever possible, or capo'd (see **page 143**) if not in an open key. Acoustic guitars are particularly effective in this context as they have a very clean, percussive type of sound. On the other hand, chords higher up the neck give a tighter, choppy sound which can be very dynamic, but with perhaps less body and warmth than their lower counterparts. Electric guitar sound is often favoured with this approach. But always remember that anything you hear on a favourite recording will very likely feature a combination of both types of chord sound to some degree.

Another important consideration is listening to what other band members are playing. If you have another guitarist (or maybe a keyboard player) also playing chords, it's likely to be more effective to play at different inversions, perhaps one at lower pitch and one higher, which will create a more interesting combination of sounds than would be achieved if both of you were playing the same inversions of chords.

If you study the sheet music of familiar songs this can be informative or not, depending upon the detail and quality of that particular transcription. Some are very basic, with little more than the lyrics, and with chords written above. Often these will be represented by simple chord box diagrams, usually in the open position, and are not necessarily what you hear on the recording. This type of music is intended only for casual reference, and isn't much use to the more serious musician. But there are other music books that are incredibly detailed and extremely accurate, and therefore tend to be rather more expensive. These types of transcription can be very educational in illustrating how the guitar parts of your favourite songs are arranged (constructed), and are well worth studying, especially if you're interested in a particular type of music or artist.

Chords in melody and harmony

Let's suppose that you have a predetermined sequence of chords, as in any song, and wish to make up a guitar solo appropriate to that situation. How do you go about doing this with no source of reference other than your own imagination? Well, you could try humming along as you strum the chords, and try to find something that sounds right. This is OK, and it does work where simple, hummable melody lines are concerned. But as we know, guitar solos are made up of lots of little tricks (bends, hammer-ons etc) and intricacies that your voice (assuming you can actually sing anyway) would be hard-pressed to imitate. So constructing a guitar solo from voice alone can be rather limiting in many ways. What you need is a clear understanding of the melodic opportunities of any given chord, and how to exploit these for best effect – which is why we've spent the entire chapter so far in understanding the note and scale construction of the most widely used chords.

If you consider any chord, there are two ways of thinking about it: either as a selection of scale notes, or as fingering patterns on the fretboard. Most experienced guitarists, whilst

being generally familiar with scales, tend to go with the second approach. This is partly because it's more visual, but also because they're used to playing numerous inversions of each chord at many positions on the neck.

This is another very good reason for knowing as many different ways of playing a chord as is possible. It gives the guitar fretboard many visual points of reference, instead of being just a succession of frets and dots.

As an example of this approach let's take a closer look at a **G** major chord, as represented by its chord notes. The fretboard diagram below (the left-handed version is on **page 229**) illustrates its various positions collectively, up as far as the 12th fret, after which it obviously repeats the pattern one octave higher. At first glance this might look like just a collection of red dots at random points on the fretboard, but if you examine it more closely you'll see chord patterns, of various inversions, and all overlapping each other. This is more clearly apparent because we've given each dot a number, and are thereby able to break the pattern down into separate chord shapes.

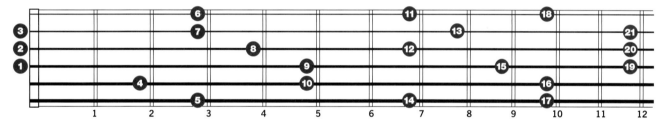

Working from left to right, the chords are as follows: dots 1, 2, 3, 4, 5 and 6 form an open G chord. Partially overlapping this are dots 5, 6, 7, 8, 9 and 10, which form a 3rd fret G bar chord; and overlapping this chord shape are dots 9, 10, 11, 12 and 13, which form a G chord at the 5th fret. From this we proceed to dots 11, 12, 13, 14, 15 and 16, which form another G bar chord (name note 10th fret). And finally, again slightly overlapping, are dots 16, 17, 18, 19, 20 and 21, which create a G bar chord at the 10th fret.

A couple of these chord shapes may be new to you, although they can be found in the more comprehensive chord dictionary on **pages 205–24**. At the moment it's more important that you study the way in which the entire fretboard can be seen to consist of a variety of chord patterns. When you begin to view the guitar neck in this way it tends to un-complicate matters, and gives the fretboard a look of greater familiarity.

All of these notes, at whatever octave, are either **G**, **B** or **D**, and therefore suitable to play, individually or otherwise, against a chord background of **G** major. So if you were composing a guitar solo, these would be your primary notes for that chord. Of course, the moment a chord change occurs you would apply the same logic to the next chord. But

playing just three basic notes, albeit at different octaves, will have a very limited melodic potential, so we need to find more notes suitable to the occasion – and the answer is to use those notes which, as you've already learnt, form the chord extensions. In other words, additional notes from the (in this example) **G** major scale.

What it all comes down to is this. When you compose a melody there are two main considerations: which key you're playing in, and which chord you're soloing over. The key, and therefore the scale, determines your basic note options, whilst the chord itself defines which of those scale notes are most likely to sound good against that particular chord. And if you look again at the scale notes **G–A–B–C–D–E–F#**, you can be sure that those which are actual chord notes

will always sound appropriate. The other scale notes are referred to as passing tones, and will work perfectly well with the chord, provided they're not permitted to sustain for too long. What is 'too long', you might wonder? And being the helpful person that I am, I'll give you some examples as illustrated above.

As played over the G chord, these snippets of individual bars will sound perfectly acceptable with that chord. Each brief sample contains some of the actual chord notes (**G**, **B**, **D**), and also some other scale notes, which enhance the melodic possibilities beyond those basic three notes. And what you'll notice is that the greater part of each phrase consists of the chord notes, whilst the non-chord

notes aren't held over for any length of time. They are, as described earlier, 'passing notes', effectively connecting the essential chord notes into a cohesive and more interesting melody line. To help you consider the relevance of this, let's find out see what happens if the opposite were the case, and those non-chord notes were allowed to dominate the melody line, with only brief appearances from the actual chord tones.

Below we see examples using more or less the same note combinations as on the previous page, but with the precedence given to the non-chord scale notes. And when you play these against a **G** major chord background I'm sure you'll agree that they sound a bit odd and out of place.

This is because, with non-chord notes sounding for most of the bar, the ear has more time to assess the natural dissonance (lack of musical harmony) between these notes and the **G** chord. But there's absolutely nothing inappropriate about sustaining these particular scale notes within the context of a **G** major key composition – it's just that they'd require other chords than a **G** major as background. Try, for instance, playing the above phrases against an **Am** chord, and you'll find that musically they sound a lot more satisfactory.

In a sense it's true that a predetermined chord sequence places limitations upon what you can play as an improvised melody within that formula. But on the other hand, it also helps to maintain the same 'feel' as in the main body of the song. Of course, there's no reason why you couldn't develop a different chord sequence for the guitar solo itself, but this is rarely done in practice, probably due to the awareness of staying true to the general theme of the music.

These rules applying to melody based around the chords are subject to the key signature of the music itself, as well as the chord being played at the time. This must be taken into consideration where the additional scale notes are concerned, although it has no effect upon the actual chord notes, which are always suitable. And staying with the **G** major chord for now, I'll explain how this works.

The **G** chord is common to three different keys (and their relative minors), in which it nearly always features. These are the keys of **G**, **C** and **D**. The reason why it's common to those keys is because their scale notes all contain the notes of **G**, **B** and **D**. This isn't so with any other keys, which therefore

don't normally (there are always exceptions) use the **G** major chord. But depending upon which key you're playing in, the key signature will influence how you play certain notes, which may be used over that basic **G** chord. You might use an **F♯** as a passing note, as would be required by the key signature of **G** major or the key signature of **D** major, but an **F** note would not be played sharp if used as a passing note against a **G** chord, when used in the key of **C** major. This is simply because the key of **C** contains only 'natural' notes. So whilst you may be thinking in terms of playing over a **G** major chord, you should, in that instance, also be thinking about using only notes from the **C** major scale.

All of these facts might sound complicated on paper, but they're naturally apparent to the ear when heard in the context of any piece of music. Some brief examples on the following page will give you the idea of how different one chord can sound, with regard to the key in which it's used. Notice the same chord sequence (but in different keys) in each four-bar phrase, which is from tonic to sub-dominant to dominant (or dominant seventh) and then back to tonic again. Be aware also of how the notes in every bar are integral to both the chord and the key signature.

Remember that this isn't a continuous 12 bars of guitar music – it's three separate four-bar phrases, the purpose of which is simply to clarify a point. In each case, and in each key, the **G** chord uses some or all of its constituent notes (**G**s, **B**s **D**s), which are suitable in each case and always sound right with that chord. But if you study the 'passing notes' you'll see that some of them vary according to the key

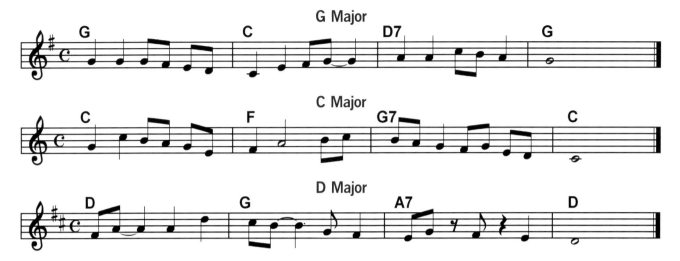

signature. In the first phrase an **F#** is used with the **G** chord; but in the next line (key of **C**) an **F** natural appears with the **G** chord, and yet both sound in tune and in context with that piece of music and with that **G** chord. In the next phrase (key of **D**) a **C#** appears as a passing note with the **G** chord, and even this sounds melodically correct. So the basic rule when composing a guitar piece of your own is to use the chord notes freely, and other passing notes with regard to the overall key signature.

Obviously, we've concentrated here on the **G** major chord as one example, but it applies with all chords both major and minor, and the extensions thereof; and a comprehensive familiarity with all chord positions makes it a lot easier to locate your notes across the fretboard. With this information in mind, it's well worth studying some sheet music and listening to the way in which different chords relate to each other and to the notes that they support. If you don't have any music available at the moment, there are many examples to be found in this book, particularly in Chapters 4 and 5, which clearly illustrate the relationship between chords and melodies played within different key signatures.

Adding some harmony

Harmony can broadly be described as simultaneously playing two or more notes which sound good together. The most immediately obvious example of harmony is simply a chord, but guitar solos also often feature note sequences played in harmony, which is what we're really talking about here.

The most straightforward approach to playing a melody line in harmony is to accompany each note with the note found a third higher on the scale in question. What does this mean? Take another look at the **C** major scale.

Counting up in 3rds from each note is convenient for locating a harmony for any given note, but it mustn't be confused with the *actual* order of scale notes as explained on **page 103**. The method indicated above is only for this specific purpose, in regard to finding the appropriate pairing of notes in a harmony situation.

From these illustrations you can see that two-part harmony is actually partial chords, in this case taken from the key of **C** major, and when pairing notes in this manner the basic rules still apply – that these notes should be applicable to both chord and scale. In the case of harmony it's simply a question of using *pairs* of notes which meet these criteria.

When playing notes together it's usually desirable to consider one of the pair as being the main melody line, with the other note complementing and enhancing it. This is done

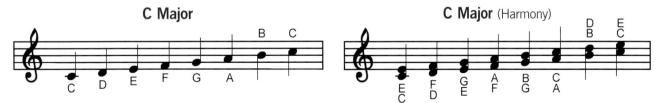

Any note can be given an 'upper 3rd' harmony very easily. Taking any note of the scale and then counting up by two notes locates the required harmony. Starting, for instance, with C as 1st and D as 2nd, then clearly E is 3rd. This works for every note in the same manner. If you want a 3rd harmony for D, then you just start counting up from that point in the scale, so D is 1st, E is 2nd and F is 3rd. How this appears in musical notation is shown in the diagram above.

by playing the main note slightly louder than the other, which is easily achieved by playing with either a downstroke or upstroke of the plectrum. Whichever note is struck first will tend to be the louder of the two. You can try this out right now by playing the harmony scale on the previous page. First run through all the notes using only downstrokes, which will cause the lower melody to be dominant. Then try playing it with upstrokes, which will have the opposite effect.

When a harmony is required for any melody line it isn't necessary that all of the harmony notes should be always in 3rds. This isn't an unalterable rule, it's only one of several options, and sometimes an alternative is unavoidable anyway due to the chords underlying the basic melody. If you consider the example above right you'll see what I mean.

In this two-bar example, bar one is easily played in 3rds, with all chord notes and passing notes beautifully harmonised against the **C** chord. But the second bar uses a combination of 3rds and, for the last note of the bar, an upper 4th (from the **G** note) harmony, in order to stay in tune with the **C** chord. In these examples I've included the tab, which will indicate a good choice of fretboard positioning for smooth and convenient playing. Should you happen to prefer an alternative, feel free to use that instead.

When using harmony notes in this way it's not always necessary for every note to be harmonised. As usual it will depend upon the sound you wish to create. Some examples of occasional harmony notes included in an otherwise single-note phrase can be seen in other chapters of this book, such as Chapter 4 (exercises 11 and 13), and many of the bends, slides etc demonstrated in Chapter 5.

Another approach to harmonising a given note is to maintain one note as harmony for several notes above or

below it in pitch. The practicality of this approach will, of course, depend upon the chord, as the harmony note will essentially be a case of sustaining a chord tone as support for the 'moving' melody line. This is typically achieved as demonstrated below.

From these examples you can see that there are sometimes several possible options regarding an appropriate harmony for any note; so how do you decide upon which one to employ in a given situation? The answer is that you should, if in doubt, experiment with the various possibilities, and let your ear decide which one is the preferable sound for that occasion. To put it simply, if it sounds right it *is* right, and vice versa.

Although rules are made to be broken, there are a couple of basic guidelines where harmonising is concerned. Generally speaking, a note can't be harmonised with another unless they're separated (in pitch) by at least three semitones. So if you take a **C** note, for instance, it wouldn't pair well with a **C#** or a **D**. Or, in the other direction, it wouldn't sound good harmonised with a **B** or a **B♭**. But I always stress that exceptions to practically any musical 'rule' can occur if used in the appropriate context. There are certainly occasions when dissonance (see **page 114**) is turned into a virtue, but this must be used with discretion, and in the light of greater experience.

The blues scale

Having just mentioned the word 'dissonance' for a second time, this seems like a perfect opportunity to reintroduce the blues. And when we consider this style it's worth remembering that this particular form also includes rock and roll, and heavy rock guitar as well, because the essentials are basically all the same. It comes down to the use of certain notes, and the technique with which it's expressed.

The basic blues scale is also often referred to as the pentatonic scale, so-called because it is primarily based around five notes, and usually just a few basic chords. This approach, of what might be called simplicity with style, all adds up to making the blues an improviser's greatest asset. And once you've learned the blues scale and how to use it, you can improvise on the spot and need hardly ever go wrong.

I suppose that the first rule of playing lead guitar for the blues would be to throw away the rulebook, because it does seem to contradict some of the things we've learned so far. But don't panic; I'm exaggerating just a little bit here, and your knowledge of chords and scales will soon make a contradictory sort of sense of all this.

The five notes of the pentatonic blues scale are as follows: 1st, ♭3rd, 4th, 5th and ♭7th. From this you can see that it's actually a minor scale, but one of the odd things about the blues is that this range of notes is used with both major and minor chords. This makes for unusual company among notes and chords, but somehow it works, and it's this quality of dissonance that's responsible for the unique and well-loved sound of the blues.

Another interesting thing about this blues scale is the way in which the notes integrate well with several chords, so that having established the key for, let's say, a three-chord blues song, the basic note pattern is the same for all three chords. In other words, it isn't necessary to rethink the scale pattern every time you encounter a chord change. Let's contemplate this, with a sample of 12-bar blues in the key of C, using notes based entirely upon a pentatonic C scale.

As you can see, this is really a very simple formula in note and scale terms, but what really makes good blues technique is the 'feel' with which it's played. This is exemplified here with slides, bends, and hammer-ons, all enhanced with lashings of vibrato.

Guitar players are actually quite fortunate where blues playing is concerned, because they only have to learn a few basic finger patterns, and then move them up or down the neck according to what key is required. On a keyboard instrument, for example, it can be necessary to deal with unruly combinations of black and white notes even in what, for guitarists, would be easy open keys. Let's be straight about this: guitar playing and the blues were just made for each other. Here are some fretboard patterns (left-handed players see **page 229**) for the pentatonic minor blues scale, as shown here in the key of **F**:

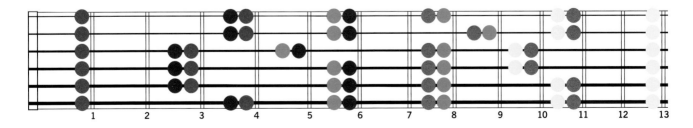

In this diagram each colour represents a blues pentatonic scale in one fixed position, and where there are two colours in one fret space this is where these patterns overlap, making the fretboard into one large pattern. The best approach, for those of you interested in becoming familiar and comfortable with the blues scale, would be learning each pattern separately, and then very soon you'll learn to work them into each other, making your playing and improvising skills flowing and versatile. When you've mastered the patterns as seen here in **F**, apply the same approach to other keys by starting from a higher fret position and working from that point.

Although this five-note scale is at the heart of all things bluesy, there are those who occasionally add to it by throwing in an extra note here and there. The additional note is usually the ♭5th, which is something of an optional extra, creating a scale of 1st, ♭3rd, 4th, ♭5th, 5th and ♭7th. Far more common even than this slight adjustment is the practice of enhancing the ♭3rd with a slight upward bend. We aren't talking about a severe bend here – not even as much as a semitone (one-fret) bend. This is more like a quarter-tone bend, which just raises the pitch slightly without actually reaching the next definite (fret) pitch. This is sometimes referred to as a 'blues curl', and on paper it looks like the illustration above right.

A partial bend like this is something absolutely typical of the blues. When applied to the ♭3rd it effectively places the note between a major and a minor. You can think of it either

as a ♭3rd played slightly sharp, or a natural 3rd played slightly flat. Try it out for yourself by applying it to some of the (E♭) notes of the 12-bar blues on the previous page and you'll realise that it's a very effective embellishment for this style of music.

When you construct a solo around any chord sequence, be it blues style or otherwise, chord and scale knowledge is always fundamental to accurate and efficient creativity. But keep in mind that the occasional unexpected note (one which isn't typical of the scale or style) can be used to good effect in the right context. For example, you may be working essentially from the pentatonic blues scale, but that doesn't mean you can never use any notes other than those five or six. Consider the following phrase, which would sound good when playing in this style, although it incorporates additional notes along the way:

This strays from the basic pentatonic scale in a couple of places, having both a B note and an F# note, but it essentially retains the right 'feel' whilst giving a wider range of versatility to your creative options.

You might wonder what point there is in having a guideline of scales to create a certain sound when it's also OK to contradict those scales from time to time. As with many situations, it's really a case of understanding the rules of the game whilst being aware of any available options. Above is another example of some additional notes being used to good effect:

If you regard this as a bluesy pentatonic phrase then the **E** natural and the **B** natural are the odd notes here. On the other hand, if you take the key signature at face value the **E♭** and the **B♭** are out of the ordinary. As always it depends upon which effect you intend to create. Try the little chord riff on the left.

This is simply a chord change with some passing notes added for good effect and again we see the use of a note untypical of the key in the **F** natural. So there are many ways of using scales, chords and dissonance to your advantage, if you learn all the rules but also know when to break them.

The country scale

In some ways country and blues are similar, and certainly the guitar styles overlap in many regards. Like blues music, country generally relies upon a few basic chords for its traditional sound, and these tend to be the straightforward major and minor chords. Country rhythm is most often played on acoustic guitar, with the emphasis on open chords and sustaining rhythm strokes. The traditional country rhythm, with alternating bass note and chord strums, can be studied by referring back to chord chart 13 on **page 28**. Obviously this is only one example, but it's very typical of the style.

Lead guitar for country music is usually played with a bright, twangy sound, including plenty of string bending and, for faster numbers, some chicken pickin' thrown in for added excitement.

It's almost illegal to play anything other than a Fender Telecaster, but otherwise any single-coil guitar will do the trick, using the bridge pickup and plenty of treble. Whereas blues players tend to concentrate upon the pentatonic *minor* for their characteristic sound, the basis for a country guitar sound is the pentatonic *major* scale. And the convenient thing about learning the pentatonic major scale is that it has exactly the same fingering positions as the pentatonic minor scale. Think back to **pages 103–4** and recall how each major scale has a relative minor scale, which contains the same notes but starting from a different 'name' note and therefore having a different sequence in which those notes are played. Look at the two comparative diagrams below (left-handed players see **page 229**):

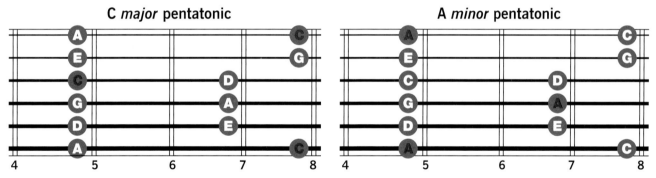

Both of these patterns are obviously identical in note structure and finger pattern, but the one above left is based around the note of C, whilst the other is based around the note of A. What this amounts to is, if you played it against a C major chord the sound would be smoother and less dissonant than if you played it with an A major chord. Same notes, different effect.

So when you're thoroughly familiar with the finger patterns across the fretboard, as shown on **page 117**, you not only have the blues scale patterns but also the country scale patterns based upon the note found three frets higher. In other words you need to visualise these identical patterns in two different ways and apply this knowledge accordingly. To clarify this, refer to the chart seen here.

Blues and country scale patterns

Minor pentatonic (blues)		Major pentatonic (country)		Minor pentatonic (blues)		Major pentatonic (country)
A	=	C		E♭	=	G♭
B♭	=	D♭		E	=	G
B	=	D		F	=	A♭
C	=	E♭		G♭	=	A
D♭	=	E		G	=	B♭
D	=	F		A♭	=	B

This easy-to-read chart is really a quick reference variation upon the major/relative minor illustrations seen on **page 104**, and very soon you'll understand these things naturally within the context of playing and creating your own solos. Notice that the pentatonic major scale is a simplified version of a standard major scale, but with the 4th and 7th absent from its structure. Similarly, the pentatonic minor scale is just a standard minor scale also missing a couple of notes, namely the 2nd and 6th.

Like the blues scale, there are occasions when you might choose to include additional notes. A popular 'extra' note for country solos might be the ♭3rd, giving more of a country/blues feel to your playing. As always there are alternatives that you may wish to explore when you've established yourself in the fundamentals of any given style. For the moment, have a go at the following country-style solo, using the bass/strum rhythm style at a tempo of around 184bpm as the basic 'feel' for this piece.

This is a typically lively country-style solo, with all the usual string bends and hammer-ons/pull-offs typical of a country guitar sound. But there are a few points worth mentioning here, to assist your understanding of the piece. Bars one and four both feature the unison bend technique as detailed on **page 75**. So the bent note is held over whilst the following note is sounded, and then released as a 'bend down' note in the next bar. This requires some care in holding the bent note steady, ensuring that its tension (and therefore its pitch) isn't inadvertently released whilst the unison note is played. It might feel tricky at first, but with practise this will soon become easy to do. Also, check out the note marked as an 'x' in bar three. This is a percussion note, played by touching, but not pressing down to

the fretboard. Although the note isn't 'sounded' in the usual sense, it does retain some pitch identity, so it's important to play at the appropriate fret (in this case first string, 10th fret). This could be seen as a variation on the chicken pickin' technique, and is useful in getting that authentic country guitar sound, particularly in solos played at a faster tempo.

Notice the unusual chord at the very end of this piece. This is a 6/9 chord, which is sometimes used to add an extra touch of class as an ending chord. Needless to say, this chord is included in the comprehensive chord dictionary on **page 218** (the left-handed version is on **page 245**). But if you just can't wait, I'll include it here in the D version used in this solo:

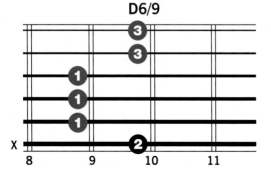

The 6/9 chord is often used as a final chord, giving a different feel as compared to a straightforward major chord. Its 'name' note can be either the note on the first string or, when played as a six-string version, the note one octave lower on the sixth string. The note indicated in black is therefore optional and can present a somewhat difficult fingering position. At lower (wider spaced) fret positions this can be best achieved by alternate fingering, holding the first and second strings with fingers four and three respectively.

Chord substitution

This is a term that causes some confusion amongst guitarists, but all it really means is taking a basic chord sequence and elaborating upon it with some appropriate alternatives. Your inclination toward doing this will largely depend upon which type of music you're playing. If you're playing rhythm guitar in a rock and roll or country band it probably wouldn't go down too well if you start embellishing basic chord sequences with extensions and substitutions, but in a jazz group it would be the normal thing to expect. This is because the traditional sound of any music form largely depends upon the harmonic structure of its chord patterns. To put it another way, rock and roll just wouldn't sound like rock and roll with a lot of added 9ths, augmented, diminished and other fancy chords.

The D6/9 chord used to end the previous example could be considered as a chord substitution, because the expected chord for this ending would obviously have been a straight D major chord,

which would have been perfectly acceptable. Substituting the D6/9 chord gives a less predictable sound, but one which is entirely appropriate and in keeping with the situation. But since it was a country-style guitar solo, the majority of the chord structure was kept simple, and to do otherwise would definitely not have been appropriate for the occasion.

To understand the basics of chord substitution let's begin with a familiar and often used chord progression. This is the C, Am, Dm, G7 pattern, with each chord being played for the duration of one bar.

The notation and tab are included here to indicate a suitable choice of inversions (see **page 111**), although obviously other possibilities are acceptable according to circumstance and taste. A basic chord progression such as this can easily be enhanced by adding scale notes to form chord extensions. With this in mind the result might be as seen below:

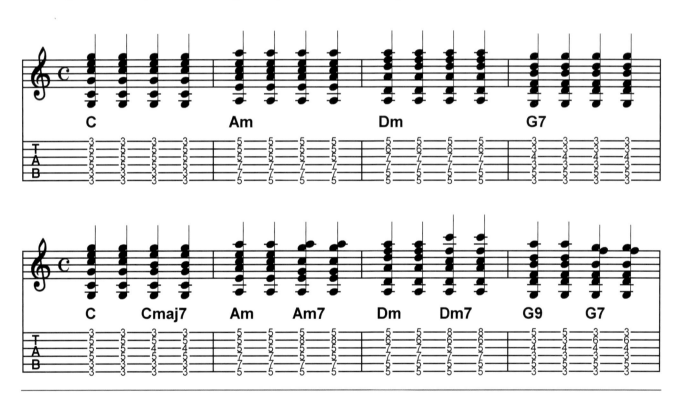

So this is a simple chord sequence that has now become harmonically more sophisticated, with nothing more than a few small adjustments. And notice how the (7th) sound quality of the (major and minor) seventh chords has been strengthened by adding upper notes which exaggerate that particular aspect of the chord.

Small variations in a chord sequence such as we see here would be fairly unobtrusive as far as other band instruments are concerned, as it's unlikely to conflict with (for example) the established bass line of the original format. But when making more

significant changes care must be taken to ensure that undesirable musical conflict doesn't occur. This won't be a problem (with suitable communication of ideas between band members) in order to dovetail the musical arrangement overall. To illustrate this point, take a look at the following chord sequence, written out in basic form for easy comparison. The top line is the standard chords, and the bottom line is the altered version. The line of notes in blue is a basic example of what a bass guitarist might be playing as an accompaniment, based upon the original unaltered version.

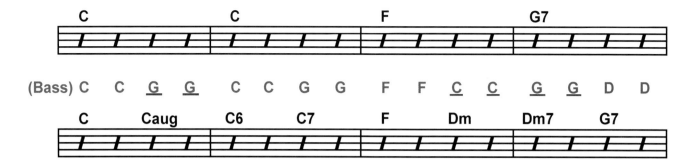

As you see, the bass notes would fit well with the original chords, but some notes (underlined) would tend to conflict with the altered arrangement. The **Caug**, for instance, doesn't contain a **G** note because it's raised by a semitone in this chord, becoming instead a **G#** note. That's just one example, but the others are equally obvious. So it isn't a good idea to arrive at band practice having worked out an elaborate variation on a basic chord sequence, and thinking how impressed everyone will be. If the other musicians are still playing from the original set of chords they're more likely to be irritated than impressed. And what if, perhaps, your keyboard player has also been hard at work doing the same thing, with his own version of the arrangement? Can you imagine the potential for musical confusion? So chord substitutions involving all but the most basic of alterations need to be arranged as a complete musical unit. These are considerations that need to be resolved with other musicians, but wouldn't be apparent when working alone. Again, it's not a problem, but it's certainly something to bear in mind.

Although there are certain fundamental rules pertaining to chord substitution, this doesn't mean that there's only one way of altering any given chord progression. As usual the main considerations are good taste, and an awareness of what's right for a particular song or style of music. If you play jazz guitar then you'll probably use chord substitution a lot, in which case the variations can become extremely complex and, at first glance, confusing. But on a more basic level even the **C**, **F**, **G7** chord sequence above can be treated in several different ways. A couple of other possibilities are shown below.

In these two variations the original version is also illustrated for direct comparison. The choice of chord inversions is up to you. When deciding on this, try to place your chord fingerings in such a way as to make the transition from one chord to another sound as smooth and natural as is possible. Remember that this is best achieved by avoiding large shifts from one neck position to another.

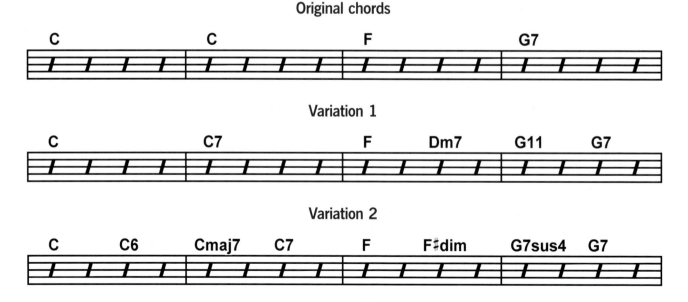

Chord substitution can essentially be applied in two ways. You can either add to the original chords with extra scale tones, such as changing **C** into **C6**, and **G7** into **G11** etc, or alternately you can insert new chords into the existing progression. This second approach is illustrated on the following page.

Original chords

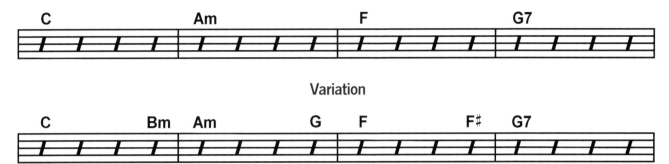

Variation

In this case we're creating a natural-sounding movement between the basic chord changes by inserting an extra chord on the last beat of each bar. Diminished chords are very useful and versatile as 'joining' chords. We've seen this already in connecting an F chord to the G7, with the use of an F#dim. Here is another example based upon the same principle:

Original chords

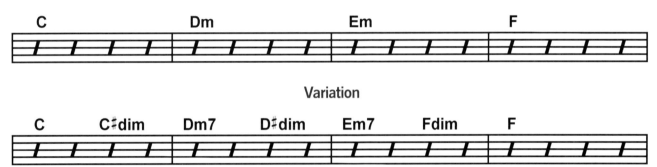

Variation

Applying chord substitution almost invariably means playing more chords per bar, and therefore requires greater fluency in chord changes. This places substantial demands upon your knowledge of chords, as well as the actual physical technique required. Jazz players have an extremely comprehensive repertoire of chords for what is perhaps the most demanding of musical styles, and what we've attempted so far is really just an introduction to what would be required if this should be your particular area of interest.

A glance at some jazz chord sequences can be a daunting experience, featuring not only numerous chords of exotic description but also frequently a different chord change on every beat of the bar. The following example gives an idea of how this might appear and, because of the importance of well-chosen inversions, I've also included the notation and tab for your consideration.

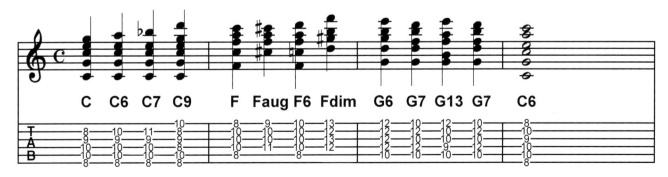

When chord inversions are carefully chosen, it happens that the upper line of notes tends to dominate the sound for melodic effect. We touched upon this subject briefly back on **page 111**, but it's even more apparent here due to the frequency of chord changes within the sequence. But, with different inversions of every chord being found all across the fretboard, this can be varied widely according to your musical intentions for the piece.

Despite the fun you can have in exploring the harmonic potential of a simple chord sequence, don't lose sight of the fact that it's supporting a melody line. This is generally the primary function of any chord progression, and whatever embellishments you make must also serve the lead melody (vocal or instrumental).

Jazz guitar chords

You might reasonably assume that any existing music you choose to play will already have appropriate chords for its melodic structure, and might therefore have asked yourself what the point would be in altering them at all. If so, the answer is likely to be 'Because it will help to give that song an authentic jazz sound which it doesn't already possess.' So, let's suppose you're playing in a jazz group and decide to do an appropriate styling of a Beatles song. You would find that the original chord sequence – suitable though it is for the Beatles' version – doesn't have much in the way of a jazz feel to it, and this is where you need to take straightforward major and minor chords and 'convert' them into more appropriate versions for the sound you're trying to achieve. How you go about doing this can be guided by what we might describe as the 'rules' of chord substitution. And, although we've learned something of this already, it's worth considering the situation in more detail for greater clarification. Here are a few of the basics to point you in the right direction:

1   The tonic chord of any key is frequently enhanced by simple additions from the scale. So in the key of **C** major, the **C** chord itself might be played as a **C6**, **Cmaj7**, **Cadd9** or **C6/9**.

2   The dominant seventh chord (**G7** in the key of **C**) could typically become a **G9**, **G11** or **G13** chord.

3   The sub-dominant chord (**F** in the key of **C**) is interchangeable with its relative minor or even minor seventh, becoming therefore a **Dm** or **Dm7**.

4   Minor chords are often embellished with their 7ths, 9ths, 11ths etc, ie **Am7**, **Am9**, **Am11**.

5   When passing chords are used in jazz they're often the same 'type' of chord as the one which follows, but played a semitone above or below the destination chord as a 'lead-in' to it. For example, **G7** to **C9** could be played as **G7**–(**B9**) **C9**, or **G7**–(**D♭9**) **C9** (see next page), wherein the chord in brackets is played on the last beat of the **G7** bar, and is therefore immediately followed by the **C9**.

6   When a dominant chord changes to a chord which is a fourth above (**G7** back to **C**), it's very common to replace that dominant chord with the seventh chord which has its root note three whole tones – six frets – higher (see next page). So, **G7** to **C** becomes **D♭7** to **C**.

These are some of the general guidelines that will make the situation easier to understand. As always there's no substitute for the experience of actually playing a range of jazz compositions, but this should help you to get started in the right direction. Of these 'rules', points 5 and 6 haven't been illustrated before and are therefore likely to be clearer with a few demonstration bars for you to play:

Original chords

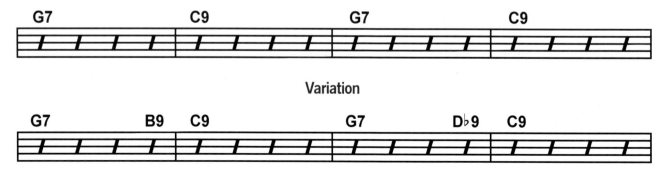

Variation

This illustrates the 'passing chord' reference, whereby a chord is inserted before the intended changeover from G7 to C9. Both variations are shown here, as it moves one semitone up toward the following chord, or alternately down. Either approach is commonly employed in jazz guitar playing.

Original chords

| Em | Dm | G7 | C |

Variation

| Em7♭5 | Dm7 | D♭7 | C6 |

The chord for consideration here (illustrating point 6, previous page) is the D♭7 which replaces the G7 in bar three, although I just couldn't resist jazzing up a few of the other chords along the way.

Even if you're not a dedicated jazz player, there's still considerable interest to be found in some of the chords that characterise this style. Quite a number of chords frequently used in jazz hardly ever occur in the more usual pop/rock songs. The Em7♭5 in the above chord sequence, and illustrated here, is one such example. (Left-handed players see **page 247**.)

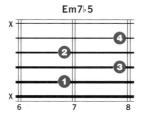

This particular chord shape takes its name from the note found on the fifth string (**E**), and is fully moveable, providing you remember to mute the first and sixth strings. But even in the more commonplace chords you'll often find unusual finger positioning, and therefore chord versions, which tend to give a different (more jazzy) type of sound. This is to do with something known as 'voicing', which is basically the choice of notes a musician decides to include in a chord. To illustrate this situation, consider the two examples below (left-handed players see **page 229**):

G7 (3rd fret)

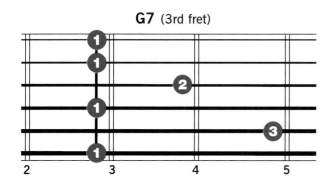

G7 (3rd fret)

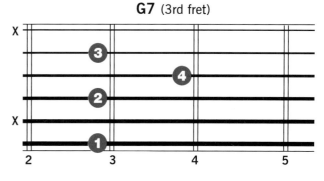

Although both of these **G7** chords are fundamentally the same version, the second example chooses to leave out certain notes. This trims the chord down to its basics of 1st, 3rd, 5th and ♭7th (**G, B, D, F**), instead

of including the additional octaves of the 1st and 5th which appear in the more familiar bar chord version. A similar picture can be observed in the **Am7** chords illustrated below (left-handed players see **page 229**):

Am7 (5th fret)

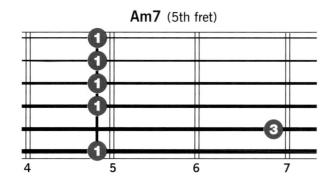

Am7 (5th fret)

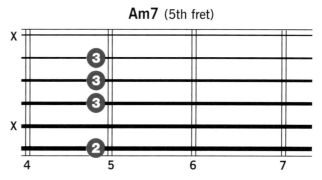

Again, any unnecessary (doubled) chord tones have been omitted, and again certain strings will have to be muted to avoid undesirable and unmusical sounds being created. Obviously these altered versions require a change of fingering, but your digits should be getting pretty versatile by now anyway, assuming you've played all the chords presented so far in this book. And just for the fun of it, here are two more nice jazzy chords (left-handed players see **page 229**).

The **maj9** chord (**C** version here) consists of 1st, 3rd, 7th and 9th, leaving out the 5th scale tone, whilst the **Dm9** (minor ninth) chord comprises the 1st, ♭3rd, ♭7th and 9th, but again no 5th. Although it's certainly possible to include the 5th note within these chords, its omission is pretty much standard practice where convenience is concerned.

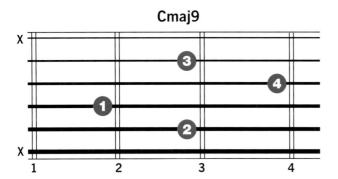

Cmaj9

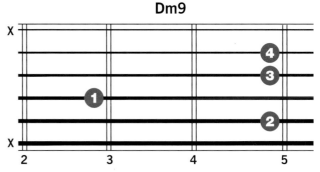

Dm9

Chord synonyms

When you start to play around with chords, by leaving out certain notes that traditionally define the status of that chord, a curious situation can sometimes occur. This is referred to as the 'chord synonym', which means that a chord (or partial chord) can be known by more than one name. To explain this, the easiest example to begin with is the note composition of a **C6** chord, when compared directly against an **Am7** chord.

If you look at the note structure of any **C6** chord you'll see that it consists of C, E, G and A. No problem so far, until you analyse the note structure of the **Am7** chord, which also (though you might think of them in a different order) contains C, E, G and A. So, here we have two chords which are notationally identical, but which are generally thought of as being two separate chords. Indeed, these chords are virtually interchangeable in factual terms,

and jazz players often substitute one for the other. But what tends to re-establish the individual chord identity to some extent is which note the bass player is inclined to emphasise, or perhaps the actual arrangement of notes within the chord itself.

Thinking of a **C6** bar chord as played at the 3rd fret, there are two C notes in that particular chord shape, which will strengthen the 'C' aspect of the chord, whereas an **Am7** bar chord played at the 5th fret contains two A notes but only one C note, thereby causing its sound emphasis to lean more toward that aspect of its tonality.

The **C6** and **Am7** chords are probably the most obvious example of chords 'overlapping' in such a direct and comprehensive manner, but when you leave out notes from chords, as described earlier, the situation becomes ever more prevalent. (Left-handed players see **page 230**.)

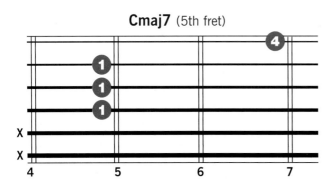

Cmaj7 (5th fret)

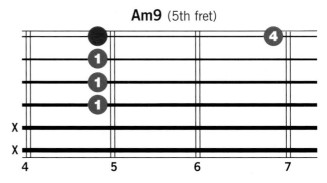

Am9 (5th fret)

When played in this form, the **Cmaj7** and the **Am9** are exactly the same structure, and would suffice in either context. Notice here that the **Am9** has the 'theoretical' root note shown in red (illustrated for your information only). This indicates a note that isn't played in this chord version, but defines the name note of the chord. So the **Cmaj7** chord is intact, in that it has all the chord notes, whilst the other is a shape commonly used minus its root note as shown here. In fact, leaving out the root note of a chord is, oddly enough, an extremely common jazz chord practice. Although it might seem a crucial note for any chord to have, the fact that it's a root note means that it's very likely to be covered by one of the other band instruments anyway.

A further 'rootless' chord that overlaps another of similar structure is the ninth, which is seen below as compared to the minor 6th. Again, the 'theoretical' root note (of the **C9**) is shown in red. (For left-handed version see **page 230**.)

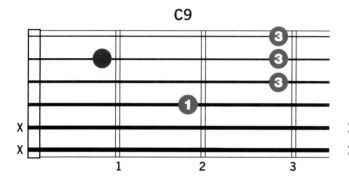

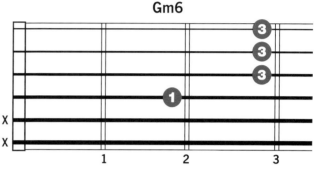

This similarity of various chords is the inevitable result of having only 12 notes to work with, and what we've looked at so far is certainly not the end of the story. The more you play with various chords and part chords, up and down the neck, the more often you'll see close relationships between certain chords. Take a look at the four-string chord seen here (see **page 230** for left-handed version):

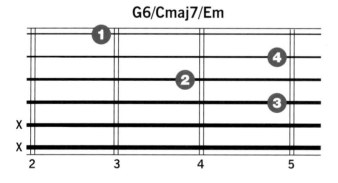

Again, we see a chord with more than one possible identity. It could be either a **G6** without a 5th, because it has a 1st (**G**), 3rd (**B**) and 6th (**E**). Or it might be a **Cmaj7** with no root note, but does have the 3rd (**E**), 5th (**G**) and major 7th (**B**). Or it could be played as an entire **Em** chord, having all of the constituent notes, 1st (**E**), ♭3rd (**G**) and 5th (**B**). So once again we have what might be considered a 'multipurpose' chord.

Now, I realise that it may appear to you that these comparisons between chords aren't entirely legitimate, simply because certain notes are absent from their makeup – that's certainly arguable from a precise point of view – but the crucial thing to understand is that the 'absentee' notes don't generally cause any problem, as far as the use of the chord is concerned. Specifically, a note that's not present in a chord can't cause any conflict with a fully notated version of that same chord. So if perhaps a keyboard is playing a 'full' **Cmaj7** chord, consisting of **C**, **E**, **G** and **B**, the fact that you may be playing only three of those notes (in the form of what's actually a complete **Em** chord, as seen here) won't clash (create dissonance) in any way with the full version.

Polychords

What might be considered a related situation to that of the chord synonym is the 'polychord'. But whereas the chord synonym is basically one chord shape with two or more possible identities, the polychord is precisely the opposite case – that of having two chords with one name. This curious situation, which isn't as complicated as it sounds, arises from the complex structure of certain chords, added to the limitations of notes available.

If you analyse the structure of a **Gmaj9** chord, for example, you'll see that it contains the notes **G** (1st), **B** (3rd), **D** (5th), **F♯** (7th) and **A** (9th). But if you consider this in greater detail, you'll realise that this range of notes could actually cover two complete (and usually separate) chords. The basic **G** major chord (**G–B–D**), and also the **D** major chord (**D–F♯–A**). Therefore the **Gmaj9** chord is technically considered to be a polychord.

When you take the time to consider this result of 'chord overlap', it becomes obvious that the more notes a chord contains, the more likely it is to contain the constituent notes of at least two basic chords. So another good example would be the **G11** chord which, when played as a 'full' chord (not partial as in some of the chord synonyms) is made up of the notes **G** (1st), **B** (3rd), **D** (5th), **F** (♭7th), **A** (9th) and **C** (11th). Break this down into smaller units and you have the combination of a **G** major chord (**G–B–D**), and an **F** major chord with its constituent notes of **F** (1st), **A** (3rd) and **C** (5th).

As with many musical situations, there are variations upon the polychord principle. A true polychord is, as described above, one that fully contains the notes of two separate chords. But there are also what might be considered to be 'semi-polychords' (my description only), which are the basic and essential notes of one particular chord, whilst containing some crucial aspect of its structure from another chord. This would usually take the form of a bass note that wouldn't normally be considered as being fundamental to that chord. And whilst this can obviously be indicated in standard notation if the chord notes are written in full, it will more often be indicated quite simply, as part of the chord symbol written above the stave. So a **C** major chord, which is intended to have a **D** note bass (for instance), would be written in chord terms as **C/D**. A version of such a chord is shown here (left-handed players

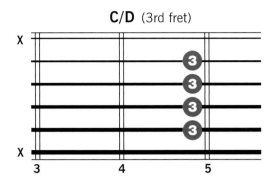

C/D (3rd fret)

see **page 230**), as what is essentially a 3rd fret **C** major bar chord, with the simple addition of a **D** as its lowest note. But, as with other situations, it may not always be necessary to include this additional note within your own chord if another instrumentalist – such as a bass guitarist – should be playing it instead.

This range of choice where chord inversions and voicings are concerned may seem a lot to learn at first, but this is exactly the reason why a knowledge of chord construction is so important, because when you understand this in a reasonably comprehensive way you'll realise that chords of every kind are to be found all over the fretboard, and indeed it's entirely permissible to make up your own chords, simply by being aware of the known 'formula' of any given chord.

Playing jazz guitar

The general approach toward playing jazz guitar is substantially different from that of rock, country or blues. You're already aware of the greater complexity of chord structures and voicings employed; but the type of equipment, and therefore the sound characteristics created, tends to be somewhat different too. Whilst rock guitarists usually go for a solid-body guitar (Stratocaster, Telecaster, Gibson Les Paul etc), with light-gauge strings, jazz players are likely to take the opposite approach. Here the inclination is toward semi-acoustic, hollow-body guitars such as the Gibson ES-175 or similar, fitted with fairly heavy-gauge strings. And instead of the bright cutting sound of the

bridge pickup being predominant, jazz players are more likely to switch over to the neck pickup instead. The end result of all this is a mellow rounded tone, with a very clean (not distorted) sound.

When soloing, jazz guitar employs a greater variety of scales than would be usual in country or rock, with string bending being a rarity instead of the norm, as in other styles. Indeed, the tendency toward heavy-gauge strings, as opposed to the rock guitarist's preference for light-gauge strings, does rather relegate any serious string bending (assuming standard tuning and therefore string tension) into the 'best avoided' category.

Getting into the modes

In any serious study of music you will, sooner or later, encounter the subject of 'modes', and seeing as how we're on the subject of jazz playing it's likely to be sooner rather than later. So let's take a tentative look at this subject. The best place to begin is probably by explaining exactly what a mode is.

Modes are scales that are based upon each note of another scale. But since you're likely to require a bit more information than that, take a look at the familiar sight of the **C** major scale here.

C–D–E–F–G–A–B–C   (Ionian mode)

When you view the scale notes in this, the usual, order they're collectively referred to as being in the Ionian mode. But if you were to write these same notes, beginning from a starting note other than **C**, they'd then collectively have a different mode name. And each time you do this – bearing in mind that there are seven possible starting points (because there are seven notes in the scale) – it will also create a new fingering pattern on your fretboard. In ascending note order, the other six modes based upon the **C** major scale are as follows:

D–E–F–G–A–B–C–D	(Dorian mode)
E–F–G–A–B–C–D–E	(Phrygian mode)
F–G–A–B–C–D–E–F	(Lydian mode)
G–A–B–C–D–E–F–G	(Mixolydian mode)

A–B–C–D–E–F–G–A	(Aeolian mode)
B–C–D–E–F–G–A–B	(Locrian mode)

So, this tells you what modes are, and the nice fancy names they have, but not exactly what they mean to you in guitar music terms. A good way to begin your understanding of modes and their uses is simply to visualise them as patterns on the fretboard, paying careful attention to the fret numbers to ensure accuracy.

Ionian

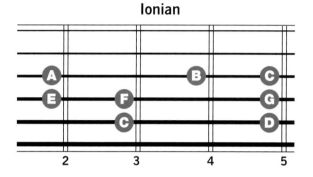

Dorian

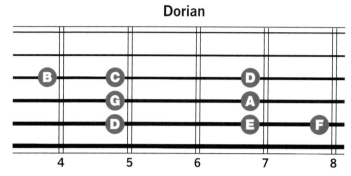

These two diagrams (Left-handed players see **page 230**) illustrate the fret positions of the Ionian mode and the Dorian mode, both of which are built from notes of the **C** major scale. When you look at them in this way, the first thing you'll notice is that they form two different fingering patterns, simply because each mode starts from a different note. This causes the 'interval' (difference in pitch) between adjacent notes to differ in places from one mode to the other. Comparing these interval patterns directly, working from the starting note of each mode (low **C** and low **D** respectively), we see the following whole tone/semitone pattern emerge:

Ionian mode
Whole tone – whole tone – semitone – whole tone – whole tone – whole tone – semitone.

Dorian mode
Whole tone – semitone – whole tone – whole tone – whole tone – semitone – whole tone.

In other words, the distance between the first note of the Ionian mode (**C**) and the next note (**D**) is two frets, or one 'whole tone'; and the same is true of the distance between the first two notes of the Dorian mode (**D** and **E**), which again is two frets. But when it comes to the distance between the second and third notes of each mode the pattern changes. Now we see an interval of two frets between **D** and **E** (Ionian) compared to an interval of one fret between **E** and **F** (Dorian), and these contrasting interval differences continue intermittently over the entire distance of the two modes.

Now, because these modes are both from the **C** major

scale all of this might appear to be entirely academic, as if you haven't discovered a new scale but simply a different perspective on the original one. And indeed, this is certainly the case when the Ionian mode starts from **C** and the Dorian mode starts from **D**. So what you need to do, in order to make it interesting, is to shift these modes around a bit, and ask yourself what would happen if you played the pattern of the Dorian mode but started from the **C** note position. (Left-handed players see **page 230**.)

Dorian

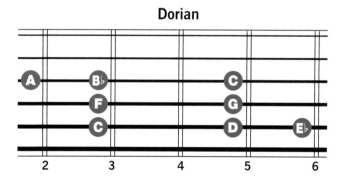

This is still the same fretboard pattern as on the previous page, but now it begins from the **C** note instead of the **D**, which should help you to regard it in a different way. And due to the fact that it contains a ♭3rd (**E♭**) it's clearly a minor scale, and therefore would be most suitable for improvising over **C** minor type chords. But notice that this isn't the same as the usual minor scale, because it doesn't have a ♭6th note within its structure. Compare this mode to the more familiar C minor scale on **page 104** and the difference is apparent. So this can be regarded as an alternative option which might be preferable in certain situations, such as playing over a **Cm6** chord, in which the 6th itself is also not flatted.

Any mode can be transferred to any key whilst retaining its individual sound characteristics, providing the note/fretboard pattern isn't altered in any way. Consider the Phrygian mode which, working from the **C** *scale* notes, forms the pattern below left, and then starting from the **C** *note* position appears as below right. (Left-handed players see **page 230**.)

Phrygian (from E note)

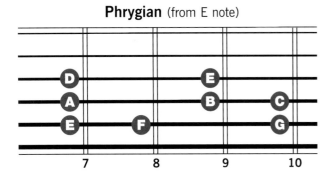

Phrygian (from C note)

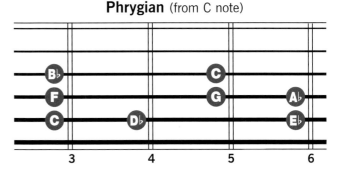

Again, as with the Dorian mode, you have another minor scale mode, this time consisting of the notes C–D♭–E♭–F–G–A♭–B♭–C, and this is again very useful with certain minor chords such as **Cm7**. But, due to its **D♭** note, it wouldn't be ideally suited to a minor ninth chord (which has a **D** natural within its structure). So let's take a couple of basic note runs, which will illustrate the use and contrasting tonal effect of these modes:

Dorian mode

Phrygian mode

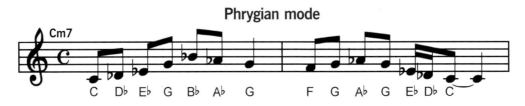

In this demonstration you see two different modal approaches to what's essentially a **Cm** chord improvisation. For easy reading I've placed one directly above the other and actually written the note names below the stave. Try playing both, with chord backing if possible, and listen to the effect created by these contrasting modes. Partly this places demands upon your knowledge of theory, but also it's simply common chord sense. The Dorian mode played over a **Cm6** is logical because it contains all the chord notes (C–E♭–G–A) plus a few passing tones. Similarly, the Phrygian mode variation uses the relevant **Cm7** chord notes of C–E♭–G–B♭ along with some passing notes. The interesting note in here is obviously the **D♭**, which adds a touch of the unexpected to the more usual run of notes. So, amid the high-sounding theoretical detail it all makes sense from our original improvising standpoint of taking the chord notes and working around them with a few little extras.

This sort of logic applies in the use of any mode. If you ask yourself 'Will this mode work with a certain chord?', the thing to do is check out which notes are in the mode compared to which notes are in the chord, and see if there's any serious conflict of note versus chord structure. Take the Lydian mode, for instance, which (starting as usual from the **C** note) is C–D–E–F#–G–A–B. This would work with many of the **C** major type chords, especially **Cmaj7** or its extension (**maj9**), but would you want to use it with a **Csus4** chord, which has an **F** natural within its structure, and therefore contrasts with the sharpened **F** in the Lydian mode? It's a matter of musical common sense rather than any difficult question of theory, and your knowledge of chord construction should simplify any such uncertainties of modal application But remember, there need be no mystery in understanding the construction of any mode. So if you should be wondering how I arrived at the notes of the Lydian mode, let's have a refresher course before going any further.

Here's how to work out the sequence of a mode:

1 Refer to the modes chart in key of **C** on **page 129**.
2 Play the note sequence of the required mode (for Lydian it would be F–G–A–B–C–D–E–F) and remember the fingering pattern in that position.
3 Decide which chord you wish to play the mode with, and transfer the pattern to that root note position.
4 Starting from the appropriate key (name) note, play the established fretboard pattern, ensuring that you don't alter the sequence of note intervals.

And if that still leaves any room for confusion, here are all the major scale modes in their key of **C** positions:

C–D–E–F–G–A–B–C   (Ionian mode)
C–D–E♭–F–G–A–B♭–C   (Dorian mode)

More about modes

It would be nice to report that this is the end of the mode story, but unfortunately such is not the case, for whilst there are other scales to be considered there are inevitably modes to be derived from them. However, taking into account your present level of knowledge in these matters, we're really talking about relatively small variations on a familiar theme.

Another well-used scale is the so-called Harmonic minor, which differs from the natural minor scale by only one note. Specifically, its 7th note is played one semitone higher, making it appear as seen below, and shown here in comparison to the natural minor scale:

C–D–E♭–F–G–A♭–B♭–C   (Natural minor)
C–D–E♭–F–G–A♭–B–C   (Harmonic minor)

Another variation upon the minor scale theme, and very popular with jazz musicians, is the Melodic minor, which not only has the raised (not flatted) 7th note, but also a raised 6th as well:

C–D–E♭–F–G–A–B–C   (Melodic minor)

As with the major scale modes, these minor scales generate modes by exactly the same process of logic as explained on the previous page.

Two other scales worth noting are the Diminished scale and the Whole Tone scale, the latter being so named because it contains no semitone intervals, which for guitarists means that it moves up (or down) by intervals of two frets each time.

C–D–E♭–F–G♭–G#–A–B–C (Diminished scale)
C–D–E–F#–G#–Bb–C   (Whole Tone scale)

C–D♭–E♭–F–G–A♭–B♭–C   (Phrygian mode)
C–D–E–F#–G–A–B–C   (Lydian mode)
C–D–E–F–G–A–B♭–C   (Mixolydian mode)
C–D–E♭–F–G–A♭–B♭–C   (Aeolian mode)
C–D♭–E♭–F–G♭–A♭–B♭–C (Locrian mode)

It's not much different in a way from moving chords around the neck. All you're doing is taking a collection of notes and transferring them to a new location, as determined by a specific name note. The key to it all is simply to think in terms of fretboard patterns instead of notes, which makes the whole thing easier for guitarists than it would be for players of numerous other (non-fretted) instruments.

Although there are seven modes to be derived from the major scale, only five are in any way new to your repertoire, because two of the modes are really old friends in disguise. The Ionian mode is simply another name for the standard major scale, whilst the Aeolian mode is obviously just the natural minor scale.

A complete 'Chromatic' scale is something you should also be aware of, which contains all notes including sharps and flats. This is more a point of reference and doesn't relate to any specific key, and is therefore of no use in creating modes as they would all be melodically identical.

Taking all of these scales into consideration, with each being the basis for several modes, we're obviously looking at a considerable number of modal options. Rather than attempting to commit to memory every single one, it's more practical to be generally aware of the scales from which the various modes originate, and utilise them as an ongoing source of reference as and when required.

When improvising any guitar phrase or solo, it's usually easiest to use the chords and your awareness of their construction as the first point of inspiration. And although it might appear more difficult to work around these advanced jazz-type chords than it is with simple major/minor triads, this isn't necessarily so. If you consider a chord such as a G11, for example, this chord contains almost all of the notes in a basic **C** major scale. So, if you were soloing around this chord in (as is likely) a key of **C** composition, it would be hard to play a wrong note because it has six out of the seven possible scale tones within its structure. Even more accessible in this regard would be the G13 chord, which has every one of them. So from this point of view the very complexity of certain chords can be turned into an improvising advantage.

I emphasise that you should avoid falling into the classic guitarist trap of using a solo merely as a chance to show off your technique. Being flash might impress yourself, or perhaps another guitarist who may be listening, but it won't mean anything to most people in your audience. Concentrate on melodic quality of note choice, and accuracy of execution, along with an awareness of its suitability within the song for which it's intended.

Other styles of playing

So far we've concentrated upon what is undoubtedly the most widely used approach for general guitar playing in popular music. This is the use of a pick or plectrum for sounding the strings, in standard tuning, which are fretted in the usual way by the left-hand fingers, or the reverse if you happen to be a left-handed player. This has proven to be an extremely versatile technique for both rhythm and lead guitar styles of playing. But it's not the only method available, and there are some alternatives that offer certain advantages to suit other situations. It's now time to explore some of the other possibilities, which will extend your range of options and enhance the potential of your music.

Acoustic fingerpicking

Along with all its undoubted virtues, there is also a disadvantage in relying entirely upon the plectrum for all your playing requirements. This is the impracticality of simultaneously, or even alternately, sounding non-adjacent strings with ease and efficiency. So if you wanted, for example, to play a note on the fourth string whilst pairing it with another note on, let's say, the second string, another approach would ideally be required. It's true that you could strum a plectrum across strings two, three and four whilst taking care to mute string three to prevent it sounding, but this isn't really the ideal solution, because the muted string would still give a percussive click, which is generally not desirable. Additionally, the clear sounding of strings two and four does, to some degree, tend to be compromised by this technique.

In this type of situation many players employ the so-called 'hybrid picking' approach, which consists of using a plectrum in the usual manner whilst utilising fingers two, three and (occasionally) four to play any additional strings as required. This technique has considerable versatility, although some find that in certain styles involving rapid arpeggiating – such as folk music or country – this can feel somewhat restrictive in constant use. Which brings us back to the merits of fingerpicking, a method of playing which effectively provides you with several independent plectrums built into one hand.

The picture below illustrates a comfortable and efficient position for your picking hand:

The first thing you'll notice, when attempting fingerstyle playing, is a difference in tone. A plectrum, being a relatively thin piece of (usually) plastic, produces a very clear and dynamic sound, whereas your fingers will create a noticeably more mellow tone. Depending upon your taste and preferred style of music this can be considered favourable or otherwise. Should you wish to retain the clarity of a plectrum there are several options available to you. The first is to adjust the tone controls on your guitar and/or amplifier in order to acquire more treble, though this suggestion is obviously less than helpful if you're playing an unamplified acoustic guitar. Another possibility is simply to pick the strings nearer to the bridge, rather than closer to the neck. But if neither of these suggestions is suitable there are a couple of other possibilities for you to consider. Some fingerpickers grow their nails a bit longer, and allow them to make contact with the strings, more or less simultaneously with being plucked by the fingertips. This gives an added 'bite' to the sound produced whilst retaining the helpful touch-sensitivity of the fingers.

Failing all other options you could always try using fingerpicks, which will definitely re-establish the familiar tone created by the good old plectrum. These implements, as pictured here, are certainly effective from the sound point of view, but are generally found to be a bit trickier to manage than actual finger contact with the strings. My own advice is to start off by picking with just your fingers, and then, once you get the hang of it, feel free to experiment with any alternatives which may appeal to you.

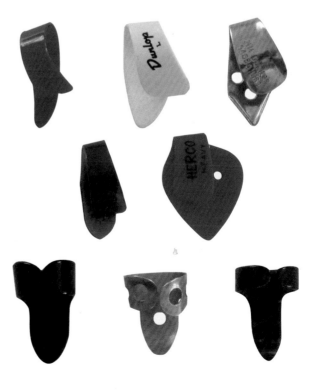

This playing position, with the palm resting lightly on the bridge, provides stability for the accuracy of movement between thumb and fingers one, two and three. The fourth finger is rarely employed in this style, due to its limitations in both size and strength. As a general rule your thumb is used for sounding the lower three strings, whilst your fingers are responsible for playing the upper strings.

Instructions regarding which finger to use on each particular string are traditionally expressed in the so-called **P-I-M-A** style of directions. All this means is that the thumb and first three fingers of your picking hand are referred to by the initial letters of their Spanish names, which gives us **P** for pulgar (thumb), **I** for indice (index finger), **M** for medio (middle finger) and **A** for anular (third finger). I mention this here for your information, as you may encounter these types of directions elsewhere, but for easier reading within this book we can continue to think of them as Thumb, 1st, 2nd and 3rd fingers, with directions expressed accordingly. And as with so many things, after a certain amount of experience you'll not require any directions at all, because your own common sense will automatically use the most convenient finger for each situation.

First of all, let's try a basic alternating string-picking exercise, in order to develop coordination skills and independent finger/thumb action. This is simply a case of playing an arpeggio with an open D chord, and picking each string with a different finger, letting all notes ring on with full sustain. Fingerpicking directions are displayed in blue, for clear contrast with the tab written below.

This is a familiar type of arpeggio piece, the like of which has been heard in many songs, particularly in the style of country and folk music. Think of it as two four-note phrases; the first starts with your thumb playing the root note of the chord (D), followed by the

Example 1

When playing an arpeggio in this style, the benefits of fingerpicking become immediately apparent. Playing this with a plectrum would entail a great deal of complicated jumping around between low and high strings, which would turn a very easy phrase into an unnecessarily complex piece of work.

other three notes; the second phrase starts on the lower 5th of the chord (A), followed again by the same three notes as before. It's not only easy to play, after a little diligent practise, but also incredibly versatile for many musical situations. And this style can be applied to most chords or chord sequences, as illustrated by the familiar C–Am–F–G7 pattern below.

Example 2

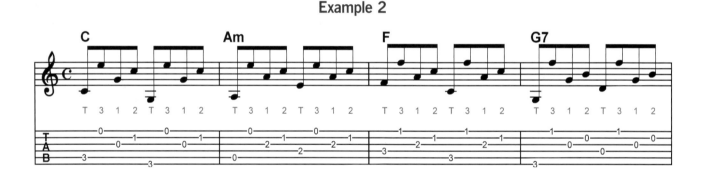

Many fingerpicking patterns can be built from just this one basic arpeggio, by simply adapting it to your own requirements and that of the song you happen to be playing at the time. Although, with practice, you can play this type of eighth-note sequence at a faster tempo than might seem feasible at this

stage, it's also possible to give a bit more 'space' to the rhythm by inserting some quarter-note phrases along the way. Try the following variation on this theme – this time in the key of A major – which includes some three-note chords to break up the arpeggio repetition somewhat.

Example 3

Example 4

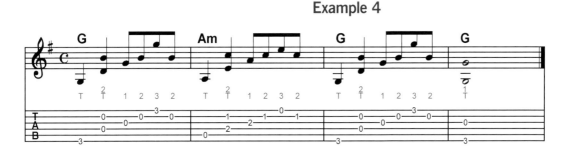

Example 5

Example 6

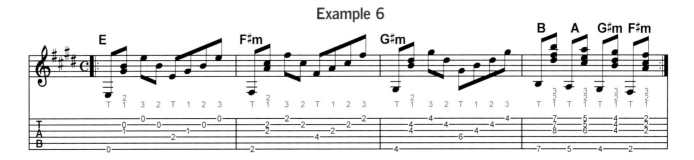

Clearly this is a formula that can be varied in many ways, and used with any chord sequence. As a rule the first note played does tend to be the root note of the chord, although there can be exceptions as determined by circumstance. Above are a few more examples for you to consider, including one in 3/4 time.

The fingerpicking exercises we've attempted up to this point have all been based upon arpeggios, and played in a repetitive rhythmic pattern. This makes it relatively uncomplicated, in the sense that all you have to do is hold down a chord and then train your picking hand into the appropriate rhythmic sequence in order to master the piece. There are, however, other ways of utilising this playing technique to enhance your ever-increasing musical versatility.

The example overleaf differs somewhat from anything we've attempted so far, whilst still applying the basic principles of fingerpicking, in order to play something that wouldn't be possible with the standard plectrum style of playing. This type of picking is typical of the rockabilly/country style that can be heard in the playing of Scotty Moore on some of the early Elvis recordings, and indeed on many other country-style guitar solos right up to the present day. Consider this piece carefully before

playing, in order to check out what's actually happening here.

This solo features a slightly tricky (at first anyway) combination of bass notes and high notes interacting with each other to create a light and lively rhythmic feel to the music, and also tends to create the impression of rhythm and lead guitar all coming from one player. But unlike the previous fingerpicking exercises this has a less predictable pattern.

The actual number of notes per bar may appear to be relatively sparse, but something of this nature would be played at a pretty lively speed anyway, thereby not allowing much time for you to get bored between notes. Obviously you should, as always, begin learning at your own convenient speed, and make no attempt to rush things until you're completely conversant with what you're doing. But eventually I would recommend a tempo of around 190–200bpm.

Before you get started there are a couple of points to be aware of. First of all, you'll notice from the tab line that some notes are doubled with their unison (same note pitch) counterparts on an open string. This isn't apparent from the actual notation, but it occurs in bars one and three. Also, you'll notice the octave sign (see **page 65**) above bars seven and eight. This applies only to the upper string notes, but

Example 7

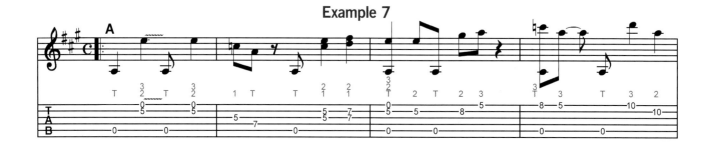

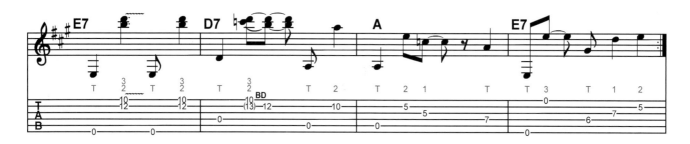

not the bass strings, as again will be apparent from the tab. Additionally, this approach will benefit from lightly damping (see page 43) the bass strings, which will tend to emphasise the upper notes as being the main melody line.

If you prefer, it's entirely possible to play a piece such as this by employing the previously described 'hybrid picking' approach (see page 133) of pick and fingers, which is how country rock players such as James Burton or Albert Lee would probably play it. Another variation on this style would be to fit a thumb pick, the like of which can be seen in the photograph on page 133 (upper row), which lends a rather more cutting tone to the bass notes, and can therefore be regarded as a compromise between pure fingerpicking and hybrid picking. It's always a question of personal preference, based upon whatever you find easier to do.

Solo guitar playing

Most styles of popular music depend upon a number of musicians playing as an ensemble (group), in order to enhance a melody to maximum effect. This is obviously beneficial simply because one instrument by itself is likely to produce a rather inadequate sound. But certain instruments, of which the guitar fortunately is one, can, when played with appropriate skill and technique, create an attractively 'full' sound without the need of any additional instrumentation, vocals or, indeed, electronic assistance.

The method by which you can play guitar as a solo performer and produce satisfactory results is, as partially demonstrated in the exercise above, by combining the main melody line with additional chord tones to build up the sound and support a melody which would otherwise sound incomplete. But when you're playing entirely alone, and not even singing over a chord-strumming rhythm or enhanced arpeggio background, it'll be necessary to elaborate further upon this basic example in order to produce the most attractive, professional-sounding results.

The principle underlying this technique can be understood quite easily if we look at a few bars of a basic melody with the chord symbols accompanying them, as we've seen throughout this book so far and, indeed, as you'll find in any standard written music arrangement.

Example 8

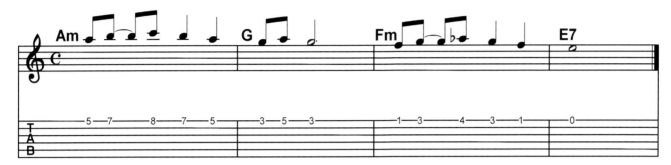

Well, it's a pretty little four-bar melody, but how do we make it sound a bit more impressive when played by only the one guitar? The easiest way is to use some sustaining chords to underscore the upper line of melodic notes.

Example 9

Be sure to sustain these added underlying notes for the full duration of each respective bar, in order to achieve the full effect – which is, I think you'll agree, a surprisingly substantial improvement for relatively little additional effort.

This is the simplest variation on the basic melody; but what if we try it yet again, this time adding a few bass notes for additional improvement?

Example 10

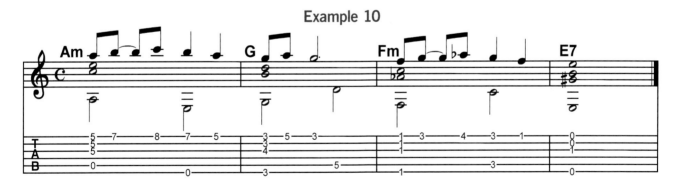

It gets better every time, doesn't it? And this type of arrangement can be applied to pretty much any piece of music you might wish to play as a solo guitar performance. As ever, it's simply a case of knowing your chord construction along with a range of inversions (see **page 111**), and applying this knowledge accordingly.

When first attempting to play in this manner there's no escaping the fact that it does take a bit of getting used to in order to play, with accuracy of timing, the upper melody in conjunction with the lower bass line. But when you get into the rhythm of things you'll find that the results are definitely worthwhile. The important thing is that in the learning stages you should take your time over each bar of music to ensure that accuracy is attained. As ever, the speed and fluency will come later, when familiarity takes over and comes to the rescue.

Any melody can be treated in this way. You don't need to acquire a prearranged transcription for every piece that you might wish to play. It's just a case of understanding the basics of how these solo guitar arrangements are constructed, and then you can create one yourself.

First of all you need to have access to as many open string notes as possible. These notes are especially important because they can be allowed to sustain easily in support of the other fretted notes. So, when arranging a guitar piece for yourself always think in terms of 'guitar-friendly' keys (see **pages 54–55**). And because you're working toward a guitar solo piece, the key doesn't have to be considered by, as is usually the case, what would suit the pitch of a vocalist. If you wish to make any pitch adjustments later there's always

the possibility of using a capo (see next section) to good effect; but start out by thinking in open keys.

As a general rule the preferred approach is to arrange things so that the principle melodic part of the music is played in the upper range of notes (the higher strings), with the lower notes providing the 'backing'. This works well due to the natural tendency of higher notes to 'cut through' more than lower notes are inclined to. And remember that any melody can be played on the upper strings, no matter what the original range might have been, simply by raising the pitch of all notes by an octave.

When playing a solo piece your intention is basically to 'fill in the gaps'. This is putting it a bit simply, but that's more or less what you'll be aiming for. You don't want the music to sound empty or lacking in rhythm just because there's no additional accompaniment. Let's take a look at another piece of single-note melody, and construct a suitable arrangement around it.

Example 11

If you think of the six guitar strings in comparison to the keyboard of a piano, one useful way of considering a possible solo arrangement is to think about the way a pianist plays the bass notes with the left hand (because this is the area of a keyboard where the lower notes are located), whilst simultaneously playing the melody and any additional chord notes with the right hand, which covers the upper range of notes. Similarly, on a guitar you might aim for the lower three

strings in playing the bass notes, and the upper three strings for chord notes and melody.

Obviously this is a rather generalised way of looking at the situation, because there will necessarily be a certain amount of overlap between lower and upper strings, as will be defined by individual circumstance, but it does give you a starting point for thinking about creating an arrangement. With this in mind, let's look quite separately at a possible bass line for the above melody.

Example 12

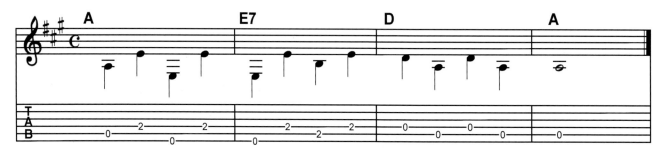

Example 13

When you look at the melody and bass line in this way it's easy to understand what we're dealing with from the timing point of view. Both parts are simple enough, with straightforward timing, so the trick is to maintain the steady rhythmic bass line whilst also playing the melody on top. And the example above shows how it looks, when both parts are played together.

Notice that of these two lines of musical notation, some notes are played as pairs (simultaneously) whilst in other places either the upper or lower of the notes may be sustaining whilst its counterpart is playing another note to maintain either the flow of rhythm of continuation of the melody. This is really the

tricky part of solo fingerpicking – getting it clear in your mind which line does what, and on which beat of the bar it's doing it.

The bass notes in this type of situation are generally permitted full sustain in the manner of fingerpicking arpeggio playing (see previous section), which in some ways it does resemble. And as this style of playing is more often than not performed on acoustic guitar, you'll want to take advantage of the instrument's natural (as opposed to electronically enhanced) sustain characteristics.

In constructing your arrangement for any piece of music, an important question is how elaborate you might wish the structure to become. As far as the example above is concerned, it could be enhanced still further by the addition of a few well-placed extra notes.

Example 14

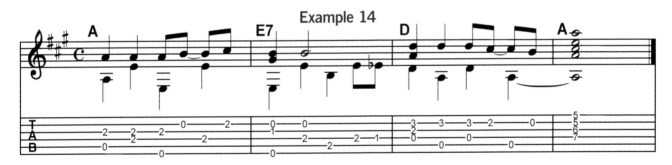

Remember, this is just a variation upon the previous arrangement. You might prefer the simpler one. It's just another example of experimenting – playing around with the chords and various options suggested thereby to see what sounds best to you.

Something which always sounds good when several notes are played together, as in bars two, three and four above, and which you can try when playing this, is to 'rake' these notes instead of just playing them straight. This means that instead of all the notes being played at exactly the same moment they're played in very rapid succession. This sounds complicated, but in fact it's extremely easy to do. It's just a question of understanding the principle involved. To 'rake' strings is really nothing more than that which naturally occurs when you hold down a chord and then run a plectrum across the strings, from low to high notes. The motion required isn't so rapid as with a strumming action, but it's much faster

than an arpeggio would ever be. It's one of those things that's actually harder to explain than it is to play. Here is a notation example of 'raking' an open E chord. It's just a quick succession of grace notes (see **page 74**) leading into the top note of the chord, which will naturally tend to be accentuated somewhat. Notice that all of these notes are permitted to sustain for the full duration of the note into which they're leading. And, of course, when this technique is applied in an actual guitar solo, as seen above, this final note is the one that is the significant melodic note as far as the overall melody is concerned.

This is something that can be practised when playing any chord or series of chord tones in the fingerpicking style. With regard to the open **E** chord as an example, just try out the following. First place your picking hand thumb on the fourth string: Next place your first, second and third fingers on, respectively, strings three, two and one. Then, very quickly and with a rippling motion, play all four strings one after the other, 4–3–2–1. You'll find that even after a relatively small amount of practice this is quite easy to achieve, and indeed, almost becomes a natural motion requiring virtually no effort at all. Nevertheless, be careful, once you get the hang of it, not to overdo the 'raking' approach. Like many things,

the effect is heightened when applied with discretion and tasteful restraint.

Anyway, back to the business of solo arranging, which can be approached from a number of different directions. Apart from the bass/treble style of playing, another approach – and one best suited to slow/medium tempo numbers – is the chordal technique favoured by jazz guitarists. This consists of taking the basic melody and playing it, for the most part if not entirely, as full chords. It needs to be added that these are generally three- or four-string chords, as opposed to six-string versions, which would perhaps sound a bit cluttered and would also require a lot more dexterity. For the purpose of easy viewing comparison the single-note melody is at the top, and directly below is the full four-string chord version, which is also fully tabbed.

Example 15

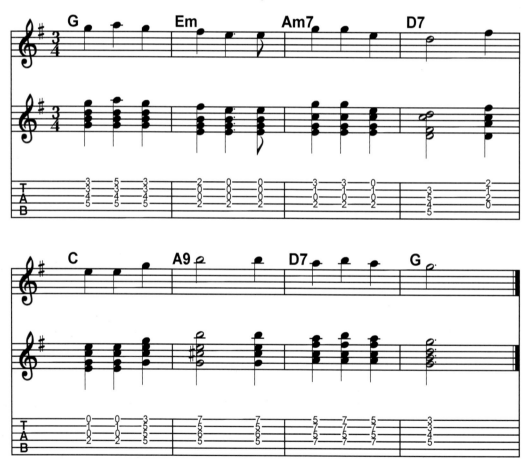

Always keep in mind that these are simply examples of a particular playing style, to illustrate how different techniques are applied and to present you with a range of options available for enhancement of the basic melody. If you think it might sound better played differently, don't hesitate to try out any variations that might occur to you. For example, you might find this

particular arrangement a bit rigid in presenting every single note as a full four-string chord. In a situation such as this I would probably work around the arrangement as presented, whilst perhaps aiming for a touch more fluidity by interposing the chordal structure with some single notes, and occasionally raking the chords to bring out the melodic content to greater effect.

Example 16

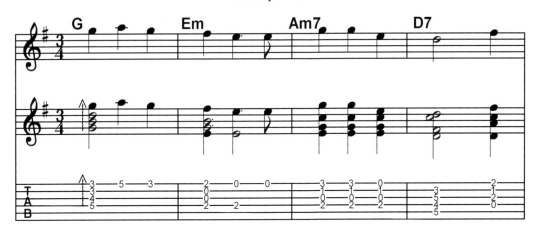

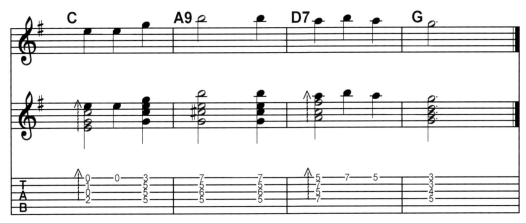

In this alternate version of the previous arrangement, take note of the 'rake' symbol introduced here at the beginning of the very first bar, and subsequently employed later in bars five and seven. This symbol has an arrow indicating in which direction the strings are played. In this case they're raked from lowest note to highest, in the manner previously explained. And although initially this new variation might be slightly more difficult to read, in practice it should actually prove somewhat easier to play.

The fact is that it's generally possible to continue creating variations upon this or any other arrangement. Once you're presented with any melody and the accompanying chords, it's entirely a matter for your own imagination and sense of what sounds attractive. Obviously there's also the feasibility factor to be taken into consideration, which basically defines what's physically possible. For instance, using the full chord technique it would hardly be realistic to play something at a very quick tempo, so this is where the bass/melody approach would be far more appropriate and considerably more practicable. But you're not necessarily confined to any one method of arrangement per piece of music. What's often more applicable is to combine these varying techniques so

that they dovetail into what would be an overall attractive and satisfying sound.

What we've played so far has been a demonstration of the possibilities of solo guitar playing. It will often be the case that an arrangement is considerably more complex than these few examples; nevertheless, the same fundamental guidelines will apply. It's still just a single-note melody, supported by some chords and perhaps a few little extras thrown in for added interest. Looking at some pieces of music as arranged for solo guitar playing can, quite frankly, be a daunting experience for those new to the skill. And with this in mind let's utilise all these lessons you've learned by having a go at the exercise on the following page.

Try to think primarily in terms of chord shapes rather than regarding everything as separate note patterns. Hold down the chord, and work the additional notes around that. Also, any accompanying notes to the upper melody, such as the G# seen at the beginning of bar one and the A note beginning bar three, can, in practice, be permitted to sustain as desired in support of the principle melody line. Finally, ensure a firm 'attack' to the hammer-on and pull-off phrases, in order to maintain adequate volume in playing these notes.

Example 17

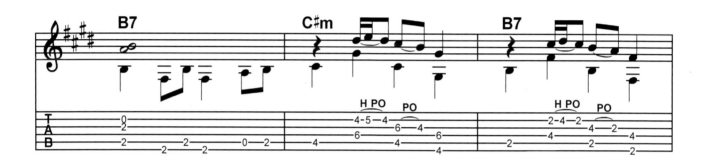

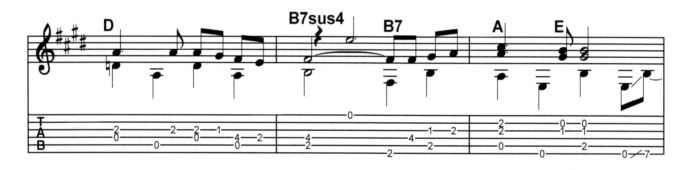

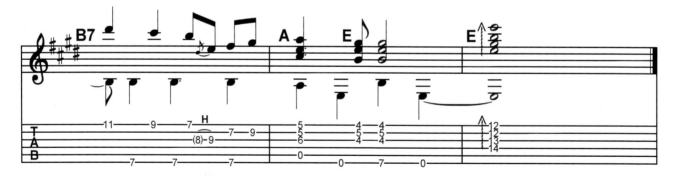

Whilst it's straightforward enough (after a little practice) to play this piece in the written key of **E**, it might not seem possible, if required, to play the same music in, for example, the key of **F**. This is obviously due to the impracticality of impossibly wide finger stretches as would occur when playing melodic phrases higher up the neck, whilst still requiring the benefit of sustaining bass notes on the open strings. But in order to allow for such inconveniences, and to make the impossible possible, is precisely why the modest little capo was invented.

Capo

The capo (an abbreviation of capotasto) is an inexpensive yet invaluable little gadget which every guitarist will find useful from time to time. The purpose of any capo is to raise the pitch of all six strings by forming a bar across the neck of a guitar. In effect this is the same as your index finger does whenever you play any bar chord. The precise design of capos varies somewhat from one model to another, as illustrated by the examples pictured below, but all serve the same purpose.

Although the use of a capo is a relatively uncomplicated business, there are a couple of points which deserve your attention and which mainly concern stability of tuning. Despite its many virtues, the capo hasn't been in development for quite as long as your index finger, and therefore has certain limitations which don't apply when forming a bar manually across the strings.

When you fit a capo to your guitar there will probably be a natural tendency to secure it as firmly as possible, in order to prevent strings rattling. This is logical enough in a way, but because the capo bar is made of a fairly sturdy material without the natural flexibility of your finger this causes it to exert more or less the same force against all six strings. And with some strings being thicker than others, what is enough pressure for, say, the first string is actually more than enough for the sixth. So the lower strings, being pressed rather more firmly than is desirable against the fretboard, can actually be 'bent' somewhat out of tune. Specifically, they'll tend to become slightly raised in pitch, and to what degree this occurs will depend upon how tightly you clamp the capo to your guitar neck.

It is, of course, possible to fit the capo first and then re-tune the strings to allow for the extra tension, and obviously when there's

time to do so and very accurate tuning is essential (such as in a recording situation) this is precisely what happens. But when you're performing on stage surrounded by impatient musicians and an expectant audience it's unlikely that you'll have this luxury. So there needs to be a musically acceptable compromise that requires only a few seconds to fit your capo with appropriate pressure at the required position on the neck.

First of all, because the thickness of guitar necks varies from one instrument to another, and indeed from one location on the neck to another (its lightest point being closest to the nut), I've found it very helpful to use the type of capo which is completely versatile in its adjustability, as opposed to some which have a general type of adjustability or fixed spring pressure; and looking at the various capos pictured below only one fits this description. Capos 1 and 3 are both of the fixed spring pressure type, capo 2 is adjustable but only by predetermined degrees. So that leaves capo number 4, which is completely adjustable by virtue of its screw-thread arrangement.

In addition to having the most efficient capo at hand, there's also the question of fitting it in the most effective manner. First, adjust the capo so that it's exerting enough pressure (but not more than is required) to secure all six strings in a reasonably even manner, and then fit the capo to the neck at the desired fret location. When doing so, the best approach in my experience is to secure it immediately behind the fret in question (as seen in the photograph below rather than midway between frets. In so doing, the fret itself provides support for the capo pressure on the strings, which are therefore less inclined to be bent in any wayward direction.

Pictured above are a variety of capos which employ various methods of attachment to the guitar neck, one of which is illustrated in action at right. Notice that capos 3 and 4 have a very slight curvature on the 'bar', whereas capos 1 and 2 are flat. The choice of which to use depends upon the profile of your guitar neck. A curved neck profile must have a capo with a curvature or else the outer strings (one and six) won't be held firmly against the fretboard. Most guitars will have this slight neck curve, but you should verify this fact before buying a capo for your instrument.

The advantage of using a capo in certain situations, instead of simply playing bar chords, is that it leaves all of your fretting-hand fingers free to form chord shapes as if you were playing in the 'open' position. So you can, in fact, change the key of a song without also having to change the fingering. This, as you'll soon discover, has numerous benefits, and we shall now consider one of the most obvious by taking a look at the simple fingerpicking chord sequence below.

Example 18

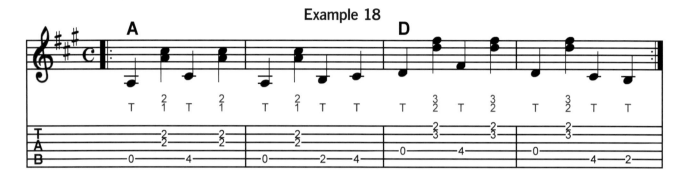

This is obviously a straightforward riff alternating between a couple of open chords, and the tab shows you the easiest way of playing it. No problem so far. But what if, having learned this, some annoying person complains that the pitch is too low for his or her voice, and therefore suggests changing it into the key of B? Then what was a very simple riff suddenly becomes a lot harder to play, and appears as you see it below.

Example 19

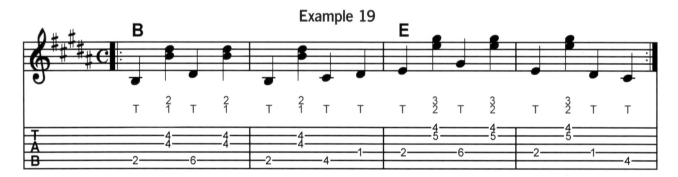

This requires a good deal more manoeuvring when compared to the original key of **A**. It's true that there are other ways of finger positioning, at other locations on the neck, but either way it would be more work than before the key change. But this need not be so. It's simply a case of capo to the rescue, applied at the 2nd fret, which effectively converts this piece back into an open key once again.

Example 20

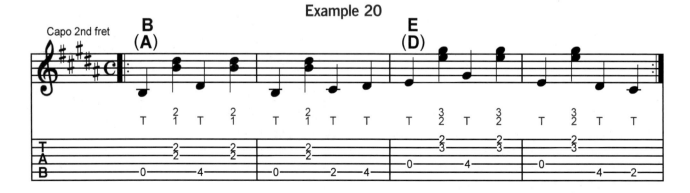

So the overall effect of all this key changing and capo-ing is that it's still transposed into **B**, but from a playing perspective you should regard it the same as if it were still in the original key of **A**. But how does this work from the notation and tab point of view? Keep reading and all shall be revealed.

First of all, take a look at the chord symbols above the stave and you'll see two different versions. The chord sequence above is the actual chords being heard, whilst the lower version of chords indicates how you should play them with the capo in place. In other words, they're the chord versions you would play if it were still in the open key of **A** major, but because the capo is acting in place of the nut (see **page 195**) the pitch is actually two frets higher, and therefore in **B** major. The pictures below illustrate how this looks in direct comparison to the 'original' open chord position.

Another important point about reading the music where a capo is used is the fact that the fret at which the capo is applied is now considered to be the 'open' string position. This has no effect upon traditional music notation, wherein the notes are written exactly the same as usual, but it does make a difference to the tab line. So if you look again at the music you'll see that because the capo is at the 2nd fret position, all tab notes are written as being two frets lower than would normally be the case. This means that a 2nd fret note such as **B** (on the fifth string) is written as an open string note. And by the same logic, a 4th fret note such as **C#** (fifth string) is tabbed as a 2nd fret note. So basically it's a case of regarding the capo as the nut and counting all other fret positions from there.

As a generalisation you'll tend to use the capo to facilitate the use of 'open' strings where standard tuning wouldn't

normally present this convenience. All of your usual open chord shapes can, therefore, be played anywhere on the neck, with each position creating a new key centre for any set of open chords. This situation has given rise to the myth that capos are only used by guitarists of limited ability who are unable to play bar chords, as a substitute for their lack of talent. You can forget this supposed 'fact' for the nonsense that it is, and be assured that capos are frequently (in fact inevitably) employed by all of the very best players, for reasons of extending the range of a traditionally tuned instrument, and not to prop up poor technique. Obviously it's true that for anyone who only wishes to learn a few basic chords the capo can indeed extend their repertoire to an impressive degree, but its principle use is to create new possibilities at any skill level, as certain things would be quite simply unplayable without this handy device.

At this point you might wish to experiment with playing some of the fingerpicking patterns shown previously by moving your capo to various locations up the neck, and finding out how it sounds from this new perspective. You'll notice that, in addition to the convenience factor, the use of a capo also tends to alter things from a tonal point of view. This is due to the shortening of scale (string) length, as the capo is effectively creating a new 'nut point' at each different fret position. Sometimes you'll find this effect pleasing, and sometimes not, depending upon your musical requirements and personal taste. And due to this and other factors (such as the progressively narrowing fret spacing), there does tend to be a limit as to how high a capo can be applied with musically helpful results. These limitations versus benefits are obviously something you'll have to consider for yourself, according to each situation.

 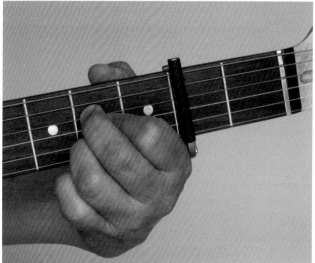

The standard open A major chord shape (above left) wouldn't be possible further up the neck without the use of a capo. However, with the versatile capo applied you can play this chord form as a B major, as in this example, or indeed any other major chord by simply securing the capo at whichever fret position is required for a convenient change of key.

Slide playing

The distinctive and generally attractive sound of slide guitar tone is created by the use of a metal tube (as illustrated right) that defines the pitch of notes. This style is also commonly referred to as 'bottleneck' playing, due to the fact that, as the name indicates, a glass tube can alternately be used in place of metal. However, the actual playing technique involved is the same in either case.

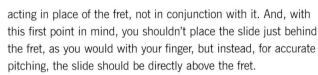

To understand how it works, first consider the way in which frets define pitch by 'stopping' the string at various, precisely designated intervals along the fretboard. Basically speaking the slide or bottleneck does exactly the same thing, except that its point of contact is on the upper surface (away from the neck) of the string instead of its underside. So in effect the slide could be regarded as a sort of moveable fret, with the consequent advantage of being able to sound those indefinable notes that occur between the fixed fret positions. And it's precisely this moveability which gives slide guitar playing its distinctive sound, similar to that of pedal steel or Hawaiian guitar.

In the 'old days', impoverished Mississippi blues players would fashion a slide out of anything available – which basically means anything with a solid edge of sufficient density to produce a halfway decent tone. Apart from the obvious bits of sawn-off metal tubing or actual necks from bottles, penknives were another favourite, along with somewhat more cumbersome (but probably close at hand) objects such as whisky glasses and beer bottles. Fortunately, for the sake of convenience, these creative improvisations of varying eccentricity are no longer really necessary, and a ready-made slide can be purchased at little expense from your local music store.

Having acquired this accessory the question arises as to how it should best be employed, in which instance I refer you to the example pictured right. There are no rules about which finger should ideally be fitted with the slide, except to say that it's usually worn on the third (pictured here) or fourth. This is partly because it tends to feel most comfortable there, but also because it leaves some of the other fingers free for fretting notes in the usual way.

Although playing with a slide looks pretty obvious, there are a few points which make it different from the usual technique. First of all you don't actually press the strings down against the frets, but instead rest the slide lightly against the string, which is acting in place of the fret, not in conjunction with it. And, with this first point in mind, you shouldn't place the slide just behind the fret, as you would with your finger, but instead, for accurate pitching, the slide should be directly above the fret.

When you make your first attempts at producing sound in this way it's likely that you'll find it difficult to play with a sufficiently light touch as to avoid making contact with the fingerboard. Not only is this a very common complaint, it's practically unavoidable, and as a result guitarists who are serious about their slide playing usually make a few adjustments to their guitar, by raising the action (see **pages 175–79**) and fitting heavier-gauge strings. The heavier strings, being under greater tension, are less likely to be pressed down too far, and also tend to provide superior tone. And because slide-playing eliminates the need for string bending the heavier strings don't have that usual drawback of being unbendable.

The obvious consequence of making significant adjustments to your guitar is that such changes are loaded with disadvantages when you return to the more usual style of playing. Slide players, therefore, are likely to possess more than one instrument, one guitar being permanently set up for slide use and the other as normal. But if you only have one guitar available it's necessary to achieve a realistic compromise regarding action etc whilst experimenting with this technique.

Try to obtain a slide that is a comfortable fit for the finger you intend to use. Anything too large will be difficult to handle, while a slide that's too close-fitting may prove to be impractical due to the tendency of fingers to curve somewhat in actual playing position. Remember that your choice of metal or glass for the slide (or bottleneck) will create differing tonal characteristics, as will the density of materials.

Sliding successfully

The use of any slide is something that requires careful handling. There are two principle hazards awaiting the enthusiastic beginner: inaccurate pitching and extraneous noise. Being accustomed to standard guitar playing, it's likely that the frets have been somewhat under-appreciated in their role as accurate and infallible pitch keepers; but when slide-playing it's you, and not the frets, that have to determine accuracy of pitch for every note or chord played. Although you're aware of the need to position your slide directly above the required fret position, it would be extremely difficult to visually determine the accuracy of this for every movement made in real playing terms. So what actually tends to happen is a combination of visual reference and ear definition. If, for example, you play any note slightly sharp or flat, your acquired musical experience so far is very likely to inform you of this fact, simply because it sounds wrong and out of tune. This will be obvious enough when you're just practising by yourself, but even more apparent when played against the background of any additional instrumentation.

The problem of unwanted noise being created by the movement of a slide is resolved by muting, using a combination of fret (slide) hand muting along with careful picking-hand technique. The actual sliding hand plays its part by lightly resting a finger against the strings just behind the slide. Usually this will be your index finger, although other finger options are obviously permissible according to your preference, and also depending upon which finger is doing the sliding. And with regard to right (picking) hand muting, most slide players find that fingerpicking the strings gives greater control over muting options than playing with a plectrum.

Now, let's get down to business with a straightforward single-note slide played on the second string. You'll notice that this is tabbed in much the same way as standard finger sliding (see pages 86–91), but the sound produced will be quite different. In order to minimise the noise factor from strings other than the intended slider, try to keep your picking-hand fingers lightly resting against the 'unused' strings.

When you're practising this first basic exercise it's not a bad idea to use a little bit of amplification, simply because this will emphasise any unwanted noise and thereby enable you to find out if your muting technique is as efficient as it should be. If you prefer to use your plectrum for this style of playing, that's perfectly OK, but you may find it a bit more difficult to achieve the necessary pick-hand muting. In this event just try to keep your hand quite close to the strings, muting with your palm and the available fingers (two, three and four). As with so many things, it's really a case of experimenting to find out what works best for you.

Having mastered this simple slide lick let's try a slight variation on that theme, this time incorporating some downward sliding for added interest. Remember to study the tab as well as the notation, because this tells you which strings and fret positions are most appropriate for ease of playing.

Although only a few notes are used in this example (overleaf) you still need to proceed with some diligence and care. When you slide up from fret 10 to fret 12 on the second string this places you neatly in position to slide down again, albeit on the next highest

Example 21

Although there's no inflexible rule about which finger should pick a given string, you might find it helpful to position your picking hand as pictured here, which will effectively mute all strings not being played. Fingers one, two and three are able to pick or mute the upper strings as necessary, whilst the thumb is in contact with strings four, five and six. This picture demonstrates the third string being played, whilst all others are muted.

string, from 12 back to 10. But when you do this, with the slide still inevitably being in contact with string two, you'll also hear that string descend back to its original pitch. This is where your muting skills will be put to the test, requiring you to silence that note as the other takes over. And obviously the same thing applies in your next manoeuvre, as you slide string two back up again, whilst silencing the first string. It's tricky at first, but just take it very slowly until these moves come naturally. There will be many times, in slide playing, when you'll want two or more notes to slide together, but this should happen only by intention, not by accident.

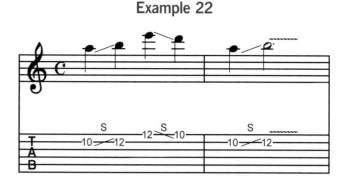

Example 22

Slide vibrato

In the example pictured above you'll see the familiar vibrato symbol above the final note, and as with any other guitar soloing style, this is an important aspect of slide technique. In fact vibrato is probably used more in this style than in standard playing styles. Partly this is for its expressive styling, which is as it should be, but to be honest it also helps minimise any inaccuracy of pitching. Vibrato in slide playing is achieved by moving the slide just slightly above and below its intended note. This is done with a rapid shimmering motion that, by moving somewhat around the note, so to speak, does tend to lessen any otherwise obvious discrepancies in your pitch precision. Although you should always aim for maximum accuracy in sliding to the right note, there's no doubt that a bit of well placed vibrato can provide occasional technical assistance too. So the message here is to be aware of this fact, but don't allow yourself to rely upon it to an unprofessional degree.

A touch of slide vibrato can add an atmospheric haunting quality to the sound of even the simplest licks. Take the following as an example of this, with essentially a bluesy feel built with very few notes and based around a **G** chord. As with normal finger vibrato (see **pages 92–93**), slide vibrato is something generally added according to individual discretion. However, in these examples I've tabbed the key vibrato points for your information.

A very popular use of slide playing is applying it to chords, such as the technique of sliding 'into' a chord from a fret or two lower, although any length of slide is permissible just as long as it sounds good within the context of the music. Also notice the opening chord notes here, which aren't written as a full bar. These are basically a 'lead-in' to the **C** chord, which is considered to be the first actual bar of written music.

Example 23

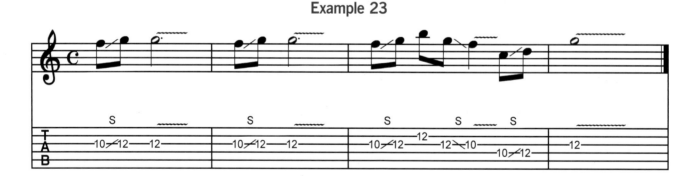

Example 24

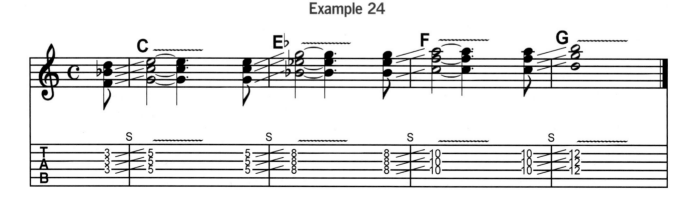

Alternate tunings

The immediately obvious limitation of slide playing is simply the fact that, because it's a straight bar, your ability to play two or more notes at the same time depends upon those notes being at the same fret position, as exemplified by the partial chords in the previous exercise. So this three-string chord is possible for slide playing, but its six-string version isn't. Unless, that is, we explore the potential of alternate tunings.

When guitar strings are tuned in the traditional manner (E–A–D–G–B–E), this provides a range of acceptable finger positions and therefore playing possibilities for a comprehensive repertoire of chords and harmonic options. But when you come to think about it, this clearly isn't the only way the instrument can be tuned. There is a virtually endless variety of string tensions that could be used to create tunings which differ significantly from the standard formula.

Perhaps the most commonly used, and very effective, method of alternate tuning is simply to tune the open strings so as to form a complete chord, without requiring any additional finger fretting at all. And there are indeed a variety of ready-made 'chord tunings' possible, generally (but not necessarily) based around a major chord. For instance, looking again at the standard open string tuning of E–A–D–G–B–E, just consider what would happen if some of those strings, specifically the third, fourth and fifth, were tuned a little bit higher in pitch. Simply by raising the pitch of the third string by one semitone, and the pitches of strings four and five by two semitones, you'd then have the six strings tuned as E–B–E–G#–B–E. Your knowledge of chord construction will tell you that this forms a complete E major chord, and by forming a straight bar (or slide) across the strings at any point on the neck this obviously creates a new major chord at every fret position. This might seem a bit confusing at first, not so much with chord patterns as with single notes or harmony lines, what with some of the notes (those on strings three, four and five) being in different places. Nevertheless, it's surprising how quickly you'll adapt to this, and to put this into visual terms the chord diagrams below illustrate what you're actually looking at. (Left-handed illustration is on **page 230**.)

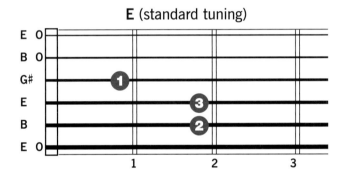

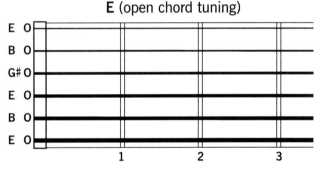

Above left is the familiar E major chord shape, consisting of three open strings and three fretted notes. Compare this with the illustration above right, which is also a full E major chord. This version requires no fretted notes due to the fact that those fretted strings (three, four and five) are already tuned to the notes which would otherwise require fret positions.

Another variation on this theme is open D tuning, attained by lowering the pitch of several strings. So we lower the first string by two semitones, lower the second string by two semitones, lower the third string by one semitone and, leaving strings four and five as they are, lower the sixth string by two semitones. This gives us the six strings tuned as D–A–D–F#–A–D, which is a D major chord. In fact you could tune the strings in ways which would form any chord at all, although in practice tunings are usually designed to minimise the amount of adjustment required by utilising some of the already tuned open strings. Two more popular options are open A tuning (E–A–E–A–C#–E) and open G tuning (D–G–D–G–B–D). It may be worth considering the fact that some tunings will increase the amount of stress on your guitar neck (and the strings) simply because some of the strings will be placed under greater tension (tighter) when tuned to higher pitch. However, this doesn't usually cause problems unless the string gauges are very heavy, in which case you could try lighter-gauge strings to counteract this situation.

Whenever alternate tunings are employed, remember that this has no effect upon the tab directions that relate only to fret positions, so you still play at the fret as directed, but a different note from the usual (tuning) is heard. The written notes, on the other hand, relate to musical pitch regardless of where they may be located on the guitar fretboard. So if you don't also refer to the tab instruction, this would entail some careful consideration regarding where that note has been relocated, because of the variation from standard tuning. This is one area where tab is extremely helpful, as a shortcut from having to do a lot of mental note shifting.

Although these types of alternate tunings are frequently utilised to facilitate slide guitar playing, this isn't the only situation in which tuning variations occur. Although not generally playing slide guitar, Keith Richards uses open chord tuning for many of his best-known riffs, and Status Quo rhythm guitarist Rick Parfitt also makes use of similar tunings to power many famous Quo numbers. In a somewhat different context, the ever versatile Dolly Parton often plays with open chord tunings simply because her fingernails are

rather inconveniently long for conventional fretting, and with all six strings tuned to a full chord it's just a case of moving an index finger bar up and down the neck; odd but effective. But for the moment let's just stay with the slide playing, and try out a basic open E chord tuning of E–B–E–G#–B–E, as illustrated on the previous page.

In this example, played at around 120bpm, you should be familiar with all the notation and tab details. Notice that certain notes in bars two, three and four are played an octave higher than written, as the tab will also indicate. The bars with triplet signs (four and eight) are groups of three quarter notes, played in the time spacing of two quarter notes. If you need refreshing on this subject, refer to **pages 25 and 63**.

Example 25

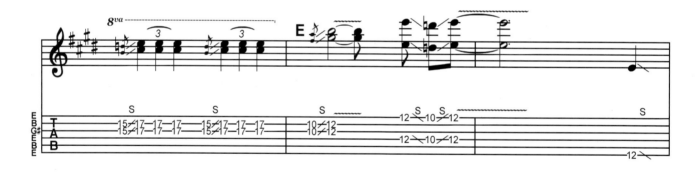

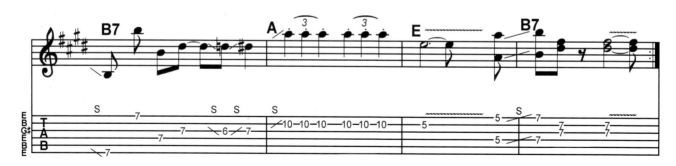

Mixing it up

Sometimes a slide can be used intermittently with standard picking, so that only certain notes in a piece of music are played with the slide whilst others are played fretted, or open, in the more usual way. As I mentioned earlier, this can be a significant factor influencing your choice of which finger wears the slide, and the following exercise, which features open A chord tuning E–A–E–A–C#–E, is easiest when played with the slide on your third or fourth finger.

Example 26

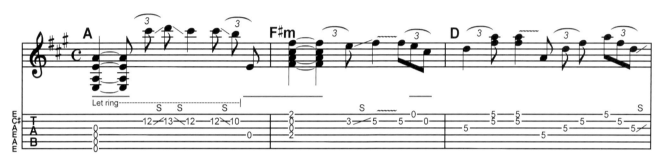

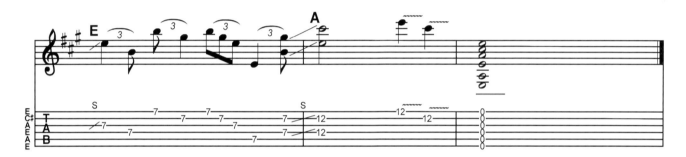

This is a slow triplet, played around 60bpm, with the non-slide parts underlined in red. As is the tradition with alternative tunings, the left-hand side of the tab stave indicates the actual pitch of the open tuned strings. When playing the chords at the beginning of bars one and two, and also the ending chord (assuming that you're playing in fingerpicking style), you'd be inclined to strum these lightly with the nail of your index finger; and because the opening chord should be allowed to ring out whilst the following notes are played it's helpful to position your slide so as to leave these lower strings unhindered. This can be achieved by simply changing the angle at which it meets the strings (this is easier with higher action), as is clearly demonstrated in the picture seen here on the right.

When playing in this manner, alternating slide and non-slide parts, take care not to apply the slide too heavily, so as to avoid creating unattractive noise in hitting the strings. Apart from this potential hazard it isn't likely to present too much difficulty after a moderate amount of practise. Remember also that the choice of tempo is to some degree a matter of discretion, and it's usually helpful to take things at your own comfortable speed, at least until you become familiar with the piece.

When playing in any non-standard tuning the basic major chords tend to be obvious, because they're usually a straight bar at the appropriate fret. But it usually requires a bit of careful thought to work out other possible chord positions, as in the F#m chord from the previous piece. And because of the practicality of workable finger positions it isn't always possible to manage a full six-string version of every chord you may require. However, it should be remembered that alternate tunings are usually employed for a specific purpose, and tend to relate to a particular song or guitar phrase without necessarily being more generally versatile, as in the familiar style of standard E–A–D–G–B–E tuning.

We should perhaps remind ourselves that tuning variations can be employed for reasons other than slide playing, and consider a few more options in this regard. The so-called 'dropped D' tuning is straightforward but often used. As the name suggests, this consists of simply lowering the sixth string by two semitones whilst all others remain at standard tuning pitch (D–A–D–G–B–E), so that the bass string is able to provide a low D note, as can be useful for compositions in the key of D (major or minor). Again, this has its limitations, being more or less restricted to that particular key. On the other hand, because only one of the strings requires tuning alteration it's easy enough re-tuning to standard pitch without much inconvenience.

There is, of course, the Keith Richards favourite of open G tuning D–G–D–G–B–D, which he has utilised with style and imagination to create virtually a whole new rhythm style of rock guitar playing. This type of riff work is typified below.

Example 27

This illustrates the effective simplicity of open chord tuning. The index finger bar creates a full chord, while intermittently applying additional notes on the 2nd and 4th strings. Note the tip of the 1st finger muting the bass string, which is not required in this particular piece.

This is just an example of the style, but it gives you the general idea, and is obviously something that would be impossible to play with standard tuning, no matter how versatile you might be. So clearly, alternate tunings do open up a range of new possibilities whilst unfortunately presenting you with the inconvenience of carrying more than one guitar when playing live.

Another tuning possibility is simply to lower the pitch of all six strings by something like a semitone, so that instead of E–A–D–G–B–E your guitar would be tuned to E♭–A♭–D♭–G♭–B♭–E♭. In this case all of the chord shapes and fretboard patterns would remain the same, but would naturally sound one fret lower in pitch. If you still intend to use all your favourite open chord shapes when playing in their usual key (C, Am, G7 etc) you could easily manage this by applying a capo to the first fret and regarding this as the 'open' position.

The reason for this 'dropped' tuning, which maybe does seem a bit pointless, has to do with string gauges (see page 169) and the relative tensions thereof. Although relatively light-gauge strings tend to be most widely used, there are those who prefer to fit their guitars with heavier strings, simply because they create a stronger sound. But the drawback to this advantage is, of course, the difficulty in string bending, and indeed general playing technique, with the heavy strings being under considerably greater tension than would be the case with light gauge strings. Remember that the heavier (thicker) any string is, the more it has to be tensioned by the machine heads (tuners) in order to reach a desired pitch. Add to that the fact that your poor old guitar neck is under quite enough stress at the best of times, and you have a couple of pretty substantial reasons for heavier

strings being tuned to a lesser tension, and therefore lower pitch. A particular case for lowered overall tuning is that of a 12-string guitar (see page 173), which requires the high octave G string to be tensioned close to the breaking point. And when fitting or tuning strings on 12-string instruments breakage of this particular string sometimes does occur, so a lowered tuning is sometimes applied for this specific reason.

Tuning all six strings to a lower pitch in this way is a favourite heavy rock technique, because of the extra-powerful sound typical of this type of music. In some cases even tuning one semitone down isn't deemed sufficient for the seriously heavy metal boys, and a de-tune of two semitones, or one whole tone, is used instead. When applying this type of tuning method – which is basically just the principle of standard tuning in relative terms, but tuned a fret or two lower – there will obviously be no particular problem regarding fretboard positioning or scale patterns. Instead it's simply a case of transposing the chords and notes to a higher key. So if you have, for example, tuned your guitar to D–G–C–F–A–D, which is one whole tone lower, then everything will accordingly have to be played two frets higher than usual. From a fingering point of view a chord sequence of C–Am–F–G7 would be played as D–Bm–G–A7. It's all simple and logical enough, and presents considerably less mental activity than working with most other types of alternate tuning.

By all means have fun experimenting with various tuning options, but be aware that if you're persistently tuning and re-tuning just the one guitar for this purpose, such frequent changes of tension on the same set of strings will certainly lead to string breakage rather sooner than would normally be the case.

CHAPTER 8
Additional information

Along with the actual musical abilities required of a competent guitarist, there are certain other odds and ends of what might be called inside information that you'll find extremely useful in your chosen field of musical endeavour. We're speaking here of those annoying things which are mostly acquired through trial and error – in other words, experience – and which, for some reason, no one ever thinks to mention, and much of which you don't find out for yourself until it's too late. By which time you may well have wasted both money and effort, as well as suffered embarrassment and missed out on important opportunities. So this section of the book is to help you avoid some of the hazards and inconveniences awaiting you, thereby making life as a working guitarist just that little bit easier.

Off the record (or CD)

Unless you intend to only ever play your own compositions (which would be limiting in many ways, not the least of which would be the lack of inspiration and experience), it's inevitable that you'll often be required to work out how to play a piece of music with only the recording itself as a source of reference. Whilst there is much information available from sheet music, and also on the Internet, there will always be occasions when this is either insufficient, incomplete or just plain inaccurate.

When attempting to learn music in this situation, no matter how the actual guitar part may sound in terms of melody or complexity, your best starting point should always be to ascertain the basic chord sequence. For whilst your role as guitarist might be the playing of riffs or flowing melody lines, you should know by this point that all of this will inevitably be built around the chords over which it's played.

Working out the chord sequence from a recording is mostly not too difficult, although it obviously varies in difficulty from one song to another, and from one type of music to another. As a general guide for you to begin with, it's true to say that country music, blues and early rock and roll are usually the easiest, being for the most part based around three or four major chords. Heavy rock leans on '5' type chords (see **page 41**) a great deal, which can somewhat blur the distinction between major or minor (because they contain no 3rd), but overall the chords used aren't harmonically complex, although they can occasionally employ rapid changes between the chords used. General types of so-called pop music, from the '60s up to date, usually include the standard bunch of major and their relative minor chords, and occasionally a few surprises. But your biggest challenge is working out the chords in jazz, which, if you were paying attention in Chapter 6, you'll know to be a rather demanding form of music.

So let's suppose you're sitting comfortably, guitar at the ready and your chosen recording ready to play. The first thing you need to do is establish which key the music is in because, based upon what you've already learned, this will instantly present you with a shortlist of the chords most likely to appear. And the easy way to figure out the key is simply to listen to the last note of the verses, or last note of the song. Any note in a piece of music which has that satisfying 'final' sound is likely to be the key note of the entire recording. As with many things this has to be regarded with due caution, because there's always the unexpected, but the natural sound of finality is a pretty reliable guide as to the key of any song. Once you've decided which is that crucial note on the recording just play the same note on your guitar and ensure that it matches the pitch of the singer/ instrument etc, and there you have the key. Either major (usually with most popular music) or minor can be verified by playing a full chord of the appropriate variety.

A word of advice here with regard to your music source, because it's essential that your guitar is tuned to the same pitch as the recording, otherwise the two will never attain musical agreement. I'm assuming that your guitar will be tuned to standard 'concert' pitch as defined by a reliable tuning source (see **page 11**), and from this logic we must further assume that the recording from which you're working will be tuned, with equal accuracy, to this same pitch, which at the point when it was recorded will almost certainly have been the case. But inconveniently it's not impossible that this situation may have been altered in some manner before the sound emanates from your loudspeakers. In fact there are several rather annoying reasons why this might have occurred, and as this is quite an interesting subject in itself we'll take a few minutes here in order to consider them one at a time.

When recorded music plays back at the same speed at which it was recorded the result is a sound identical in pitch to that of the original recording. But if it's played back at a different speed a very strange thing happens, which is simply that the original pitch is altered along with the tempo of the music. Specifically, when it's speeded up on playback the sound goes up in pitch, and conversely when it's slowed down the sound goes down in pitch, with the actual degree of pitch change being dependant upon the severity of tempo variation. Now it's true that modern computer technology can counteract this effect, but this is a fairly recent situation, and the greater amount of recorded music was produced long before such things were possible. In fact there are many times when it's been the specific intention of a recording artist or engineer to alter the original pitch of a recording, for perfectly valid musical reasons, which might indeed improve the sound but makes it a bit difficult for you to play (guitar) along with.

A typical reason for speeding up a recording might be that having worked for many hours, or even days, recording a song, somebody decides upon further consideration that it would sound better if it were faster. The options then would be to either re-record the entire song at a faster tempo, or to speed up the tape (before there were hard-disc recorders) by simply adjusting the tape speed control. And bearing in mind that studio time costs money, the record company wouldn't be all that happy with the idea of several more days spent recording exactly the same song over again when it might not even turn out to be a profitable hit record. It's true that if you happened to be Elvis Presley or the Beatles then studio time and its concurrent expenses probably wouldn't have been an obstacle, but this would have been the exception, not the rule. For most bands back in the '60s the clock was always ticking, and studio time demanded results. So with a little bit of cautious tweaking of the dial, you instantly have a faster piece of music, with band, audience and the record company all quite happy. It's a fact that there would be a limit to the extent of tape speed alteration, because too much change can make the vocal sound a bit weird, but usually a small degree of adjustment would be satisfactory anyway.

Another reason why a recording could be 'in between' pitches would be to do with your music-playing device. It's unlikely to be the case nowadays, but if you were working from an actual record player these can be unreliable in terms of their rotation speed accuracy, thereby creating another potential pitch change hazard. And the same applies to cassette tape players, which don't always run precisely at the correct speed. But most probably you'll be working from a CD, PC, Minidisk or similar, and these are extremely reliable with regard to their fidelity of production, which certainly makes things a lot easier than they once were. However, this cannot cancel out the fact that some recording speeds were adjusted at source, without recourse to modern pitch/tempo correction facilities. And so you'll just occasionally find it necessary to counterbalance this inconvenience by your own effort and initiative.

Fortunately for you the guitar is an instrument of widely variable pitch, and if you cannot match your guitar (at standard concert pitch) to the recording, then what you must do is adjust your overall tuning until it's the same as the recorded track. This isn't really difficult because, supposing the recording appears to be slightly sharp (too high) for the key of G, but not quite high enough for the next key pitch of A♭, you can assume that somewhere along the line things have gone astray somewhat, and then you can choose between either tuning up to the recording and learning it as in the key of G, or tuning down to match the recording and learning it in the key of A♭. The probability, incidentally, is that the song was actually recorded in G and has become artificially faster, rather than vice versa. This conclusion is partly based upon the well-known guitarist preference for 'open' keys, and partly upon my own findings from personal experience. Nevertheless, some people prefer to tune down and maybe transpose later on, rather than subject their strings to the stress of greater tension. Whichever option you prefer, I would emphasise that it's important to reach accurate tuning agreement with the recording, because this will make your job a great deal easier, especially when trying to figure out some difficult or rapid chord changes and complicated solos.

Having attained satisfactory pitch you can now start on the fun part – actually working on the song itself. No doubt every guitarist has his or her preferred method in this area, and you'll also develop your own, but here are some guidelines and suggestions (some of which we very briefly touched upon in Chapter 6) for you to consider as a generally effective approach.

1   The first and last chords of a piece are likely to be the tonic chord (see **page 105**).
2   The penultimate chord is often the dominant (see **page 105**) or dominant seventh. The next most likely is the sub-dominant.
3   Remember that chord changes occur as the song and its melody dictates, and not necessarily at fixed or regular intervals of every bar or every other bar, etc, so use your ears to identify when the change to another chord takes place. This can also be more than once in the same bar.

4   If a chord sounds odd or unusual in some way, this usually suggests a chord that is not typical of that key – for example, in the key of **C** major standard chords such as **F**, **G7**, **Am** etc would all have a familiar and 'natural' sound within that chord sequence, because these chords are built entirely of notes which occur in the **C** major scale. However, if a chord containing any notes not from that scale were introduced, such as **Gm** for instance, then this would have a different 'feel' to it, which should alert you to a possible variation from the norm.
5   There will be times when a chord is hard to identify. Perhaps it sounds almost like a **C** major but somehow that doesn't quite fit; in such an instance try chords related to the **C** chord, such as **Am** (which has two out of three identical notes). If that doesn't work either, consider any of the extensions built upon that basic **C** major chord, like **C6**, **Cmaj7**, **Cadd9** etc, or it might even be an unexpected **Cm** chord instead.
6   The melody line can also give you clues as to which chord is underlying, because of your knowledge regarding which notes work well with which chords. This is particularly helpful if several vocal harmonies are being sung, because this can provide you with every note in the chord. If, for example, the song is in the key of **D** major and several voices are heard, with one voice singing a **B** note, another singing a **D** note and a third voice singing an **F#** note, then it's a pretty fair bet that the chord in question is a **Bm**.

If, despite the information above, you're still stuck regarding one particular chord, you can always resort to my long-winded but failsafe final strategy. This is simply to play that particular section of the music over and over again, trying a different chord on each occasion until you hit the right one. First try all the major chords (it's not that bad, there are only 12), next try all the minor chords, and because most chord variations are based upon one or the other the chances are that you'll find something very close to the correct chord, if not the exact one. If you still have no luck, go for the augmented and diminished chords, which are only another seven possibilities, and this should pretty much nail it. But don't look so worried, because this is really going to extremes, and in the vast majority of songs it won't be anything like this much trouble anyway.

When attempting to work out solos, riffs, etc, the difficulty of so doing varies widely, depending upon the melodic content involved. If you wanted to learn something like the Rolling Stones famous *Satisfaction* riff, or perhaps the riff from Led Zeppelin's *Whole Lotta Love*, you can hardly go wrong. The melody is simple, contains very few notes, and is uncluttered and familiar. These being exactly the same qualities which make them so catchy and compulsive, we have a happy situation all round.

Moving on from this point, the next level of difficulty are those melodies which may be substantially more complex in terms of note quantity, but are still easily comprehensible to the ear. Into this category would be some well-known guitar pieces such as

Gary Moore's *Parisienne Walkways*, Fleetwood Mac's *Albatross*, or perhaps any number of famous instrumentals by the Shadows. For whilst these contain many more notes than the simple repetitive riffs, they still have those same virtues of being clear, uncluttered and usually familiar. So, up to this level of difficulty it's not much more than a question of listening carefully, and a bit of trial and error.

Things start to become slightly more complicated when you move up to the next level of virtuosity. This is where solos contain passages of several notes being played simultaneously, or maybe quite a lot of single notes but played at very high speed. Listen to Brian May's imaginative guitar work from the Queen classic *It's a Kind of Magic* as an example of this type of playing. In this song the high speed proliferation of 16th notes makes for rather challenging work if you intend to learn it, simply because although it sounds great in its entirety, the ear actually has great difficulty in analysing the individual note structure of the piece.

Another area where guitar work can present a learning challenge is in country music. Despite being built upon generally basic chord patterns, some of the lead guitar parts can be tricky – what with numerous bends and sometimes quick-fire alternating bass/treble runs, the clarity of tone often belies an impressive complexity of technique. Taking all of these various styles and their musical demands into account it becomes obvious that there will be times when some seriously hard work stands between you and your need to decipher the lead guitar work of a chosen song. Consider the following points as a helpful guide to ease your burden:

1 When faced with a challenging solo, begin by just listening carefully several times over to the specific part causing difficulty. This will help to familiarise your ears to the overall sound and structure of the piece.
2 Always be completely clear about the chords underlying each bar of the solo, riff, etc as it progresses. Then, as you work out the melody, bar by bar, you'll be guided (by the chords) as to which notes are most likely to be employed in its construction.
3 Work out the basic melody first, and where notes are harmonised (two or more played together) you can fill in those details later on. Given the key, scale and chords, it's usually pretty obvious which notes will provide the harmony. If in doubt, refer to **pages 115–116**.
4 Remember your scales and think accordingly. If it's a blues solo it will usually be notes from the traditional blues scale (**pages 116–119**), or if it's country music, think in that type of scale instead (**pages 119–120**). If you generally don't know which type of scale relates to which type of music, stay after class and write 100 times 'I should have paid more attention in Chapter 6'.
5 When you find a song particularly heavy going, just work on it one small amount at a time. Take a rest and come back to it later. It's no good getting tired and irritated, because your concentration will lapse, with careless and inaccurate results.

6 If all else fails and you simply can't make out the exact notes from a certain passage, remember that probably no one else can either. So why not indulge in some creative originality and just improvise something appropriate of your own? This doesn't work with a world famous riff that's familiar to all, but it's pretty much guaranteed to pass unnoticed amid a flurry of notes so indistinct that even you, despite your best efforts, can't identify.

A favourite trick for working out fast guitar runs is simply to slow down the recording playback speed when possible. This is hardly a new idea, as you might think. In earlier decades eager guitarists would take a 45rpm (revolutions per minute) record and adjust the record player to its 33rpm setting for a slower playback. It would tend to sound a bit strange perhaps, and obviously lower in pitch, but it definitely made it easier to work out a fast instrumental passage. This was a popular technique because everyone had a record player capable of at least two playback speeds, but the feasibility of a similar approach today depends upon having equipment capable of slowing down digital recording playback. There are certainly devices purpose built for this, available as a guitar accessory, but another possibility is to acquire a modestly priced multi-track recorder with variable speed capability. At the time of writing this book there are quite a number of such devices available, with more appearing at increasingly frequent intervals. In fact several more have probably arrived on the market whilst I've been completing this paragraph, which means that they're getting less expensive all the time, and many second-hand models will be available. One example is pictured below, this being a miniature four-track hard disk recorder with the requisite speed variation available.

You can then record the required song on to the unit at the recorder's standard recording speed, and then slow it down enough to be helpful. If you can obtain one of these it should make lighter work of learning those fast, incomprehensible solos. Playing them back at full speed on your guitar is, however, another matter, so don't forget to make constructive use of your slides, hammer-ons and pull-offs, as learned in Chapter 5.

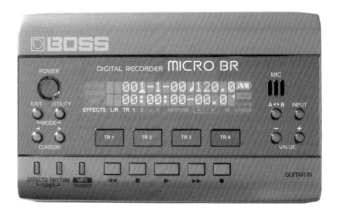

Getting the sound

Now that you've managed to work out the notes of your favourite guitar solo, riff, whatever, you'll probably want to make it sound as authentic as possible. It's a peculiarity of guitar players that they usually want to sound like someone else. No one ever expects a singer to sound like another singer (unless, of course, it's an intentional impersonation), and you don't expect a drummer to change his tone and technique with each different song. But guitar players are nevertheless expected to sound like every other guitar player as the occasion demands. So, whatever the reasoning, it's quite a useful skill to be able to create a reasonable facsimile of the original sound. And whilst there are numerous reasons why you're unlikely to duplicate such tonal qualities exactly, it's generally possible to achieve an acceptable similarity.

Any electric guitar tone that you've ever heard sounds the way it does for a remarkably wide variety of reasons, some of which are easily modified, perhaps by the flip of a switch, and some of which are less easy to define because they're matters of individual technique. And whilst I can't state this as a positive fact, I doubt if this applies equally to any other instrument in general use. If we look even casually into this subject you'll begin to see what I mean.

When any note is played on a guitar there are many things that can influence the way it sounds. These are from a purely equipment point of view, without even taking individual playing technique into consideration:

1 The materials from which the instrument is made. This is mainly wood, but also hardware such as the bridge, frets and nut. For more on this subject refer to Chapter 9.
2 Type and gauge of strings, along with any special tunings or tensions which can affect tone.
3 The type and quality of pickups.
4 The actual pickup used. This could be bridge position, middle position or neck position, or even any combination of those three depending upon the applicable wiring and switching options available.
5 Adjustment of any volume or tone control fitted to the guitar.
6 Use of any so-called tremolo (vibrato) arm, as may be fitted to various guitars.
7 Possible use of a capo.
8 Type of amplifier, and settings made to that unit.
9 Choice of clean or distortion tones used, and the extent to which these may be applied.
10 Use of any effects, either as part of the amplifier or separate units.

If you're interested in the sound of one particular player you should begin by looking at the equipment he or she is using. Their favourite choice of guitar is usually pretty obvious, because you can see that for yourself in any number of photographs. But remember that this isn't necessarily a fixed situation, as the actual instrument used on a particular recording may be something entirely different, chosen to create a tone that their regular guitar couldn't provide. But despite this fact it's a reasonable starting point to assume that a Jimi Hendrix song features a Fender Stratocaster, and it's well known that Hank Marvin has a likewise preference. George Harrison used a Rickenbacker 12-string on many of the mid '60s Beatle songs, most famously on the opening chord (**G7sus4** at the 3rd fret position) of *A Hard Day's Night*. Roger McGuinn made an entire career out of a similar instrument, as exemplified by the Byrds classic *Mr Tambourine Man*. As I also mentioned earlier, most country players go for the Fender Telecaster. Blues players often prefer the Gibson Les Paul, or similar, for its slightly heavier tone, as do many heavy rock guitarists. And I won't be giving out any prizes for knowing which instrument Brian May holds dearest to his heart – his beloved home-made red guitar is probably one of the most famous rock music icons ever.

Identifying other equipment used by your favourites is less easy, simply because they don't wear amps or effect pedals around their necks. Sometimes this side of the sound is rather generally known, such as Pete Townshend and his use of Hiwatt amplification, or James Burton's Fender Twin Reverb combination amp, but more often than not you'll need to make an educated guess – even more so in the case of additional equipment such as effects.

Since you probably don't have the availability of many different types of equipment anyway, this is where a certain amount of compromise becomes part of the equation, wherein you'll be using one guitar and amp set-up for everything. So, approaching the situation from this point of view let's start getting versatile.

When analysing a guitar tone in an attempt to reproduce that sound, start by identifying the very obvious things first before moving on to the finer detail. Most immediately apparent will be the distinction between a clean or a distorted (overdriven) sound, which doesn't take much thinking about, if at all. But degrees of this distinction are significant too, as some apparently clean tones feature just a touch of distortion. And the reverse also applies, when relatively little actual amp or pedal distortion is applied and the player uses a heavy picking technique instead. So try to get this aspect of the sound reasonably correct to begin with, and then make some adjustment to the tone controls in order to refine the actual quality of that sound. If you want a fairly crisp overdrive avoid too much middle tone, or if you want a rich full sound apply some mid tone but back-off the treble.

Guitar amps and effect units generally have only bass, middle and treble controls, so with a moderate amount of experimentation it's usually not too difficult to find a reasonable approximation of the tone you want. Keep in mind that the guitar and its pickups place certain limitations upon what's possible. All the tone adjustment available won't make a single-coil pickup sound exactly like a high-output twin-coil humbucker, or vice versa, but it certainly gets you nearer the target. Don't overlook your guitar tone control either, because this can take the sharp edge from a normally twangy single coil when you require a more mellow sound. Also, the bridge pickup will provide a lot more bite and energy than a neck or middle pickup, and most (but not all) rock guitar sounds lean toward use of this pickup.

Apart from tone qualities generated by the equipment itself, take time to consider how the playing technique will also affect this side of things. If you're trying to capture the sound of your favourite guitarist, don't just listen – remember to observe as well. Does he or she pick near to the bridge, or closer to the neck, and is the picking done with a plectrum or fingers? – because both of these points are important in defining accuracy of tone. If you're seeking a clear twangy sound, chances are you'll be picking very close to the bridge. This is logical enough, but also consider an alternative possibility: increase the amount of amp treble and pick the string closer to the neck. You still get a clear tone, because of extra treble from your amplifier, but the different picking location gives a less penetrating kind of twang. It might sound a bit contradictory but it does work, and presents you with another sound option that might be just right.

Another influential but easily overlooked factor is the thickness of a guitar pick. The heavier the plectrum, the heavier (more bass sounding) the tone. A very thin plectrum, along with its thin tone, will also give a more 'clicking' type of sound as it plays across the strings. It's not possible to ascertain the gauge of the pick used on any specific recording, but it's easy and inexpensive to try out several different types until you find your preferred choice for the occasion.

Fingerpicking can also vary the usual range of tone, apart from naturally being different in tone due to density of materials. Some players are inclined to pull the strings slightly away from the fretboard whilst fingerpicking, with the result being a light 'snapping' sound as the released strings hit the frets. Again, one more possibility which might get you closer to the magic tone you're seeking.

Something which very obviously influences the sound is the use of 'effects'. Broadly speaking, this term refers to a sound that can't be achieved using just the guitar and amplifier. As a general rule these effect units (a subject covered more comprehensively in Appendix 1) are in the form of foot-switchable pedals, making them easily – and therefore intermittently – applied as required. Where these are part of a 'sound', your job is to decide which one, or ones (several may be applied simultaneously, thereby adding to your confusion), are applicable. As you gain some experience in using these their various sound qualities will become reasonably familiar to you.

The popularity of different effects has varied throughout the decades, which is another guide as to which ones may have been featured on any given recording. The delay (echo) effect is one that seems to have survived the whim of fashion, having made its early appearances as a tape echo (see page 196) unit in the '50s and been central to the early sound of rock and roll. The delay sound has similarities to, but also significant differences from, reverb (see page 199), which, although available as a separate unit, is also standard to most guitar amplifiers. Reverb itself is widely used, to create a 'spacey' sound, and is certainly a feature of many guitar tones,

although it's much more generally used to lend ambience to many aspects of a recording.

Tremolo effect (volume fluctuation – see page 199) is a traditional feature of early '60s music but also appears elsewhere. This is easily identifiable where used, although its popularity has decreased in more recent times. A similar fate applies to the wah wah pedal (also known as a 'crybaby' effect), which reached the height of its popularity in the late '60s (think Hendrix), as did the now rarely seen Uni-Vibe (Jimi again). Compressor units (see page 200) are an established favourite with country lead guitarists, although they're heard more as a central feature of the technique than a distinct effect as such. And although it hardly qualifies as an actual effect, a basic volume control pedal can also feature strongly in the country guitar sound. This is because it can be used to diminish, or even completely eliminate, the initial 'attack' (sound of the note beginning) which is characteristic of any guitar string being sounded – and this, especially when combined with string bending, tends to replicate the sound of a pedal steel guitar. Finally, the familiar stereo chorus pedal's peak of popularity began in the '80s and continues today – an attractive sound when used with discretion, especially on arpeggio-type playing.

These aren't the only effects available, but it gives you an idea of how electronic devices can alter an otherwise basic tone into something more elaborate. In seeking to replicate guitar tones you'll frequently encounter these sound modifiers, and with experience and experimentation you should be able to approximate the degree to which any effect is applied. Refer to Chapter 9 for an individual reference on effects, as well as how they can best be used.

So when you're looking for just the right sound to express a particular piece of music, remember that there are many variables in reproducing a guitar tone, and try to reduce the odds by approaching your task in a methodical way. To summarise the above information, consider the points below:

1 Identify the basic tone as clean or distortion, and the extent to which this applies.
2 Decide which pickup is most likely being used. It only takes a moment to try the available options.
3 Adjust the bass, middle and treble controls to get closer to the right sound.
4 Consider the playing technique as far as it's known. Or experiment with fingers, various plectrums and string picking positions to see which appears favourable.
5 Decide if any effects are required, and if so which ones. Adjust these accordingly.

After you've established what appears to be a satisfactory tone, give it a rest and listen to it later on, or even the next day. This is helpful because your ears tend to become 'bored' after hacking away for hours at minimal changes to tone and effects. If it still sounds good a day later you're probably on to a winner. But keep in mind that the room you're in will also have an acoustic quality which may vary elsewhere. Once again, time and experience will be your best guide.

Vocal accompaniment

The actual quality or extent of your vocal abilities isn't really the business of this book; but if you do possess some vocal talent it's likely that you'll either be inclined or required to express this additional skill whilst playing your guitar. Some people have no difficulty at all in doing both at the same time, whilst others find it to be something of a coordination problem. If the latter applies to you, some patience and application is usually all it takes to put things in order.

My advice would be to start with a song of limited rhythmic complexity and not too many chords, ensuring that you can manage all the chord changes without difficulty. Remember that your brain needs to cope with two completely different tasks simultaneously, so the last thing you need is to be partially unfamiliar with either one. So if the chords or strumming action require more than the minimum of mental effort, then you haven't practised the piece thoroughly enough.

On the vocal side of the things, begin by finding a key suitable for comfortable pitching of your voice in all registers (pitch levels) as required by the song in question, and ensure that you're effortlessly familiar with the melody. You should next decide whether to learn the words off by heart or read them as you perform the song. My personal preference is to commit the song lyrics (and chord sequence) to memory, because although it's harder work at first, the words then will flow easily without really having to think about them at all.

So now that you can play the rhythm guitar part fluently, and know the song well, it's time to put the two together. Any difficulties in so doing are probably going to involve your strumming hand rather than the fretboard work, the difficulty being that you're attempting to strum a rhythmic pattern – let's say straight eight to the bar rhythm strokes – whilst trying to sing to a vocal rhythm that's somewhat different. It's like thinking about two rhythms at the same time, and there's a danger of one inadvertently 'following' the other, with the vocal most likely leading the chaotic way. It's time to back-up a little and simplify matters even further.

Put down your guitar for a moment and try this approach. Tap your foot at the tempo of the song, in a steady 1–2–3–4 beat, and try singing along in time with that. This shouldn't prove too difficult, as you've probably done this many times without even thinking about it. Next transfer this foot-tapping to your strumming hand, again with a simple 1–2–3–4 motion, and do this for a while until you get into the feel of it. Step three is to pick up your guitar and continue the same simple motion, but don't worry about your chord changes – just lightly mute the strings instead which will provide a rhythmic 'clicking' sound – and practise this to the point of effortless boredom. Finally, hold down a chord and continue the same pattern until you can sing to this steady rhythm of four to the bar.

When you can sing along to this very basic rhythm beat, gradually increase the rhythmic complexity until you reach the desired strumming pattern correct for the song. In other words, start with simple quarter-note strums, adding the occasional eighth strum, and work your way into a full eight to the bar by way of gradual progress. Some guitarists will also find it helpful to play along with the recording for a while, listening to the way in which the vocal melody interacts with the guitar rhythm, before attempting to perform the song for themselves. But above all else, the most essential aspect of any approach is to ensure a thorough familiarity with your guitar part in the song, and then practise putting the two together afterward.

Although most vocalists, when playing guitar, prefer to play rhythm instead of lead, for very obvious reasons, there are also occasions when the other approach is preferred or required. This usually takes the form of the lead playing being worked around the vocal, as typified in Mark Knopfler's playing on *Sultans of Swing*, or the B.B. King approach of play a bit, sing a bit. This style of playing mostly requires a fluency of technique and basically the ability to mentally switch back and forth between guitar and vocals, since you're not actually and literally doing both at the same time. Alternately, where there's only one guitarist in a band the tendency is to play rhythm whilst singing, and throw in the essential lead licks where desired. This is really a case of basic necessity when playing live, as demonstrated by many over the years such as Chuck Berry, Buddy Holly, Pete Townshend, Wilko Johnson, Jack White and numerous others.

If you need to play a riff and sing at the same time this usually isn't as difficult as you might think. The trick here is to think of the riff in rhythmic terms, which is entirely plausible because of the repetitive nature of any riff. So what this amounts to is getting into the pattern of playing the riff in the same way you would with playing a chord rhythm. Sure, it's a little bit more tricky, but it's generally possible with a reasonable level of playing skill and experience.

Avoiding mistakes

So there you are, on stage rockin' away, and with all your friends in the audience. The moment comes for your soaring, heart-lifting guitar solo. Up goes the volume as the spotlight falls upon you, looking cool and sounding great. And then it happens – halfway into that carefully worked out and much rehearsed solo you hit a wrong note. In one split second you go from feeling like the number one person in the room into wishing you were somewhere else entirely. Yes, we've all had the experience, because it happens to all musicians, and whilst some playing errors are usually not too apparent, there's nothing quite like a cutting guitar tone to make the mistake obvious to all. And if you think you've got problems in a small club, playing to maybe just a few dozen strangers and a few friends, this is a relatively small amount of pressure to be under compared to some other situations. Can you imagine how Brian May must have been feeling, playing one of the most famous tunes in the world (the British national anthem), every note familiar to all, entirely solo, standing on the roof of Buckingham Palace, being watched by billions, during the 2002 Golden Jubilee? Happily all went well for him, and mostly it will for you too (assuming you've put it the hours beforehand), but just occasionally things do go wrong, and it's good to know how to reduce the risk of such embarrassment, or at least minimise the effect when it does happen.

The way I see it, mistakes can be broadly divided into two categories: those which occur because you've forgotten what you're supposed to be playing, and those which result from your hands making the wrong move. Looking at the first type, the obvious thing is to ensure that you've practised a song sufficiently to know exactly what you need to play. Certainly it's a fact that too many guitarists make mistakes simply because they haven't learned the music thoroughly enough, but even so the most familiar piece can also become suddenly unfamiliar at a crucial moment. It's true to say that when your brain is cluttered up with dozens, or perhaps even hundreds, of songs, solos riffs etc, confusion does arise from time to time which may involve even a fairly simple number. Why this occurs is hard to ascertain, but perhaps it's just an occasional case of musical overload, and probably happens to even the most talented players sooner or later. When it happens you're unlikely to have time to relearn the music or think about it for a while, because you'll probably be on stage, halfway through a song, and with only a split second to react. Not an ideal situation, as I'm sure you'll agree.

What you can do, however, is a quick exercise in damage limitation, by falling back on your improvising skills; and although you may have forgotten what you usually play, it's perfectly possible to play something a bit different, which may not be your very best work but will suffice in this musical emergency. It's unlikely that you've actually forgotten which song you're playing (if you have it's probably time to cut back on the illegal substances), and the overall tempo will give you the right feel for improvisation, so make a point of at least remembering the key (or write it on your song set list) and play something appropriate around the chords.

This approach is dependant upon your level of improvisational skill, but if in doubt just keep it fairly simple, don't get too fancy or try too hard, and don't attempt to use too many notes. And although you, and possibly the band, will notice the difference, the audience will remain entirely unaware of your sudden change of plan.

The other type of mistake – when you accidentally hit the wrong chord or string – is a bit more problematic, but there are ways to prepare for such an eventuality which will minimise the likelihood of it happening in the first place, or at the very least reduce the audible effect when it does occur.

Do I really need to tell you that those who practise the most make mistakes the least? OK, so assuming you've covered that angle what else is left? – because even the most dedicated and hard-working musicians will occasionally trip over a note. First of all, prepare your guitar to be in optimum playing condition, with a good comfortable action (see **pages 175–79**). This just makes everything so much easier to play, and reduces any potential difficulties immediately. But in addition to this you need to actually see what you're doing. Yes, it sounds too stupid to be true until you find yourself playing in a dimly lit club but with the stage lights glaring right into your eyes. Then, all of sudden, you find that the neck position markers, which seemed fine before, are almost invisible to you, and now you can't even tell which fret you're aiming for. That sort of situation is bad enough when you're playing chords, but when soloing up and down the fretboard it can become virtually impossible. But for once the remedy is dead easy, as illustrated by the picture above.

All you need do is apply some larger side dots over the inadequately small original ones. The best colour is definitely white, and basic cellulose – such as car body paint – is usually fine for the job, and is also reasonably long-lasting. If you use a spray, which gives a smoother finish than applying by brush, this can be messy, so mask off the rest of your instrument accordingly. I also have to include a note of caution here regarding the possibility of an unfavourable chemical reaction between cellulose paint and any lacquer or varnish on your guitar, although I've never personally experienced such a conflict. To be on the safe side you should test a small inconspicuous area first, to ensure compatibility between your guitar's finish and the intended marker paint. Incidentally, if you're dealing with a particularly expensive or 'classic' instrument you need to be aware that its financial value might be diminished by any alteration from its original status – even, for example, a fully professional refinish job which genuinely improves its appearance.

Having ensured that your guitar is in excellent playing condition, as it should be at all times, we come to the subject of skill and technique. In this department my first advice would be not to play beyond your ability, because it's not much use working out a really flashy piece of guitar work unless you can execute the piece efficiently pretty much every time. Obviously you'll want to progress and extend your capabilities over time, but this should be done at home, not at a public performance. And if you still find something difficult to play when you're practising in private, it isn't somehow going to become easier in front of an audience.

Even following all the above advice, and after years of experience, there's still no escaping the fact that just occasionally you're going to hit a wrong note; so we need to minimise the audible effect of this upon your adoring fans. Most playing errors seem to feature the picking hand rather than the one doing the fretwork (for advice on picking accuracy, refer to **page 27**), which means that either you hit a wrong note or you fail to play the right one by missing the string entirely. In the latter case the effect isn't usually too horrendous, especially if it's in a fast run of notes, because you'll be sounding the following note before most people in the audience even register your oversight. And if it's a solo created by yourself, no one except you, and maybe the band, knows what it was really supposed to sound like anyway.

If the opposite happens, and instead of missing the intended string you accidentally hit another one, it will – unless you're very lucky – sound pretty awful and be apparent to everyone. This is where those really embarrassing and ear-tormenting moments occur, when usually they could be prevented by the use of one simple technique with which you're already familiar. The answer is, of course, muting any strings that aren't required to sound.

Although muting can be done by either hand, especially when fingerpicking, on this occasion left-hand (fret hand) muting is generally easiest and most versatile for the situation. And just to give you an idea of what I'm talking about here, and the virtues of its application, let's try a little experiment first. Pick up your guitar and play a G# note at the 6th fret of the fourth string. Play this several times so that your ears get used to that being the note you expect to hear. OK, now 'accidentally' just miss that fourth string, hitting the un-muted open fifth string, or maybe the equally un-muted open third string instead. Unless you happen to be tone deaf (a slight problem for a musician) this will sound really awful.

So now let's try it another way. Ensure that your fretting finger is placed in such a way that it holds down the required fourth string, but also mutes both of the adjacent strings. This isn't very hard to do – as shown in the picture, you simply flatten the angle at which your

finger meets the string, thereby increasing its spread across the neck. This will permit the intended fourth string to sound quite clearly, whilst also completely preventing strings three and five from accidentally doing likewise. Now if you miss your target string all you'll get is an almost inaudible, and musically inoffensive, click, as you accidentally strike an unintended string. So although you may have a 'missing' note, the overall result will be considerably less noticeable, and massively less embarrassing, than sounding a wrong note.

Although less common than picking errors, fretboard inaccuracies sometimes occur – probably as a result of not looking, or being unable to see, where your fingers are going. Any visibility difficulties can usually be resolved by improved position markers along the edge of your guitar neck, as mentioned earlier; but if you're significantly short-sighted and don't want to wear glasses on stage it's really a choice between wearing contact lenses or continuing to hit the wrong notes – although it should be mentioned that there have been some notable players who are completely blind, such as Jeff Healey and Jose Feliciano, and therefore play entirely by feel. So by comparison wearing your spectacles on stage (Buddy Holly, Hank Marvin, Roy Orbison, Jarvis Cocker) isn't really that big a deal anyway.

If, as sometimes happens, you land at the wrong fret position, the quickest way out of there is to simply slide up or down to the intended correct fret position. If done quickly enough this can even sound as if you intended to make the slide for effect purposes, but if not this approach will at least get you back on track in the least noticeable way.

Working with other musicians

At some point in your musical career it's likely that you'll want to, or find it necessary to, join a band. This situation has numerous difficulties, annoyances and inconveniences attached to it, but also one major advantage in the shape of improved sound possibilities. It's true that with the hi-tech equipment available today it's quite possible to create a full and professional sound by using artificial backing tracks, to which you could add your own guitar playing and vocals, and then perform as a solo artist – a great many club-type performers prefer this approach, simply because it means that they'll get all the money and less of the hassle – but you'll get far less individuality in your sound, because all the other solo performers are using pretty much the same stuff, which tends to sound depressingly monotonous after a while. So let's assume you intend to join, or start, a band and take it from there.

A significant number of young bands are formed by several friends getting together with a desire to make music, or more likely a desire to get rich and famous. This latter motive is understandable enough, but is rarely sufficient to go the distance. By this I mean that after a few months of struggling through vague rehearsals, with people of limited musical ability, the novelty starts to wane, disillusion sets in and the band, such as it is, begins to fall apart. The fact is that for any band to start from nothing and work up to a reasonable level of efficiency a considerable amount of dedication is required from all concerned. So if your intention is to press-gang a few friends into joining your incipient group, the likelihood is that you'll be plagued by apathy, unreliability and a general lack of talent.

But let's suspend reality for a moment and suppose that I'm

wrong, with every band member being as reliable and dedicated as I presume you to be. In this happy situation you'll require two characteristics above all: a reasonable level of maturity all round, and at least one person with some organisational ability. The maturity is important because you're working in close proximity to the insecurities, shortcomings and personality differences of several people, for long periods of time, and will need to be tolerant of each other on many levels. The organising ability is necessary or else nothing constructive will be achieved. All you'll have are regular band get-togethers with nothing to show for it.

The usual scenario for disorganised bands, even when they're individually capable musicians, will initially manifest itself in the following way. Everyone arrives at the rehearsal hall, brings in their equipment, sets it up, tunes their guitars, and then waits. Silence reigns for a few moments, as everyone glances around at everyone else, and finally someone looks at the founder member (probably you) and says, 'So, what are we going to do then?' And this is why you need to exert some degree of control over what will otherwise degenerate into random guitar doodling, and intermittent snatches of semi-learned chord sequences, at the end of which your band will have achieved exactly nothing. The only one to profit will be the person who is renting you the rehearsal hall. So let's consider another approach.

At least a week before group practice your band should decide upon a couple of songs, agreeable to all and not excessively difficult to play or sing. And during that week every band member should thoroughly learn his or her own particular part for those songs. Once decided upon, avoid any last-minute changes of plan in this regard, otherwise you'll be right back to square one again. Oh yes, one more thing – ensure that you know which key it will be played in, as defined by the vocal range of your singer(s), because any unnecessary key transpositions can waste practice time, particularly if there are any fancy solos or harmonies involved. If you follow these relatively simple bits of advice you should find your rehearsals to be enjoyable and productive.

The other way of getting together with other musicians is to join an already functioning band that is looking for an additional guitarist. In many ways this is easier for you, because it's really a question of fitting into a band where most of the hard work has already been taken care of, although – initially at least – you'll have less control over the musical situation and less say in group policy. But first you have to get the job.

Your first point of contact with any band is likely to be from an advertisement in a local paper, or maybe pinned up on the notice board of a music shop. The Internet is obviously another medium of contact, but because this is rather wide-ranging you need to ensure that any ads relate to your area, or it just won't be practical from a travel point of view.

When you respond to an advertisement, make sure you find out pretty accurately what they're looking for, and what sort of working order the band is already in, or you may find yourself joining up with a bunch of time-wasting loonies who are, in

themselves, no more than optimistic beginners. Fine if that's what you want, but don't just assume that because their ad reads well they must be experienced semi-professionals with dozens of gigs waiting. There are more rubbish bands out there than good ones, whatever type of music you may be interested in playing.

Having satisfied yourself on this point, one way or the other, try to find out some of the songs they'll be wanting you to play at the audition, and preferably in which key. This is a huge benefit to you, simply because you won't arrive completely unprepared, and will therefore give a much better account of yourself and your abilities. There are two reasons why you may be unable to resolve this question. One is because they only play their own compositions. If that suits you, ask if they can send you a recording sample to learn from, or otherwise you'll just have to improvise. The second reason is because you're into a completely different type of music from them, and are therefore unfamiliar with their repertoire. If this is the case, it's almost certainly a waste of time from everyone's point of view, because they'll hire someone who's more in accord with their requirements and has similar musical interests.

A non-musical but essential requirement at any audition is that you should 'look the part'. Despite the usual assumed air of nonconformity, it's surprising how bands usually adhere quite firmly to the conventions of dress and appearance traditionally associated with their particular kind of music. So even if you're a dedicated heavy metal fan, it's no good showing up with your guitar and amp but dressed like a bank manager. They'll probably be polite enough to hear you play, but unless you're absolutely brilliant, or even if you are, you still won't be likely to get the job.

Another mistake you might easily fall into is not bothering to take your own gear – apart from, presumably, your guitar – because someone has assured you over the phone that they'll have something for you to plug into. It certainly sounds a lot easier than carrying around a heavy amp and a bag full of effects pedals, so you just take the basic minimum necessary; after all, it's only an audition, not a gig, and they'll surely understand (being musicians themselves) that you sound even better with your own gear. Don't fall for that one, because the fact is that people say a lot of things, but when it comes down to it you'll be expected to sound your very best, whatever you may have been told over the phone, and whatever piece of junk they allow you to play through. The only way to ensure a good sound is by using equipment with which you're familiar, and can utilise to best effect. So don't take chances; take your own gear instead.

Finally, remember that many people are hopelessly disorganised, and they may be trying out several other guitarists who've all been given the same supposed audition time, leaving you to wait around for ages whilst others are playing first. So do try to ascertain a realistic appointment time, rather than a hypothetical one, to hopefully avoid this tedious situation. You should make sure of arriving on time, and there's no reason to expect any less courtesy in return.

Playing live

Yes, this is what it's all about. After all the hard work at home and at rehearsals, you finally get to appear in front of an audience – a bit nervous probably, and inexperienced certainly, but with sensible preparation there's no reason why it shouldn't work out just fine.

If you've joined up with an already functioning band of reasonably experienced musicians they'll probably know what they're doing, and will have a set-up routine which will be quite straightforward for you to fit into. But I'll assume the worst, which is that you'll have to deal with everything for yourself and be responsible for making everything work out well. With that in mind let's take all the essentials into consideration.

First of all, at the earliest stage of arranging the gig you should try to ensure that your band and the audience to which you'll be playing are reasonably compatible in musical terms. Regardless of what you might have seen in the movies, it's going to be more or less impossible to win over a club full of blues fans if you happen to be playing country, reggae, jazz or whatever else doesn't appeal to them. This is really just common sense, but it does happen, especially if you book through an agent, who might not really know or care what you're all about anyway. So if in doubt you should try to visit the club some time beforehand, and check it out for yourself.

The next thing is to be certain of knowing enough songs to fill out the required performing time. This is likely to be somewhere around two hours or just over, which won't be non-stop but will have one or two breaks along the way. Exactly what constitutes enough songs obviously depends upon their length, but if we assume an average length of three minutes per song you would obviously need 20 songs for every hour of playing time. In reality it will be somewhat fewer numbers than this because of gaps between songs, chatting to your audience, introducing the songs and so on. But it's also possible that you might play some numbers a bit faster than you did at rehearsal, what with nerves etc, so be on the safe side and consider that it's better to have songs to spare than not enough. Besides, if it all goes well you may be asked for an encore or two at the end of the night. So keep a couple of strong numbers aside for this possibility.

What may well surprise you at your first gig is a substantial difference in sound quality between one room and another. For various reasons the building in which you're playing will possess certain acoustic characteristics which you will be unable to alter to any significant degree, and which can prove either beneficial or detrimental to your sound as a band. If you're accustomed to practising in a familiar room or hall you'll have grown used to the sound of that particular place, and will – perhaps without really having thought about it – have adapted your volume, tone and effects to that situation.

The subject of acoustics could probably fill a book of its own, but as far as you're concerned the main problem is usually too much echo, which will be caused by many hard, sound-reflective surfaces such as walls, chairs, windows and even the dance floor. And what with several sound sources within your band twanging and banging away at various times and volumes, an echo-laden room can make your best efforts sound like a real mess. The opposite of this, of course, is a completely 'dead' room with no discernible echo whatever, which will have lots of soft surfaces such as curtains, soft chairs, carpets and even the audience itself to absorb the sound. The thing is, you can always *add* echo or reverb if required, by use of electronic devices, so this isn't really a problem; but *removing* unwanted excessive echo from any room is a real nuisance, which can ruin your performance.

Unfortunately, very few people in the audience will know the first thing about acoustics and its less attractive effects upon your music, so they'll just think you're a lousy band and you'll unfairly end up taking the blame. So when you arrive at any venue, make certain that you do so in plenty of time in order to have the best chance of sorting out any difficulties regarding acoustical problems, or anything else which may arise. I can assure you that if anything's going to break down, or any leads, connectors etc become dodgy, it's more likely to happen at a gig than at any other time. All things considered I'd recommend arriving a couple of hours before performance time, or, if this isn't possible for any reason, try to make it with at least 90 minutes to spare. Anything much less than that really is cutting it pretty fine, and if a mishap does occur you'll be in bit of a mess, especially if you're still new at the game.

Getting back to the problem of excess echo, the obvious first thing to do is cut back on whatever artificial reverb or delay you normally use. Also, it's common for drummers to carry around a medium-size piece of carpet material upon which to set up their kit, which will not only help acoustically but also minimise the possibility of the kit (especially the bass drum) moving around during the performance. Remember that whatever sound is coming from your amps, drum kit and so on will also be picked up by the microphones and re-amplified through the PA (public address) system, which may produce additional noise problems such as feedback (see below). So try to keep the microphones at a low level, and sing close up into them rather than turning them up in volume and standing further back. Try not to play at too high a volume, in order to minimise the echoey sound, and keep in mind that the problem will ease somewhat when the audience arrives, simply because their bodies and clothing are all made of helpfully sound-absorbent materials.

The problem known as 'feedback' is a high-pitched, screeching noise caused by the signal going into the microphone, out of the loudspeakers and then being picked back up by the microphone and amplified once again. If left uncontrolled this sets up a repetitive continuity of sound, and produces the truly awful noise with which you're probably familiar. In order to prevent this, a typical small band set-up, as seen on the following page, places the vocal microphones well behind the path of its loudspeakers.

If despite your best efforts feedback does occur, the quick way to

stop it is simply to switch off or lower the volume of the instrument causing the problem. Usually this will be a microphone, but certain other instruments are also capable of creating feedback, especially amplified acoustic or semi-acoustic, guitars which are too close to their own amplifier speakers. Certain tone frequencies can either create or exaggerate feedback problems, especially bass frequencies, and in this case it may be necessary to compromise your preferred tone settings in order to reduce the problem.

A specific problem I once encountered involved an unhealthy interaction between an amplified acoustic guitar and the sound generated by the bass player. Every time he played a low **A** note it caused the soundboard of the acoustic guitar (see **pages 185 and 198**) to vibrate alarmingly and produce severe feedback. The obvious compromise solution in that instance was to fit a capo and play the song in **B♭**, which meant that all of the problematic **A** bass notes became **B♭** bass notes, which caused no problems at all.

As mentioned in Chapter 1 (**page 7**), solid-body electric guitars, although they can produce feedback if played at too high a volume and close to the speakers, do tend to be highly resistant to this problem because of the relatively high density of the body. You may be aware that some guitarists do, on occasion, deliberately create controlled feedback for sound-effect purposes, but this is definitely not something I'd recommend until you really know what you're doing, no matter how big a Hendrix fan you might be.

Sound check

Although some clubs, bars etc will be reasonably well equipped from your point of view, by having a proper stage of adequate size and suitably close to the power supply, this will certainly not always be the case. Many times you'll be expected to cope with insultingly inadequate facilities, and told to set up in a small corner of the room with either no stage at all or one barely large enough for performing mice, and miles away from a single dodgy-looking power socket to be shared by the entire band. So be sure to carry a couple of multi-socket extension leads with a good length of cable, and use a power trip-switch to protect yourself from any risk of unsafe electrical connections. Yes, I know all about health and safety regulations, but

this is the real world, and even with responsible club facilities things can sometimes go wrong.

As if you don't already have enough to deal with, some clubs are fitted with volume detectors that, if your sound exceeds a certain decibel level, will cut off the power to your equipment. You will normally be given about ten seconds warning of this impending power cut by a series of multi-coloured lights within your range of vision. During this brief 'warning' period you'll have to either quickly reduce volume or lose power completely. These sort of devices, which will usually have been installed because of noise complaints from local residents, are a real menace to musicians, and it's very distracting trying to play, sing, control effects and other equipment whilst also having to keep one eye upon the volume warning lights. On the positive side it should be said that most clubs aren't (at the time of writing) fitted with these annoying devices, and among those which do have them some of the more sympathetic club managers will allow you to use a power supply not connected to that system. Failing such helpful options, most bands will make the best of things by playing at what's usually an inappropriately minimal volume level, and then try to avoid playing at that same venue on any future occasion.

When your equipment is set up it's time to do a sound check, to ensure that all instruments and voices are correctly balanced (in terms of volume) relative to each other. In order to do this correctly, someone who can be trusted to have a good ear for such things will need to go out into the general area where the audience will be and listen carefully whilst the band plays and sings. Not everyone is good at this, and certainly no one not closely involved with the band should be entrusted with this extremely important task. So don't ask the barman, the club owner, wives, girlfriends, or general hangers-on to do this for you, and certainly don't rely upon the opinion of any audience members who may be present. It's usually best, and frequently the only option, to do it for yourselves. This means that a suitable band member (meaning one who is neither singing nor playing a non-portable instrument such as keyboard or drums) must wander around the room and listen, intermittently giving useful and hopefully accurate advice such as 'vocals too quiet', or 'rhythm guitar too loud'. In order to perform this task you'll obviously require either an extremely long guitar cable or, more conveniently, a wireless transmitter system (see **pages 202–203**) that will permit complete freedom of movement. Listen carefully to the sound from various locations in the room until it all sounds reasonably correct. I say 'reasonably' because you'll never get it absolutely perfect for every song by just sound checking one or two partial numbers. So again it's a bit of a compromise, but by using this approach it usually works out generally well.

An important consideration for any band is deciding whether to generate instrumental sound only from the backline (behind your playing position) amps, or to 'mic up' everything through the PA system, for what's likely to be a superior sound mix. And in case you're unfamiliar with this situation I'll explain what I mean by taking you on a little musical trip through time.

Many decades ago there was obviously no such thing as 'electric' music as we know and love it today. So way back in the earlier part of the 20th century the popular dance bands, led by people such as Glenn Miller, Benny Goodman, Tommy Dorsey, and so on, relied entirely upon acoustic instruments like trumpets, clarinets, violins and sometimes a fairly unobtrusive drum beat for their sound. In a situation like this, any problems regarding volume were likely to be the exact opposite of what they are today; and instead of the usual complaints about a band being too loud, it would more likely be a case of not being loud enough in anything other than moderately-sized venues. So if a bandleader needed more volume from, say, the brass section, the only thing he could do would be to hire more musicians to increase that aspect of the sound. OK, now if we move forward in time to the late 1940s, and especially into the '50s, electric amplification was becoming widely used, first on vocals and then, most notably, through the invention of the electric guitar. Indeed, without the invention of the magnetic pickup (see **pages 184–93**), rock and roll and its numerous musical offspring would simply not have been possible.

When it became possible to amplify music it was entirely feasible for a limited number of performers to make enough noise to fill out a large club or dance hall, without the sound being lost to people sitting some considerable distance away from the stage. As a result the early rock and roll bands would set up on stage with a drum kit, an electric guitar and amp, a bass guitar and amp (taking over from the traditional stand-up bass) and, if they could afford it, maybe a vocal harmony group. All OK so far. But the next problem occurred when certain acts became so popular that they found themselves playing in extremely large concert halls and, later, stadiums. At this point even the largest guitar amps weren't really up to the job, and groups such as the Beatles were, rather optimistically, attempting to be heard in Shea Stadium (New York) by an audience of around 60,000 screaming teenagers. The next brave effort was probably that made by the Who, in setting up large banks of loudspeakers behind themselves so that audiences would stand some reasonable chance of actually hearing the sound from the stage. The drawback in this approach is that whilst audience members positioned some considerable distance from the band might have a reasonable volume level for their ears, those persons actually on the stage itself would be, almost literally, deafened by their own massive speakers.

As a result of this somewhat ill-advised activity some well-known musicians later suffered severe hearing problems, which clearly indicated the need for a different approach and permits me to get to the point of my story.

The favoured approach nowadays tends to be something called 'sound reinforcement', which entails the on-stage amplifiers being kept at a volume level suitable for the hearing of the band members themselves, and then placing in front of each on-stage loudspeaker a microphone which picks up the sound of (for example) your guitar amp, and then transmits that sound to the audience via the main PA system. So in effect it's entirely possible for your amplifier to be relatively quiet from your point of view, but nevertheless permit its sound to be heard much louder by the audience. In practice it isn't always necessary to use a microphone, because a direct line can usually be taken from the guitar amp into the main sound system; but the overall principle is exactly the same, although obviously without any ambient noise being picked up from sound sources other than the actual guitar amp itself.

When this type of set-up is employed all sound sources on the stage become entirely controllable through one overall sound system, and can therefore be volume-balanced far more effectively than would otherwise be possible. This generally includes the drums, which will obviously require several microphones, one for each aspect of the kit (snare drum, bass drum, cymbals etc). So taking all this into consideration, you'll require a mixing desk capable of handling around 16 different channels to effectively fulfil the requirements of an average small group. And although a stereo mix (with different instruments 'panned' to either the left or right speaker) is usually possible, it's also inadvisable, because this would only be effective for those audience members positioned central to the PA speakers. Everyone else would be hearing only certain parts of your musical output, and therefore receive an inadequate sound. So it's usually best not to get too fancy in this regard, and just stick to mono for live work.

If, through choice or necessity, you decide to opt for the 'backline only' approach this can still be reasonably satisfactory in smaller venues, but because the drums will be heard entirely acoustically (not amplified) they'll tend to dictate the volume of all other instruments. It's not much good having your amplifiers either so loud or so quiet that the drums are heard disproportionately to everything else, and because some drummers are naturally louder than others there can be no specific rule other than to let common sense be your guide.

Being prepared

In the way of general advice, it's important to carry spares of anything which could either break down or be mislaid. This includes the obvious items such as picks and guitar strings, which should be a complete new set and not some tatty old ones left over from a previous string-change. Also carry a small set of tools comprising various screwdrivers, wire cutters, pliers, insulating tape, solder and iron, which will become invaluable at some time in the future. Less

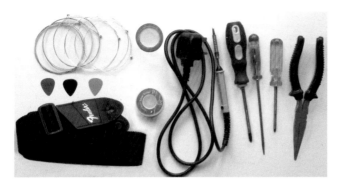

likely, but crucial in the event of breakage, is a spare guitar strap. These are generally pretty reliable, but somebody sometime will be caught out by using a dodgy, frayed strap, and your foresight will then pay off.

If a breakdown does occur during your performance don't panic, because it usually turns out to be something reasonably fixable. Instead of trying to fix it whilst the band plays on around you it's much better to take a short break and work on the problem together. Inform the audience of the temporary pause due to equipment failure, and they'll usually be entirely understanding whilst you sort out the difficulty. If you treat it as some kind of embarrassing secret they'll just wonder what's going on, and maybe get a bit impatient, which doesn't help anything. Work through the problem in a logical manner in the following order, trying out the simplest things first:

1 If there's been a complete and sudden loss of sound the most likely cause will be a failed connection of some description. So first of all try switching to another pickup in case the one you've been using has failed. This is rarely at fault, but it only takes a second to check out so do this before looking further.

2 The next check, and a far more likely culprit, will be a faulty guitar lead, so check that by simply replacing it with another one which you know to be functional. And if you're using any effects or other devices between guitar and amplifier, eliminate possible faults in this chain by connecting your guitar directly into the amp.

3 Next, although it sounds almost too obvious to mention, make certain than your guitar amp is still connected to its power source, both at the power point itself and also where the power lead meets the amp. If this appears OK, ensure that your amp is actually producing sound by plugging something else into it (spare guitar, microphone, whatever). If there's still no sound, but the amplifier power light is on, remember that the connection between amp and speakers may have failed.

4 If you still have no sound, and if any remaining doubt exists with regard to your guitar, just plug it directly (no effect pedals in between) into another amplifier, or perhaps the PA system, to ascertain that the instrument is actually functioning.

By this point you should know where the problem lies, either with your guitar, its amplifier or something in between. If the fault cannot be fixed easily you'll have to effect a compromise solution to get through the evening. It's usually possible to amplify your guitar through other equipment, and although the sound might not be as good it's a case of better than nothing. Any fault in the effects chain can be resolved by simply removing that particular unit from the signal path and making do without that effect.

The least likely problem is that your guitar output has completely packed up, which will almost certainly be a break in the wiring. If you or someone else in the band carries a spare guitar, that's great. Otherwise, if all pickups are non-functional and no alternative exists you'll have to take a longer break and check out the wiring. More information on this subject can be found on **pages 186–195**.

Your set list should be prepared in good time to avoid on-stage discussions (or even arguments) about which song to play next, and keep close to hand anything which you will, or might, need during the performance, such as capo, bottleneck slide and definitely several spare plectrums. Regarding the last, the usual practice is to have them located where you can quickly grab another when you accidentally drop the pick whilst actually playing. Common ploys used are tucking a few plectrums under the edge of the guitar scratchplate (see **page 195**) or attaching them to a microphone stand with sticky tape. Although a spare pick or two resting on top of your amp may seem close enough, this isn't very helpful if you happen to be singing into the microphone when the plectrum slips from your grasp.

Tune up in good time before going on stage so that you can just pick up your instruments and play immediately, which is what will normally be expected. Having said this, if there's a significant time-gap between tuning up and playing it's as well to check that your tuning is still accurate. This is because any change in temperature will cause the strings either to expand (if it gets warmer) or contract (if it gets colder), with predictable results on your guitar's pitch accuracy.

And finally, whilst I have it in mind, one other simple but rather essential point. If you're not using a wireless transmitter (see **page 202**), be certain to loop the cable around your guitar strap before plugging it into the instrument. This approach, pictured below, ensures that you won't accidentally unplug yourself whilst playing by inadvertently stepping on the wire trailing across the stage. It's a very old trick, but failure to adopt this simple precaution will certainly cause you embarrassment sooner or later.

CHAPTER 9

Maintenance and repair

Guitars are generally reliable and mostly trouble-free, but like any other mechanism they do require at least a very basic level of attention from time to time, and when that time comes you can either seek out the services of a guitar technician or go for the do-it-yourself approach. Some repair jobs are probably best left to experienced hands, but many things in need of attention are reasonably straightforward, and well within the capabilities of any competent individual. For a description of all guitar features that will be a necessary reference within this section, refer to page 195.

String changing

The simplest maintenance job you need to do on your instrument is changing the strings. This is something you really do have to manage yourself, simply because of the frequency with which it will occur. Apart from the regular string change necessary to keep your guitar in good playing order, it's likely that sometimes a string will break at a gig. When this happens you'll need to do the job quickly and efficiently, without pausing to consult a repair manual.

Although removal and fitting of strings isn't a complicated business, you might be surprised at how many guitar players make an unsatisfactory job of it. The most common error lies in untidy or insufficient winding of the string around the capstan, or tuning post. Take a look at the examples pictured below, to see the right and wrong ways this can be done.

Guitar strings themselves are of varying gauge (thickness), which is measured as thousandths of an inch. Reading from high (thin) to low (thick), a typical set of electric guitar strings might be 9 (first string), 11 (second string), 16 (third string), 24 (fourth string), 32 (fifth string) and 42 (sixth string). This is just one example, as various other gauge sets are available, or you can compile your own set from individual strings if you have some particular preference. String sets are commonly referred to by description of the thinnest string, so the above example would be a 'set of nines'.

The thinner strings are 'plain', which means that they have no coating such as the winding seen on the heavier strings, which is there to increase the string thickness as opposed to making extremely thick 'un-wound' strings.

Example 1 displays untidy winding, which not only looks messy but is also potentially unstable.

Example 2 is insufficiently wound around the capstan and will probably slip, which will result in loss of tuning.

Example 3 winds upward to the top of the post. This will create unnecessary stress on the capstan and machine head in general.

Example 4 shows how it should be done. This has sufficient winding which goes downward on the post, and with no messy string overlap. An effective and reliable fitting.

Traditionally, descriptions of steel string types fall into two basic categories, roundwound and flatwound. These terms apply to the outer string surface of the wound strings in the set, as can be observed by close examination of the thickest string. By far the most commonly used are the 'roundwound' variety, generally used by all rock, blues and country players. The 'flatwound' string type is somewhat softer in tone, and is sometimes preferred by jazz guitarists. If you do decide to try flatwounds – which are somewhat uncommon today – it will be necessary to specify this fact when you buy strings, or else you'll certainly be handed the more usual roundwound variety.

When fitting a complete set of new strings the first task, obviously, is removal of the old ones, in which regard there are basically two schools of thought. Some players prefer to remove and replace each string one at a time, in order to maintain a steady tension on the guitar neck, whilst others, including myself, will first remove the entire set, which affords the opportunity to give the area a good overall clean-up before fitting the new strings. If you do choose to remove all the strings remember to unwind them gradually as a set, so that a fairly even neck tension is maintained at all times.

Before you begin removal take care to notice exactly how the strings are fitted to your guitar at the bridge end. With so many different models available, it's wise to study the correct attachment method for your particular instrument, although a few basic fitting designs predominate, as you can see below.

Your own guitar will very likely feature one of these bridge designs or similar, simply because so many instruments have been based upon so few basic models. But if you do have something different, it isn't likely to present any problems for you to work out how the string fitting is arranged.

When you remove the old strings, be certain to dispose of them in a responsible manner, bearing in mind that they have sharp ends – especially the thinner strings – which would be rather painful to step on. It's also inadvisable to leave lengths of very strong wire laying around, which could be a risk to small children or animals. My own method is to wind them around in the same manner as that of the new string in its packet, and then place them in that same packet prior to disposal.

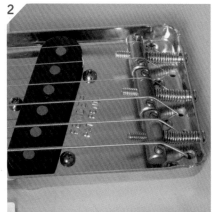
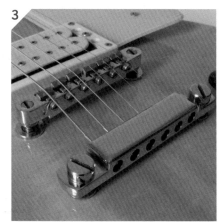
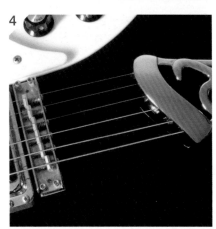

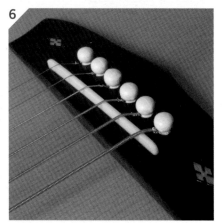

Fender Stratocaster (1) and Fender Telecaster (2) type bridges feature 'through the body' string fitting. Gibson Les Paul (3) and this Rickenbacker design (4) have a fitting separate from the bridge itself, over which the strings pass, but to which they are not attached. This 12-string electric guitar (5) has a combination of fittings to deal with the greater number of strings. Steel string acoustic guitars (6) have a bridge with holes into which the string ends are located, to be held in place by pins.

Acoustic guitar string change

In the case of an acoustic guitar, you should unwind the string before attempting to remove the bridge pin that secures the ball end in place (see illustration below). A specific tool for this can be obtained from a music store, or they can be gently lifted out with a pair of pliers. But take it easy, because they're only made of (usually) plastic, although wooden or metal bridge pins can afford superior tone if you care to purchase a set.

Notice that there's a difference between strings fitted to an acoustic guitar as opposed to an electric. Most obviously, the wound strings are of a different colour, which is because they have bronze windings instead of being nickel-wound. Also, acoustic strings are usually of substantially heavier gauge than electrics, with a typical set being something like 12 (first string), 16 (second string), 24 (third string), 32 (fourth string), 42 (fifth string) and 52 (sixth string). This heavier gauge is to generate greater volume and superior tone, with string bending not being regarded as much of a priority for acoustic playing. Incidentally, if you're more usually accustomed to playing an electric guitar, these heavier strings can be a bit rough on your fingers at first, although you do get used to them after a while.

At its other end the string is threaded through the hole in its appropriate capstan (tuning post) and bent sharply at an angle, as illustrated here. All strings will be longer than is strictly necessary for the job, so you'll be able to allow plenty of slack to wind securely around the post, as explained on **page 169**. The lower strings, being thicker, should be wound at least a couple of times on the post, whilst the thinner strings can be wound many more times, for secure and effective tuning stability.

Leaving the correct amount of slack for an appropriate winding of each string can be a bit hit and miss – there's either too much or too little. But if you find that you've over or underestimated the situation, just wind back a little, readjust and try again.

A word of warning here: as you're winding the strings accurately on to their posts there is a tendency to lean forward, over the machine head, to check on the winding. As you do so, be very careful of any excess string length, which can give you a vicious poke in the eye if you're not careful. With this hazard in mind, I always put a bend near the string end (see photo above right) to reduce its sharpness and therefore the danger of accidental stabbing.

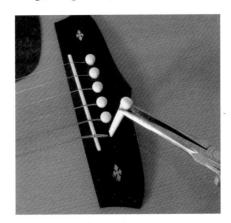

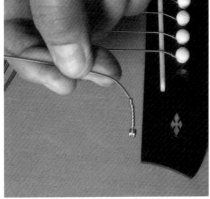

1 Release tension on the strings first, and then remove the pins that secure each string into its location at the bridge. These are all held in place by pressure alone, as they're tapered to ensure a snug fit into their respective holes. Almost certainly they'll be too tight to lift out with your fingers, so the careful use of a suitable tool will be required. These pins are generally durable, but will occasionally snap under pressure; so it's useful to carry a spare set in your guitar case, and absolutely essential if you're actually gigging at the time.

2 Before locating the ball end of each new string into its hole, it's helpful to put a bend in the string near to the end, as shown here. This is to reduce the likelihood of the string popping back out, along with the bridge pin, when you tighten the string up to its correct pitch tension.

3 Place the string into the appropriate hole and replace the pin, pressing down firmly as far as it will go. Although the pins, and indeed the holes, are of a standard size it sometimes happens that, for various reasons, pins may become loose and won't retain a secure fit. If this happens, try another pin from the spare set which you've no doubt purchased for such an occasion.

All strings should be wound from top to bottom of the post, with the winding going to the inside and not the other way round – ie the string should tighten (go up in pitch) when you turn the key anticlockwise. When you're satisfied that all strings are wound securely, with the correct tension for pitch, snip off the excess ends with wire cutters and dispose of safely.

New strings have quite a lot of 'stretch' in them which, when played, causes the guitar to go out of tune rather quickly. So the solution to this problem is to deliberately stretch them yourself before actually playing, which is really a very simple procedure, as illustrated below.

This action is necessary for all six strings (or 12 in the case of 12-string guitars – see **page 173**), and applies to both acoustic guitar strings and electrics, although in both cases you'll probably find that the lower strings have more stretch in them than the thinner strings.

Although this stretching might appear to be a bit abusive toward your lovely new set of strings, and would seem to create a risk of breakage, neither is actually the case. The fact is that guitar strings, particularly when new, are incredibly durable, and any new string which actually does break under such circumstances is most likely faulty in the first place, and would soon have snapped under normal playing pressure.

If you don't bother to stretch a new set of strings they'll gradually stretch anyway in their own good time. This will, however, be extremely inconvenient to you, because you'll spend most of your playing time out of tune, and intermittently retuning throughout your performance, the entertainment value of which is likely to be rather lost on you, your fellow musicians and your audience.

When the strings are tuned up to correct pitch, take a firm hold of any string and pull it away from the fretboard. Repeat this action at varying points along the entire length of that string to ensure that it's evenly stretched overall.

When you check the tuning again you'll find that this particular string is significantly out of tune, having dropped noticeably in pitch. Retune the string and repeat the procedure several times, as necessary. When the string no longer requires tuning back up again, it is sufficiently stretched for playing stability.

Electric guitar string change

Many of the same rules apply here as when dealing with acoustic string changes, except that the method of attachment at the bridge will be different.

If you check the pictures on **page 170** you'll see that the strings for Fender guitars and their many imitations are usually fitted through the body, from the guitar's rear. Other designs are removed from a tailpiece on the face of the instrument. These types of design usually have parts that are secured in place only by the pressure of the strings themselves, and will therefore come away when all the strings are removed, as illustrated by the photograph right, which displays a Rickenbacker 330 bridge and tailpiece.

This isn't a problem, as these parts are easily refitted and held secure once the new strings are in place. But be aware of these 'unsecured' pieces of hardware, to avoid having them dropping off unexpectedly and possibly becoming damaged.

Reattach the new set of strings in the appropriate manner for your guitar, and wind them accurately on to the machine heads as described in the section relating to acoustics.

Newly fitted strings will have a slightly different tonal quality compared to the old strings that you have been accustomed to hearing. This might surprise you after your very first string change, with their somewhat brighter and more twangy character, and actually some people find this sound rather pleasing, so that they tend to fit a new set of strings for any special occasion, such as recording. But whether or not you like this particular sound it doesn't last for very long, and after a fairly short time of being played the more familiar 'played-in' tone will be re-established.

Exactly how often a set of guitar strings should be changed is another matter of widely differing opinion. It's true that some bands (with money to spare/waste) change strings – or, more likely, get their roadies to change strings – before every gig. And it's equally true that some players don't bother to fit new strings until it becomes unavoidable due to breakage, or until the old strings are so coated in rust and dirt that even moderate tuning accuracy becomes a lost cause.

The sensible approach is to wipe clean your strings after each playing session or gig, because you'll be surprised at how much dirt can be acquired, particularly in warm playing conditions where perspiration is an issue. This will maximise the realistic working life of the strings, and also keep them clean and pleasant to use. String life overall depends upon how much they're played, so in that sense there's no precise rule about when to change them. But, as a rough guide, assuming you play one gig every week and practise an hour per day in between, it's not a bad idea to fit a new set every month to six weeks.

Some guitar headstocks, notably those with all six machine heads on one side, have so-called 'string trees', or guides under which certain strings should pass (see picture above), and without which the result would be unnecessary stress on the headstock and machine heads. They secure the strings firmly between the nut (see page 178) and machine heads and, although simple in design, are important. They cause the string to 'break' firmly over the nut, whilst also meeting the tuning capstan at an angle suitable for efficient winding and secure tuning.

12-string guitars

In the case of 12-string instruments the strings are set in pairs, as illustrated in the picture here, and which can also be noted from the bridge close-up on **page 170** (example 5). Each pair consists of one string of the usual approximate gauge and with standard tuning, alongside another string which, on the lower four strings, is tuned one octave higher, whilst the two upper string pairs are tuned in unison.

As a general rule the higher, thinner strings are the uppermost of the pair (from the player's point of view), as can be clearly seen here. This is standard procedure for most 12-string guitar set-ups, although the Rickenbacker Company do employ the reverse approach.

When buying strings for any 12-string guitar, you can, as with the standard six strings, either purchase a ready-made set (consisting of six pairs), or perhaps buy a standard six-string set and then match the upper octave strings yourself. Either way, it's not a bad idea to buy an extra 'upper third' string whilst you're at it, because due to the necessities of tuning it to a high **G** pitch this string needs to be extremely thin, and is therefore inclined toward breakage.

With this potential hazard in mind, I tend to avoid stretching this particular string after fitting, partly because the risk of breaking it is too great, but also because such an extremely thin string has very little in the way of excess stretchability anyway.

A useful ploy with 12-string guitars (to avoid string breaks) is to tune all strings a semitone lower than usual (see **page 153**), and then perhaps apply a capo in order to enjoy the benefits of open-string chords.

Machine heads

Also referred to as tuning heads, or simply tuners, these remarkable examples of small engineering are both extremely efficient and generally reliable – so much so that I personally can't recall having ever experienced any significant problem with them, on any guitar of moderate quality. This is because in recent years most manufacturers have fitted the fully enclosed, permanently lubricated type, as opposed to the 'open' variety, which are clearly vulnerable to damage, dirt and rust. Both types are pictured below.

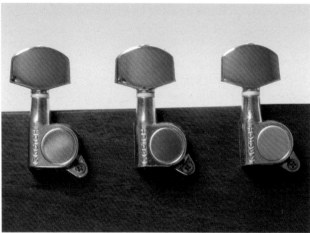

The machine heads pictured above (top) are fitted as two complete units of three per side. Fitted to a metal plate, the mechanism and gearing are clearly visible. Although convenient to see, therefore enabling you to understand their construction, they're somewhat inconveniently exposed to any potential damage. The example immediately above displays an enclosed gearing design of individual unit machine heads, which are more or less failsafe and protected from the outside world.

Due to the fact that tuning is a rather exacting business, it's necessary for good quality machine heads to work to a very high degree of precision. So although gear ratios vary somewhat, anything above 10:1 would be considered suitable for satisfactory tuning accuracy. This means that for every ten complete turns of the winding mechanism, the actual tuning post (the part with the string wrapped around it) will turn once.

If, for any reason, you find it necessary to replace machine heads, it's obviously simpler to replace those fitted individually, because the other type will need to be replaced in sets of three, and will therefore be 'spaced' in a predetermined and unalterable way – and unless you're lucky enough to obtain a new set which has the same distance of spacing between each tuner, they won't fit into the headstock of your guitar. This would create numerous difficulties in making significant adjustments to the headstock itself, which would be a lot of work and inconvenience in order to obtain a satisfactory result. So if this situation does arise, my recommendation would be to purchase an entirely new set of individual unit machine heads, and fit them in place of the old ones. At worst this will only require that you fill the old screw holes and possibly enlarge the capstan holes somewhat, to permit access for the new ones.

Old screw holes can easily be filled by cutting slim strips of moderately hard wood that will fit into the holes. These fillings can be coated with wood glue and inserted carefully, where they'll provide a strong and solid base for any necessary drilling. If you do any drilling, remember to 'stop' the drill bit so that it doesn't go all the way through, and thereby impair the appearance of the front of your guitar headstock. When the glue has dried, any bits of wood sticking obtrusively out of the holes can be trimmed level with a sharp knife.

The individual machine heads are often secured in place only by the nut around its capstan, in which case they'll be 'locked' into position by a small protrusion that fits into a hole in the rear of the headstock, as will be self-evident by the design of the unit, an example of which can be seen at the top of the page.

Checking and adjusting the action

The 'action' of a guitar describes its general state of adjustment, in terms of how playable it is. So a guitar with good action is considered to be one which feels comfortable and well set-up for optimum efficiency and ease of use. By contrast, poor action can render an essentially well-made instrument virtually unplayable even for a skilled guitarist, and an impossibility for the beginner.

A good deal of this good action/bad action controversy concerns the height of the strings, with regard to their proximity to the fingerboard. This particular feature is commonly referred to as either 'high action' or 'low action', and examples of both can be seen here.

Both types of setting have their virtues or otherwise: a high action gives cleaner tone (because there's little chance of strings touching the frets as they vibrate), but is harder to play, whereas a low action is easy to play (because it's easier to press the strings down on to the fretboard), but any hard strumming or picking can cause strings to rattle against the frets. It's probably true to say that most players lean toward a relatively low action, whilst keeping in mind that moderation is usually the best compromise.

If you decide that the action on your guitar is unsatisfactory, there are several areas of adjustment that, individually or collectively (depending upon where the problem is), can correct the situation. But this assumes that the guitar itself is essentially in good working order – in other words, undamaged. If you purchased the guitar from new, this will almost certainly be the case; but if, for whatever reason, a new instrument does have a fault, take advantage of the guarantee to have any problems corrected.

If you've acquired a second-hand guitar on which the action can't be adjusted, as will be explained in the following sections of this book, then the fault is most likely to be a twisted neck. This unfortunate situation is visually apparent if you look down the neck from the headstock point of view, as some of the frets won't run parallel to the others as they should. If you compare the two pictures (right) you can see how this appears.

If you're unlucky enough to experience this problem, which is usually caused by storing the guitar in damp conditions, you'll need to refer the job to a skilled guitar repair technician, although even then the only remedy is likely to be a replacement neck. Needless to say, you should check any potential second-hand purchase for this possibility, and hold on to your money if a guitar neck appears at all doubtful. Working from the likelihood that all is basically OK, but in need of some adjustment, setting the action on a guitar depends upon the appropriate interaction between three basic components: the nut, the bridge and the truss rod.

Low action

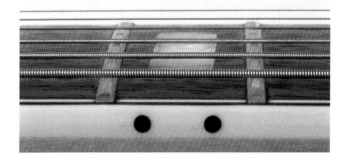

High action

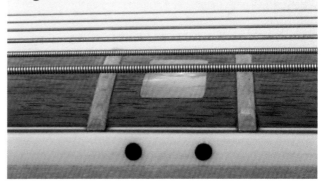

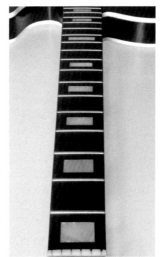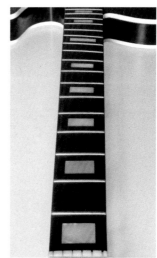

The example above left is a guitar neck in good condition, with all frets laying parallel to each other over the full distance of the fretboard. However, the other example shows that this alignment fails to maintain its consistency, becoming apparent around the 12th fret, due to a distortion in the guitar neck.

Truss rod adjustment

A set of steel strings, when tuned to concert pitch (see **page 5**), will exert a considerable force on the neck of a guitar. For this reason a metal rod is fitted within the neck itself, to counteract pressures that would otherwise cause distortion and damage. This is called a truss rod, and is adjustable in terms of the precise degree of tension required to balance out a particular set of strings, bearing in mind that a set of heavy-gauge strings exert greater force than lighter strings, simply because they need to be tightened more to attain pitch.

If you look just casually along the edge of your fretboard it does visually appear as if the neck is perfectly straight, although in fact this isn't usually the case, nor should it be for optimum playing efficiency. A well-adjusted truss rod should be set so that the neck, under normal string tension, is very slightly curved, in order that the strings can vibrate freely without touching the frets.

The slight dip in the neck (which shouldn't be confused with the entirely different matter of a twisted neck), is most apparent around the 7th fret, and can be visually detected if you run a straight edge along the frets between fret 1 near the nut, and the fret located where the neck meets the body. This is around fret 16/17 on a Fender Stratocaster, for example, but will vary according to the design of your particular guitar. Upon careful inspection you will, when the rod is correctly adjusted, notice a very small gap where the straight edge doesn't quite touch the frets at this midway point (fret 7).

If you don't have a reliable straight edge for reference, the popular technique is to use the string itself, by applying a capo at the first fret and then pressing the string down manually at the 'body fret' described above. This will certainly provide an extremely accurate straight edge for you to check the neck curvature, and is easiest to see by using the lowest, and therefore thickest, string for this purpose.

There is no exact measurement that determines the precision of the truss rod adjustment, in terms of the actual amount of curvature required, so most people are inclined to adjust it entirely

as a matter of what 'feels' right. However, as a guide for you to consider what sort of degrees we're talking about here, a light to medium-gauge plectrum would slip between (7th) fret and straight edge without difficulty. So this is a fairly small gap, but nonetheless significant for maximum efficiency of operation. And if the gap appears too small, perhaps even non-existent, or alternately too great, then you must effect an adjustment to the truss rod.

First you'll need to locate the adjuster, and ensure that you have the correct tool for the job, which is usually a hexagonal (Allen) key, but can be otherwise according to the make of guitar. In the majority of cases you'll find the adjuster location to be at the base of the headstock, probably concealed by a small cover. Some alternatives can be seen in the pictures below.

If you purchased the guitar from new, it's not uncommon for an appropriate adjuster key to be included with the instrument. But if not, any reasonably comprehensive tool distributor can sell you the correct item, which can be of either metric or US (non-metric) size, depending upon the instrument's country of origin and vintage. Do be careful to ensure that the tool fits correctly, because truss rod adjusters can sometimes be a bit hard to turn, and a loose-fitting Allen key or spanner would very likely cause damage that could render any further adjustment practically impossible, even with the correct tool.

The adjustment itself is simple. To increase the neck relief (gap between 7th fret and straight edge), loosen the truss rod by turning the screw thread anticlockwise; to reduce the neck relief, turn the screw thread clockwise. A truss rod is unlikely to require more than a small adjustment, so do it very gradually by approximately quarter turns, whilst checking on the change in neck relief each time. Remember that good action depends upon other factors also, and if the truss rod does appear to need further adjustment later you can usually do so without much inconvenience.

In the rare event that a truss rod thread is too stiff to be turned under moderate pressure, you should refer the situation to a skilled guitar technician, rather than risk causing expensive damage to the rod, or perhaps even to the neck itself.

Above left is a standard design for truss rod concealment as exemplified by the Stratocaster design, along with many others. Whilst the adjustment area is the same, the Rickenbacker guitar has two truss rods, which should be adjusted by equal degrees for correct tension balance.

There are also occasions when a truss rod adjuster is located at the other end of the guitar neck, as seen in the acoustic guitar above, where access is gained through the sound hole. Rather more inconvenient is the example above right, where the neck must be removed to reach the truss rod adjuster.

Bridge height adjustment

Although there are several designs for the guitar bridge, most are relatively easy to adjust on an electric guitar, whereas the acoustic guitar bridge requires a certain amount of care and DIY skill. So let's begin by taking a look at some of the most commonplace bridge types.

As with any adjustment regarding comfortable action, there are no specific measurements involved in adjusting the bridge height. If it feels right to you, and produces a good sound, then it is right. However, if you do feel that the bridge on your guitar is in need of some adjustment, the job (at least where electrics are concerned) isn't hard to do.

If, before starting, you suspect that the nut (see next section) is of questionable accuracy, it may be helpful to apply a capo at the first fret, because this will establish a satisfactory level at the nut end of the fingerboard.

The basic principle of bridge height adjustment is to achieve a string level which doesn't vary too much along the overall length of the neck, although it will usually be the case that the strings are closest to the frets at the nut, and gradually move slightly further away as they go higher up the neck. Also keep in mind that the neck on most guitars has a slight camber to it, and so the bridge must be set in sympathy with this contour. On a Les Paul type bridge this will be taken care of already by the design of the bridge unit itself, and will therefore present no problems, providing you adjust each side equally.

The individual bridge saddles on the Stratocaster bridge type require slightly more attention in this regard, so that collectively they also follow the neck camber. These height differences aren't considerable, because the neck camber is only slight, but they're significant in terms of playing comfort and, to some extent, pickup response. It simply means that the outer string saddles (strings one and six) are set lowest, with strings two and five saddles set slightly higher, followed logically by the saddles for strings three and four set highest of all. This is really just common sense, and again you should be careful to adjust each saddle by the same degree, which will maintain the original profile matching the shape of the neck.

If you're not satisfied that the bridge saddles are already accurate in terms of matching the neck camber, the easiest way to check on this is by making a visual assessment of the situation. This can be done by simply sighting along the strings from the rear end of your guitar. From this angle you'll be able to see the staggered heights of the saddles quite clearly, and assess the situation to decide whether any change is required. If so, make small adjustments, starting from the two centre saddles (strings three and four), which should be more or less even, and working gradually downward in height from there.

Although a low action is a generally attractive proposition, you should also check intermittently from the playing perspective, because excessively low set strings will not only be inclined toward fret buzz, but may also make string bending difficult. This is because your fingers will slip over the top of the strings, and be unable to grip well for bending. So, not too low, OK?

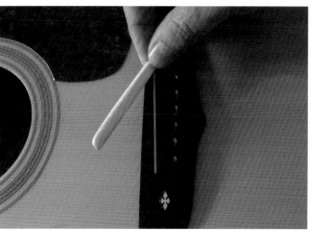

The Les Paul design (top) is easiest to adjust, because it's a single-piece unit sitting on two screw-thread adjuster wheels, one at either end of the bridge.

The Fender style bridge, on the other hand, is a bit more complicated in that it consists of six individual saddle units, each of which must be adjusted as a separate piece, by means of a very small Allen key. Each saddle is situated upon two correspondingly tiny screws, which should be turned by equal amounts to raise or lower as required.

The acoustic guitar strings (left) rest on a simple one-piece saddle, which can be easily removed from its seating location. There is no designated adjuster mechanism, but it can be trimmed carefully if the strings are set too high. Alternately it can either be raised by shims or replaced if they're too low.

The bridge of an acoustic steel string guitar isn't ideally suited to adjustment, but if necessary this can be done by removing the piece of plastic or other material upon which the strings rest, as seen on the previous page. It's then possible to reduce the height of the string action, either by carefully sanding down the base of the saddle, which will reduce all string levels equally, or by increasing the depth of the usually very slight groove in which each string sits.

Alteration to the saddle base is something that must be done with considerable accuracy, or the base may not be seated firmly along its entire length. This will have an adverse effect upon the resonance of sound quality, because the strings won't be properly in contact (albeit indirectly) with the guitar body. It's especially problematic if your guitar is electric/acoustic, in which case its

contact transducer (see **pages 187–88**) will most likely be located at this position, and poor contact will again affect sound quality and also volume. So if you have any doubt about your ability to achieve a perfectly even finish to the saddle base, it's probably safer to attempt saddle depth reduction across the upper edge. This might be a bit more time-consuming, but it's a safer option for the inexperienced hand.

Neither option should be attempted without some reservations, because even if done with accuracy this type of adjustment is clearly irreversible, and if you overdo it the only satisfactory remedy is to replace the saddle piece itself. So if you're unhappy with the string height on your acoustic guitar, I recommend exploring the other options (truss rod, nut) first, adjusting the bridge saddle only if entirely necessary.

The nut

I've left this for last because, like the saddle of an acoustic guitar, adjustment to the nut is very easy to get wrong, and hard to put right. Having said that, it's been my experience that many new guitars tend to have the strings riding too high over the nut, and are therefore likely to be in need of some attention.

If you press down any string at the first fret it will be pretty obvious whether or not the action is difficult at this location. Assuming you've already satisfied any doubts regarding the truss rod or bridge, then the problem rests with the nut. But before making any changes here it's helpful to get a clearer picture of exactly how things are supposed to be. So let's try the following method of assessment.

Fit your capo at the 1st fret (if you don't have a capo you can check this by holding down the bass string manually), and then look closely at the degree of string-to-fret clearance at the 2nd fret which, because of the capo, is effectively the first playing fret. You'll see that's it's fairly close, but with sufficient room for the strings to vibrate freely without rattling against the frets. In this situation you would have a low, comfortable action for playing chords, and it's especially beneficial for bar chords.

Now, remove the capo and check the string clearance again, this time at the 1st fret. If the nut's already well adjusted the strings should be only slightly higher than they were at fret 2 when the capo was fitted. And similarly, the playing action at this fret should be equally comfortable, even for bar chords. However, if there's a significant difference in action, with greater playing effort required, then your guitar nut definitely needs attention.

Each of the strings will be seated into a narrow groove, the width of which approximately equals the diameter of its accompanying string. So if you intend to recess these grooves further, to lower the string height, you'll need suitable tools for the job. These will normally comprise a set of fine 'needle files', which will provide a size range to cover all six (or possibly twelve) strings.

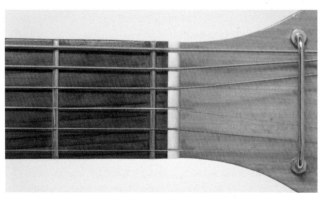

The usual situation is as seen in the upper picture, whereby the depth of the grooves in the nut will determine string height in this area of the fretboard. However, there's a less common situation, as illustrated in the lower photograph. This guitar has a 'zero fret' adjacent to the nut, which, although not apparent from this angle, sits higher than all the other frets. This fret will, therefore, determine the string height, because the nut grooves are (or should be) cut lower than the zero fret. In this situation the grooves in the nut act as string guides only, and providing you ensure that all strings are in fact resting firmly on the zero fret no problems are likely to occur regarding the nut itself.

Although apparently straightforward, this particular job shouldn't be undertaken too casually, because the nut and its correct adjustment are crucial to the efficient working of your guitar.

Each string recess should be angled slightly downward in the direction of the headstock. This will ensure that the string itself has one, and only one, definite point of contact with the nut, which, for accurate tuning, should be where it meets the fretboard. This will ensure correct 'scale length', this being the distance over which an open string can vibrate – in other words, the distance between nut and bridge.

Carefully file the groove in a straight line with, in each case, a needle file no wider than that dictated by the original groove width. Keep in mind that this task should be done with extreme caution, because it's very easy to overdo the depth required and so end up with a string rattling against the 1st fret. And I do emphasise that this is very likely to happen if you're at all impatient. So you must keep checking the string to 1st fret level, and resist any temptation to rush the job by doing too much filing between 'fittings'.

If you've released tension (even partially) on the strings, in order to remove them easily from the nut, remember that this will also ease the curvature of the neck because of reduced tension on the truss rod (see **page 176**). This will have a significant influence upon your assessment of the string clearance from the frets, so don't forget to retune the strings to correct pitch before checking the results of your work.

When you're reasonably satisfied that all string recesses in the nut are comfortably playable, try to resist the temptation of going too far. Instead, try playing the guitar as normal for a week or so, to see how it feels under realistic working conditions. You can always trim a bit more later on if necessary.

If, for whatever reason, the nut grooves are cut too low, then you'll have to replace the nut with a new one. Most music stores stock a variety of pre-cut nuts, in various sizes, and if you take the old one with you it's just a case of finding a matching size, including string spacing (the distance from one string to the next), which can be trimmed as necessary.

Removing the old nut from your guitar is usually not at all difficult, as they're only glued lightly in place. Some are set into a groove, in which case the method I always use is to place the head of a suitably sized screwdriver under the edge of the nut, and tap gently upward until the nut comes away. In another design the nut isn't set into a groove at all, but merely seated at the very end of the fretboard. This makes things even easier – you simply place the screwdriver head behind the nut and tap in a forward direction for removal. Both situations are pictured below. In either case, before replacing with a new nut remember to clean the area of any debris, such as remains of the old glue, so as to ensure a smooth, clean surface for the new nut.

Cutting a new nut

It may be necessary for you to make an entirely new nut from a completely blank piece of material. This will occur if you can't find an appropriate 'pre-cut' type (which is more than likely if you have a left-handed guitar), or if you wish to upgrade from the standard nut already fitted to one made of a superior material, such as brass. In this situation you can acquire a suitable 'blank' for the purpose. These are usually a bit harder to find, compared to the pre-cut type, but are available from the more comprehensive music shops or online.

The new blank piece of bone, graphite, brass or whatever should be made using your old nut as the pattern. First cut it slightly oversize using a hand saw, and then form the more exact shape by securing it in a vice and using a variety of files to contour the shape as required. Take your time over this because you'll want it to be seated snugly into the groove (as applicable), to ensure the best possible fit.

To obtain a smooth finish, I always use progressively finer grades of wet and dry abrasive paper, which will leave it smooth but with a matt finish. If you're dealing with a non-absorbent material like brass

the nut can be polished up nicely by using a mild liquid abrasive, such as metal polish. However, in the case of an absorbent material like bone this would be inadvisable, in which case you can gloss it up with a fine grade wire wool, or alternately a piece of clean rag, and then simply polish it with enthusiasm and considerable patience.

To cut the grooves accurately (using needle files), mark their respective positions using the original nut as your guide and, although it's easier to get started with the nut still secured in the vice, the finer detail of correct groove depth should always be completed with the nut fitted to your guitar. Any general-purpose glue will suffice for attachment, because the nut will, in practice, be very firmly held in place by the strings themselves. Refer to the information on the previous page, and remember again to use the original nut as your guide to the correct string spacing and groove width. The grooves needn't be too deep, providing that when tuned to pitch/tension they're sufficient to prevent the strings from popping out, especially when string bending.

Intonation

Correct intonation refers to the guitar's ability to play notes of accurate pitch at every fret position along the entire length of its neck. For this reason it's obvious that the position of each fret is absolutely crucial, and with any well-made instrument great care is indeed taken to ensure the accuracy of fret placement. So with all frets where they should be, and with a reliable tuning reference ensuring that you tune each open string with failsafe precision, it's hard to see how anything could possibly go wrong. Unfortunately there's just one more potential pitfall that can interfere with this happy state of musical affairs, but it's one that can usually be corrected with relative ease.

If you think about an open string, you're looking at a perfectly straight length of wire that will unfailingly play the note to which it's tuned. In the case of the lowest string this will normally be an E note; then if you were to press down that string at the 12th fret you're effectively shortening its vibrating length by half, which will then also produce an E note, but one which should be precisely one octave higher than that of the open string. However, when you fret a note, at any location, something interesting occurs to the string itself. In pressing it downward against the fretboard you're actually bending the string very slightly, out of its otherwise perfectly straight alignment. And you know what happens to a string when it's bent (see **pages 73–80** if you don't). Yes, that's right, it goes upward in pitch. And of course, the higher the action the further it must be pressed to meet the fretboard, which causes an even greater degree of bend and therefore pitch change. With a well-adjusted action this bend won't be very great, but it will be significant in causing the fretted note to be ever so slightly sharp of its intended true pitch. And any discrepancies of this type will also tend to become more apparent as you go progressively higher up the neck.

For this reason the bridge saddles of an electric guitar are adjustable in a horizontal, as well as vertical, direction (see photo). Correct adjustment of the bridge allows you to compensate for this 'bending' situation by moving back the saddles just enough to counteract the effect of such unintentional string bending.

Although bridge designs vary somewhat, the method of adjustment is more or less identical in all cases, and will be fairly apparent upon examination of the bridge on your own instrument. There's an established formula for working out the correct saddle position for each string, for which you'll require a suitably sized screwdriver, as illustrated here, and a reliable pitch reference source such as an electronic guitar tuner. The method for correct adjustment is perfectly straightforward, requiring no specialised skills, and is as described here.

1 Begin with all strings tuned up to standard pitch.

2 Play a 12th fret harmonic (E) on the sixth string, and take careful note of the exact pitch reading, as displayed on your electronic tuner. If you're unfamiliar with how to produce harmonics refer to pages 93–95.

3 Now, press down the same string at the 12th fret, play the note, and again check the exact pitch reading on your tuner.

4 If the harmonic note and the fretted note produce exactly the same pitch reading, then the intonation is correct on that particular string, and you can move on to check the next one. However, if there's any difference whatsoever between the harmonic and the fretted note, read on.

5 If the fretted note reads higher than the harmonic, you should move that string's bridge saddle back slightly (away from the direction of the neck), and recheck until both notes read the same.

6 If the fretted note reads lower than the harmonic, you should move the saddle forward slightly (toward the neck) until both notes are of identical pitch.

7 Continue to repeat this process until all strings have been similarly adjusted, at which point your guitar intonation will be correct.

Notice that when you adjust any bridge saddle the overall pitch of that string will be altered. You may then wish to retune the string before making further adjustment. But note, for your convenience, that it's not essential to continually retune the open string to exact pitch, which can be tediously time-consuming when setting intonation. It's only necessary that both harmonic note and fretted note, when compared, should be of the same pitch, although they don't have to be at perfect concert pitch during this procedure.

Sometimes the bridge saddles, especially on the lower strings, might not move back quite far enough, because of the tension spring behind the screw, which can take up too much of the available adjustment range. In this instance I've always found it perfectly acceptable to remove any inconvenient springs, as seen on strings five and six in this picture on the following page, to allow for greater saddle adjustability.

You should be aware that old and worn-out strings can never be expected to attain satisfactory intonation. So if your strings have

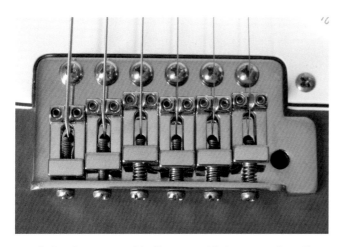

seen better days you need to fit a new set before even attempting the procedure described above.

Special mention should be made of the bridge saddle layout on the Fender Telecaster which, traditionally (it doesn't apply to all models), has the six strings set in pairs over three saddles (as pictured on **page 170**), so that instead of each string

being separately adjustable these instruments feature a 'shared' arrangement, whereby strings one and two are resting on one saddle, strings three and four share a saddle, and strings five and six likewise. Needless to say, where this situation exists a certain amount of compromise must be the answer when setting the intonation.

The recommended method for adjusting a three-saddle Telecaster bridge is to work from one particular string of each pair. So, when adjusting for the two upper strings you check, and make settings to, the first string. On the middle pair, adjust for the fourth string. Finally, check and adjust string number six for the lowest two strings.

Acoustic guitar bridges are non-adjustable, being pre-set so that the lower strings are set slightly further back compared to the higher strings. This is generally considered acceptable, assuming the overall bridge height isn't excessive. Also, any differences are less apparent than would be the case on an electric guitar because the traditional design of acoustics does tend to limit any likelihood of playing high up the neck, and will therefore naturally minimise the demands upon very exacting intonation setting.

Frets

Should you experience any general tuning or intonation problems, it's unlikely that the cause will turn out to be related to the frets. In my experience any halfway decent instrument can usually be relied upon to be fitted with an accurately positioned set of frets.

The rule for fret placement, although critical, is actually pretty straightforward, and depends upon measuring the scale length (distance between nut and bridge) and then continually dividing that distance by 18. Bearing in mind that the scale length (around 25in or 63.5cm for acoustics, and slightly longer for electrics) of each string varies somewhat for the reasons of intonation setting described earlier, this measurement is generally taken from the first-string distance between nut and bridge.

If you were fitting a full set of frets yourself, the first action would be to divide (mathematically speaking) this scale length by 18, and then fit the 1st fret in position at 1/18 of the total distance, nearest the nut. You would next divide the remaining distance – that is, between the newly fitted 1st fret and the bridge – by 18, and fit your 2nd fret in position accordingly. You would then divide the distance between this 2nd fret and the bridge by 18, and fit the 3rd fret in position, and so it would continue until all frets were accurately in place along the entire length of the neck. By this method the length being divided will obviously diminish with every fret, which therefore clearly explains (to those of an enquiring mind) why the frets become progressively closer together as they move higher up the neck.

This is a very generalised description of the exacting process of actually fitting frets correctly. In fact the division measurement is very fractionally less than 18, although the difference involved is

so small it can hardly be measured. With this in mind, there are certain checks and balances referred to as the operation proceeds, such as being aware that the 12th fret should be precisely at the halfway point, and the 7th fret two-thirds of the distance from nut to fret 12. Resorting to these reference points helps prevent any gradual accumulation of error which might otherwise occur by sticking too rigidly to the 'division of 18' rule.

In more general terms, fret care falls into two categories. There's the possibility of jagged or very slightly overhanging edges, which is sometimes the case in a lower price-range instrument; and, rather inevitably, there is fret wear caused by constant pressure and friction from the strings. Clearly, any rough edges can make the guitar uncomfortable, or perhaps even painful, to play, but fortunately the solution is well within the ability of anyone possessing basic DIY skills. All you need is a fine file (not too rough) and some masking tape.

Use the masking tape to protect the area around the problem fret and, as shown here, carefully file down the excess fret overhang at a slight angle. As you do this, it's quite likely that you'll also wear through the masking tape, so be ready to renew this as necessary to avoid risk of damage to the adjacent woodwork.

Any fret wear caused by time and the consequent string indentations will be slightly more problematic. In this case it eventually becomes necessary to replace some, or all, of the frets. The first few frets, near the nut, are usually the most heavily worn, simply because this area of the neck generally gets played more than higher up.

Removal and replacement of frets isn't a job for the amateur, because of the risk of damage to the fretboard – unless you really do know what you're doing, in which case you probably won't need my advice anyway. Otherwise this job should definitely be referred to a specialist.

As a matter of more routine maintenance you can, and in my opinion should, clean and polish the frets from time to time with very fine grade wire wool. This is best done when changing the strings, so that all strings are removed for easy working. As always the fretboard should be protected with masking tape, which is easily removed when work is completed. Then the fretboard itself can be pampered. Rosewood (dark-coloured, as pictured on the previous page) can be treated with either lemon oil or almond oil, which can be easily applied with cotton wool and will protect the wood from the risk of dehydration over time. My own approach is to apply the oil – without overdoing it, incidentally – and then leave it overnight to be absorbed into the wood before actually playing the guitar. Maple (light-coloured wood, as pictured above right) doesn't require such treatment.

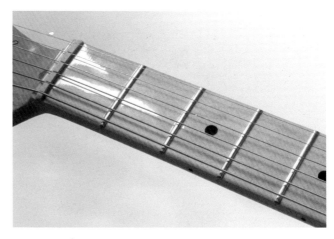

If you should own a guitar with a coated or lacquered fretboard (usually evident simply by its slightly glossy appearance, as in the case of the Telecaster pictured here), no abrasion or oil of any type should ever be applied during fret and neck cleaning. Instead, this type of neck can be polished up in the same manner as the guitar body. Enthusiastic buffing with a soft cloth usually does the job in both cases.

When attempting to polish any part of your guitar, don't use any sort of liquid abrasive, such as Brasso or T-Cut. Although these will certainly produce an excellent shine their abrasive action means that if used over any length of time they'll gradually wear away the surface coating on your guitar body. For this reason products of this nature are definitely not recommended for cleaning your beloved guitar. Always opt instead for a non-abrasive polish or, my personal choice, a soft clean rag and a few minutes' hard work.

Tremolo (vibrato) adjustment

As briefly explained elsewhere in this book (page 203), a so-called 'tremolo arm' is, in fact, a vibrato device. The simple distinction is this: tremolo refers to a fluctuation in volume, whereas any fluctuation of pitch, such as that afforded by this mechanism, is more correctly termed 'vibrato'. However, this incorrect description is so widely used and long-established that it's hard to avoid, simply for reasons of convenience.

There are essentially two principle designs for these devices: the Bigsby unit and the Fender design. Bigsby 'tremolo' units and their numerous variants, such as the model pictured here, are mounted on to the face of a guitar, and if required can be fitted to an instrument that wouldn't normally possess one, such as a Gibson Les Paul or a Fender Telecaster.

The Fender Stratocaster version, in contrast to the Bigsby, is actually 'built in' to the instrument, with a design integral to the guitar body itself. These models require slightly more in the way of general maintenance, due to an occasional need to adjust spring tension via the rear body plate, as can be seen on the next page.

The principle involved is ingenious, and something of a design classic, although not complicated to understand once you're aware of its method of operation. The tremolo 'block', through which the strings pass from rear to front, is held steady by two opposing forces: the string tension pulls it forward, whilst the

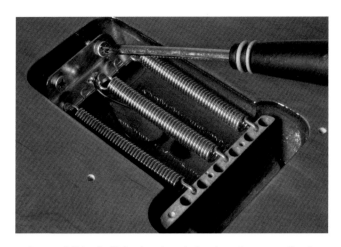

springs pull it back. String tension obviously varies, according to the pitch required for normal tuning, and also according to the gauge of strings fitted to any particular instrument. Consequently the springs are also adjustable, by means of the screws securing them to the inner body. So in order to adjust spring tension you need only turn these screws (as pictured above) either clockwise or anticlockwise as necessary.

Looking at the front body surface of the guitar (see picture above right), the Fender-type bridge/tremolo mechanism is at its most stable when seated flat against the guitar. This is easily achieved by tensioning all springs to sufficiently counterbalance the opposing pull of the strings when tuned to working pitch. But it's unwise to over-tighten these springs, because this would make it difficult to operate the tremolo with a comfortable degree of pressure action on the bar.

Begin by tightening all (usually three) springs so as to hold the bridge against the body – taking care to adjust the screws by equal degrees for an even pull – and then try out the device for 'feel'. If this seems satisfactory to you, try out some string bending of the fretting-hand variety. This will increase string tension to the point where it pulls the bridge slightly forward, thereby detuning all other strings to a certain degree which, depending upon what these other strings are being used for, may prove to be problematic. In other words, if these strings are still sounding you won't want them to suddenly drop in pitch. But if they're silent it can't make any difference. This will depend somewhat upon your playing style, and is the reason why country players often 'lock off' (see below) the tremolo mechanism, because they often bend some strings whilst simultaneously sounding others that are unbent. If, however, you prefer to leave the device 'active', but wish to minimise 'detuning pull' from bent strings, it can be helpful to increase spring tension in order to somewhat resist this inconvenience.

When the bridge is resting against the body, as described above, it's clear that the tremolo device can only be used to bend pitch downward, as it's physically impossible to lift the bar from this position. In order to permit upward movement of the lever and therefore of note pitch, you'd need to ease spring tension to a point that allows the bridge plate to attain some clearance from the body.

Although some players do this – and feel free to try it for

yourself – this isn't something which I consider to be a satisfactory arrangement, simply because the reduced spring-pull creates an instability of the bridge, which is then overly sensitive to very slight, and sometimes unintentional, degrees of pressure. And, of course, this again is a particular nuisance when string bending.

The actual bar itself is fitted to the instrument by means of a screw thread, so that it's easily detachable for fitting the guitar into its carrying case. The only problem with this is the fact that the thread is rarely, if ever, a close fit. This means that when fitted and in normal playing position the bar tends to hang loosely down, as dictated by gravity, instead of maintaining a reasonably horizontal profile, as would usually be required.

The long-established solution to this problem is simply to wrap several turns of plumbers' tape around the thread before fitting (pictured below), which may seem primitive but is actually an extremely effective method of improving the fit between bar and bridge for a more efficient playing action.

If you should own a guitar with a tremolo device already fitted, but prefer not to use it at all, it's common practice to render the mechanism inoperative using one of two methods. One way is to simply tighten the springs to the point where normal string tension (even when bending) is unable to counteract the spring pull – this is probably the quickest fix, but may be somewhat stressful on the springs, especially where only the standard three are fitted. The other, and perhaps somewhat more satisfactory, approach is to place a suitably sized object, such as the small wooden block seen overleaf, behind the tremolo via the rear access point, which will certainly prevent any forward movement of the bridge.

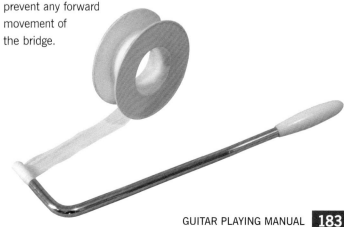

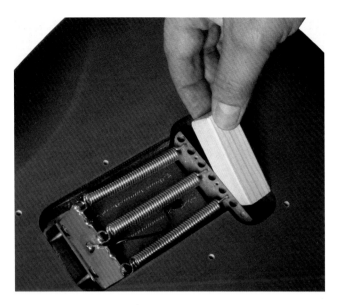

The Floyd Rose so-called 'floating bridge' tremolo is a variation upon earlier designs, in which, to permit upward movement, the body is recessed directly under the bridge. This type of tremolo is extremely effective in normal operation, but can be somewhat more difficult to deal with in other ways. And because it should lie completely parallel to the body, the delicate balance of spring-to-string tension requires that greater care must be taken when making any adjustments, so that the springs will precisely counteract the force of whatever gauge strings may be fitted. Also, there's a potential hazard awaiting you if a string breaks during performance. This is clearly an undesirable event in the best of circumstances, but especially so with a floating bridge tremolo fitted. In this situation the missing string causes an immediate loss of tension from the forward pull of the strings and, because the bridge isn't resting against a firm surface, the springs pull the bridge backward, thereby causing all remaining strings to go drastically out of tune.

Locking nut and adjuster tailpiece

A common problem regarding the use of tremolo (vibrato) devices generally is the fact that once you've pressed the bar down to lower pitch, and then released it, all strings may not return accurately to their normal pitch. The reason for this is usually because the string gets 'caught' in the nut on its return journey and, despite the strong pull of the springs, is unable to reacquire its previous tension. With this long-standing problem in mind the locking tremolo nut was invented, which effectively clamps the strings into a fixed position over the nut, rendering any movement impossible at that point. Naturally this also means that the usual method of tuning with the machine heads will be disabled, so guitars equipped with a locking nut are also fitted with a micro-tuner bridge mechanism for use once the strings are set to their standard pitch.

First of all you fit and tune your strings with the locking nut in its 'unlocked' position, which is easily achieved by releasing the Allen screws that hold it in place. Next you stretch out all

the strings in the normal manner (see **page 172**). When this is complete, and your strings are fully tuned back up to pitch, you secure the nut into its locked position, and subsequently make any other tuning adjustments at the bridge end of the string.

Assuming, however, that you have a guitar with a standard type tremolo device, as with a Fender Stratocaster, and no locking nut or tuner bridge device, there's always the more traditional method of smoothing the way for strings over the nut. First of all make certain that all nut grooves are as smooth as possible by taking care over the filing procedure if necessary (see **pages 178–79**). Then apply something slippery to the grooves to further reduce any chance of them interfering with the movement of the strings. This can be something as simple as rubbing graphite from a pencil into the grooves, which is pretty effective. Or, with an absorbent substance such as a bone nut, you might carefully apply some Vaseline to the grooves, giving it time to soak in before replacing the strings once again.

Pickups and electronics

The sound of an electric guitar is entirely due to the invention of the magnetic pickup, which appears to have tentatively originated some time during the 1920s, designed primarily as an optional attachment to the standard acoustic guitar. The idea wasn't fully developed until somewhat later, when the principle of a guitar entirely dependent upon its pickup – and therefore possessing no effective acoustic sound of its own – was originated. And although a wide variety of pickups are now available, to provide different sound options, all of them function in essentially the same way as those early models.

A guitar pickup is, in its basic form, simply a magnet surrounded by several thousand windings of copper wire, which convert the physical energy of string vibration into an electrical signal. This is then amplified to the point where it can vibrate the cone of a loudspeaker and so be converted back into (much louder) sound once again.

Looking at any pickup in its fully dressed appearance is a bit misleading in terms of its actual function. In order to understand it more clearly, and without any of the usual aesthetics, take a look at this very basic version of a single-coil pickup, as seen on the next page.

The pickup must be located on the guitar body in close proximity

Although the appearance of a pickup may vary somewhat from one guitar to another, as illustrated above, you'll find that underneath its fancy chrome or plastic cover there's always a magnet (or sometimes several individual magnetic 'pole pieces') surrounded by a considerable length of wire.

to the strings so that they pass through the magnetic field surrounding the magnet, and because the strings themselves are made of steel they're naturally responsive to magnetism. Whilst the strings are motionless all is peaceful within this magnetic field, and no sound is created. However, as soon as a string begins to vibrate it will disturb the tranquillity of the field and electrical current will be generated.

Before this ingenious device existed guitar players were, due to lack of volume, usually confined to a rhythmic backing role within a large dance band. So they must have been delighted, and probably amazed, to finally be able to hear themselves clearly above the brass section, and perhaps even take the occasional solo.

When the initial novelty wore off certain drawbacks began to become apparent in this sudden conversion from acoustic to

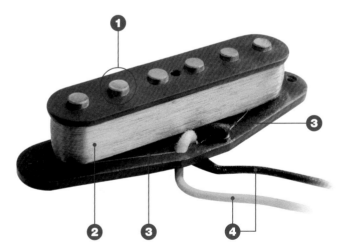

The pole pieces visible on the upper surface of the pickup (1) are the magnets, which are in turn surrounded by several thousand turns of insulated copper wire (2), known as a coil. At either end of this continuous single length of wire you can see two very fine strands (3). These are connected to the output wires (4), which directly, or more often indirectly (because of various switches and the usual volume/tone controls etc) – send the signal to the output jack plug socket of the guitar.

amplified sound, the main one being feedback (see **pages 164–65**), which, as we've already discovered, can be a real nuisance for guitarists even now, particularly where amplified acoustic instruments are concerned.

The problem with fitting a pickup to any acoustic guitar lies in the fact that the body is hollow, and the soundboard (the upper surface with the hole in it) is designed to vibrate. And, of course, these two factors are normally not only assets but essential characteristics for an acoustic guitar, because they create and amplify its sound. But when a pickup is fitted a good deal more stability is required, so the logical answer was to mount the pickup on a body surface of greater density.

Whenever guitar innovations are being discussed the name of Les Paul always comes up quite early in the conversation. He was well-known as not only a great guitar player, but also a noted innovator of guitar and other recording technology. In the 1930s he was among those working on the development of the electric guitar, and attempting to overcome the problems of feedback whilst improving electric guitar sound generally. What he did was simply to mount a pickup on a single solid length of maple wood, which represented the distance from nut to bridge, and accordingly fitted this with a set of strings. When connected to an amplifier the result was, in effect, the very first solid-body electric guitar, producing a sound with excellent sustain and no feedback.

Twin-coil (humbucker) pickups

Twin-coil (humbucker) pickups consist of two separate coils, wired together in series, in order to resist any electrical interference noise, as could occasionally be problematic with the single-coil design. Having two coils together also provides a somewhat more powerful sound than singles traditionally featured on Fender guitars. This alternative pickup design is generally the preferred choice for those who require a 'bigger' sound, such as that originally featured on the Gibson guitars, and subsequently many others in more recent years.

Connections and fault diagnosis

If you refer to this picture of a standard single-coil pickup you will observe that it has only two wires leading from it, indicated here as **A** and **B**, which are respectively the 'hot' or live wire and the 'ground' or earth wire. The small socket to which it connects, in order to receive the jack plug, is also shown. This has, very logically, two connection points, to which the pickup wires are attached. Wire **A** (white) from the pickup connects to the socket location that will meet the centre point, or tip, of the jack plug when it's inserted. Wire **B** (black) from the pickup connects to the socket location that'll ensure contact with the outer sleeve of the jack plug.

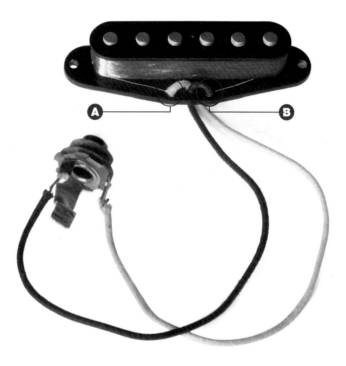

This, in essence, is how a pickup is wired in its basic form, to permit effective connection with an amplifier. Clearly nothing could be simpler – just two wires and two points of connection; this is so straightforward that even the most helpless or hopeless DIY person could hardly go wrong. But if you look at the typical wiring layout of any electric guitar it always appears a great deal more complex than that. There are two main reasons for this apparent complexity. First, because there's usually more than one pickup fitted, and therefore more wiring; and second, the fact that various controls and switches are fitted between pickup and output.

Looking at a tangle of wires, switches and volume/tone controls it's very easy to get discouraged before even attempting to understand how it all works – which would obviously be essential if you should ever need to effect a repair. But it so happens that the basic essentials of any electric guitar circuit are actually rather easy to comprehend, if you consider each component individually and so understand what it is, and how it works.

A standard volume control, as pictured here, is technically known as a potentiometer. This is, in fact, a 'variable resistor', and the name itself tells you exactly what it does, which is to vary the amount of resistance between a pickup and its output. So as you turn the rotary dial from maximum down to minimum level you're actually increasing resistance to the flow of current, with the result being a gradual reduction of volume. This device works because the pickup wire is connected to one end of a resistive track and the output is connected to the other, so that the potentiometer acts as an adjustable barrier between these two points, allowing for an alteration of signal strength. More resistance equals less volume, and less resistance equals more volume.

The tone control seen here operates on a similar principle, being also a potentiometer/variable resistor. But the difference here lies in the fact that a small capacitor is added to the circuit, which causes higher frequencies to be reduced as the dial is turned. This creates a 'resistance' to treble tone as opposed to volume. But remember that passive (not powered) controls such as these can only cut a given volume or frequency, and not actually increase it. In other words, the basic sound or volume produced by any pickup can be reduced, or 'resisted', but in order to boost either volume or tone a powered amplifier of some description would be required.

Apart from these rotary volume and tone controls, the most commonplace component in the average guitar circuit will be the pickup selector switch, two examples of which are pictured here.

This type of switch is required whenever more than one pickup is fitted to the guitar, which is likely to be the case with most, although not all, electric guitars. It simply provides a route for the signal from either pickup to the output socket. Types of switch vary, depending mainly upon the number of pickups fitted to a particular instrument. Generally speaking, these switches cover between three and five available switching options, permitting any pickup to be used individually or in conjunction with another pickup.

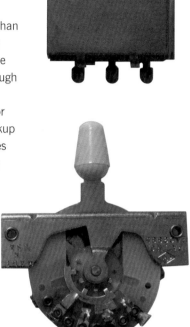

A guitar with two pickups, such as a Gibson Les Paul or a Fender Telecaster, will have three switch positions. This allows either the bridge pickup or the neck pickup to be used by itself, while a 'middle' position activates both together. A Fender Stratocaster, however, has three pickups, and is fitted with a five-position selector switch. This allows the options of bridge pickup alone, bridge and middle pickups together, middle pickup alone, middle and neck pickups together, and neck pickup alone. This hasn't always been the case with the Stratocaster, as the earlier models were fitted with a three-way switch so that each pickup could only be used alone. But as many players discovered, it was possible to carefully 'balance' the selector switch between two settings (the favourite trick was to put a match stick into the groove to hold the switch in place), which would enable two adjacent pickups to be heard at the same time. Eventually this odd state of affairs reached the attention of the Fender company, who did the sensible thing and designed the five-position switch fitted as standard today.

Acoustic guitar pickups

Although an acoustic guitar can be fitted with a standard magnetic pickup, as was the case in earlier times, this is now rarely seen. The reasons for this are partly because this method tends to produce a tone not entirely faithful to the natural tone of such instruments (being halfway between acoustic and electric in its sound characteristics), and also the fact that acoustic guitars are best served by bronze-covered lower strings – a material which isn't responsive to magnetism. Although the inner core, being made of steel, will produce some response on these particular strings, in order to work most efficiently with a magnetic pickup an acoustic guitar would ideally have to be fitted with a set of electric guitar strings, creating a double compromise in fidelity of sound quality. Despite these misgivings some players still employ these attachable pickups, an example of which can be seen below, designed to fit conveniently into the sound hole.

Two methods of amplifying your acoustic guitar, both of which are easily fitted but offer somewhat different tonal characteristics. The magnetic pickup here is basically identical to that fitted to any electric guitar, and will therefore produce similar sound qualities.

For these reasons the contact transducer, an example of which is seen below, has now become the preferred option, having the obvious benefits of amplifying a more naturalistic acoustic tone.

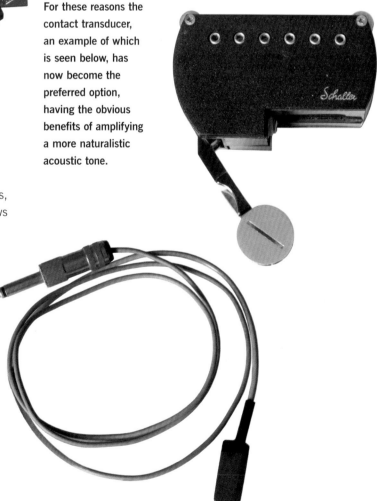

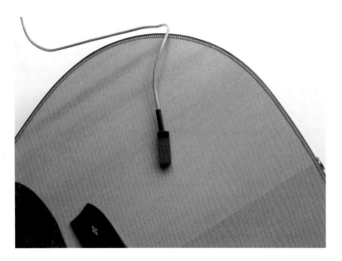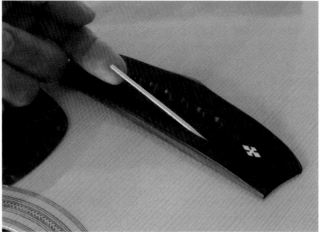

On the left is a direct contact transducer, attached to the acoustic guitar soundboard. Fitting this device inside the body entails more work but makes for a neater finish. The more popular method now is to place a pickup under the bridge saddle, as displayed above right. This is entirely unobtrusive, and will produce excellent results.

Instead of responding to string vibration by application of a magnetic field, as with a traditional pickup, the 'contact transducer' is sensitive to the vibration of the soundboard of an acoustic guitar. With the version pictured above this would be attached directly to the instrument body, and would output the sound via a jack plug socket in the usual way. As with an electric guitar pickup, the tone and volume can be modified by fitting suitable controls between transducer and output. The device itself can be attached to either the front (outward-facing surface) of the soundboard, as pictured above left, or perhaps on the inner surface for reasons of appearance. The results are similar either way.

In more recent years this type of pickup has been modified and improved upon by placing it directly under the bridge saddle. This approach, as seen above right, is extremely efficient, and is somewhat more aesthetically pleasing. Although you can fit one yourself, to any acoustic guitar, they do tend to benefit from the addition of active (powered) circuitry, which greatly enhances the tone qualities, along with the usual volume control. An alternative is to simply place an equaliser pedal (see page 199) between guitar and amplifier. If you buy an 'electro-acoustic' guitar with a bridge transducer already fitted this will generally include a built-in EQ.

If you're an acoustic player this type of pickup is extremely useful, especially for live work, because you can move around freely without having to maintain a steady distance from a microphone, which would be the only other option to achieve a reasonably faithful amplified acoustic guitar tone. But don't forget to take into account the type of amplification used, which can either enhance or detract from the true acoustic quality desired. The average guitar amp is designed primarily to work with electric guitar, and will colour the tone accordingly. There are now guitar amplifiers available built specifically for use with

acoustics, which would be a preferable option for the discerning player. A less expensive alternative would be to plug into the main PA system, as this will generally be of very high fidelity (able to produce an accurate sound), and would therefore be suitable for this purpose.

Replacement pickups

One likely reason why you might need to intervene, with regard to pickups and their associated components, is that you may wish to upgrade one or more of the pickups by replacing it/them with a superior quality model. This is quite a common situation with guitarists who have an instrument that is considered favourable in other ways. Instead of replacing the entire guitar, it's much cheaper – and relatively simple – to buy some new pickups.

In a purely functional sense it's true that any pickup will work with any guitar, but the physical size, and therefore the fitting, of the pickup is obviously a bit more exacting. This is no problem at all with popular models of guitar, because a great many very high quality replacement pickups are now available, and are designed to fit exactly into the instrument with no additional modifications being necessary. If, however, your guitar is among the less common types it may be helpful to take it with you when pickup shopping, as a guide to fitting requirements.

When you buy any decent pickup it will include a wiring diagram detailing which wires go to which location on the switches and potentiometers etc. On single-coil pickups this will be fairly obvious anyway, but on twin-coils there may be several wires to consider, and more than one alternative for connections. Usually all the standard options will be shown, but if in doubt keep it simple and copy the wiring connections from the old pickup which you've just removed. With this consideration in mind, always make out a sketch diagram of the original wiring, indicating the colour of each wire and where it goes, before removing anything.

Selecting a new pickup isn't always a straightforward procedure, because until you've fitted it into your guitar it isn't possible to decide if you like the sound. Certain companies can be very helpful in this regard, as they'll often permit a 'trial period' for you to make the final decision. During this time they'll allow you to choose an alternative if so required, on condition that you return the first pickup unaltered. This means that you should not have trimmed the wires at all whilst fitting the pickup for testing.

In general terms of quality you can rely upon names like DiMarzio and Seymour Duncan, because they simply don't make inferior pickups. Beyond that it's really just a question of what type of sound you wish to achieve. And, although most pickups will be described in some way, there's nothing quite like hearing it as fitted into your own guitar, and played through your own amplification.

When fitting high quality pickups to a relatively inexpensive instrument, you may be surprised to find that a couple of good pickups can cost as much, if not more, than the original cost of the guitar itself. Obviously the price will vary somewhat depending upon how good the new pickups are. But if you economise too much you might find that the new ones are little better, if at all, than the old ones. Apart from the tonal characteristics, a peculiar feature of some cheaper pickups is that they may tend to be 'microphonic', which means that they can be inconveniently sensitive to sounds other than the string

vibrations – if, for example, you tap your plectrum against the bridge, body or anywhere near the pickup, the sound may be clearly heard through the amplifier.

The actual 'pole pieces' (see **page 185**) visible directly underneath each string are often height-adjustable by means of a screw thread, in order to compensate for any differences in individual string volume and varying string distances from the pickup itself. Although this isn't the case on all types of pickup, Fender Stratocaster-type pickups often feature pole pieces of differing, although fixed, heights to address this situation.

Finding the fault

If one or more of your pickups fails to work this doesn't necessarily mean that you need to buy a new one. Indeed, it's more likely that the situation is repairable, in which case your first task is to locate the component or connections at fault. And because the pickups themselves are of a very basic structure the problem will almost always be that of a faulty connection somewhere in the circuit.

Before attempting any serious analysis, just take a careful look at the pickups and wiring. Many times the problem will be immediately obvious, such as a disconnected wire, in which case you only need to reattach the connection with solder and the problem is solved.

Soldering is a relatively simple procedure, and is the basis for all electrical connections within a guitar circuit. The picture below shows you the equipment required to carry out a repair job to your guitar electrics.

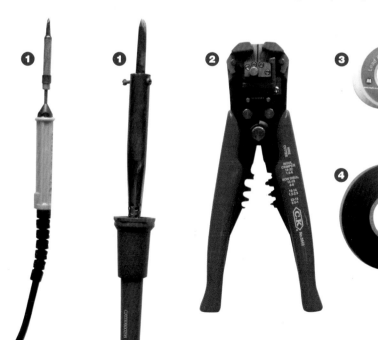

❶ A soldering iron of medium power, such as 15W for light connections or 50W for any job requiring more heat, such as attaching or removing wires from the rear casing of a potentiometer.

❷ Wire cutters/strippers to provide a new clean wire for attachment.

❸ Solder with flux core to secure the connection.

❹ Insulating tape, as may be required to prevent short circuits.

When the iron is heated sufficiently to melt the solder, simply apply it to any connection you wish to remove and lift the wire or component away. Take care not to handle the connective point with your fingers until it's had time to cool down, or you'll quickly learn not to do so again. For this reason you'd be wise to acquire a pair of long-nose pliers for safe handling during all soldering work.

Try not to keep the hot iron in contact with any components for longer than is necessary to get the job done, or damage may result from overheating – which is another good reason for having two soldering irons of different power capacities. The heavier powered iron is really too hot for light connections such as the fine wires attached to selector switches, and should only be used when the lower powered iron is insufficient.

When making a new connection, remove any debris (such as stray bits of wire) from the previous connection and ensure that all areas to be soldered are perfectly clean. This can be achieved with some medium grade abrasive paper and a little effort. Newly cut wires will obviously be clean anyway, but the point to which they attach may be less so. Any parts, including freshly bared wires, which have never been soldered before will require 'tinning', as will the tip of a new soldering iron. This is simply a case of applying a light layer of solder to the surface in question before attempting to join any parts together.

When making the connection it's essential that the two parts be held together, without any risk of movement, during the few seconds required for the solder to solidify. In the case of wires being attached to a switch they can often be twisted around the

connection beforehand, and will thus remain stable whilst you are soldering, but when attaching the earth wires to the back of a potentiometer this isn't possible, and you'll have to use a suitable tool to hold the wire in place.

If you're unfamiliar with such matters and find yourself with a stray wire that's obviously broken away from its correct place, you may be in some doubt as to where this should be reattached. The mystery may well be solved by the discovery of a remaining bit of frayed-looking wire still attached to a switch or potentiometer. The actual length of the disconnected wire could also be helpful, as it may only be sufficient to reach certain areas and therefore couldn't possibly have broken away from a more distant part of the circuit. Easiest of all would be a detached earth wire coming from a pickup, which would usually have to be connected to the casing of the volume potentiometer, as exemplified in the photograph below right.

If no obvious solution presents itself you'll need to track down the fault through a process of elimination. This can be done in a perfectly straightforward manner, and naturally assumes that you've already established the efficient operation of all external equipment (see page 167) such as amplifiers, effect pedals, connecting cables and any other items that, if faulty, may be preventing an operational pickup from transmitting a signal through to its destination.

In tracing any breaks or poor connections in a guitar circuit, there's a very useful piece of equipment called a multi-tester or multimeter. Although these devices have a range of uses and settings, we're concerned here only with using it to ascertain the

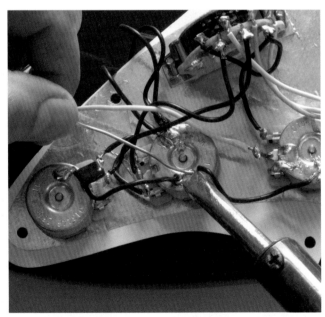

Two examples of likely soldering jobs in a typical guitar circuit. In the case of attaching the wire to a pickup selector switch you'll only require a low-powered iron, such as the 15W model shown here. The other example, above right, requires a higher-powered iron because the casing of the potentiometer will absorb much of the heat required to do the job. But in either situation be careful to avoid touching (intentionally or otherwise) any heated area with your fingers. The solder 'wire' itself can clearly be seen in these pictures, as a small amount of it is melted on to the area to ensure a firm connection.

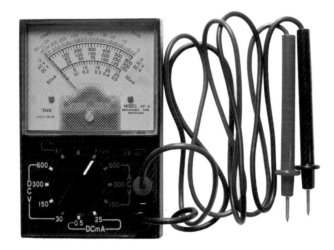

efficiency of connections in a guitar circuit. This doesn't involve any mains power or dangerous voltages, as might be the case with amplification equipment. All we're dealing with is a basic ability to verify that the circuit contains no flaws that are not visually apparent.

Other types of multimeter are available, with a digital readout as opposed to the needle indicator of the model shown. For this type of work, however, I find that the model with a needle is easier to read, as compared to a fluctuating series of numbers that can be somewhat confusing and, indeed, unnecessary when simply trying to verify the efficiency of basic circuit connections.

For our purposes you'll need to set the meter to its 'ohms' setting, which is done by turning the central dial accordingly as displayed in the photograph below.

Before use, the first thing you should do is to 'zero' the meter. To do this you touch both probes together, as shown in the picture below, to ensure that the indicator is pointing to zero. If it doesn't read zero, and assuming that the unit has a correctly functioning battery inside, an adjustment can be made by turning the adjuster wheel indicated in the picture until the zero reading is achieved.

To give you an idea of how this works in practice, take a look at the readings on the meter. This concerns the top line only, as this is the 'ohms' readout. At the far right the reading is zero. When this reading is attained, as for example in touching the two probes together, this means that there's no resistance to the flow of current – in other words, a perfect connection. But at the other extreme is a reading of infinite resistance (with the needle at far left), which means that there's complete resistance to the flow of current. This reading will be seen when there is a breakage in the circuit, or when, for example, the probes aren't making contact with each other. So on zero resistance the circuit is complete; but on infinite resistance the circuit is broken.

Although we can, for convenience, witness the operation of the meter by making or breaking contact between its two probes, exactly the same situation applies if you place something between these two points. If you touch one of these probes to one end of a 'good' wire, and the other probe to its opposite end, your reading will indicate zero resistance. But if there's a break in that wire your reading will indicate infinite resistance. Using this method you can easily detect any flaws in the circuit connections.

Multimeter 'zeroing. Note adjuster wheel indicated at right.

The multi-tester or multimeter shown here is an invaluable aid in tracking down suspect connections in your guitar circuitry. It's a battery-powered device with a needle indicator that provides you with a visual reference, telling you if an electrical signal sent from any given point in the circuit is actually reaching its destination. The voltages involved in the multimeter and generated by the pickups are extremely small, and therefore completely harmless to the user.

The photographs above and on the left show you how to select the 'ohms' setting, and also how to set the meter to zero, which indicates that the signal flow is uninterrupted. This is also the reading you would expect to see in practice, when attempting to establish that there's a good connection between wires and switches.

There are a number of methodical steps you can take to find out where a fault lies. By working through these it's almost inevitable that you'll track down the problem:

1 Begin by trying all the pickups, one by one, to ascertain if more than one is apparently not working.

2 If all pickups are silent it's highly unlikely that there's a fault with any pickup as such. More likely there'll be a common cause, such as shared wiring or potentiometer breakdown. You must ensure that all likely areas are investigated. Check connections to the output jack plug socket (see **page 195**), and if they're OK test all wires leading from the pickup selector switch to the potentiometers. If everything seems correct so far it's possible that the internal workings of the volume control are faulty. For information on testing a potentiometer see **page 194**.

3 If only one pickup isn't working the problem may well be an unreliable selector switch. There are several ways to verify this, but the most definite is to swap the wires around with a pickup that is working correctly. So let's assume that your bridge pickup is producing no sound, but the neck pickup is perfectly all right. All you need do is to remove (de-solder) the wire leading from the bridge pickup to the switch, then also remove the wire leading from the neck pickup to the switch. You then simply reattach each wire to the connection point previously occupied by the other wire. Having done this you can now test the 'faulty' bridge pickup by selecting what would normally be the switch setting for the neck pickup. Now, if the bridge pickup produces sound but the neck pickup doesn't (on the 'bridge' pickup setting, of course), you can be certain that the problem is a faulty selector switch. Pickup selector switches commonly fail from time to time, and although repairs are sometimes possible it's usually best to replace a faulty switch with a new one.

4 If, for whatever reason, you're still in doubt about any pickup, and/or connections pertaining to them, there's one absolutely foolproof test you can apply. Disconnect the suspect pickup wires from all switches, potentiometers etc and then connect it directly to the amp with a reliable cable, as in the picture above right. This connection eliminates any confusion from internal components. If the unit is away from its usual strings, gently tapping the pole pieces as shown will test for sound. If, however, you still have no sound then the pickup itself is definitely at fault.

Remember that the magnetic pickup, clever device though it is, still only consists of a magnet with a lot of wire wrapped around it, and, because a magnet can hardly 'break down', any fault must be in the wiring; but to properly check this out you should first disconnect and remove it from the guitar for easy handling.

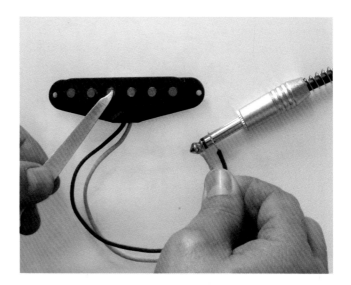

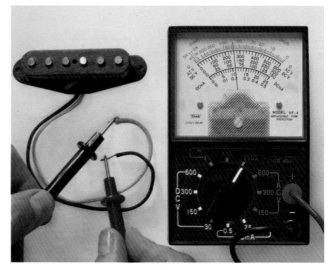

You can easily get a multimeter reading from the pickup by simply touching one probe to the positive wire, and another probe to the earth wire. It doesn't matter which probe goes to which wire, because you'll be completing the circuit either way – assuming there's no breakage within the pickup wire.

The typical meter reading from a 'good' pickup, as seen above, will indicate some resistance, but it's enough to know that a reading exists to determine that a signal is getting through.

If no reading whatever is registered on your meter (the needle doesn't move at all) then there must be a disconnection somewhere in the coil itself, or perhaps at its output wires, requiring further investigation.

It's essential that you overlook nothing in your search for the problem. Basically this means checking every possible point at which a break in the circuit might have occurred, and it's best to do this in a methodical step-by-step manner. So let's first eliminate from our investigation the output wires, which connect the coil to the selector switch. You can easily do this by touching one probe to the end of the wire and the other probe to the point at which it meets the pickup itself, as clearly displayed in the picture below.

There may be several wires leading from a pickup, depending upon its complexity of design, but with a test as basic as this it doesn't actually make any difference what a particular wire happens to do within the overall circuit. All that matters is locating each end of a given wire and applying the meter accordingly. In some twin-coil models you may be surprised to notice that two of the numerous wires are soldered together, and will usually be covered with insulating tape. This is the point where the two coils are connected, and you should check that this is a secure connection.

I know that some things may be difficult to reach, but if you can satisfy yourself that all external wires are OK then the problem must lie within the coil itself. This might seem like a daunting prospect, considering how much coil winding there is, but in my experience a coil wiring problem is often nothing more than a disconnection at the point where it meets the output wire, and if this is the case you can usually tell by careful scrutiny (the wire is very fine) of that area.

If there is a break at this point all is not yet lost, because you may be able to fix it yourself. This is especially likely if it occurs at the end of the wire on the 'outside' of the coil winding. In this event you can carefully unwind a single turn of the wire to give yourself something to work with.

Remember that the wire is coated with insulation, a small portion of which will have to be removed before attempting to solder it back into place; and because the

wire is rather delicate you'll find it hard, if not impossible, to bare the end with abrasive paper or similar. So what I have found effective is to 'melt' the plastic coating away by stroking it carefully with the 'clean' (solder-free) end of a low-power soldering iron. Being less heat-resistant than the inner wire, if you do this a few times the coating will dissolve away, leaving a clean bare end of wire accessible for soldering. But do this with care, because the fine wire itself will also melt if overheated. So keep checking this wire with your multimeter, and when you get a reading (indicating bare, uncoated wire) you'll know that it's ready to solder.

If the coil wire has broken away leading to the 'inner' end of its winding this is somewhat more problematic, because it isn't possible to unwind any excess slack for easier working due to the fact that this end of the wire disappears completely into the coil itself. But if you do have a little bit to get hold of it may still be possible to extend the join, simply by using a short length of fine fuse wire to connect the 'too short to reach' coil wire with its main output connection. As with many repair jobs, a little creative improvisation can save the day.

Although rare, it's not impossible that there may be a fault elsewhere within the coil, which is completely inaccessible to you. In this event the coil will require rewinding, which isn't a job you can manage without specialist equipment and the necessary know-how. The only alternative would be to purchase a new pickup. But if you were happy with the sound of the old pickup a rewind job might well be the preferred (although not always the cheaper) option.

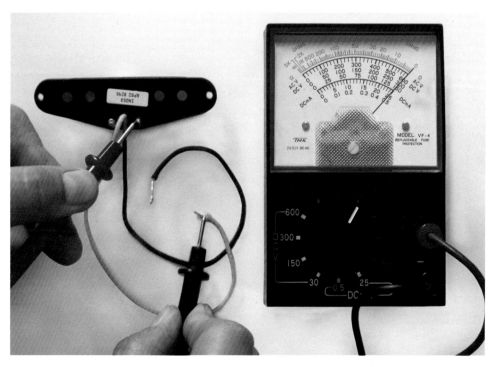

This simple test will verify the efficiency, or otherwise, of the wires leading from coil to switch. With a single-coil pickup there are only two such wires, and both can easily be checked by this method. Other pickup designs may, however, be less easily accessible, particularly where humbucker (twin-coil) pickups are concerned. In such cases it may be necessary to carefully remove any surrounding objects such as insulating tape or pickup covers.

Potentiometers

It's not at all difficult to measure the abilities of any variable resistor (potentiometer) with the assistance of your helpful multi-tester. In this regard there are two different readings you may wish to ascertain. One is the overall resistance of the unit, and the other is the smooth (or otherwise) operation of its resistor track across the entire range.

The maximum resistance of any potentiometer is usually clearly marked on its outer casing, which for a typical guitar volume potentiometer might be something like 250k. This rating will generally be sufficient to 'resist' the output of its pickups – in other words it would be capable of completely silencing the volume when fully turned down. However, because the rear casing is often obscured by solder, attached earth wires etc, you may be unable to read the capacity of a potentiometer, in which case you must use your multimeter to find out what it actually is.

Remove the potentiometer from your guitar, first taking care to make a note of all wiring connections. Then take its reading by touching a tester probe to each of its outer lugs, as pictured here. In the case of, for example, a 500k unit, at a casual glance the meter needle might not appear to be giving a reading at all. But this can be deceptive, because with the reading being very close to the far left of the scale a closer inspection is sometimes required to reveal the facts. So, since we assume that your meter was properly 'zeroed' before testing (see **page 191**), this procedure will accurately indicate the resistance capacity of the potentiometer being tested.

This type of information will be helpful if you should wish to replace the potentiometer with a new one due to flaws in its operation, such as noise being generated when the dial is rotated or any 'dead spots' (places where the signal is interrupted). It's true that sometimes this can be corrected by the application of switch cleaner, which can usually be

purchased from an electronics component store, but there are always those occasions when it'll be necessary to replace the unit, in which case you'll need to know the rating of the potentiometer in question.

The other test referred to is when you have a potentiometer that is operational but faulty. In this situation you can connect one probe to an outer lug of the unit and the other probe to the centre lug. If you then rotate the dial you'll see the resistance change gradually across its operational range from 'full on' to 'full off'. What you're looking for here is a gradual movement across the dial as opposed to any surprises, such as a sudden point of resistance, indicating a flaw in the track. Again, it's possible to apply switch cleaner to the wiper track, which can correct the problem. This is most effectively achieved by prising away the rear cover to gain clear access to the track, as can be seen in the picture above. But take care, when you're doing this, to ensure that you can put it back together again, firmly and correctly.

Tone control

Most of the problems mentioned so far, with regard to potentiometers, are concerned with the volume control, but there may also be problems with the tone controls, such as noisy or erratic operation; and of course, there's also the particular inconvenience of a tone control that doesn't actually do what it's supposed to do, which is to adjust the tone. Assuming that all the wires are intact, and the potentiometer itself is OK, such faults inevitably concern the capacitor, as described on **page 186**. So if you have a tone problem, first ensure that the capacitor is firmly connected to its relevant points. This may vary from one layout to another, but is generally obvious because of its positioning within the circuit. If in any doubt about the connections simply re-solder the capacitor to ensure a firm fixing. If this fails to solve the problem, take the capacitor with you (as a sample) to an electronics supplier and replace it with a new one.

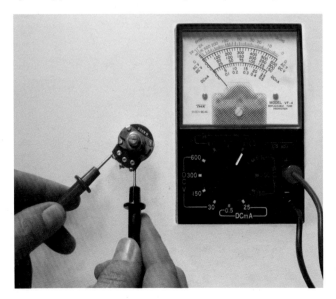

A common complaint about passive tone controls on guitars is simply that they appear to have very little effect across some of the range, and only take audible effect when the dial reaches a certain point. This is certainly a justifiable comment on most guitar tone controls, but is so common as to hardly constitute a 'fault' as such. The fact is that they're not very sophisticated tone controls units, in comparison to those found on amplifiers, but they do offer a certain convenience, being close at hand, and it's generally best not to expect too much of them apart from that.

Additional information

Electric guitars have a wire connecting the bridge unit to the casing of a potentiometer. This is an additional safeguard against any unwelcome electrical hum. So if your guitar does appear to suffer excessively from this problem, it may be that this connection has become disconnected or broken.

This particular wire is attached by solder to the volume potentiometer, along with several other connections, and is accessed at the other end by simply removing the bridge plate under which it rests, making a secure but usually not soldered contact with the bridge. Being nothing more than a short length of wire this can hardly go wrong unless, of course, there's an actual breakage. But beware of anything interfering with the integrity of its bridge contact, such as paint, dirt or possibly even rust. This wire is not identically located on all types of instrument. On the Fender Stratocaster, for example, its attachment point can be found at the 'claw' securing the tremolo springs in place.

Due to the wide variety of electric and electro-acoustic guitars available, it wouldn't be possible to cover every eventuality that you might encounter in a guitar circuit. But when attempting to understand the wiring and switching options, and how they work on your particular instrument, keep in mind that it's still essentially a case of pickup wires leading to the output jack plug socket. Everything else is just an optional extra, designed to extend the range of sound possibilities and your control over them. So when a fault occurs you can be reasonably certain that all you're really looking for is a dodgy connection somewhere. It might appear to be a great deal more complex than this, simply because wires, switches, potentiometers etc are substantially different from each other in terms of their physical appearance. Nevertheless, each of these items can be regarded as simply being part of the pathway between pickup and output. If this pathway is clear, the signal can pass through without impediment.

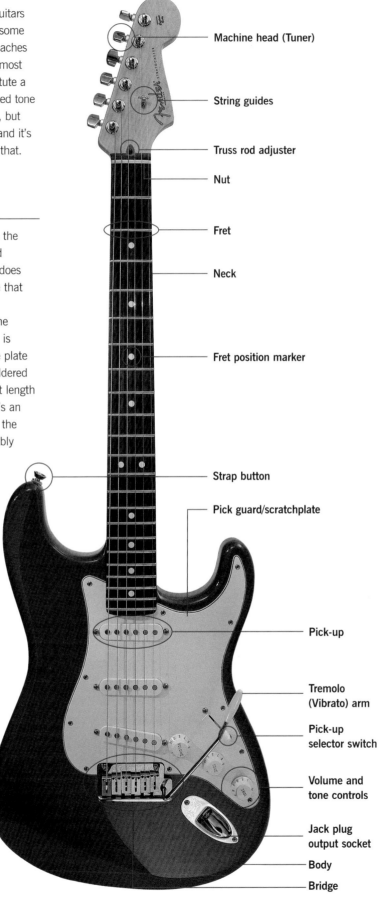

Machine head (Tuner)

String guides

Truss rod adjuster

Nut

Fret

Neck

Fret position marker

Strap button

Pick guard/scratchplate

Pick-up

Tremolo (Vibrato) arm

Pick-up selector switch

Volume and tone controls

Jack plug output socket

Body

Bridge

Equipment and effects

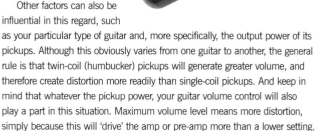

In its original form the guitar, being entirely acoustic, is a complete and self-contained instrument, if somewhat limited in its volume output, and it's precisely because of this limitation that the electric guitar came into existence during the early part of the 20th century, creating a whole new range of sonic possibilities and eventually giving rise to a number of accessories and effects.

Whilst most players will use at least some effects to enhance their sound, this is something that requires restraint and experience, along with an awareness of what will blend well with other instruments in the band. There's a long-standing myth that effects are somehow able to compensate for a lack of basic talent, but this is really the exact opposite of the truth. The fact is, the greater the range of effect devices you have, the greater the skill required to use them well. So with this in mind the following information relates to the most commonly used, and indeed generally useful, sound modifiers available, and will serve as a guide to what equipment you may wish to acquire and how best to use it.

Distortion

Starting with what's certainly the most popular of all, it's probably debatable as to whether this actually constitutes an 'effect' as such, being originally the accidental by-product of an overdriven valve amplifier. But now an extremely wide range of (usually) floor-mounted units exists, designed to create, in a more convenient and controllable manner, exactly that same sound. Their success in this particular regard is a subject of some controversy among guitar players, but nevertheless, each has its own sound, and all of them can be used to create the 'heavy' guitar tone characteristic of rock music.

The attractive sound qualities of what might normally be considered an undesirable misuse of amplification has been known about and utilised for many decades now, and certainly since well before anyone ever used the term 'heavy metal'. Valve amplifiers, when driven to their volume limits, just naturally tend to distort, as Chuck Berry, Eric Clapton and many others discovered when using amps too small (in power) for playing in large halls back in the 1950s and '60s. Probably to everyone's surprise, the resulting distortion of sound proved extremely popular with audiences, and therefore useful to guitarists everywhere. But because it's often impractical to turn amp volume up to the point of distortion a device was needed which could overdrive the guitar tone before it actually reached the amplifier. These early models didn't really sound much like the quality tone produced by an overdriven valve amp (they were commonly called 'fuzz boxes' as a description of their harsh but nonetheless useful sound), but despite their limitations they paved the way for further development.

These devices, two of which are pictured here, are essentially pre-amps – which means that they're amplifiers which occur between a guitar and its main amp, thereby adding certain sound qualities (in this case distortion) that the main amplifier doesn't, or need not be required to, possess. Any typical distortion/overdrive unit will have two essential controls. The gain or drive control will, as it's raised, increase the amount of distortion, and this is used in conjunction with the volume or level control, which determines the overall output to your main amplifier. So what this means is if you increase the gain, whilst keeping the volume at a lower level, you'll get more extreme distortion.

And if you reverse these settings, a cleaner sound will be produced. So by balancing one control against the other you have a range of sound options, from fairly clean right up to very distorted.

Other factors can also be influential in this regard, such as your particular type of guitar and, more specifically, the output power of its pickups. Although this obviously varies from one guitar to another, the general rule is that twin-coil (humbucker) pickups will generate greater volume, and therefore create distortion more readily than single-coil pickups. And keep in mind that whatever the pickup power, your guitar volume control will also play a part in this situation. Maximum volume level means more distortion, simply because this will 'drive' the amp or pre-amp more than a lower setting.

Another consideration you may wish to utilise is the main amp gain/volume levels. Although any distortion pedal will be quite capable of generating plenty of distortion by itself, some players are inclined to set their amplifier controls so as to add its own extra touch of power. The amp controls would be set so that (as with the pedals) gain is increased, whilst master volume is reduced. The only thing to note here is that even when you switch off the actual pedal itself, you won't have a completely 'clean' sound without accompanying amp adjustment. As always it's a question of what works for your own personal playing requirements. So be aware of all the options, and experiment for best results in accordance with your style and type of music.

Echo/delay

The earliest echo/delay units were based, rather ingeniously, upon the principle of tape recording. The original note would be recorded on to the tape and then, as the tape continued along its path, would pass over several playback heads, thereby causing the note to be heard again. The actual number of repeats would depend upon how many playback heads were activated at the time, whilst the rate of repetition could be adjusted by altering the speed of tape travel. The tape, being on a continually revolving loop, would finally pass over an erase head before being recorded anew, and so on.

The most famous of these 'tape echo' units, the almost legendary Wem Copycat, still holds a place of special affection amongst guitarists of a certain vintage, who will testify that nothing else can equal its character of sound. And whilst to some extent this is true, tape echo also has its drawbacks, as anyone who's ever used one will be aware, such as tape breakage, the need for regular maintenance and limited time-delay versatility. Nevertheless, these devices served well for many years, and early rock and roll guitarists like Scotty Moore (Elvis Presley's lead guitar player) depended upon the tape echo as a crucial part of their sound.

With the attendant shortcomings as incentive, analogue delay units appeared in the early '70s, which varied in design from the Carlsbro unit picture here (actually around A4 size in reality) to smaller types, more conveniently built into small pedal form.

Either way, these new analogue delays required no tape to produce the echoes, and demanded no real servicing. Although effective and widely used, however, the quality of sound on the actual echo itself tended to degrade rapidly with successive repeats. But by the 1980s all such problems had become redundant with the advent of digital delays, which can produce an extremely comprehensive range of delay times whilst maintaining clarity of signal reproduction.

It does seem to be a peculiarity of guitarists that, as soon as a new and apparently superior method of creating a sound is devised, they start to complain that it lacks the 'character' or 'warmth' (that word gets used a lot) of the old system; and many people found that digital delay, with its strict uniformity of echo repeat, was perhaps just a little bit too sterile. So just as tape echo had its loyal adherents, to some extent the analogue system also became lamented when digital appeared. As a result there have recently been attempts to duplicate, with digital technology, the benefits (and, in some respects, the drawbacks) of both tape echo and analogue delay, so there are now delay units which offer a choice not only of echo settings as such, but also of the actual type of echo preferred.

Apart from any peculiarities regarding the supposed method of echo reproduction, modern delay units have three essential controls, although the descriptive terms can vary from one device to another. One control determines the actual delay time – this means how soon the repeated note follows the original. A second control determines how many such repeats will occur. And the third control sets the volume of such repeats - this can be from almost no audible echo whatever, right up to the echoes being equal to, or even greater than, the volume of the original note. With such a versatile range of adjustability, these delay units can be used in a variety of ways, although in general purpose terms there are a few which tend to be most useful, whilst the more extreme use of echo requires careful control and a very exacting approach to timing.

A discreet application of echo can easily enhance a guitar's tone, by giving it an ambience it might otherwise lack and making a 'bigger' sound. When applied in this way your best guide is your own ears, which means that you just happen to like the sound in the context of the song but without necessarily timing the repeats to actually match the tempo, which considering the accuracy of most drummers is probably just as well.

Try setting the echo to something like 195ms (milliseconds), with maybe two or three repeats, which should be of lesser volume than the original note. If your particular unit doesn't refer to milliseconds but just has a generic adjustment dial, this means a steady repeat but not too slow. As always, just experiment until you find a sound that is attractive to you, but without overdoing the amount of echo or else it can sound a bit messy and lacking in focus.

Another useful approach is the classic '50s rock and roll delay sound, which is achieved by setting a fairly quick repeat of similar volume to the original note, but with only a single repeat. This is generally referred to as 'slap back' echo. Guitar maestro Albert Lee devised an interesting variation on this style by timing the repeat to match the tempo of the song – the original note is played on the beat whilst the repeated note is timed to occur precisely halfway between one beat and the next. For a standard rock and roll riff this would be as illustrated here.

If you set your delay unit so that the repeat is of equal volume to the

In this example the first note of every pair is played in the usual way, whilst the second (as underlined in red) is generated by the delay unit, set to the tempo appropriate for the song.

original note it will sound as if you're playing twice as many notes but with only half the effort, which can be useful when playing at a fast tempo.

Many delay units have a 'tap tempo' availability, which is very helpful when attempting to match your delay to the beat of a song. This enables you to actually set the delay speed whilst playing, by literally tapping your foot (on the delay unit switch) in time with the song, which will then set the speed automatically.

A somewhat less exacting approach, and therefore probably more versatile, is to set the delay for a so-called 'doubling' effect. This simply means that you set a very rapid repeat time, with the echo level approximately equal to that of the original note, giving the impression of two guitars playing together.

In recent times digital delays have become increasingly versatile, adding to their range of options, such as stereo delay whereby the repeated notes bounce alternately between left and right speakers. This assumes, of course, that your amplification has stereo capability, or that you employ two different amplifiers. There's also something called reverse delay, which, upon its repetitions, effectively duplicates the original note but played backwards. This is a bit like some of the ideas from the late '60s 'psychedelic' era, where a guitar (or other instrument) would be recorded in the usual way, after which the tape would be simply turned over and literally played backwards. And whether or not you find this unusual effect useful, or indeed usable in a live situation, is entirely a matter for your own discretion. Still, it's another sound option which may prove effective in the appropriate context.

It can be very entertaining, sitting at home experimenting with the numerous possibilities of a delay unit. But remember that when you're actually playing in a band the situation can change somewhat, requiring perhaps an adjustment to your original settings. To some extent this applies to most effects, but is particularly apparent where delay is concerned because what seemed like a sufficient degree of echo whilst playing solo can get lost among the sound of other instruments. And, of course, the same thing applies to whichever room you find yourself playing in, because, as mentioned earlier (page 164), some rooms possess a certain amount of natural echo (often too much for convenience), whilst others will be exactly the opposite. This isn't usually too much of a problem, but rather something to be aware of and something you'll grow accustomed to. So start by using your delay with discretion, making tasteful adjustments as necessary.

Chorus

The idea of a chorus effect is basically to simulate the sound of two guitars playing identical parts together, and thereby enabling one guitarist to play, in a live situation, what would previously have only been possible in a multi-track studio recording. So if, for example, you record a rhythm guitar on to one track, and then play the same thing over again on another track, the playback of both together can enhance the sound to a notable degree.

You might expect that when two guitars play identical chord and rhythm patterns together the result would simply be to create a louder version of the single guitar sound, and in theory this would be the case, but in practice the result is otherwise, for two reasons. First of all, it's not actually possible to play exactly the same thing twice, because of fractional differences in your

FRONTLINE
Stereo Chorus

technique, which create millisecond variations in the way you pick or strum the strings. Because they're so small these differences cannot be perceived as any sort of timing error as such, but they do create enough variation to be advantageous when the two versions are heard together. Another reason is due to any small tuning discrepancies (again, not significant enough to be noticeable in isolation) which might arise between any two recorded parts, and assist in creating a 'wider' sound when both versions are heard in simultaneous playback.

This practice of recording the same part twice had actually been in use for many years before guitar chorus pedals were ever thought of, and was used extensively in recording vocals, when it's generally referred to as 'double tracking', which lends the same aural advantage of greater 'width' to the sound. You'll certainly have heard this effect on many recordings, whereby the same vocalist would twice record his or her lead vocal, or even harmony, for simultaneous playback. In such cases the average listener is usually not aware that they're hearing two ostensibly identical vocal tracks being presented as if they were one.

The idea of an actual device to simulate double-tracked vocals (as opposed to literally recording them over again) seems to have originated at Abbey Road studios in the 1960s, when it was referred to as ADT or artificial double tracking, as devised by engineer Ken Townsend, to remove the time-consuming necessity of having to record vocals twice. At that stage it was created by the use of two tape machines with the same recorded signal, one of which would be using a variable oscillator to alter the speed and thereby put it slightly out of sync with the original.

A chorus unit is able to recreate these effects from only one guitar, by splitting the signal from your guitar into two separate parts. But if both signals remained unaltered there would be no sonic advantage whatsoever, because the sound coming out of the pedal would still be the same as that which went in. So the chorus unit adds a time-delay fluctuation to one of these two signals, putting it slightly out of time and (because it's fluctuating and unstable) out of tune with the original, unaltered sound. In this sense it differs from that which could be achieved from a delay unit, which would produce a fixed-rate time delay with no pitch alteration at all.

A chorus pedal generally has three main controls: rate (speed of fluctuation), depth (degree of fluctuation) and effect level (amount of effect added to the original sound). And because these controls have a wide range of adjustment, the typical chorus unit can be used to create sounds well beyond the basic doubling effect originally intended. So, for example, instead of putting the sound just slightly out of pitch with the original, as in manual double-tracking, it's possible to alter the pitch to a far more drastic degree if desired. The actual advisability of doing so is a bit questionable, for very obvious reasons, but the point is that a chorus unit does offer a variety of options.

If you keep the rate (speed) fairly low, but raise the depth level, you get the double-tracking effect, which is generally useful but especially good for rhythm work. On the other hand, increasing the rate whilst setting a lower depth level creates more of a 'shimmering' effect, particularly good for sustained chords and arpeggio playing. If you get over-ambitious, raising both the rate and depth controls to a higher setting, it will sound completely out of tune and therefore awful. So yet again we're back to the general rule of restraint and tasteful understatement.

Flangers and phasers

These devices, based upon the principle of time and tonal variations, produce some of the more eccentric guitar sounds available, sometimes to the point where it hardly sounds like a guitar at all. According to an old story, the name 'flanging' came about because a recording engineer played back a tape whilst lightly resting his thumb against the edge of the spinning tape reel, or flange as it's sometimes called, producing an interesting variation on the original sound. There are other versions of how the term originated, but basically a flanger can perhaps be described as a variation on the chorus effect, but with additions to the usual rate and depth controls, offering even greater extremes of sound.

The phaser tends to create a swirling sound, which mimics the effect of a rotating speaker unit known as the 'Leslie' speaker (literally two rotating speakers in one cabinet) whilst being far more convenient to use.

This effect can be particularly dramatic when distortion is also applied. However, although it's possible to obtain many weird and interesting sounds whilst playing around with it at home, don't forget to consider how such extremes will (or won't) work effectively when applied to an actual piece of music within the context of other instruments in a band. So, as with the chorus effect, these devices are generally best employed with some restraint, or else rather un-musical noises can result.

Wah wah

Sometimes referred to as a 'cry baby', due to its characteristic sound, this is an elaboration on a basic tone control; but instead of being adjusted by hand, as with your guitar tone, the wah wah is really the same thing built into a foot pedal (pictured), which is played by a rocking motion, thereby rapidly sweeping the tone from bass to treble. What sets it apart from simply twiddling your guitar tone, apart from the convenience of foot operation, is its active (powered) circuitry, which enables a far greater extreme of tonal variation and so creates a rather more dramatic effect.

Although simplistic in principle the wah wah requires a certain amount of skill for best effect, because you must play guitar whilst maintaining an appropriately rhythmic motion on the pedal. This effect can work well on both rhythm and lead guitar, especially when used in conjunction with hammer-ons and string bending techniques.

A more recent alternative to the traditional wah wah pedal is the 'auto-wah', which, as the name implies, requires no manual action. It is instead activated by the force with which the strings are sounded. However, although it's easier to use, the auto-wah does tend to be less expressive than its manually operated counterpart.

An interesting approach sometimes used is the 'fixed wah' sound, which is simply a case of setting the pedal in a given position instead of the usual rocking action. This takes advantage of the wah wah's distinctive sound qualities for interesting tonal effect.

Volume pedal

A volume pedal does exactly the same as the volume control on your guitar, in that it can reduce the maximum available output of the instrument, although, being passive (not powered), it can't actually boost the amount of volume. But it does have the advantage over a guitar volume in that it leaves your

hands free to concentrate upon playing, which is a pretty significant fact, and opens up a range of useful possibilities.

Most obviously, a volume pedal makes it easy for you to switch smoothly from playing rhythm, or maybe backing riffs, and then effortlessly raise the volume level for playing a solo, which – especially when playing live – really is a great deal easier than adjusting the volume by hand, or perhaps trying to pick louder when required.

Another attractive option is to reduce, or even completely eliminate, the initial 'attack' (sound of a note beginning), which is very prominent and characteristic on guitar. This is because the guitar is an instrument that has a very sharp attack, unlike, for example, many wind instruments, where the note begins rather more gently.

The technique involved is straightforward enough. You back off the volume level, pick the string, and then immediately raise the volume. This creates a unique sound wherein the note appears to begin without the usual picking sound. An early exponent of this approach was George Harrison, an imaginative but often underrated guitarist, who can be heard using a volume pedal on several Beatles recordings. Perhaps he was inspired by the country sound of pedal steel guitar, where it's an essential part of the sound. Indeed, any electric guitar on a clean setting can be used to simulate the pedal steel tone. Try some string bending whilst gently raising the volume 'into' the bend – it takes a bit of practise to get the feel of this, but it does open up some new and useful possibilities.

Some of the more elaborate volume pedals, such as the one pictured above, have a 'minimum level' control. This is simply an additional volume control built into the circuitry that, if required, prevents the pedal, at its lowest setting, from completely shutting off all volume, instead allowing you to define the lowest volume required. I would definitely recommend this additional feature as being worth the extra expense because it allows greater ease of use, particularly for live work, where it can simply be 'full on' for lead playing or 'full off' for rhythm.

Tremolo

It's that word again; but unlike tremolo picking (see **page 101**) or the tremolo arm (**page 203**) this is another

guitar effect pedal, which on this occasion creates a fluctuation in volume. If you've ever encountered a vintage guitar amplifier, such as the legendary Fender Twin reverb from around the early 1960s, you'll know that this was once a standard feature of the combo amp itself, and could be conveniently activated whilst playing by the operation of a foot-switch. But oddly enough the tremolo seems to have become virtually obsolete as an amp feature by the '70s, and was also hard to come by as separate unit. It was presumably as a result of this rarity that the effect more or less disappeared from use for many years. I seem to recall searching around for one in all the second-hand music stores without much success, until I eventually acquired the Schaller model seen here. But now, happily, the tremolo unit has been rediscovered, and if the sound appeals to you it shouldn't be hard to find.

In principle the tremolo is one of the simpler effects, having nothing at all to do with delay, pitch variations or phase shifting. It's a volume effect and nothing else. But basic though this may be, it is an attractive sound which can be especially effective on arpeggio playing or sustained chords, although its use is by no means limited to those styles only.

The tremolo controls are generally those of rate (speed of fluctuation) and depth (degree of fluctuation), although on some models the actual waveform is also adjustable, between triangular and square. The audible (as opposed to technical) difference between these two options is basically that with square wave the volume fluctuation jumps suddenly from low to high, with nothing intermediate between the two extremes, while the triangular wave is somewhat less 'sudden', moving from low volume to high in a more gradual way, covering, so to speak, all the intermediate volume points in between.

Equaliser

An equaliser (often just referred to as EQ) is essentially an elaboration upon the usual bass, middle and treble range of tone control, but with a far greater degree of individual adjustment for each particular tone band. If you look at the model pictured here you'll see that it's arranged as a series of 'faders', all situated parallel to each other.

A 'fader' does exactly the same as any rotary level control, but has a sliding action as opposed to the perhaps more familiar circular motion. This arrangement of faders is convenient, because it permits you to literally see where you are in terms of the actual frequency curve. Each fader covers a certain specific range of tonal frequency, which is specified on the unit itself. Although this will typically be displayed in terms such as '6.4k', '3.2k' etc, the evidence of your own ears will certainly provide the most workable guide for all practical purposes.

An equaliser pedal has several advantageous features that make it an asset for enhancing your guitar sound. First of all it permits you to shape your tone very precisely, beyond that offered by standard amplifier tone controls. Also, it can be helpful in eliminating feedback because it allows you to filter out the particular tone frequency that may be causing the feedback to occur. And because it's foot-switchable you can instantly change tone and volume, from perhaps a suitable rhythm sound to something more dynamic for your lead guitar work.

Reverb

Although this is certainly one of the most widely used effects, being a feature of almost every decent quality guitar amplifier, there are variations on the reverb (reverberation) sound that may require something a little more versatile. In its basic form, the reverb unit, as in most amps, consists of a spring with a transducer – a device that converts physical energy into electrical current – at each end. The signal takes time to travel the length of the spring, thereby creating the reverb sound. Although the comparison with echo is unavoidable, there are also certain differences that prevent your digital delay pedal from being able to create reverb. The delay can be heard as a distinct repeat, no matter how finely adjusted, whereas reverb is less distinct as individual repeats and creates a feeling of 'space' around the sound. If you require something a bit more adjustable than your basic amplifier reverb can provide, you may find that a separate digital reverb pedal will be worth the investment as part of your effect set-up.

Reverb is something which most electric guitar players, and indeed many acoustic guitarists, use to some extent, as it gives a live, natural quality to your playing without which the tone can be lacking in sparkle, especially in rooms with little or no natural ambience.

Generally speaking you'll probably be inclined to use it discreetly for rhythm work, adding a somewhat more lavish reverb sound for your arpeggios and solos. As always, be careful not to overdo things or it may cause the sound of your guitar to (heaven forbid) get lost among the other instruments in your band.

Compressor

It's hard to think of the compressor as being an 'effect' because it's more like a self-adjusting volume level control. The basic idea is to even out the volume level at which the strings are played, or to compensate for any natural volume differences between individual strings. It can also increase the amount of audible sustain by raising volume levels as the natural volume of the note diminishes.

When you play any note or chord on a guitar the sound will sustain for a relatively short time until, as the string vibrations diminish, the sound fades away. So the note volume is loudest when first sounded, becoming progressively quieter thereafter. Placing a compressor between guitar and amplifier can significantly change this situation. This is because it sets a 'threshold' level, which will first prevent the note from exceeding a specified volume and then will progressively amplify the sound as it fades away. The result is a very even volume level throughout the duration of any sustained note or chord. In effect this means that no matter how forcefully you strike the strings, the volume output will be no greater than if you play very lightly, and, of course, vice versa. As with all effect units there's a wide margin of how the unit can be adjusted and you'll often prefer a less extreme setting, applying just a moderate amount of compression. This would allow some volume variation according to force applied, whilst also giving the advantage of greater sustain.

Compressor pedals generally have two controls to define the sound. The amount of compression is controlled by a threshold control, which might also be referred to as sustain. The other is an 'attack' control, which determines how quickly the compression will begin. Country guitarists like to set a very fast attack with moderate sustain, which can create a very 'tight' picking sound that is particularly effective on chicken pickin' (see **pages 98–100**). On the other hand, compression can be used for increasing the effect of distortion in heavier guitar styles by creating even more sustain than the distortion itself can provide.

A discreet use of compression can be especially helpful in any recording situation, where it helps to control the amount of guitar (or any other instrument) signal and so prevents the volume from varying too much in accordance with your personal playing technique. This avoids the danger of 'overloading' the recording device and thereby producing unwanted distortion.

A couple of things to be aware of when using a compressor: firstly, because severe compression settings reduce the effect of your usual picking definition too much of it can cause your guitar to get 'lost' in the overall band sound, unless you compensate by increasing the amp volume accordingly; also, due to its effect of increasing low volume levels a compressor will similarly raise the sound of some things that aren't intended to be heard, such as the sound of your fingers sliding across the strings, or unintentional plectrum noises scratching or tapping away during supposedly quiet passages in the music.

Noise gate

Again, although not an effect as such the noise gate is a very useful device to include in your pedal line-up. This is because the more effect units you have, the more background noise is likely to be generated, and what the noise gate does is to create a barrier (or gate) between your guitar plus attached devices and the amplifier until such time as you wish to 'open' that gate in order to allow your guitar sound to come through. It works by setting a volume level or 'threshold', below which no sound can pass through. In other words, any background hiss, although sufficiently audible to be considered a nuisance, isn't actually loud enough to trigger the noise gate. However, when you begin playing in the usual way this produces more than enough volume to open the gate. Obviously, once the gate 'opens', all sound – including background hiss – will pass through, but because you're also playing your guitar this noise will now be rendered unobtrusive, due to being masked by the guitar music.

As always, designs vary, but the noise gate usually has two essential controls. One is the 'threshold', which defines the level at which it will open. This should be set at a level greater than that produced by any unwelcome noises, but not so high that it fails to immediately respond to your normal playing volume. The other is a 'release' control, which holds the gate open until the note has sufficiently faded away. Although not complicated to adjust, these two controls should be set at a sensible balance to prevent the noise gate closing too soon and clipping the fade-out of your sustained notes and chords. It's for this reason that a noise gate shouldn't be placed 'after' a delay or reverb in the sequence of connected effects (see next page), as it would then be likely to cut off the fade-out on these.

Acoustic simulator

The devices covered so far aren't the end of the effects story, although they are the most well established and certainly the most widely used. Several others are available and are well worth a mention, so let's take a quick look at the other clever little electronic wonders that you should be aware of and may wish to include in your effects repertoire.

The acoustic simulator is exactly what you always hoped for, but never thought possible: a pedal that makes an electric guitar sound just like an acoustic. Sounds too good to be true, and to some extent it is. So let's be honest about this; if you're after a top quality acoustic guitar tone you'll still need to play a top quality acoustic guitar. However, if you just need something that can provide a reasonable facsimile of acoustic tone, perhaps for some rhythm work within a band context, then this could be the answer.

The usual basic controls on this device are 'body' (which means bass) and 'top' (treble). Try using the neck pickup with the acoustic simulator, because you'll find it more likely achieves a softer and therefore more acoustic-sounding tone (you'll probably also find it helps to increase the bass level). Try just a touch of reverb too, or even chorus (but only a little bit), for better results.

Harmoniser

The idea here is that you play a single note and the unit adds a suitable harmony. So, if you were to play a **C** note the harmoniser would add an upper 3rd (**E**), or perhaps a lower 5th (**G**). Exactly which harmony you'll get is likely to depend upon how you adjust the settings regarding the key you're playing in, as well as the versatility of the particular model of harmoniser. The better ones have a so-called 'intelligent' pitch shifter, in which the particular note desired as harmony to the note played can be very specifically determined. If your knowledge of harmony is rather limited this can obviously prove musically hazardous when using a harmoniser of any description. It also means that you skipped over **pages 115–116**, where you'll find enlightenment in this crucial aspect of musicianship.

When using any harmoniser you need to be aware of its limitations regarding the speed and accuracy with which it can detect and respond to the input note. It can only detect one note at a time, and if a previous note is still sounding, even very quietly, this can confuse the device and result in some incorrect, and very unmusical harmony notes. Also, you need to ensure that the harmoniser is receiving a strong (loud) signal from your guitar, or else it may not read the note correctly. So it's probably best to have your pickup giving full volume into the harmoniser, and if you want to be heard quietly then turn down the volume at some stage after the harmoniser, not before. This is one example of how the order in which your effect pedals are connected can be important. For more information on that particular subject, refer to the following information.

Effect connection order

If you're using several individual effect units they'll obviously need to be connected to each other, creating a continuous link between guitar and amplifier. The procedure is straightforward enough. The lead from your guitar is plugged into the 'in' socket of the first effect, and another lead goes from that effect unit's 'out' socket which then connects to the 'in' socket of the next effect, and so on, until the effect chain reaches the amplifier. These connecting leads, incidentally, are referred to as 'patch leads', which are usually very short for obvious reasons and can be purchased as such instead of using a full-length guitar cable for the job. And although each effect can be powered individually by a 9v battery it makes better sense to power them all from one multi-output power converter.

For general convenience purposes most guitarists, because they're likely to be using a number of devices and not just one, tend to arrange them in a fixed position which can be quickly set up at gigs, rather than having to take each separate unit out of its box, place it in position and connect it up every time. This usually involves a bit of DIY, with all the effect pedals arranged in order and attached to a piece of board along with the power converter. A convenient alternative is to simply purchase a ready-made pedal board unit, designed specifically for this purpose.

Although the series of effects can be connected in any order at all, this random approach is unlikely to produce the best results for your sound. This is because any individual effect unit can, for a variety of reasons, influence the sound of those that follow. An obvious example of this would be the interaction between a volume pedal and an overdrive/distortion unit. Suppose the distortion is preceded by the volume pedal – every time you lower the volume, this will also reduce the strength of signal going into the distortion unit. The result of this will be to reduce not only the volume, but also the level of distortion, thereby creating a 'cleaner' sound.

Unless you actually want this to occur (and some players do), it's probably best to put any overdrive/distortion device *before* the volume pedal, not *after* it. There are other examples that can emphasise the importance of pedal connection order, and for personal choice you may wish to experiment in this regard, but for generally favourable results the following is an effective set-up, starting from your guitar:

1.Compressor – 2.Wah wah – 3.Overdrive/distortion – 4.Equaliser – 5.Flanger/phaser/pitch shifter/acoustic simulator – 6.Volume pedal – 7.Noise gate – 8.Chorus – 9.Delay – 10.Tremolo – 11.Reverb

– and then into your amplifier. Keep in mind that this sequence isn't unalterable, and you should always experiment to see if you prefer any alternatives. Obviously you may be using fewer effects than the above list, in which case you need only omit any missing items from the sequence.

Effect looping

You may be aware that many guitar amps are equipped with something called an 'effects loop', which is simply an alternative method of connecting effect pedals to the amplifier. This will be seen as two jack plug sockets on the front or rear of the amplifier, specified as 'send' and 'return' – which is simply another way of saying, respectively, 'out' and 'in'. This might sound complicated, but all it really means is that you connect a lead from the 'send/out' of the amplifier and plug it into the input socket of your first effect unit. Then you take another cable and connect it to the output of the final effect in your chain, which is then plugged into the 'return/in' of your amp effect loop. The guitar itself is simply plugged straight into the usual amp input, instead of being routed through the effect pedals. It all sounds a lot more confusing than it really is, which is why I've included a picture of a single effect pedal and amplifier to show how it looks in practice. As with connecting devices in any situation, just ensure that the 'out' of one device connects to the 'in' of the other. This might sound perfectly obvious, but it's very common to accidentally get them the wrong way round at some stage in the sequence and then spend ages trying to figure out why nothing appears to be working.

Be aware that connecting your effects to the loop, as opposed to straight into the amplifier's main input socket, can, as with any connection situation, alter the sound of certain devices in the chain – as an example, my own experience is that looping doesn't work well with distortion effects. But, depending upon how elaborate your effect set-up is, you may find it convenient to use the loop for some effect situations, if not all.

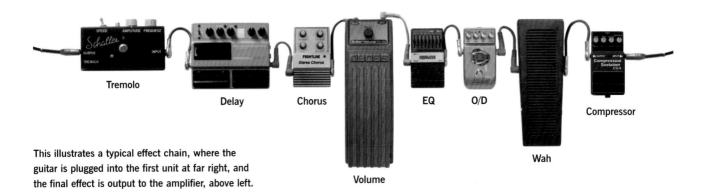

Tremolo　　**Delay**　　**Chorus**　　**EQ**　　**O/D**　　**Wah**　　**Compressor**

Volume

This illustrates a typical effect chain, where the guitar is plugged into the first unit at far right, and the final effect is output to the amplifier, above left.

Multi-effects

You could save yourself some inconvenience by considering the purchase of a good quality multi-effect unit. This takes the form of a single item that contains pretty much every effect you're likely to need.

The model pictured here is a very comprehensive example of its kind, which has since been superseded by later variations on the theme – although newer doesn't always mean better where effect devices are concerned. This is because most of the usual effects still perform basically the same function as they always did. A wah-wah pedal still does exactly the same as when Jimi Hendrix was having so much fun with it back in the '60s, and George Harrison's beloved volume pedal still just alters the volume. So if you're choosing a multi-effect unit it's probably most relevant to ensure that it has all the effects you'll actually require, along with a decent number of 'patches' – a patch being the name given to any collective arrangement of effect settings accessible with one press of a pedal. The less expensive models may not necessarily be of poorer quality in terms of sound reproduction; they might simply contain fewer effects – fewer patches – and therefore be less versatile.

Opinion is somewhat divided among guitarists regarding the merits of multi-effects, as opposed to a series of individual pedals. This is mostly because some people find it a lot easier to reach down and adjust a single pedal by the tweak of a dial than have to reprogram a multi-effect unit over perhaps several different patches to suit the acoustics of a particular room. On the other side of the argument, the multi-effect, once programmed, permits you to change from one type of sound to another, perhaps completely different, sound at the single touch of one pedal. This means that you could, for example, be using a low volume clean rhythm sound, with light reverb and a touch of chorus, then switch instantly to heavy distortion with digital delay and flanger, at a higher volume level, by just one foot action.

A compromise can also be achieved between these two options, whereby you might wish to use certain favourite individual effect pedals while also including a multi-effect unit as part of the chain. In this situation you could perhaps use a separate delay or reverb for easy overall adjustment to suit the acoustics of any particular room, whilst gaining the benefits of the multi-effect for most of the other sound options.

This is just one point of view, but obviously there are a number of possibilities that might appeal to you according to your particular requirements. But remember that any combination of effects, in whatever form, become part of the overall sequence, and should therefore be taken into consideration when deciding the order of your effect chain, as explained on the previous page. One option to consider in this context is to place some effects directly between guitar and amplifier, whilst linking others into the effect loop.

Amp simulation

During the past 50 years or so, many amplifiers have attained almost as great a status in rock and roll legend as some of the classic guitars, and as a result some of the more famous models have become either extremely rare or alarmingly expensive, and sometimes both. But guitarists still seek out those golden tones from their favourite recordings and naturally wish to emulate them, which is where amplifier simulation comes into the picture.

In recent years a great deal of time, expense and technological expertise has been invested in attempts to produce a device that will enable you to play with the benefits of classic amp tone, but without the massive financial expenditure of buying or hiring numerous amplifiers and then carrying them all to the recording studio to achieve the desired sound. And whilst this is just about feasible for those who can afford it, the problem of reproducing that sound live is an even greater impracticality.

The first to design a widely used and practical amp simulator was the Line 6 company, whose famous 'Pod' model has now become almost a legend in its own right. This has proven to be an extremely efficient recording device for guitarists, as it enables a direct connection between guitar and recording desk without the need of any other obvious equipment (traditional amp/speaker units) along the way. It's true that you could always plug directly into a recorder with any effect pedal etc, but the problem would be to achieve a convincing guitar tone which genuinely sounded as if it were coming from a miked-up Fender Twin Reverb, or whatever, with all the necessary ambient characteristics pleasing to the ear.

Although the Line 6 Pod is easy to use in a recording situation, its lack of convenient (foot-switchable) adjustability wasn't entirely suited to live work, which soon occasioned the company to design a floor-mounted model that operates in pretty much the same way as any multi-effect unit, which in many ways it does resemble. Indeed, there are numerous multi-effect units that, as with the model pictured here, now often feature amp simulation as yet another facet of their versatility.

These devices detail numerous models of amplifier which can, with reasonable accuracy, be simulated, along with all the usual range of guitar effects such as chorus, delay and so on. If you do decide to go the amplifier simulation route in an effort to achieve your ideal sound, don't forget that any guitar tones you hear on record will also have been influenced by several other factors apart from the amp and its speakers – not the least of which will be the guitar itself, plus the player's technique and the type of recording equipment involved at that time. So think of these devices as another useful tool, but not necessarily the end of the musical rainbow.

Wireless transmitter

One problem familiar to all working guitarists is the inconvenience of wires trailing all over the place, just waiting for you to trip over them or accidentally disconnect one whilst playing. And without a doubt, the most annoying of all these wires is the one connecting your guitar to its amplifier. This is even more apparent when it first plugs into some effect pedals along the way and thereby assumes an extremely inconvenient location around your feet and ankles.

In an effort to minimise some of these difficulties, clever technically minded people have long since invented the wireless transmitter, two examples of which can be seen in the photograph on the next page. The earlier designs, as exemplified by the model at the right of the picture, feature a battery-powered transmitter that attaches to your guitar strap or belt, from which a short wire connects to the guitar output socket. This sends the guitar signal to its receiving

unit, which is in turn connected directly to the amplifier. These devices first became popular in the '80s and created a new freedom for stadium rockers around the world. In more recent years, with a view toward even greater convenience, a new design has become popular, as seen on the left of the picture.

This tiny transmitter operates on exactly the same overall principle as the earlier model, except that, having a much smaller transmitting unit, it can be plugged directly into the guitar, supported entirely by its own jack plug connector. In some cases the design of this input connection is 'guitar specific', to some degree at least. This means that you would need a different design transmitter for a Fender Stratocaster or similar model, as opposed to something like a Telecaster. This is simply related to the shape of the guitar input layout, and has nothing to do with any other technical specification. Other models, including the one pictured here, are more versatile in their fitting arrangement, having a spring-loaded jack-to-transmitter connection that would therefore be suitable for either situation.

A point to be aware of when using these devices is the fact that they can sometimes conflict with other such equipment that may be operating on the same frequency. This doesn't often cause problems, but just occasionally you may find that your guitar sound is being transmitted to another sound system operating nearby, or indeed vice versa. So if you find yourself experiencing any odd behaviour from your sound equipment, it may be that your guitar transmitter, although normally reliable, is either transmitting or receiving to or from another piece of equipment. Some of the more sophisticated wireless transmitters permit adjustment to their frequency to counteract this, but if you encounter any difficulties in this regard it's always possible to resort to the old-fashioned method of direct cable communication with your amplifier.

Tremolo (vibrato) arm

This clever device differs from all other items mentioned in this chapter because it's not actually an additional piece of equipment, but is part of the guitar itself. The picture here displays a typical example as fitted, in this case, to a Yamaha Pacifica guitar, and features the tremolo design that first appeared in 1954 on the Fender Stratocaster. More detailed information on the operation and adjustment of this device can be found on pages 182–84, but for now we'll look at its functional benefits.

The purpose of a tremolo is simply to alter the pitch of notes, or entire chords, by shifting the position of the bridge or tailpiece to which the strings are attached. This differs from the pitch change created by string bending in that a tremolo arm permits you to lower the pitch, as opposed to string bending which can only raise note pitch.

Over the years the use of this bar has tended to become ever more extreme, as those of you who are into heavy metal will surely be aware – although this isn't to say that an understated approach doesn't have its benefits also. Probably the most distinctive use of the tremolo arm (technically this is an incorrect description for what is actually a vibrato mechanism – see page 182) is the understated but very skilful technique of Hank Marvin, who in the early 1960s, as lead guitarist of instrumental group the Shadows, really did create an entirely new type of guitar sound, which continues to be much imitated to the present day. His approach is to maintain a light grip on the bar whilst playing, and thereby shape the sound of notes in much the same way as the natural vibrato would in the voice of a singer. The actual length of the bar itself played a part in that sound by creating a natural tendency to pick closer to the neck of the Stratocaster, creating a gentler twang as opposed to the harsher, more cutting tone obtained when picking near to the bridge.

This device can actually change the note pitch to a significant degree if so required, by several semitones in fact, although this tends to cause excessive slackness in the strings, and a more restrained application is most often desirable. A suitable way to begin experimenting with a tremolo is to apply a gentle pressure-and-release to the bar at the end of phrases, where a note or chord is sustained. Try not to apply too much pressure or it can sound somewhat out of tune. The rate at which you apply this 'press and release' approach will be determined more or less instinctively by the tempo of the music, although such restrained use isn't normally set rigidly to any particular time discipline as such. A similar style works well for any sustained chord played at the very end of a song, adding an extra touch of class to what otherwise might be an unremarkable ending.

A more dramatic tremolo application can be created by giving the arm a more severe but very rapid quiver, and is most suitable on faster tempo numbers. This is guaranteed to add considerably to the feeling of speed and excitement, and is somewhat easier than attempting to achieve a similar effect with normal string bending. Again, this type of tremolo movement isn't set to any specific sense of timing, but is more a matter of the right 'feel', as determined by the song and your personal interpretation of what sounds good. However, be aware that if you use the tremolo arm to sound what is distinctly another note, by holding perhaps an F note and then bending it down to the point where it becomes clearly an E note, then this is really like playing two separate notes in the usual way, and therefore the timing does become an essential factor.

As with string 'pre-bending' (see page 76), you can also apply the tremolo before sounding the note. This means that you press the bar down, pick the note and then allow the tremolo arm to return to its normal position. This can be particularly effective with a distortion sound, especially if you raise the volume at the same time as gradually releasing the bar.

Harmonics (see pages 93–95) can also benefit from this device, simply because you can add vibrato (see pages 92–93) to an open-string harmonic, which, precisely because it's un-fretted, could not be given the more usual finger vibrato technique.

APPENDIX 2 Complete chord reference

The section that follows is a dictionary of all the chords you're ever likely to need. Learn the basics first (majors, minors etc) and then acquire other chords as you require them. All chord shapes in this reference are based upon the standard guitar tuning of E–A–D–G–B–E. Alternative tuning methods as described on **pages 149–52** obviously require alternate finger patterns, which can be determined as a matter of individual initiative, with reference to the information on chord construction in Chapter 6.

Chords in this section are placed in two categories. First comes a collection of 'open' chord shapes, these being chords which contain one or more 'open' (not fretted) strings. You'll notice that some open chords have more than one possible variation, such as the **A7** chord, which has two different versions, or the **Em** chord, which is also playable in

more than one 'open' fingering. This section is followed by a wider range of chord patterns that can be considered as 'moveable', in that they can be used at any location on the neck, having a different key centre at every fret. Due to the fact that these moveable chords are of identical fingering whatever the neck location, it would be pointless to illustrate every single chord shape at all fret positions. Instead, one example of each category is shown, from which all other position names can be determined according to the location of its root (name) note. If you're unfamiliar with notes along the guitar fretboard, refer to **page 30** for easy clarification.

Instructions on how to read chord diagrams generally can be found on **page 15**. In addition, the method used here, with regard to moveable chords only, is to clearly indicate which note of the chord determines its name. The illustrations below clarify this method for your information.

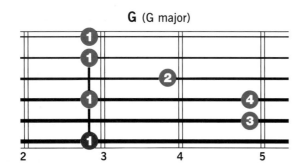

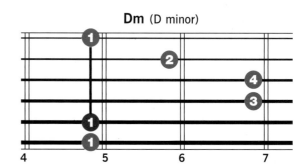

The two examples here, of a **G** major chord and a **D** minor chord, clearly highlight in red the 'name note' principle employed in this chord dictionary. So, the key note of the **G** major shape (above left) is found on the sixth string, at the 3rd fret; whereas the key note of the **D** minor shape is located on the fifth string, at the 5th fret. Moving any chord shape either up or down the fretboard changes its key note, and it therefore becomes a different chord.

Most chord shapes actually contain more than one note position that could be used to determine its name. The **G** major chord above has three such notes, whilst the **D** minor has two. But to identify all such notes in the following pages would be both unnecessary and visually confusing, so we use one note for reference in each chord shown, which will always be the lowest available root note in that particular chord shape.

Any strings that are to be played 'open' are marked with an 'O', whilst any notes not to be sounded in a chord are marked with an 'X', as illustrated in this example of a **D** major chord.

The number inside each circle indicates which finger is used to secure the string against the fretboard. Occasionally a chord note on the lowest string may be held by the thumb (indicated by a 'T' in the circle), as referred to on **page 108**. The technique of muting any strings which aren't intended to be heard is explained in Chapter 2 (**page 16**), Chapter 3 (**pages 37 and 40**) and Chapter 6 (**pages 108 and 110**). For those

of you who are left-handed players, I realise that it can be difficult to read chord diagrams intended for right-handed reading, so I've included an equally comprehensive dictionary of left-hand chord shapes, which includes every chord as displayed in the standard right-hand version; this appears on **pages 231–51**.

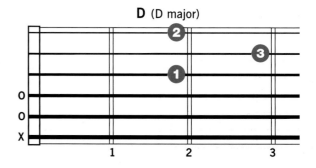

Basic open chords

Due to the nature of open chords, being dependent upon open strings, not every chord can have an 'open' version. The following section may therefore appear somewhat random in its selection, and is consequently listed in order of chord type, such as major, minor etc, and then in alphabetical order within those categories.

Also remember that some chords – those that are either sharp or flat – will have more than one name, so that, for example, C#m is the same chord as D♭m. In these cases the more commonly used name is indicated. If you need any more information on this subject, refer to **page 29** for a more comprehensive explanation.

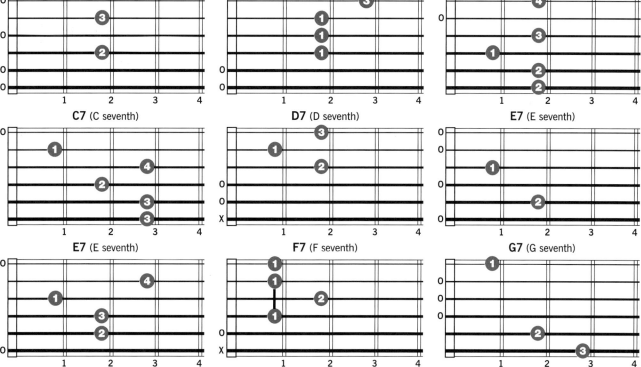

Major chords (1st, 3rd, 5th)

A (A major) **C** (C major) **D** (D major)

E (E major) **F** (F major) **G** (G major)

Seventh chords (1st, 3rd, 5th, ♭7th)

A7 (A seventh) **A7** (A seventh) **B7** (B seventh)

C7 (C seventh) **D7** (D seventh) **E7** (E seventh)

E7 (E seventh) **F7** (F seventh) **G7** (G seventh)

Minor chords (1st, ♭3rd, 5th)

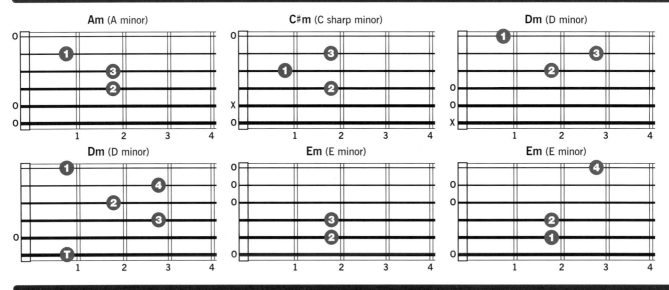

Minor seventh chords (1st, ♭3rd, 5th, ♭7rd)

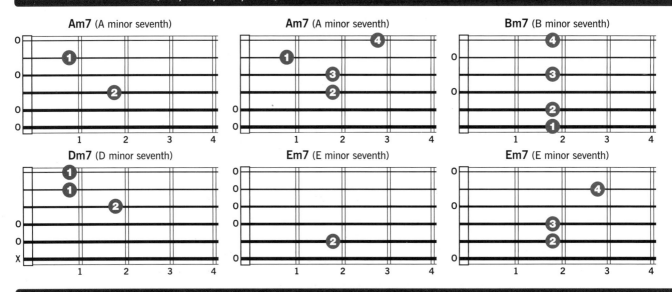

Major seventh chords (1st, 3rd, 5th, 7th)

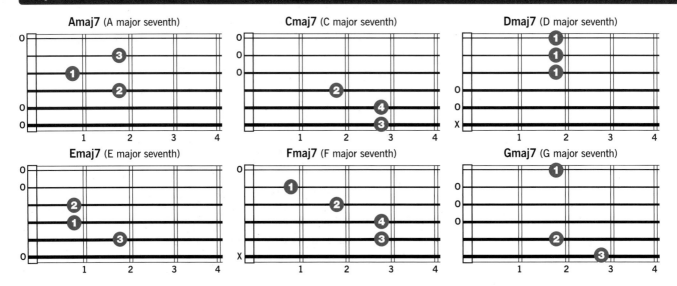

Sixth chords (1st, 3rd, 5th, 6th)

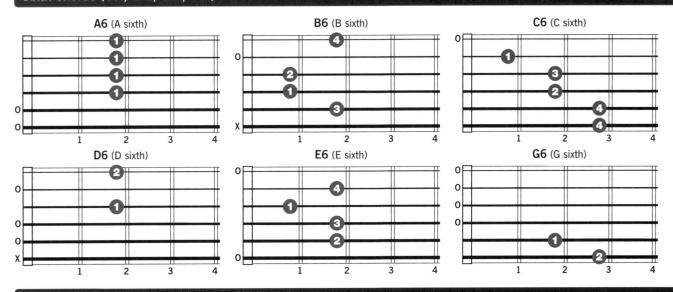

A6 (A sixth) B6 (B sixth) C6 (C sixth)
D6 (D sixth) E6 (E sixth) G6 (G sixth)

Minor sixth chords (1st, ♭3rd, 5th, 6th)

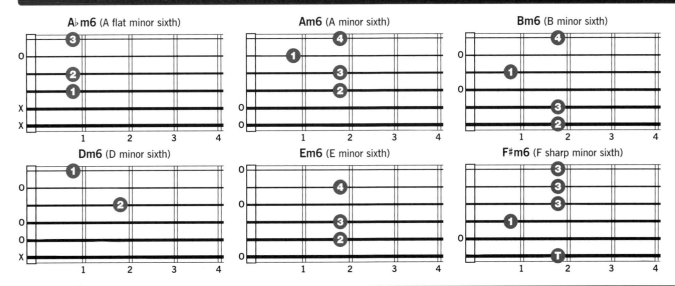

A♭m6 (A flat minor sixth) Am6 (A minor sixth) Bm6 (B minor sixth)
Dm6 (D minor sixth) Em6 (E minor sixth) F#m6 (F sharp minor sixth)

Ninth chords (1st, 3rd, 5th, ♭7th, 9th)

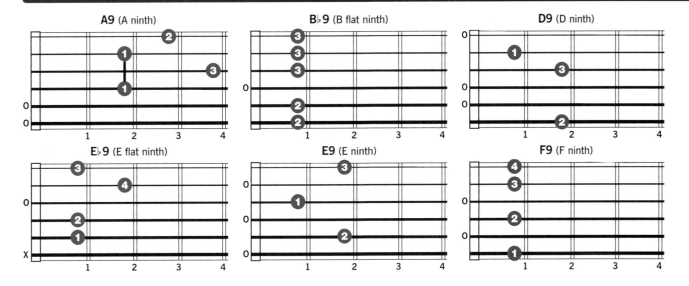

A9 (A ninth) B♭9 (B flat ninth) D9 (D ninth)
E♭9 (E flat ninth) E9 (E ninth) F9 (F ninth)

Minor ninth chords (1st, ♭3rd, 5th, ♭7th, 9th)

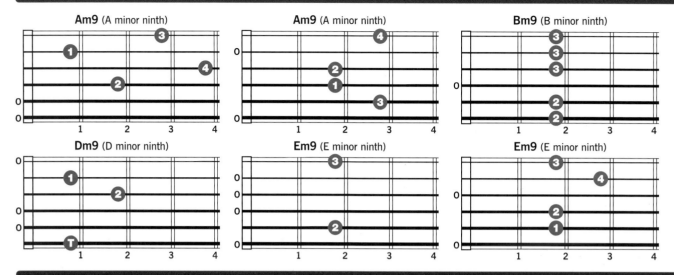

Major ninth chords (1st, 3rd, 5th, 7th, 9th)

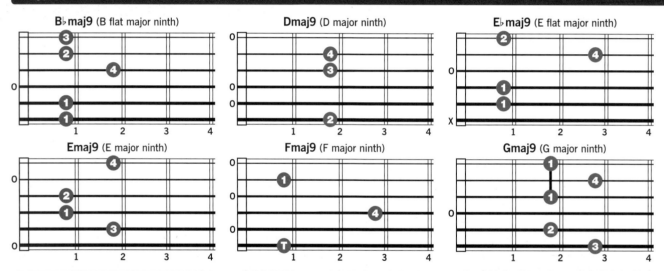

Eleventh chords (1st, 3rd, 5th, ♭7th, 9th, 11th)

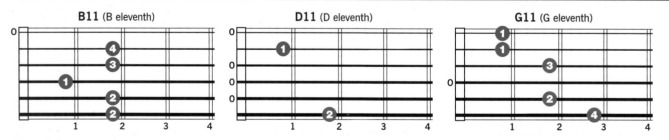

Thirteenth chords (1st, 3rd, 5th, ♭7th, 9th, 11th, 13th)

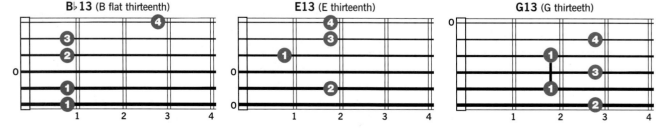

Suspended fourth chords (1st, 4th, 5th)

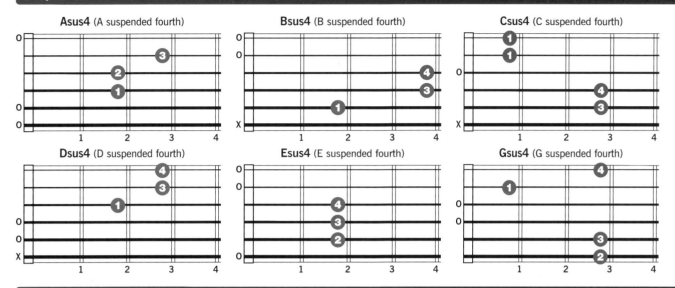

Seventh suspended fourth chords (1st, 4th, 5th, ♭7th)

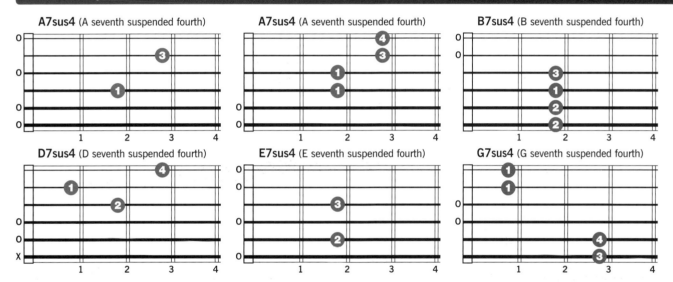

Added ninth chords (1st, 3rd, 5th, 9th)

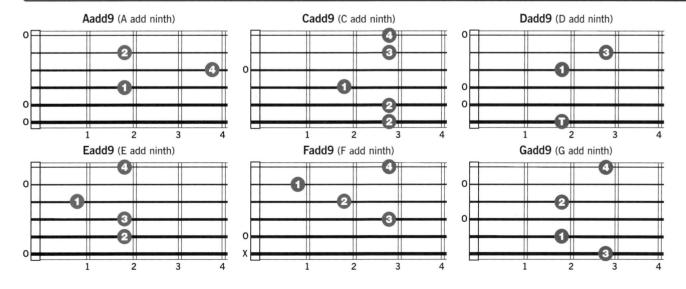

Sixth/Ninth chords (1st, 3rd, 5th, 6th, 9th)

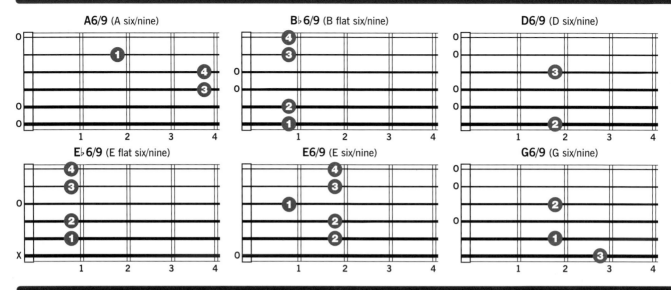

Augmented chords (1st, 3rd, #5th)

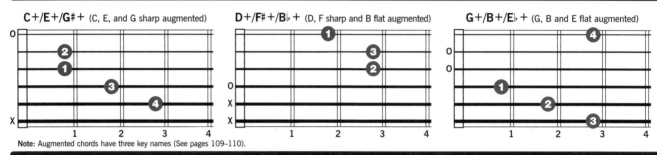

Note: Augmented chords have three key names (See pages 109–110).

Diminished chords (1st, ♭3rd, ♭5th ♭♭7th)

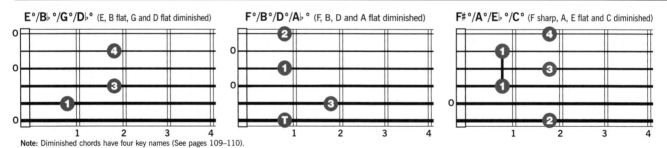

Note: Diminished chords have four key names (See pages 109–110).

This covers all the essential open chords and quite a few more. It will be recognised that I have, for each chord shape, included the maximum number of notes conveniently playable for that particular chord. But this doesn't necessarily mean that every note has to be included on all occasions. Sometimes it will be preferable to play a four- or five-string version of a chord instead of the full six-string option. More on this subject can be found on pages 39–40, and also by referring to the very comprehensive chord construction information in Chapter 6.

All fingerings shown (with regard to which finger holds down which particular string) are those generally found to be convenient for reasons of comfort and practicability. However, if you find an alternative that suits you better, that's perfectly all right too. This is one of those things to which you'll adapt naturally in the course of time and experience, and will, to some extent, depend upon which chord you've just played and which chord you're about to play next. As long as you manage to form the correct chord shape, efficiently and quickly, it's entirely acceptable to vary the fingering according to personal preference.

Moveable chords

Moveable chords are broadly referred to as 'bar chords', due to the preponderance of such chord types in this category. However, the fact is that any chord shape which doesn't include open strings is also equally versatile, in that it can be used at any position on the guitar neck, creating a new chord of its particular type (ie major, minor etc) at each fret position. And, precisely because these chord shapes can be applied at any position on the guitar neck, the moveable chord diagrams are illustrated without any specific fret numbers, each one instead having a red 'name' note to identify its pitch.

In addition to the information on **page 204**, which should be referred to in connection with this section, it's worth remembering that where chords are concerned there are often alternatives and variations that can sometimes be useful to know about. I've tried to include any such options that I would consider to be worthwhile,

such as the two alternate ways of fingering the first major chord shown, or the 'black' note, indicating a chord note that's entirely valid but often omitted, due to either difficulty of fingering or simply because the chord usually sounds better without that particular note being included. An immediately obvious example can be seen in one of the major chords shown below, where the 'black note' on the sixth string (the third chord tone) is usually omitted, because most players prefer the sound created when the fifth string (root) note is lowest.

It's a fact that certain chord shapes are more widely used than others of their type. These more 'popular' versions are the first few illustrated in each category. Most likely they'll be the ones you'll be inclined to learn first, but each particular chord shape will have its own sound characteristics, and all versions will be useful to know about at some point in time.

Major chords (1st, 3rd, 5th)

Major chord (1)

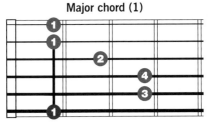

Major chord (1) (Alternate fingering)

Major chord (2)

Major chord (2) (Alternate fingering)

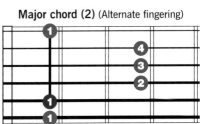

Major chord (3)

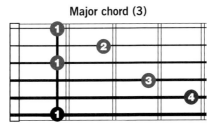

Major chord (4)

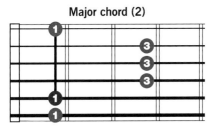
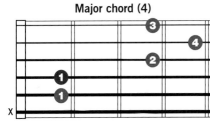

Seventh chords (1st, 3rd, 5th, ♭7th)

Seventh chord (1)

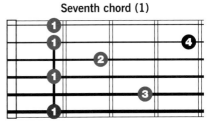

Seventh chord (2)

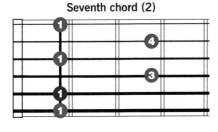

Seventh chord (3)

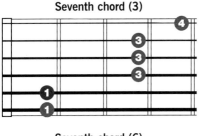

Seventh chord (4)

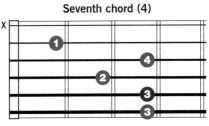

Seventh chord (5)

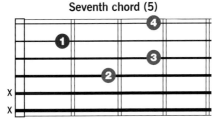

Seventh chord (6)

Minor chords (1st, ♭3rd, 5th)

Minor chord (1)
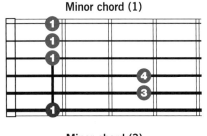

Minor chord (1) (alternative fingering)

Minor chord (2)
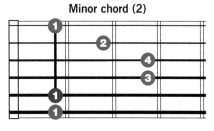

Minor chord (3)
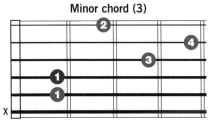

Minor chord (4)
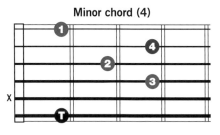

Minor chord (5)
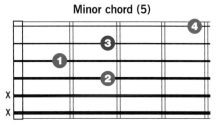

Minor seventh chords (1st, ♭3rd, 5th, ♭7rd)

Minor seventh chord (1)
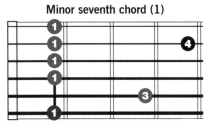

Minor seventh chord (2)
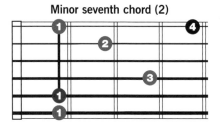

Minor seventh chord (3)
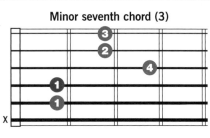

Minor seventh chord (4)
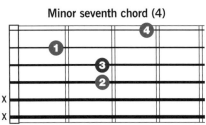

Minor seventh chord (5)
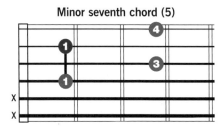

Minor seventh chord (6)
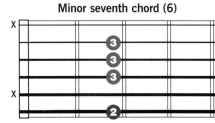

Major seventh chords (1st, 3rd, 5th, 7th)

Major seventh chord (1)
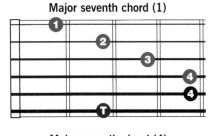

Major seventh chord (2)
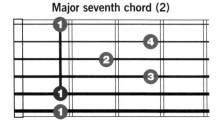

Major seventh chord (3)
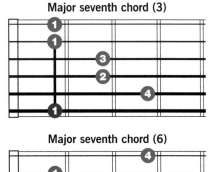

Major seventh chord (4)
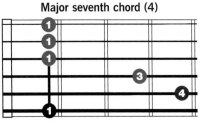

Major seventh chord (5)
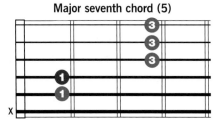

Major seventh chord (6)

Minor/major seventh chords (1st, ♭3rd, 5th, 7th)

A variation on the basic minor seventh in that the 7th note is 'natural', or not flat. Written, for example; Amin/maj7

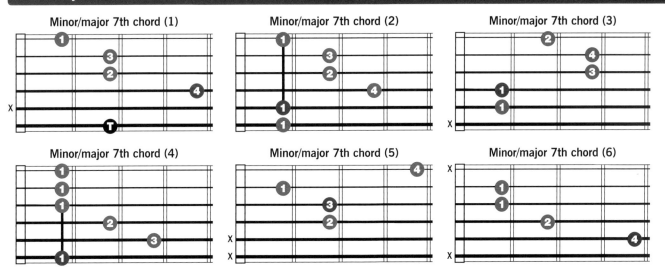

Minor/major 7th chord (1) Minor/major 7th chord (2) Minor/major 7th chord (3)

Minor/major 7th chord (4) Minor/major 7th chord (5) Minor/major 7th chord (6)

Sixth chords (1st, 3rd, 5th, 6th)

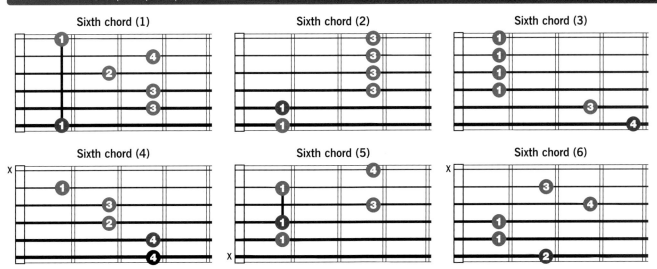

Sixth chord (1) Sixth chord (2) Sixth chord (3)

Sixth chord (4) Sixth chord (5) Sixth chord (6)

Minor sixth chords (1st, ♭3rd, 5th, 6th)

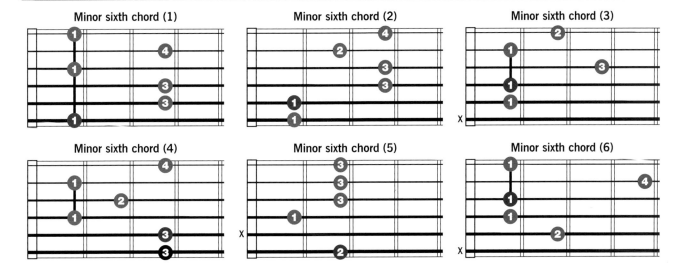

Minor sixth chord (1) Minor sixth chord (2) Minor sixth chord (3)

Minor sixth chord (4) Minor sixth chord (5) Minor sixth chord (6)

Ninth chords (1st, 3rd, 5th, ♭7th, 9th)

Ninth chord (1) Ninth chord (2) Ninth chord (3)

Ninth chord (4) Ninth chord (5) Ninth chord (6)

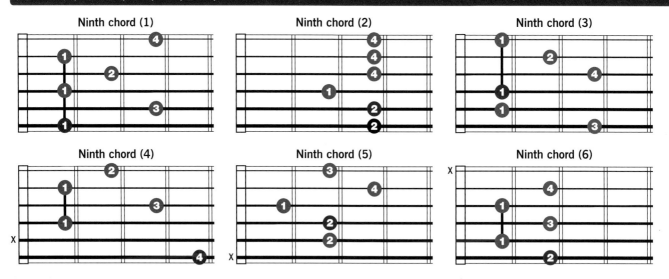

Minor ninth chords (1st, ♭3rd, 5th, ♭7rd, 9th)

Minor ninth chord (1) Minor ninth chord (2) Minor ninth chord (3)

Minor ninth chord (4) Minor ninth chord (5) Minor ninth chord (6)

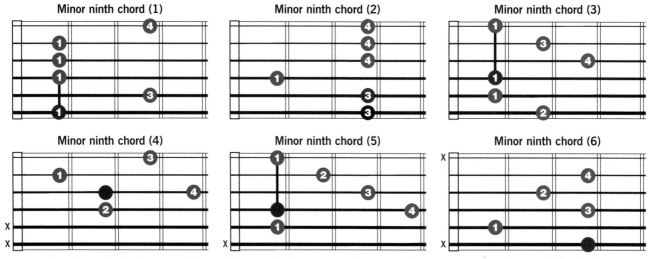

Note: Some of the more complex chords may not contain the 'root' (name) note (page 227). Where applicable, this note (although not played) is indicated in red, but without a fingering number.

Major ninth chords (1st, 3rd, 5th, 7th, 9th)   This varies from the basic 'ninth' chord, in that the 7th is not flatted. Written, for example; Amaj9 or A 9.

Major ninth chord (1) Major ninth chord (2) Major ninth chord (3)

Major ninth chord (4) Major ninth chord (5) Major ninth chord (6)

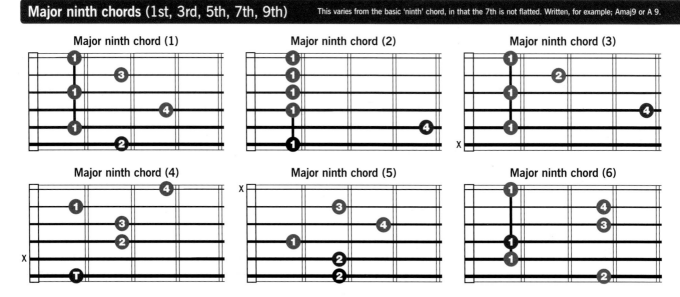

Eleventh chords (1st, 3rd, 5th, ♭7th, 9th, 11th)

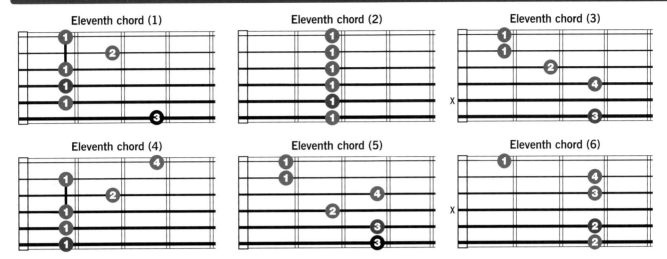

Eleventh chord (1)   Eleventh chord (2)   Eleventh chord (3)

Eleventh chord (4)   Eleventh chord (5)   Eleventh chord (6)

Minor eleventh chords (1st, ♭3rd, 5th, ♭7th, 9th, 11th)

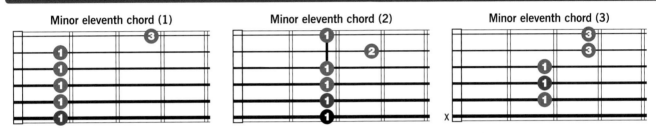

Minor eleventh chord (1)   Minor eleventh chord (2)   Minor eleventh chord (3)

Thirteenth chords (1st, 3rd, 5th, ♭7th, 9th, 11th, 13th)

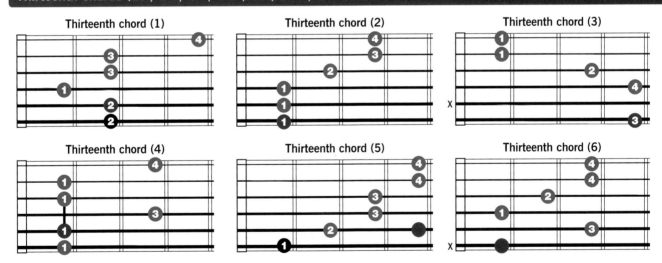

Thirteenth chord (1)   Thirteenth chord (2)   Thirteenth chord (3)

Thirteenth chord (4)   Thirteenth chord (5)   Thirteenth chord (6)

Minor thirteenth chords (1st, ♭3rd, 5th, ♭7th, 9th, 11th, 13th)

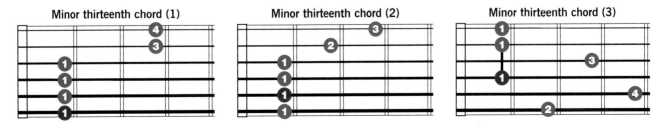

Minor thirteenth chord (1)   Minor thirteenth chord (2)   Minor thirteenth chord (3)

Major thirteenth chords (1st, 3rd, 5th, 7th, 9th, 11th, 13th)

A variation on the usual thirteenth chord, in that the seventh is not flatted. Written example Amaj13 or A△13.

Major thirteenth chord (1)

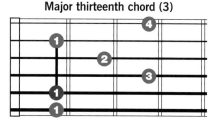

Major thirteenth chord (2)

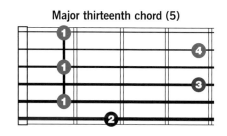

Major thirteenth chord (3)

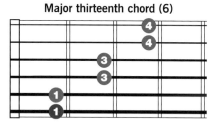

Major thirteenth chord (4)

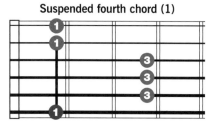

Major thirteenth chord (5)

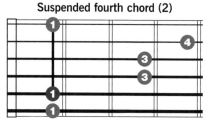

Major thirteenth chord (6)

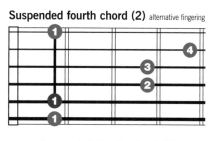

Suspended fourth chords (1st, 4th, 5th)

Suspended fourth chord (1)

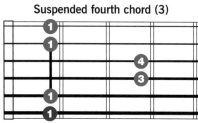

Suspended fourth chord (2)

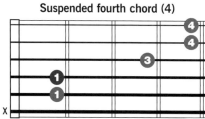

Suspended fourth chord (2) alternative fingering

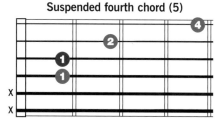

Suspended fourth chord (3)

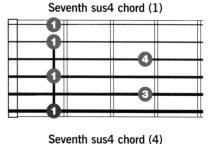

Suspended fourth chord (4)

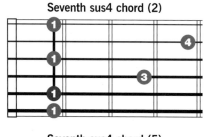

Suspended fourth chord (5)

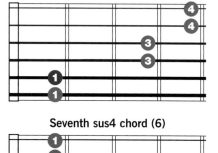

Seventh suspended fourth chords (1st, 4th, 5th, ♭7th)

Seventh sus4 chord (1)

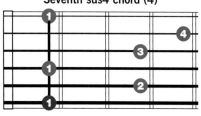

Seventh sus4 chord (2)

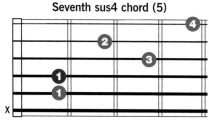

Seventh sus4 chord (3)

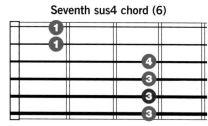

Seventh sus4 chord (4)

Seventh sus4 chord (5)

Seventh sus4 chord (6)

Suspended second chords (1st, 2nd, 5th)

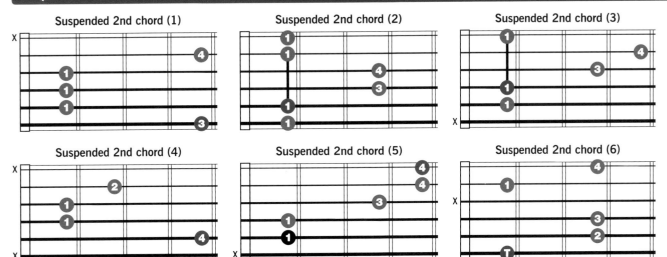

Suspended 2nd chord (1)   Suspended 2nd chord (2)   Suspended 2nd chord (3)

Suspended 2nd chord (4)   Suspended 2nd chord (5)   Suspended 2nd chord (6)

Added ninth chords (1st, 3rd, 5th, 9th)

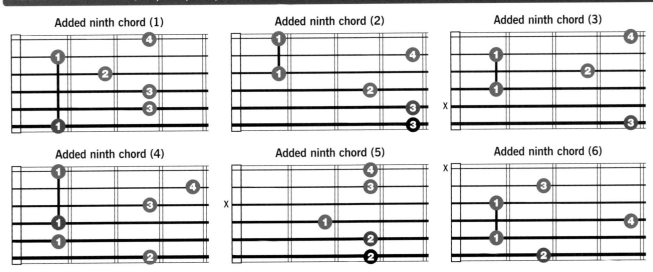

Added ninth chord (1)   Added ninth chord (2)   Added ninth chord (3)

Added ninth chord (4)   Added ninth chord (5)   Added ninth chord (6)

Minor added ninth chords (1st, ♭3rd, 5th, 9th)

The usual basics of a minor chord with the addition of a ninth. Written example Am add9 or Am/9

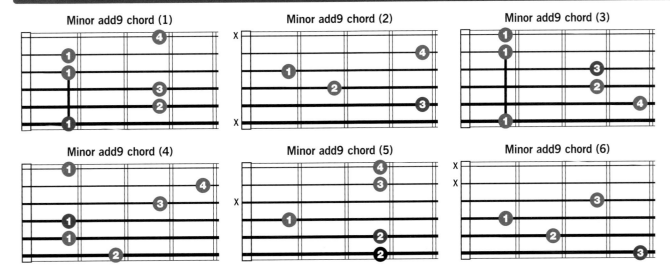

Minor add9 chord (1)   Minor add9 chord (2)   Minor add9 chord (3)

Minor add9 chord (4)   Minor add9 chord (5)   Minor add9 chord (6)

Sixth/Ninth chords (1st, 3rd, 5th, 6th, 9th)

A sixth chord with the ninth added. Written, for example as; A6/9

Six/Nine chord (1)
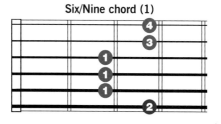

Six/Nine chord (2)
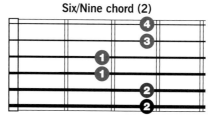

Six/Nine chord (3)
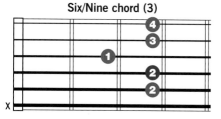

Six/Nine chord (3) Variation, with additional note
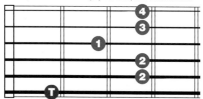

Six/Nine chord (4)
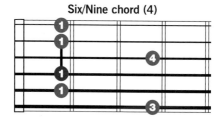

Six/Nine chord (5)
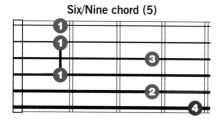

Minor sixth/ninth chords (1st, ♭3rd, 5th, 6th, 9th)

Minor chord version of the above. Written example; Am6/9

Minor six/nine chord (1)
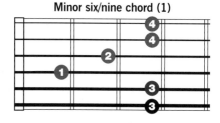

Minor six/nine chord (2)
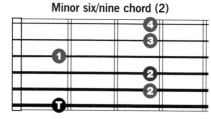

Minor six/nine chord (3)
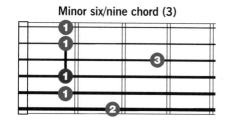

Augmented chords (1st, 3rd, #5th)

Augmented chord (1)
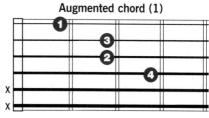

Augmented chord (2)
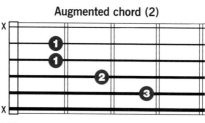

Augmented chord (3)
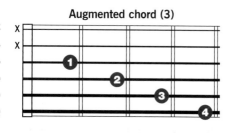

Note: Augmented chords have three key names (see pages 109–110).

Seventh augmented chords (1st, 3rd, #5th, ♭7th)

The basic augmented as above, but with the addition of the flatted seventh. Written, for example; A7aug or A7+

Seventh aug chord (1)

Seventh aug chord (2)

Seventh aug chord (3)
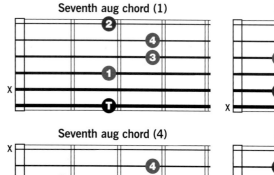
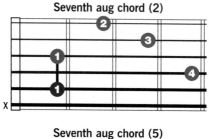
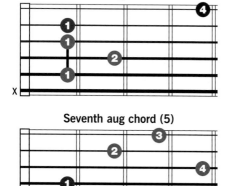

Seventh aug chord (4)

Seventh aug chord (5)

Seventh aug chord (5)

Minor seventh augmented fifth chords (1st, ♭3rd, #5th, ♭7th)

The minor seventh chord, with the fifth raised by one semitone. Written example; Am7+5 or Am7#5

Minor 7th aug 5th chord (1)
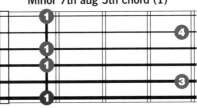

Minor 7th aug 5th chord (2)

Minor 7th aug 5th chord (3)

Major seventh augmented fifth chords (1st, 3rd, #5th, 7th)

A major seventh with the fifth being raised by one semitone. Written, for example; Amaj7+5 or A△7+5

Major 7th aug 5th chord (1)
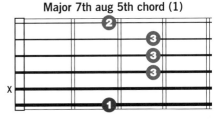

Major 7th aug 5th chord (2)
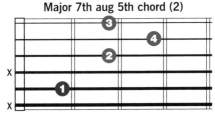

Major 7th aug 5th chord (3)
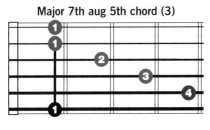

Major 7th aug 5th chord (4)
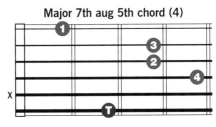

Major 7th aug 5th chord (5)
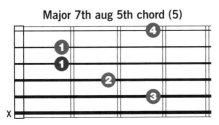

Major 7th aug 5th chord (6)
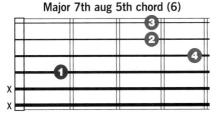

Diminished chords (1st, ♭3rd, ♭5th, ♭♭7th)

Technically a diminished seventh chord. See page 91. Written, for example; Adim or A°

Diminished chord (1)
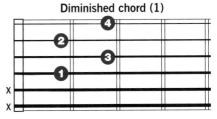

Diminished chord (2)
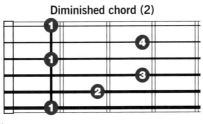

Diminished chord (3)
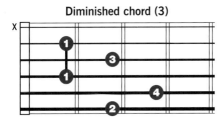

Note: Diminished chords have four key names (see page 109–110)

Diminished fifth chords (1st, 3rd, ♭5th)

The basics of a major chord, but with the 5th being 'diminished', or lowered by one semitone. Written, for example; A-5

Diminished fifth chord (1)
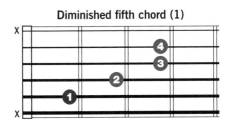

Diminished fifth chord (2)
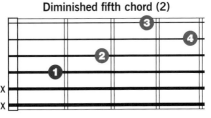

Diminished fifth chord (3)
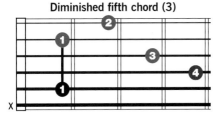

Diminished fifth chord (4)
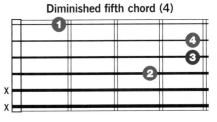

Diminished fifth chord (5)
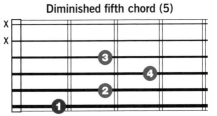

Diminished fifth chord (6)
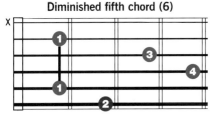

Seventh diminished fifth chords (1st, 3rd, ♭5th, ♭7th)

A variation on the previous chord, having the addition of a flatted seventh. Written, for example; A7-5 or A7♭5

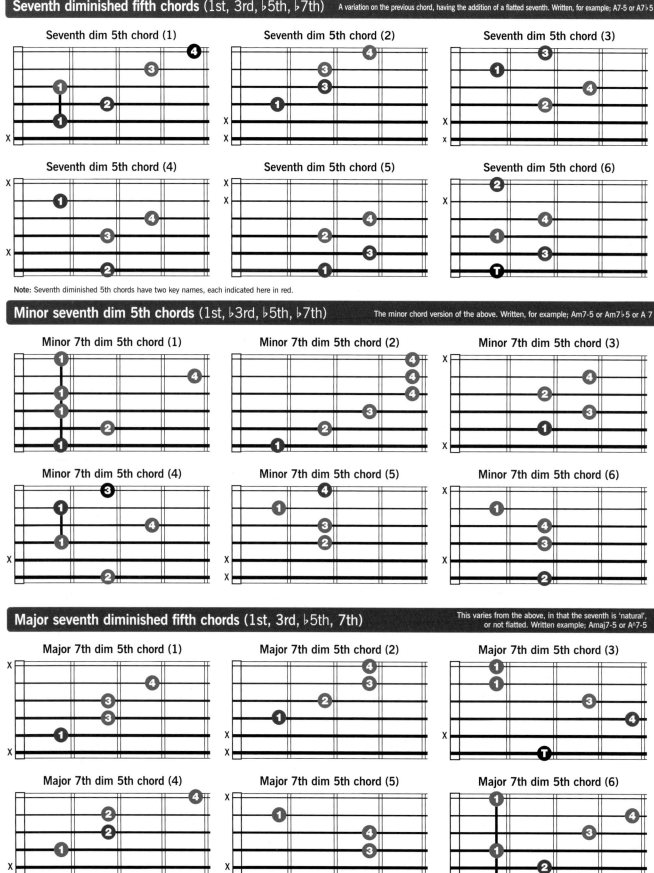

Note: Seventh diminished 5th chords have two key names, each indicated here in red.

Minor seventh dim 5th chords (1st, ♭3rd, ♭5th, ♭7th)

The minor chord version of the above. Written, for example; Am7-5 or Am7♭5 or A⌀7

Major seventh diminished fifth chords (1st, 3rd, ♭5th, 7th)

This varies from the above, in that the seventh is 'natural', or not flatted. Written example; Amaj7-5 or A△7-5

Additional chords

The range of chord types covered so far is, quite frankly, considerably greater than most players are likely to require, or indeed even be aware of. The obvious exception to this, of course, is jazz music, which places high demands upon a guitarist's knowledge of chords, and musicianship in general. And if this should be your particular area of interest, it really is essential that you have a firm understanding of harmony and chord construction. So if you have, for any reason, skipped somewhat too casually over Chapter 6 of this book, I strongly suggest that you reconsider your cavalier approach and go back over it without further delay.

Those of you who've been rather more diligent will be aware that as chord names and types become ever more complex we enter an area where various chords can somewhat overlap with each other, to the point where a chord with a long sophisticated name might actually contain the same notes as a far simpler-sounding chord with which you may already be familiar. This curious phenomenon of 'chord synonyms' has already been

explained in some detail (see **page 126**), and with several examples, and as you peruse this chord dictionary you might notice a few others which fit into that category, such as (for example) **Gsus4** containing the same notes as the less frequently encountered **C2** chord; or the fact that a straightforward **Fadd9** chord has the same four notes as the more elaborately named **Am7#5**. None of this apparently peculiar chord logic need present any confusion; it's just something to be aware of, as you'll encounter it from time to time.

It's perfectly feasible, and occasionally essential, that you may create your own chord shapes for a particular type of chord. This isn't at all difficult once you've acquired sufficient knowledge of chord construction, in which regard I refer you once again to Chapter 6. However, in order to be as comprehensive as possible, and provide you with a quick reference, I'll continue this chord dictionary with a range of those chords which are generally less familiar to guitarists, but which may nevertheless be required on occasion.

Ninth augmented fifth chords (1st, 3rd, #5th, ♭7th, 9th)
Ninth chord with an augmented or sharpened fifth. Written example; A9#5 or A9+5

Ninth aug 5th chord (1)
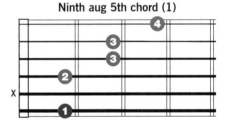

Ninth aug 5th chord (2)
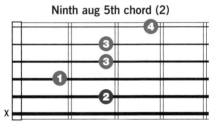

Ninth aug 5th chord (3)
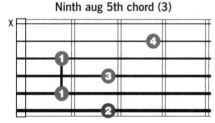

Ninth diminished fifth chords (1st, 3rd, ♭5th, ♭7th, 9th)
Ninth chord with a diminished or flatted fifth. Written example; A9♭5 or A9-5

Ninth dim 5th chord (1)
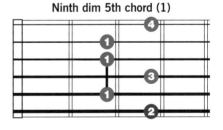

Ninth dim 5th chord (2)
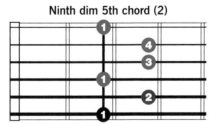

Ninth dim 5th chord (3)
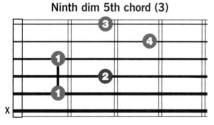

Minor ninth dim fifth chords (1st, ♭3rd, ♭5th, ♭7th, 9th)
Minor ninth chord with a flatted or 'diminished' fifth. Written example; Am9-5 or Am9♭5

Minor 9th dim 5th chord (1)
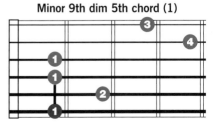

Minor 9th dim 5th chord (2)
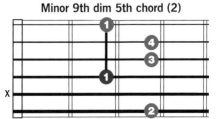

Minor 9th dim 5th chord (3)
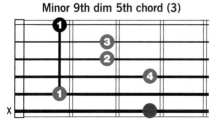

Note: Some of the more complex chords may not contain the 'root' (name) note (page 127). Where applicable, this note (although not played) is indicated in red, but without a fingering number.

Seventh augmented ninth chords (1st, 3rd, 5th, ♭7th, #9th)

Variation upon the ninth chord, whereby the ninth is sharpened or augmented. Written as, for example; A7+9 or A7#9

Seventh aug ninth chord (1)

Seventh aug ninth chord (2)

Seventh aug ninth chord (3)

Seventh diminished ninth chords (1st, 3rd, 5th, ♭7th, ♭9th)

The ninth in this case is flatted or diminished. Written example; A7-9 or A7♭9

Seventh dim ninth chord (1)
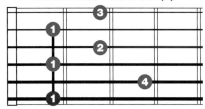

Seventh dim ninth chord (2)
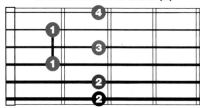

Seventh dim ninth chord (3)
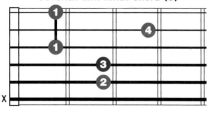

Minor seventh dim ninth chords (1st, ♭3rd, 5th, ♭7th, ♭9th)

Minor seventh with a flatted or 'diminished' ninth. Written as, for example; Am7-9 or Am7♭9

Minor 7th dim 9th chord (1)
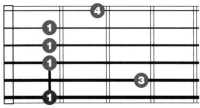

Minor 7th dim 9th chord (2)
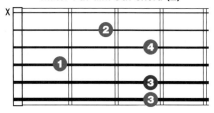

Minor 7th dim 9th chord (3)
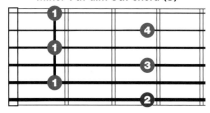

Seventh aug fifth aug ninth chords (1st, 3rd, #5th, ♭7th, #9th)

Seventh chord with a sharpened fifth and a sharpened ninth. Written as, for example; A7#5#9 or A7+5+9

7th aug 5th aug 9th chord (1)

7th aug 5th aug 9th chord (2)
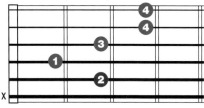

7th aug 5th aug 9th chord (3)
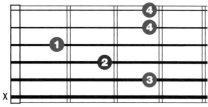

Seventh dim 5th dim 9th chords (1st, 3rd, ♭5th, ♭7th, ♭9th)

In this chord both the fifth and the ninth are diminished, or played one semitone flat. Written as, for example; A7-5-9 or A7♭5♭9

7th dim 5th dim 9th chord (1)
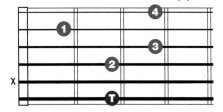

7th dim 5th dim 9th chord (2)

7th dim 5th dim 9th chord (3)
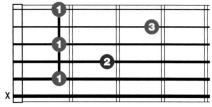

Seventh aug 5th dim 9th chords (1st, 3rd, #5th, ♭7th, ♭9th)

Seventh chord with an augmented or sharpened fifth, and a diminished or flatted ninth. Written example: A7+5-9 or A7#5♭9

7th aug 5th dim 9th chord (1)

7th aug 5th dim 9th chord (2)
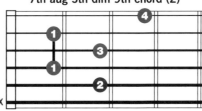

7th aug 5th dim 9th chord (3)

Seventh dim 5th aug 9th chords (1st, 3rd, ♭5th, ♭7th, #9th)

The reverse situation to the above. A seventh chord with a flatted fifth and a sharpened ninth. Written example; A7-5+9 or A7♭5#9

7th dim 5th aug 9th chords (1)
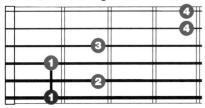

7th dim 5th aug 9th chords (2)
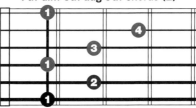

7th dim 5th aug 9th chords (3)
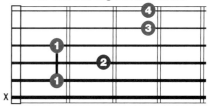

Seventh eleventh chords (1st, 3rd, 5th, ♭7th, 11th)

Different from a standard eleventh chord in that it contains no ninth. Written example; A7/11 or A7 add11

Seven eleven chord (1)
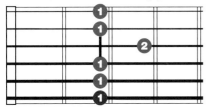

Seven eleven chord (2)

Seven eleven chord (3)
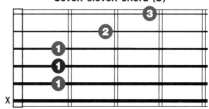

Minor seventh eleventh chords (1st, ♭3rd, 5th, ♭7th, 11th)

Minor chord version of the above. A minor seventh with an added eleventh. Written example as; Am7/11 or Am7 add11

Minor seven eleven chord (1)
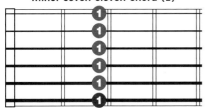

Minor seven eleven chord (2)
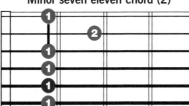

Minor seven eleven chord (3)
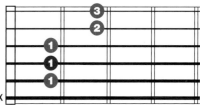

Major 7th aug eleventh chords (1st, 3rd, 5th, 7th, #11th)

Major seventh chord with the addition of an augmented 11th. Written as, Amaj7+11 or A△7#11

Major 7th aug 11th chord (1)
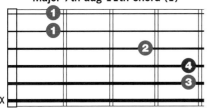

Major 7th aug 11th chord (2)
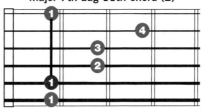

Major 7th aug 11th chord (3)
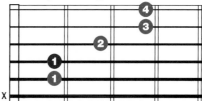

Ninth aug eleventh chords (1st, 3rd, 5th, ♭7th, 9th #11th)

A variation upon the standard eleventh chord, that note being augmented or sharp. Written as A9+11 or A9#11

Ninth aug eleventh chord (1)

Ninth aug eleventh chord (2)

Ninth aug eleventh chord (3)

Major ninth aug eleventh chords (1st, 3rd, 5th, 7th, 9th, #11th)

Written, for example, as Amaj9+11 or A△9#11

Major ninth aug 11 chord (1)

Major ninth aug 11 chord (2)
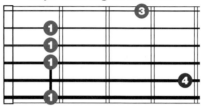

Major ninth aug 11 chord (3)
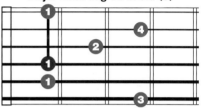

Thirteenth aug 9th chords (1st, 3rd, 5th, ♭7th, #9th, 11th, 13th)

Written example; A13+9 or A13#9

Thirteenth aug 9th chord (1)
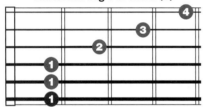

Thirteenth aug 9th chord (2)

Thirteenth aug 9th chord (3)

Thirteenth dim 9th chords (1st, 3rd, 5th, ♭7th, ♭9th, 11th, 13th)

Written example; A13-9 or A13♭9

Thirteenth dim 9th chords (1)
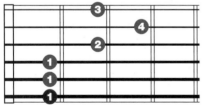

Thirteenth dim 9th chords (2)
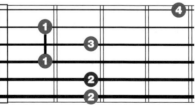

Thirteenth dim 9th chords (3)
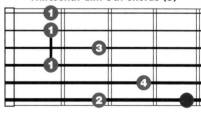

Note: Some of the more complex chords may not contain the 'root' (name) note (page 127). Where applicable, this note (although not played) is indicated in red, but without a fingering number.

Thirteenth aug 11th chords (1st, 3rd, 5th, ♭7th, 9th, #11th, 13th)

Written example; A13+11 or A13#11

Thirteenth aug 11th chords (1)
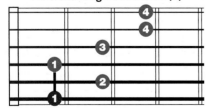

Thirteenth aug 11th chords (2)
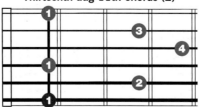

Thirteenth aug 11th chords (3)
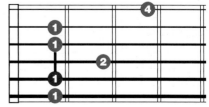

Left-handed players' reference

The information contained in this section is intended to make easier reading of certain illustrations for those of you who are playing your guitar in the left-handed manner. This is to say that when you're holding the instrument in normal playing position your left hand takes care of the picking or strumming, whilst the right hand is concerned with holding down the strings against the fretboard. For the majority of you who are right-handed players, I would mention that this part of the book contains nothing that hasn't already been covered elsewhere.

Obviously, most of the information in this book relates equally to both right-handed and left-handed playing, otherwise I would have to write an alternative edition specifically for that purpose. All musical information is obviously identical, so it really becomes a case of how you're looking at certain visual references, which is something that can be potentially confusing, especially for the beginner.

Some left-handed players don't have any real difficulty in mentally translating the 'mirror image' of a photograph or diagram in accordance with their requirements. But it isn't really an ideal situation to have to deal with when you already have more than enough to do in learning

to play the instrument itself. So, helpful as ever, I've cross-referenced points from certain chapters of this book with this special left-handed guide. Be aware, however, that not all photographs and illustrations in this book have a left-handed version. In many cases this would be unnecessary, as no visual 'confusion' is likely to arise from, say, the picture on **page 14**, which displays the correct handling of a plectrum; or the picture on **page 37** demonstrating the index finger muting of the bass string.

What this means is that whenever it might be convenient to view something from the left-handed point of view, that particular illustration will be indicated as having a left-handed version available at a specified page within this chapter. And conversely, all such illustrations contained in this chapter are accordingly cross-referenced back to the point of origin. In other words, it tells you on which page the original right-handed illustration can be found, and therefore in which context it applies. So if you, as a left-handed guitarist, wish to see how something looks from your perspective, simply check the appropriate reference for easy viewing. We begin with the diagram and photographs from **page 15**.

Ref: page 15
Chord diagram (enlarged version)

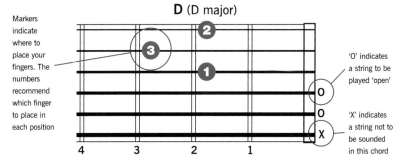

Markers indicate where to place your fingers. The numbers recommend which finger to place in each position

'O' indicates a string to be played 'open'

'X' indicates a string not to be sounded in this chord

This assumes that you're looking over the neck of your guitar, with the headstock – where the tuners are – off to the right but not pictured (to save space).

Ref: page 15
Overview of the guitar neck

Ref: page 30
When viewing this chart of notes along the fretboard, or indeed any other such diagrams, chords etc, always keep in mind that in these illustrations you're looking over your guitar neck, and so the lowest (and thickest) string is nearest your viewpoint, and consequently at the bottom of the picture below.

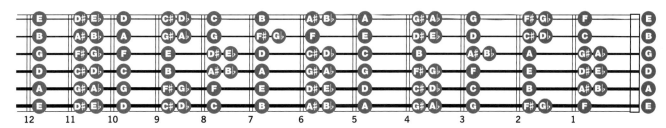

Ref: page 31

Demonstration of the bar chord principle, in this case an F major at the 1st fret. The thumb positioning for this type of chord tends to be somewhat different from that required for open chords.

Ref: page 31

Lower thumb positioning, as required for efficient application of bar chords.

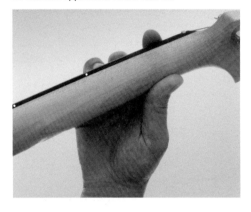

Ref: page 32

Bar chord diagram

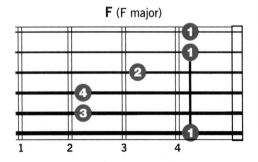

Bar chords, such as the one pictured above, are illustrated in a manner similar to that of open chords. The only significant difference is that where one finger covers several strings, only those strings not secured elsewhere are actually numbered. So although only strings one, two and six are shown with a number, the bar actually goes across all six strings.

Ref: page 35

The two options for securing the second major bar chord.

Comparisons between full and abbreviated chord forms

Ref: page 40

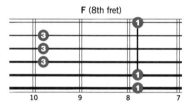
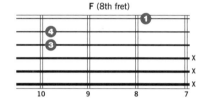

Ref: page 40

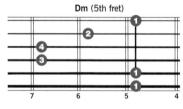
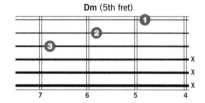

Ref: page 40

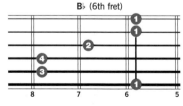
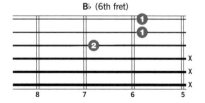

Although left-handed versions of all chords are illustrated in the complete chord dictionary which follows in the next section of this book, this doesn't include the so-called 'abbreviated' versions as shown above right. This is because they don't constitute additional chords as such, but are merely variations upon the full six-string versions, and may be usefully employed in a manner convenient to certain situations, as has already been explained on **page 40**.

Ref: page 41

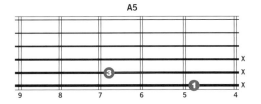

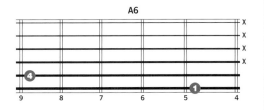

Ref: page 42

Ref: page 42

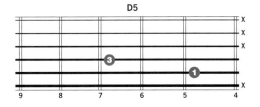

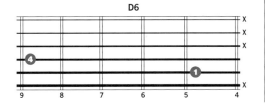

C major scale finger positioning

Ref: page 50

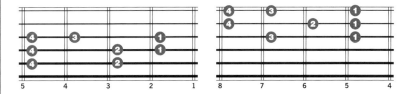

When applying these scales, don't forget to take note of the fret positions at which they're played.

C and D scales comparison

Ref: page 50

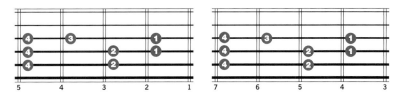

A major scale finger positioning

Ref: page 55

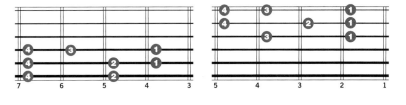

Two-octave scale in A

Ref: page 55

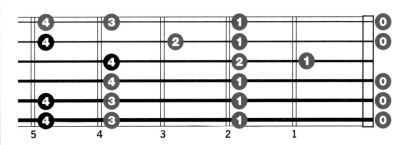

In this diagram the letters 'O' are the recommended open string positions.
The notes of A–D–B–E are also shown in black at their fretted positions, as
this can be optional. The lowest note of E must be played open.

Ref: page 78

Pressure for creating a behind-the-nut bend can be applied in either a downward or (as would apply in standard string bending) sideways movement. Either method can be effective, but if the string grooves in your guitar nut are rather shallow, sideways movement can dislodge the bent string from its groove. When attempting to master this type of bending technique, it will become apparent that the main area of stress is on your fingertips, as the lack of fretboard support causes the string to cut in rather forcefully.

Ref: page 89

A 'before and after' illustration of the double-string slide technique. Beginning with your first finger on the first string at fret 7, and your third finger on the second string at fret 8, slide the first finger up to the next (8th) fret whilst sliding the third finger up by two fret positions (to the 10th fret). It tends to be easier if you concentrate mainly on the two-fret slide, as applied by your third finger. The other finger movement is then inclined to naturally end up in the right place.

Ref: page 92

These pictures illustrate two methods of applying vibrato. Above right is a rapid movement across (perpendicular to) the fretboard. This method tends to be preferred by rock guitarists. Below right is the so-called 'classical' approach, whereby the rapid movement applied is horizontal to the fretboard. Both techniques have their virtues and are equally worth learning.

Ref: page 94

Illustrated here is the method of playing a 12th fret harmonic, which produces a note of the same pitch (but different sound characteristics) as the fretted 12th fret note on whichever string it's applied. Below is the technique required to fret a note with your right hand, whilst using your left hand to produce its harmonic note 12 frets – and therefore one octave – higher.

Ref: page 96

In this photograph the right hand is holding down a (C) note at the 5th fret in the usual manner. The left hand is both lightly touching the same string over the 17th fret, and simultaneously picking that string with the plectrum. This requires an adaptation to your plectrum technique, as it's necessary to handle the pick between the thumb and second finger, leaving your first finger free to touch the harmonic point over the appropriate fret.

Ref: page 97

The trick here is getting just the right grip on the plectrum, holding it close to the playing edge so that the tip just slightly protrudes beyond your thumb. When striking the string, ensure that the thumb is touching an appropriate harmonic point. Both pick and thumb should hit the string more or less simultaneously, in order to create the required harmonic sound.

Ref: page 113

'G' chord finger positions

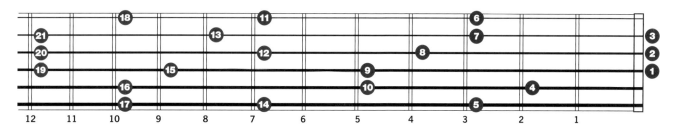

12 11 10 9 8 7 6 5 4 3 2 1

Working from right to left, the chords are as follows: dots 1, 2, 3, 4, 5 and 6 form an open **G** chord. Partially overlapping this are dots 5, 6, 7, 8, 9 and 10, which form a 3rd fret **G** bar chord. And overlapping this chord shape are dots 9, 10, 11, 12 and 13, which form a **G** chord at the 5th fret. From this we proceed to dots 11, 12, 13, 14, 15 and 16, which form another **G** bar chord, this time at the 7th fret. And finally, again slightly overlapping, are dots 16, 17, 18, 19, 20 and 21, which create a **G** bar chord at the 10th fret.

Ref: page 117

Pentatonic scale (in 'F')

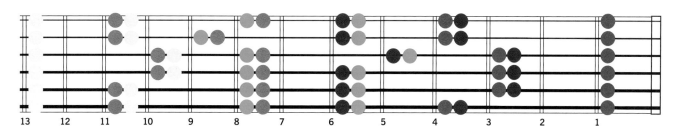

13 12 11 10 9 8 7 6 5 4 3 2 1

Comparison of pentatonic scales

Ref: page 119

C MAJOR Pentatonic

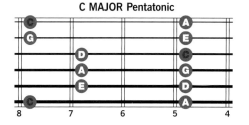

8 7 6 5 4

Ref: page 119

A MINOR Pentatonic

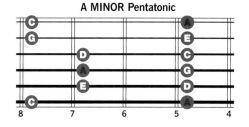

8 7 6 5 4

Note the identical fingering pattern and identical fret positions of the two diagrams immediately above. These two patterns are therefore the same in terms of notation, but would be applied in different ways. Played against a **C** major chord the sound would be smoother and less dissonant (see **page 111**) than if you played it with an **A** major chord, where the dissonance would create a more typically bluesy effect.

Chord voicing alternatives

Ref: page 125

G7 (3rd fret)

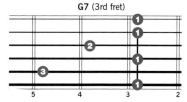

5 4 3 2

G7 (3rd fret)

5 4 3 2

Ref: page 125

Am7 (5th fret)

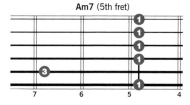

7 6 5 4

Am7 (5th fret)

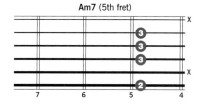

7 6 5 4

Ref: page 126

Cmaj9

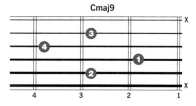

4 3 2 1

Dm9

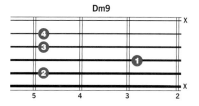

5 4 3 2

Chord synonyms

Ref: page 126

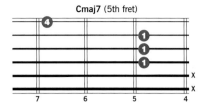

Cmaj7 (5th fret)

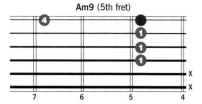

Am9 (5th fret)

Ref: page 127

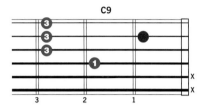

C9

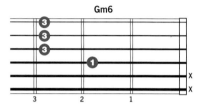

Gm6

Ref: page 127

Illustrations above and left are examples of 'chord synonyms', as explained in detail on **pages 126–7**. These are chords, or partial chords, which can be known by more than one name. It isn't uncommon for these chord synonyms to be played without the 'root' or name note being included. In such examples as are shown here this particular identifying note is illustrated in red, so that you can understand where the name of a chord is located. This 'red note' isn't intended to be actually played as part of the chord; it's for location identifying purposes only.

Example of a **C** major chord with a **D** bass note. This is based upon the 'polychord' principle, as explained on **pages 127–8**.

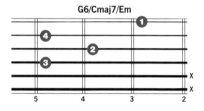

G6/Cmaj7/Em

Ref: page 128

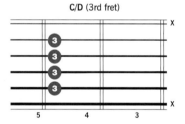

C/D (3rd fret)

Alternative tuning to 'open E' chord

Ref: page 149

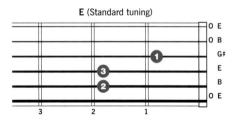

E (Standard tuning)

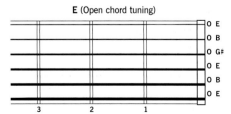

E (Open chord tuning)

Modes

Ref: page 129

These illustrations demonstrate the use of modes which, for a guitarist, can be regarded as taking a pattern of fingering on the guitar fretboard and then shifting that pattern to another position by simply starting from a different note, thereby creating a new scale. This principle is explained on **pages 128–31**.

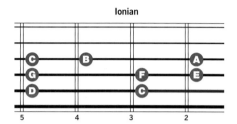

Ionian

Ref: page 129

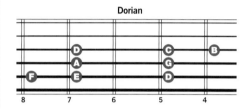

Dorian

Dorian

Ref: page 130

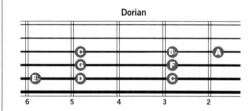

Phrygian (From E note)

Phrygian (From C note)

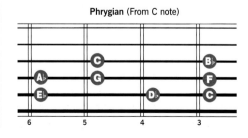

Left-handed chord reference

The section that follows is a comprehensive chord dictionary for left-handed guitarists. Learn the basics first (majors, minors etc) and then acquire other chords as you require them. All chord shapes in this reference are based upon standard guitar tuning of E–A–D–G–B–E. Alternative tuning methods as explained on pages 149–52 obviously require alternate finger patterns, which can be determined as a matter of individual initiative, with reference to the information on chord construction in Chapter 6.

Chords in this section are placed in two categories. First comes a collection of 'open' chord shapes, these being chords which contain one or more 'open' (not fretted) strings. You'll notice that some open chords have more than one possible variation, such as the A7 chord, which has two different versions, or the Em chord, which is also playable in more than one 'open' fingering. This section is followed by a wider range of chord patterns that can be considered as 'moveable', in that they can be used at any location on the neck, having a different key centre at every fret. Due to the fact that these moveable chords are of identical fingering whatever the neck location, it would be pointless to illustrate every single chord shape at all fret positions. Instead, one example of each category is shown, from which all other position names can be determined according to the location of its root (name) note. If you're unfamiliar with notes along the guitar fretboard, refer to page 225 for easy clarification.

Instructions on how to read chord diagrams generally can be found on pages 225–26. In addition, the method used here, with regard to moveable chords only, is to clearly indicate which note of the chord determines its name. The illustrations below clarify this method for your information.

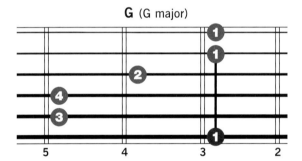

G (G major)

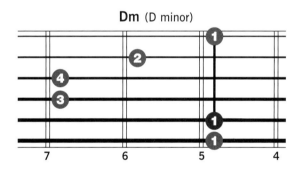

Dm (D minor)

The two examples here, of a G major chord and a D minor chord, clearly highlight in red the 'name note' principle employed in this chord dictionary. So, the key note of the G major shape (above left) is found on the sixth string, at the 3rd fret; whereas the key note of the D minor shape is located on the fifth string, at the 5th fret. Moving any chord shape either up or down the fretboard changes its key note, and it therefore becomes a different chord.

Most chord shapes actually contain more than one note position that could be used to determine its name. The G major chord above has three such notes, whilst the D minor has two. But to identify all such notes in the following pages would be both unnecessary and visually confusing, so we use one note for reference in each chord shown, which will always be the lowest available root note in that particular chord shape.

Any strings that are to be played 'open' are marked with an 'O', whilst any notes not to be sounded in a chord are marked with an 'X', as illustrated in this example of a D major chord.

The number inside each circle indicates which finger is used to secure the string against the fretboard. Occasionally a chord note on the lowest string may be held by the thumb (indicated by a 'T' in the circle), as referred to on page 108. The technique of muting any strings which aren't intended to be heard is explained in Chapter 2 (page 16), Chapter 3 (pages 37 and 40) and Chapter 6 (pages 108 and 110).

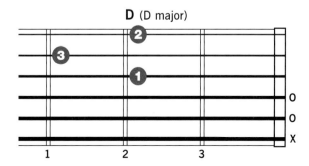

D (D major)

Basic open chords

Due to the nature of open chords, being dependent upon open strings, not every available chord can have an 'open' version. The following section may therefore appear somewhat random in its selection, and is consequently listed in order of chord type, such as major, minor etc, and then in alphabetical order within those categories.

Also remember that some chords – those that are either sharp or flat – will have more than one name, so that, for example, C#m is the same chord as D♭m. In these cases the more commonly used name is indicated. If you need any more information on this subject, refer to **page 29** for a more comprehensive explanation.

Major chords (1st, 3rd, 5th)

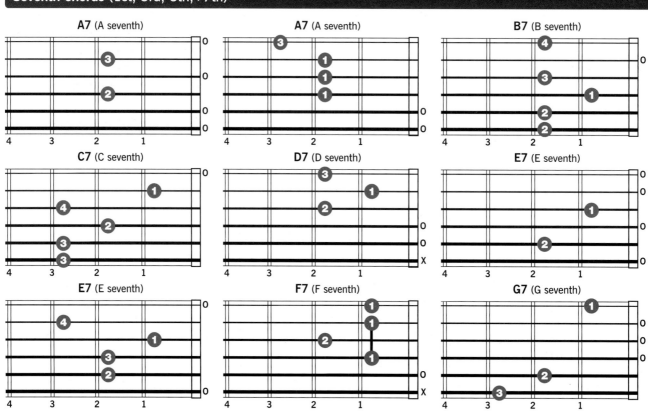

Seventh chords (1st, 3rd, 5th, ♭7th)

Minor chords (1st, ♭3rd, 5th)

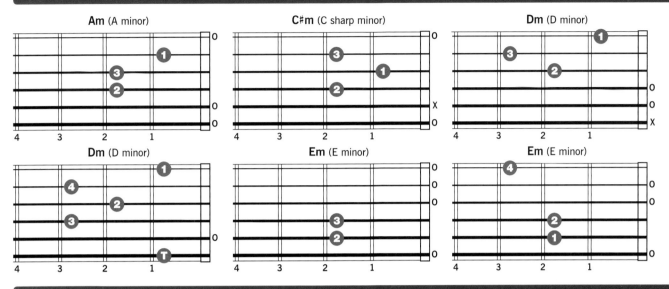

Am (A minor)   C#m (C sharp minor)   Dm (D minor)

Dm (D minor)   Em (E minor)   Em (E minor)

Minor seventh chords (1st, ♭3rd, 5th, ♭7rd)

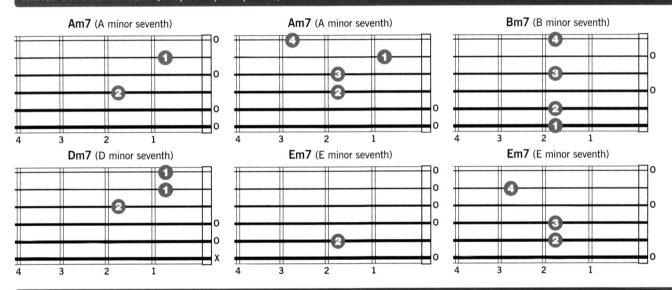

Am7 (A minor seventh)   Am7 (A minor seventh)   Bm7 (B minor seventh)

Dm7 (D minor seventh)   Em7 (E minor seventh)   Em7 (E minor seventh)

Major seventh chords (1st, 3rd, 5th, 7th)

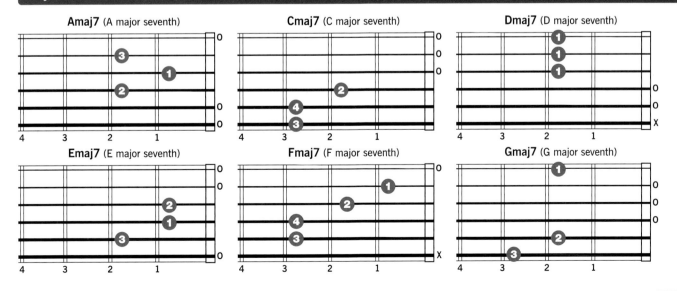

Amaj7 (A major seventh)   Cmaj7 (C major seventh)   Dmaj7 (D major seventh)

Emaj7 (E major seventh)   Fmaj7 (F major seventh)   Gmaj7 (G major seventh)

Sixth chords (1st, 3rd, 5th, 6th)

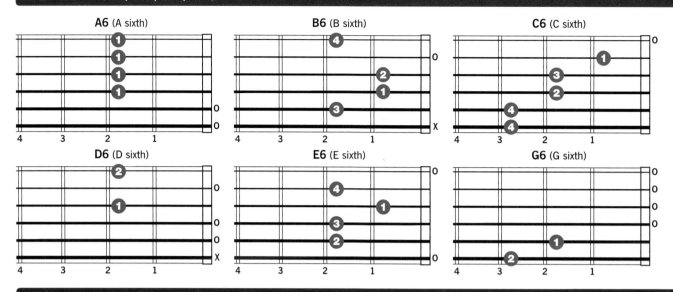

Minor sixth chords (1st, ♭3rd, 5th, 6th)

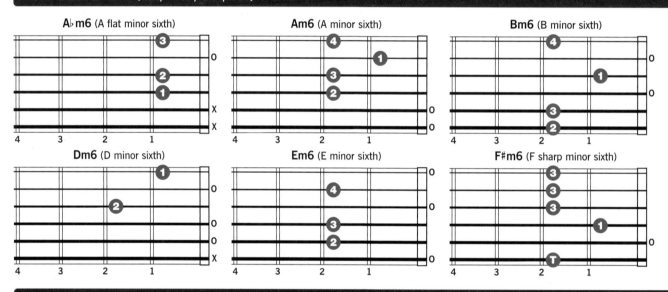

Ninth chords (1st, 3rd, 5th, ♭7th, 9th)

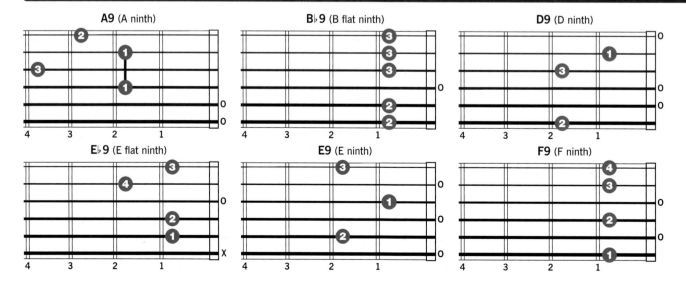

Minor ninth chords (1st, ♭3rd, 5th, ♭7th, 9th)

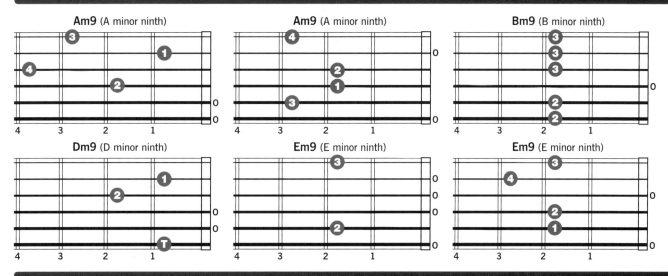

Am9 (A minor ninth) Am9 (A minor ninth) Bm9 (B minor ninth)
Dm9 (D minor ninth) Em9 (E minor ninth) Em9 (E minor ninth)

Major ninth chords (1st, 3rd, 5th, 7th, 9th)

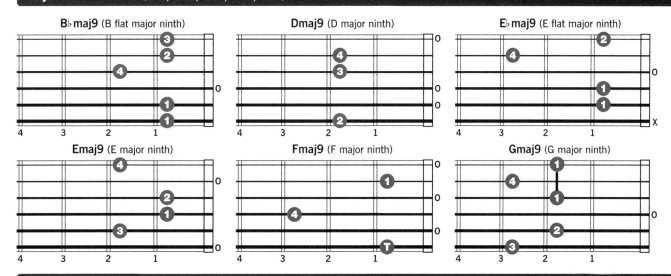

B♭maj9 (B flat major ninth) Dmaj9 (D major ninth) E♭maj9 (E flat major ninth)
Emaj9 (E major ninth) Fmaj9 (F major ninth) Gmaj9 (G major ninth)

Eleventh chords (1st, 3rd, 5th, ♭7th, 9th, 11th)

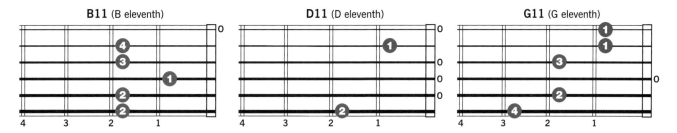

B11 (B eleventh) D11 (D eleventh) G11 (G eleventh)

Thirteenth chords (1st, 3rd, 5th, ♭7th, 9th, 11th, 13th)

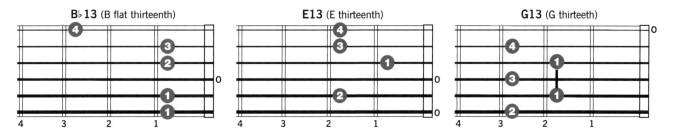

B♭13 (B flat thirteenth) E13 (E thirteenth) G13 (G thirteeth)

Suspended fourth chords (1st, 4th, 5th)

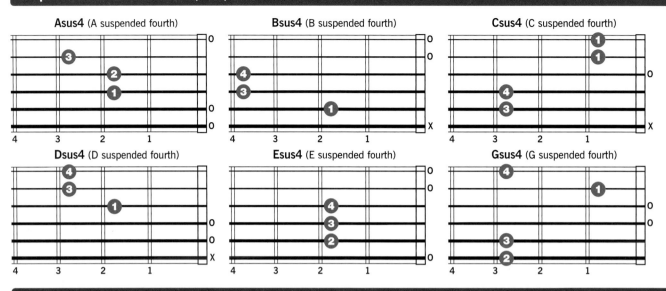

Asus4 (A suspended fourth)

Bsus4 (B suspended fourth)

Csus4 (C suspended fourth)

Dsus4 (D suspended fourth)

Esus4 (E suspended fourth)

Gsus4 (G suspended fourth)

Seventh suspended fourth chords (1st, 4th, 5th, ♭7th)

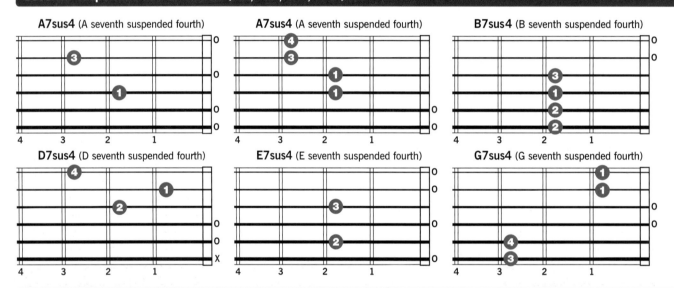

A7sus4 (A seventh suspended fourth)

A7sus4 (A seventh suspended fourth)

B7sus4 (B seventh suspended fourth)

D7sus4 (D seventh suspended fourth)

E7sus4 (E seventh suspended fourth)

G7sus4 (G seventh suspended fourth)

Added ninth chords (1st, 3rd, 5th, 9th)

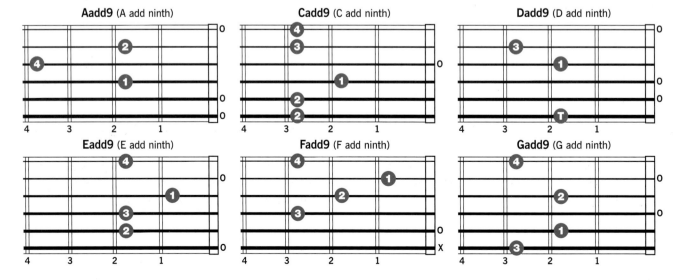

Aadd9 (A add ninth)

Cadd9 (C add ninth)

Dadd9 (D add ninth)

Eadd9 (E add ninth)

Fadd9 (F add ninth)

Gadd9 (G add ninth)

Sixth/Ninth chords (1st, 3rd, 5th, 6th, 9th)

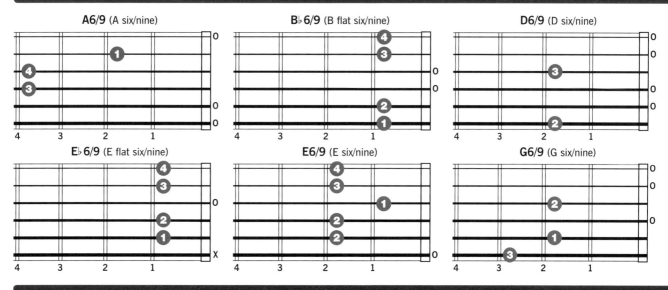

A6/9 (A six/nine)   B♭6/9 (B flat six/nine)   D6/9 (D six/nine)

E♭6/9 (E flat six/nine)   E6/9 (E six/nine)   G6/9 (G six/nine)

Augmented chords (1st, 3rd, #5th)

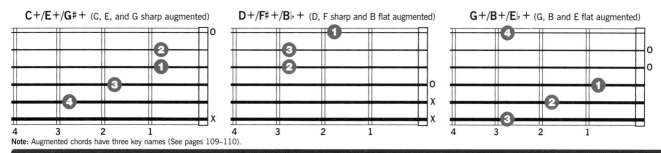

C+/E+/G#+ (C, E, and G sharp augmented)   D+/F#+/B♭+ (D, F sharp and B flat augmented)   G+/B+/E♭+ (G, B and E flat augmented)

Note: Augmented chords have three key names (See pages 109–110).

Diminished chords (1st, ♭3rd, ♭5th ♭♭7th)

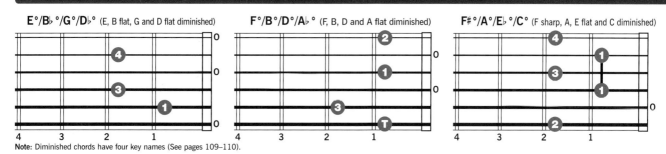

E°/B♭°/G°/D♭° (E, B flat, G and D flat diminished)   F°/B°/D°/A♭° (F, B, D and A flat diminished)   F#°/A°/E♭°/C° (F sharp, A, E flat and C diminished)

Note: Diminished chords have four key names (See pages 109–110).

This covers all the essential open chords and quite a few more. It will be recognised that I have, for each chord shape, included the maximum number of notes conveniently playable for that particular chord. But this doesn't necessarily mean that each note has to be included on all occasions. Sometimes it will be preferable to play a four- or five-string version of a chord instead of the full six-string option. More on this subject can be found on **pages 39–40**, and also by referring to the very comprehensive chord construction information in Chapter 6.

All fingerings shown (with regard to which finger holds down which particular string) are those generally found to be convenient for reasons of comfort and practicability. However, if you find an alternative that suits you better, that's perfectly all right too. This is one of those things which you'll adapt to naturally in the course of time and experience, and will, to some extent, depend upon which chord you've just played and which chord you're about to play next. As long as you manage to form the correct chord shape, efficiently and quickly, it's entirely acceptable to vary the fingering according to personal preference.

Moveable chords

Moveable chords are broadly referred to as 'bar chords', due to the preponderance of such chord types in this category. However, the fact is that any chord shape which doesn't include open strings is also equally versatile, in that it can be used at any position on the guitar neck, creating a new chord of its particular type (ie major, minor etc) at each fret position. And, precisely because these chord shapes can be applied at any position on the guitar neck, the moveable chord diagrams are illustrated without any specific fret numbers, each one instead having a red 'name' note to identify its pitch.

In addition to the information on **page 231**, which should be referred to in connection with this section, it's worth remembering that where chords are concerned there are often alternatives and variations that can sometimes be useful to know about. I've tried to include any such options that I would consider to be worthwhile,

such as the two alternate ways of fingering the first major chord shown, or the 'black' note, indicating a chord note that's entirely valid but often omitted, due to either difficulty of fingering or simply because the chord usually sounds better without that particular note being included. An immediately obvious example is the major chord shown below, where the 'black note' on the sixth string (the third chord tone) is usually omitted, because most players prefer the sound created when the fifth string note (root note) is lowest.

It's a fact that certain chord shapes are more widely used than others of their type. These more 'popular' versions are the first few illustrated in each category. Most likely they'll be the ones you'll be inclined to learn first, but each particular chord shape will have its own sound characteristics, and all versions will be useful to know about at some point in time.

Major chords (1st, 3rd, 5th)

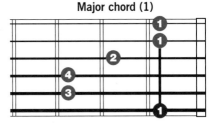

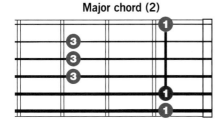

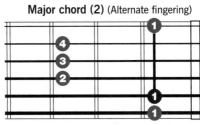

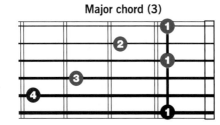

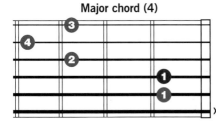

Seventh chords (1st, 3rd, 5th, ♭7th)

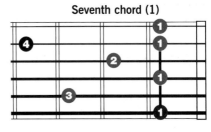

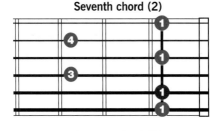

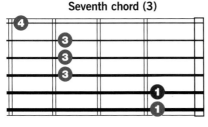

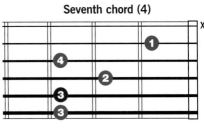

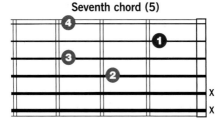

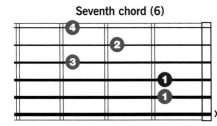

Minor chords (1st, ♭3rd, 5th)

Minor chord (1)
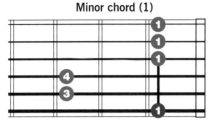

Minor chord (1) (alternative fingering)
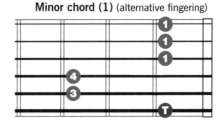

Minor chord (2)
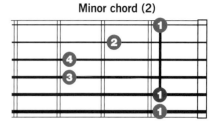

Minor chord (3)
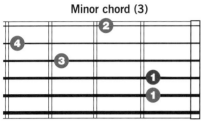

Minor chord (4)
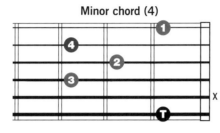

Minor chord (5)
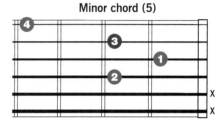

Minor seventh chords (1st, ♭3rd, 5th, ♭7rd)

Minor seventh chord (1)
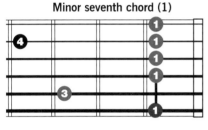

Minor seventh chord (2)
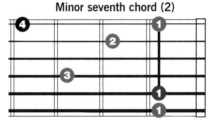

Minor seventh chord (3)
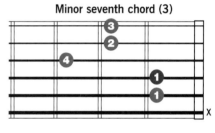

Minor seventh chord (4)
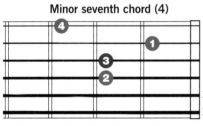

Minor seventh chord (5)
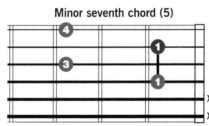

Minor seventh chord (6)
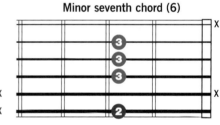

Major seventh chords (1st, 3rd, 5th, 7th)

Major seventh chord (1)
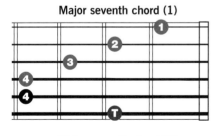

Major seventh chord (2)
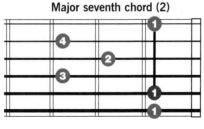

Major seventh chord (3)
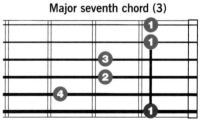

Major seventh chord (4)
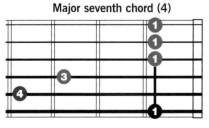

Major seventh chord (5)
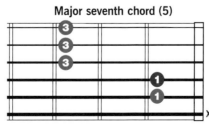

Major seventh chord (6)
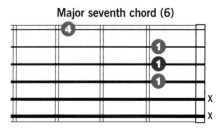

Minor/major seventh chords (1st, ♭3rd, 5th, 7th)

A variation on the basic minor seventh in that the 7th note is 'natural', or not flat. Written, for example; Amin/maj7

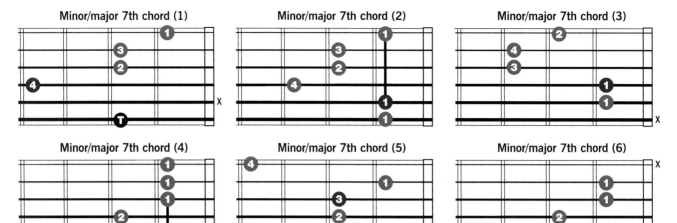

Minor/major 7th chord (1) Minor/major 7th chord (2) Minor/major 7th chord (3)

Minor/major 7th chord (4) Minor/major 7th chord (5) Minor/major 7th chord (6)

Sixth chords (1st, 3rd, 5th, 6th)

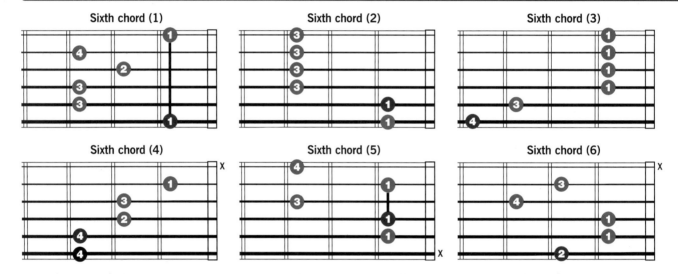

Sixth chord (1) Sixth chord (2) Sixth chord (3)

Sixth chord (4) Sixth chord (5) Sixth chord (6)

Minor sixth chords (1st, ♭3rd, 5th, 6th)

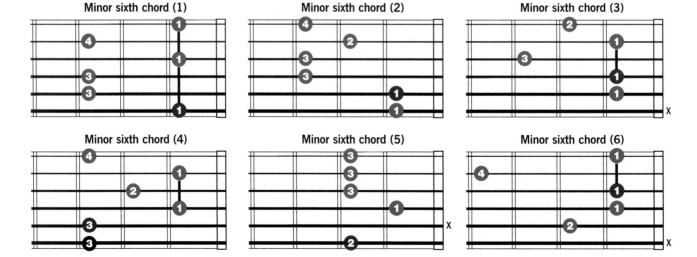

Minor sixth chord (1) Minor sixth chord (2) Minor sixth chord (3)

Minor sixth chord (4) Minor sixth chord (5) Minor sixth chord (6)

Ninth chords (1st, 3rd, 5th, ♭7th, 9th)

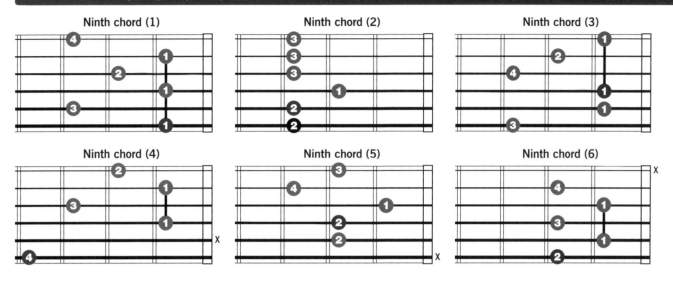

Ninth chord (1) Ninth chord (2) Ninth chord (3)

Ninth chord (4) Ninth chord (5) Ninth chord (6)

Minor ninth chords (1st, ♭3rd, 5th, ♭7rd, 9th)

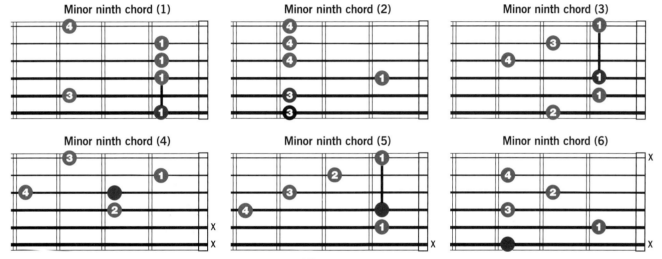

Minor ninth chord (1) Minor ninth chord (2) Minor ninth chord (3)

Minor ninth chord (4) Minor ninth chord (5) Minor ninth chord (6)

Note: Some of the more complex chords may not contain the 'root' (name) note (page 227). Where applicable, this note (although not played) is indicated in red, but without a fingering number.

Major ninth chords (1st, 3rd, 5th, 7th, 9th)   This varies from the basic 'ninth' chord, in that the 7th is not flatted. Written, for example; Amaj9 or A 9.

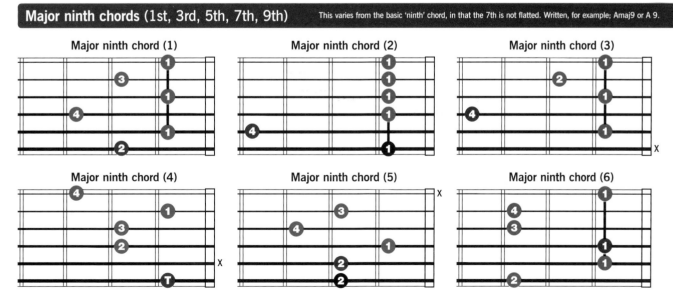

Major ninth chord (1) Major ninth chord (2) Major ninth chord (3)

Major ninth chord (4) Major ninth chord (5) Major ninth chord (6)

Eleventh chords (1st, 3rd, 5th, ♭7th, 9th, 11th)

Eleventh chord (1)
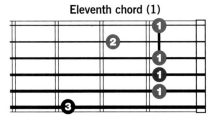

Eleventh chord (2)
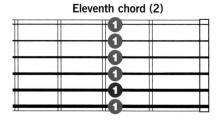

Eleventh chord (3)
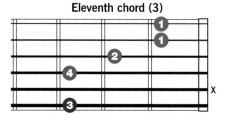

Eleventh chord (4)
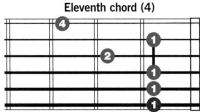

Eleventh chord (5)
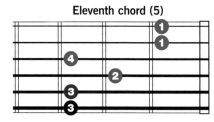

Eleventh chord (6)
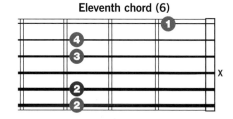

Minor eleventh chords (1st, ♭3rd, 5th, ♭7th, 9th, 11th)

Minor eleventh chord (1)
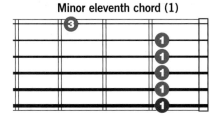

Minor eleventh chord (2)
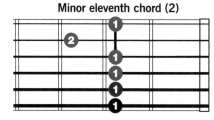

Minor eleventh chord (3)
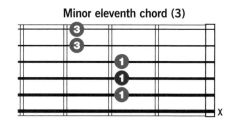

Thirteenth chords (1st, 3rd, 5th, ♭7th, 9th, 11th, 13th)

Thirteenth chord (1)
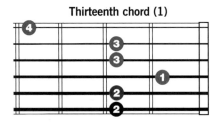

Thirteenth chord (2)
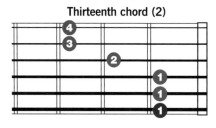

Thirteenth chord (3)
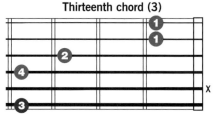

Thirteenth chord (4)
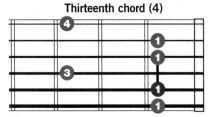

Thirteenth chord (5)
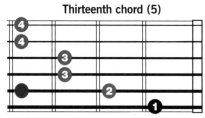

Thirteenth chord (6)
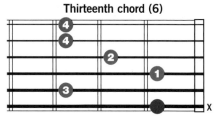

Minor thirteenth chords (1st, ♭3rd, 5th, ♭7th, 9th, 11th, 13th)

Minor thirteenth chord (1)
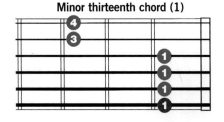

Minor thirteenth chord (2)
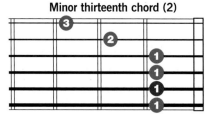

Minor thirteenth chord (3)
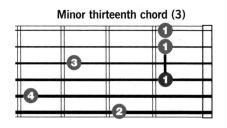

Major thirteenth chords (1st, 3rd, 5th, 7th, 9th, 11th, 13th)

A variation on the usual thirteenth chord, in that the seventh is not flatted. Written example Amaj13 or A△13.

Major thirteenth chord (1)
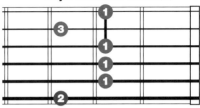

Major thirteenth chord (2)
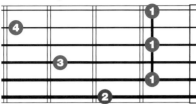

Major thirteenth chord (3)
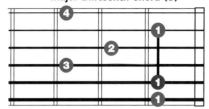

Major thirteenth chord (4)
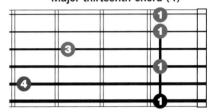

Major thirteenth chord (5)
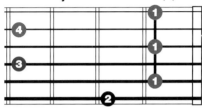

Major thirteenth chord (6)
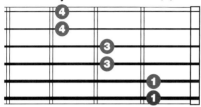

Suspended fourth chords (1st, 4th, 5th)

Suspended fourth chord (1)
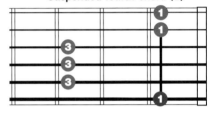

Suspended fourth chord (2)
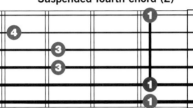

Suspended fourth chord (2) alternative fingering

Suspended fourth chord (3)
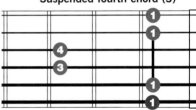

Suspended fourth chord (4)
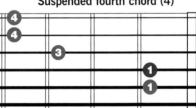

Suspended fourth chord (5)
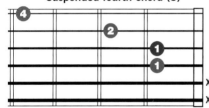

Seventh suspended fourth chords (1st, 4th, 5th, ♭7th)

Seventh sus4 chord (1)
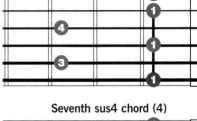

Seventh sus4 chord (2)
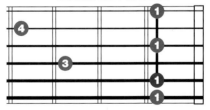

Seventh sus4 chord (3)
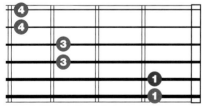

Seventh sus4 chord (4)

Seventh sus4 chord (5)
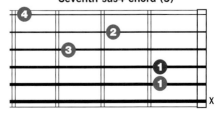

Seventh sus4 chord (6)

Suspended second chords (1st, 2nd, 5th)

Suspended 2nd chord (1)
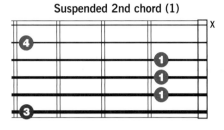

Suspended 2nd chord (2)

Suspended 2nd chord (3)
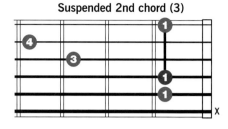

Suspended 2nd chord (4)

Suspended 2nd chord (5)

Suspended 2nd chord (6)
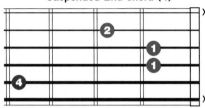
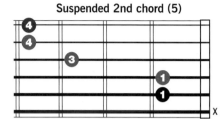
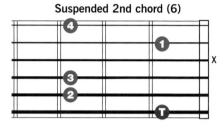

Added ninth chords (1st, 3rd, 5th, 9th)

Added ninth chord (1)

Added ninth chord (2)

Added ninth chord (3)
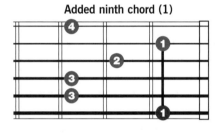
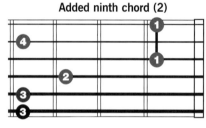
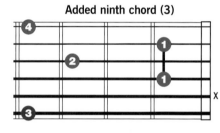

Added ninth chord (4)

Added ninth chord (5)

Added ninth chord (6)
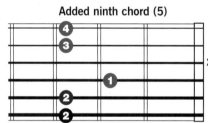
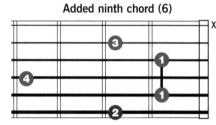

Minor added ninth chords (1st, ♭3rd, 5th, 9th)
The usual basics of a minor chord with the addition of a ninth. Written example Am add9 or Am/9

Minor add9 chord (1)

Minor add9 chord (2)

Minor add9 chord (3)
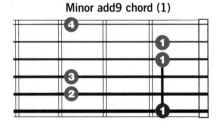
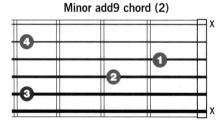
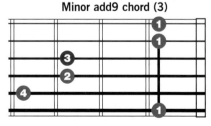

Minor add9 chord (4)

Minor add9 chord (5)

Minor add9 chord (6)

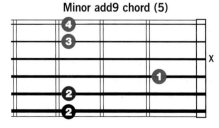
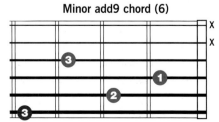

Sixth/Ninth chords (1st, 3rd, 5th, 6th, 9th)

A sixth chord with the ninth added. Written, for example as; A6/9

Six/Nine chord (1)
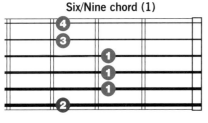

Six/Nine chord (2)
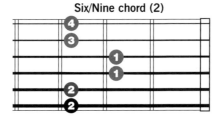

Six/Nine chord (3)
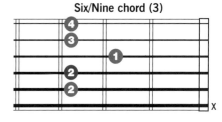

Six/Nine chord (3) Variation with additional note
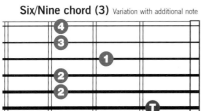

Six/Nine chord (4)
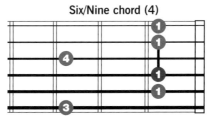

Six/Nine chord (5)
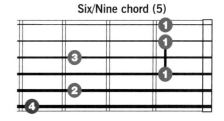

Minor sixth/ninth chords (1st, ♭3rd, 5th, 6th, 9th)

Minor chord version of the above. Written example; Am6/9

Minor six/nine chord (1)
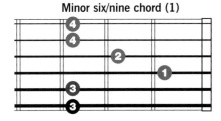

Minor six/nine chord (2)
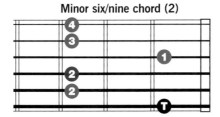

Minor six/nine chord (3)
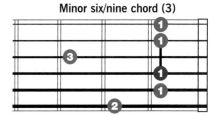

Augmented chords (1st, 3rd, #5th)

Augmented chord (1)
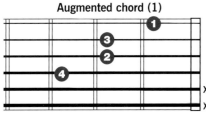

Augmented chord (2)
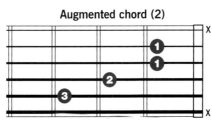

Augmented chord (3)
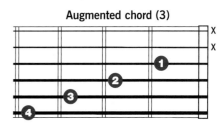

Note: Augmented chords have three key names (see pages 109–110).

Seventh augmented chords (1st, 3rd, #5th, ♭7th)

The basic augmented as above, but with the addition of the flatted seventh. Written, for example; A7aug or A7+

Seventh aug chord (1)
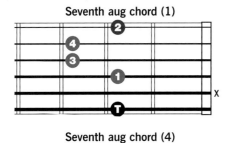

Seventh aug chord (2)

Seventh aug chord (3)
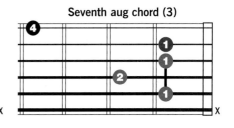

Seventh aug chord (4)

Seventh aug chord (5)
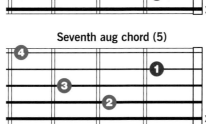

Seventh aug chord (5)
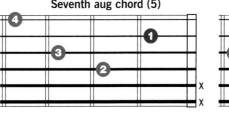

Minor seventh augmented fifth chords (1st, ♭3rd, #5th, ♭7th)

The minor seventh chord, with the fifth raised by one semitone. Written example; Am7+5 or Am7#5

Minor 7th aug 5th chord (1)
Minor 7th aug 5th chord (2)
Minor 7th aug 5th chord (3)

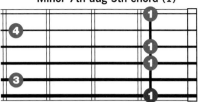

Major seventh augmented fifth chords (1st, 3rd, #5th, 7th)

A major seventh with the fifth being raised by one semitone. Written, for example; Amaj7+5 or A 7+5

Major 7th aug 5th chord (1)
Major 7th aug 5th chord (2)
Major 7th aug 5th chord (3)

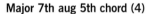

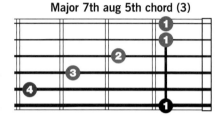

Major 7th aug 5th chord (4)
Major 7th aug 5th chord (5)
Major 7th aug 5th chord (6)

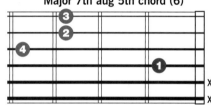

Diminished chords (1st, ♭3rd, ♭5th, ♭♭7th)

Technically a diminished seventh chord. See page 91. Written, for example; Adim or A°

Diminished chord (1)
Diminished chord (2)
Diminished chord (3)

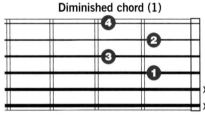
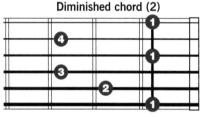
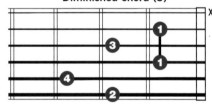

Note: Diminished chords have four key names (see pages 109–110)

Diminished fifth chords (1st, 3rd, ♭5th)

The basics of a major chord, but with the 5th being 'diminished', or lowered by one semitone. Written, for example; A-5

Diminished fifth chord (1)
Diminished fifth chord (2)
Diminished fifth chord (3)

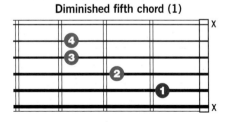
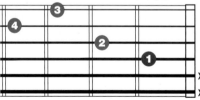

Diminished fifth chord (4)
Diminished fifth chord (5)
Diminished fifth chord (6)

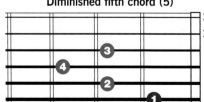

Seventh diminished fifth chords (1st, 3rd, ♭5th, ♭7th)

A variation on the previous chord, having the addition of a flatted seventh. Written, for example; A7-5 or A7♭5

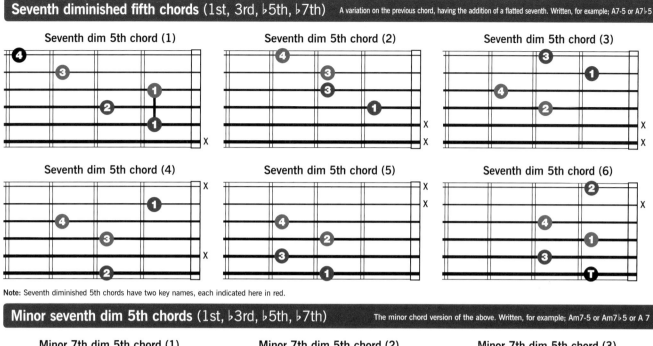

Seventh dim 5th chord (1)

Seventh dim 5th chord (2)

Seventh dim 5th chord (3)

Seventh dim 5th chord (4)

Seventh dim 5th chord (5)

Seventh dim 5th chord (6)

Note: Seventh diminished 5th chords have two key names, each indicated here in red.

Minor seventh dim 5th chords (1st, ♭3rd, ♭5th, ♭7th)

The minor chord version of the above. Written, for example; Am7-5 or Am7♭5 or A 7

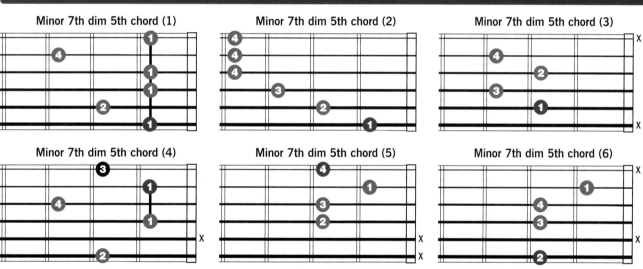

Minor 7th dim 5th chord (1)

Minor 7th dim 5th chord (2)

Minor 7th dim 5th chord (3)

Minor 7th dim 5th chord (4)

Minor 7th dim 5th chord (5)

Minor 7th dim 5th chord (6)

Major seventh diminished fifth chords (1st, 3rd, ♭5th, 7th)

This varies from the above, in that the seventh is 'natural', or not flatted. Written example; Amaj7-5 or A△7-5

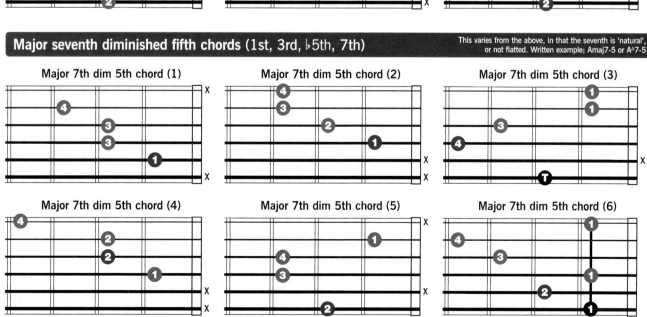

Major 7th dim 5th chord (1)

Major 7th dim 5th chord (2)

Major 7th dim 5th chord (3)

Major 7th dim 5th chord (4)

Major 7th dim 5th chord (5)

Major 7th dim 5th chord (6)

Additional chords

The range of chord types covered so far is, quite frankly, considerably greater than most players are likely to require, or indeed even be aware of. The obvious exception to this, of course, is jazz music, which places high demands upon a guitarist's knowledge of chords, and musicianship in general. And if this should be your particular area of interest, it really is essential that you have a firm understanding of harmony and chord construction. So if you have, for any reason, skipped somewhat too casually over Chapter 6 of this book, I strongly suggest that you reconsider your cavalier approach and go back over it without further delay.

Those of you who've been rather more diligent will be aware that as chord names and types become ever more complex we enter an area where various chords can somewhat overlap with each other, to the point where a chord with a long sophisticated name might actually contain the same notes as a far simpler-sounding chord with which you may already be familiar. This curious phenomenon of 'chord synonyms' has already been

explained in some detail (see **page 126**), and with several examples, and as you peruse this chord dictionary you might have noticed a few others which fit into that category, such as (for example) **Gsu4** containing the same notes as the less frequently encountered **C2** chord; or the fact that a straightforward **Fadd9** chord has the same four notes as the more elaborately named **Am7#5**. None of this apparently peculiar chord logic need present any confusion; it's just something to be aware of, as you'll encounter it from time to time.

It's perfectly feasible, and occasionally essential, that you may create your own chord shapes for a particular type of chord. This isn't at all difficult once you've acquired sufficient knowledge of chord construction, in which regard I refer you once again to Chapter 6. However, in order to be as comprehensive as possible, and provide you with a quick reference, I'll continue this chord dictionary with a range of those chords which are generally less familiar to guitarists, but which may nevertheless be required on occasion.

Ninth augmented fifth chords (1st, 3rd, #5th, ♭7th, 9th)   Ninth chord with an augmented or sharpened fifth. Written example; A9#5 or A9+5

Ninth aug 5th chord (1)

Ninth aug 5th chord (2)

Ninth aug 5th chord (3)

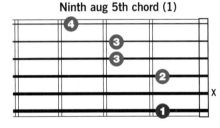
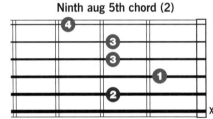
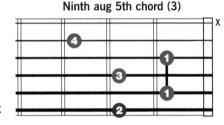

Ninth diminished fifth chords (1st, 3rd, ♭5th, ♭7th, 9th)   Ninth chord with a diminished or flatted fifth. Written example; A9♭5 or A9-5

Ninth dim 5th chord (1)

Ninth dim 5th chord (2)

Ninth dim 5th chord (3)

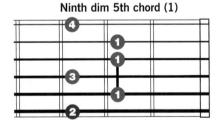
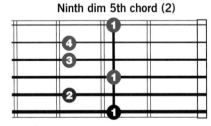
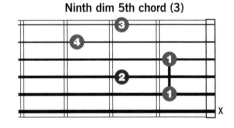

Minor ninth dim fifth chords (1st, ♭3rd, ♭5th, ♭7th, 9th)   Minor ninth chord with a flatted or 'diminished' fifth. Written example; Am9-5 or Am9♭5

Minor 9th dim 5th chord (1)

Minor 9th dim 5th chord (2)

Minor 9th dim 5th chord (3)

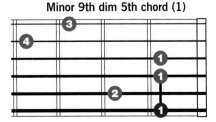
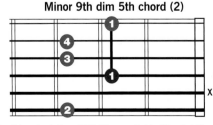
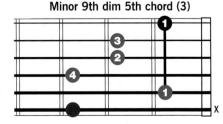

Note: Some of the more complex chords may not contain the 'root' (name) note (page 127). Where applicable, this note (although not played) is indicated in red, but without a fingering number.

Seventh augmented ninth chords (1st, 3rd, 5th, ♭7th, #9th)

Variation upon the ninth chord, whereby the ninth is sharpened or augmented. Written as, for example; A7+9 or A7#9

Seventh aug ninth chord (1)

Seventh aug ninth chord (2)

Seventh aug ninth chord (3)

Seventh diminished ninth chords (1st, 3rd, 5th, ♭7th, ♭9th)

The ninth in this case is flatted or diminished. Written example; A7-9 or A7♭9

Seventh dim ninth chord (1)
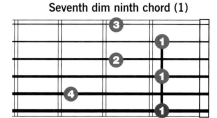

Seventh dim ninth chord (2)

Seventh dim ninth chord (3)
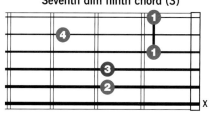

Minor seventh dim ninth chords (1st, ♭3rd, 5th, ♭7th, ♭9th)

Minor seventh with a flatted or 'diminished' ninth. Written as, for example; Am7-9 or Am7♭9

Minor 7th dim 9th chord (1)
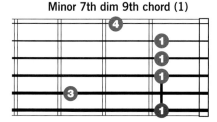

Minor 7th dim 9th chord (2)
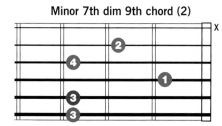

Minor 7th dim 9th chord (3)
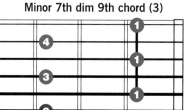

Seventh aug fifth aug ninth chords (1st, 3rd, #5th, ♭7th, #9th)

Seventh chord with a sharpened fifth and a sharpened ninth. Written as, for example; A7#5#9 or A7+5+9

7th aug 5th aug 9th chord (1)
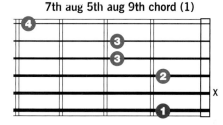

7th aug 5th aug 9th chord (2)
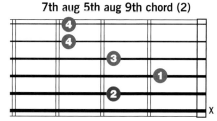

7th aug 5th aug 9th chord (3)
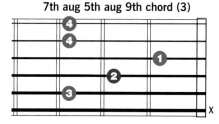

Seventh dim 5th dim 9th chords (1st, 3rd, ♭5th, ♭7th, ♭9th)

In this chord both the fifth and the ninth are diminished, or played one semitone flat. Written as, for example; A7-5-9 or A7♭5♭9

7th dim 5th dim 9th chord (1)

7th dim 5th dim 9th chord (2)
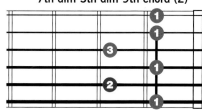

7th dim 5th dim 9th chord (3)

Seventh aug 5th dim 9th chords (1st, 3rd, #5th, ♭7th, ♭9th)

Seventh chord with an augmented or sharpened fifth, and a diminished or flatted ninth. Written example; A7+5-9 or A7#5♭9

7th aug 5th dim 9th chord (1)
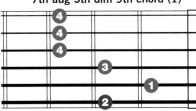

7th aug 5th dim 9th chord (2)

7th aug 5th dim 9th chord (3)
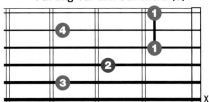

Seventh dim 5th aug 9th chords (1st, 3rd, ♭5th, ♭7th, #9th)

The reverse situation to the above. A seventh chord with a flatted fifth and a sharpened ninth. Written example; A7-5+9 or A7♭5#9

7th dim 5th aug 9th chords (1)
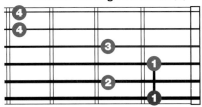

7th dim 5th aug 9th chords (2)
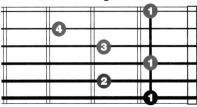

7th dim 5th aug 9th chords (3)
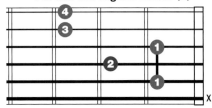

Seventh eleventh chords (1st, 3rd, 5th, ♭7th, 11th)

Different from a standard eleventh chord in that it contains no ninth. Written example; A7/11 or A7 add11

Seven eleven chord (1)
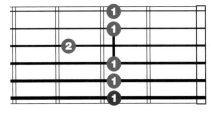

Seven eleven chord (2)

Seven eleven chord (3)
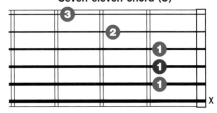

Minor seventh eleventh chords (1st, ♭3rd, 5th, ♭7th, 11th)

Minor chord version of the above. A minor seventh with an added eleventh. Written example as; Am7/11 or Am7 add11

Minor seven eleven chord (1)
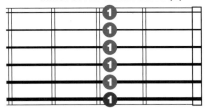

Minor seven eleven chord (2)
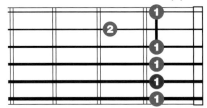

Minor seven eleven chord (3)

Major 7th aug eleventh chords (1st, 3rd, 5th, 7th, #11th)

Major seventh chord with the addition of an augmented 11th. Written as, Amaj7+11 or A△7#11

Major 7th aug 11th chord (1)
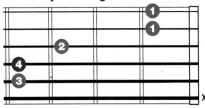

Major 7th aug 11th chord (2)

Major 7th aug 11th chord (3)

Ninth aug eleventh chords (1st, 3rd, 5th, ♭7th, 9th #11th)

A variation upon the standard eleventh chord, that note being augmented or sharp. Written as A9+11 or A9#11

Ninth aug eleventh chord (1)

Ninth aug eleventh chord (2)

Ninth aug eleventh chord (3)

Major ninth aug eleventh chords (1st, 3rd, 5th, 7th, 9th, #11th)

Written, for example, as Amaj9+11 or A△9#11

Major ninth aug 11 chord (1)
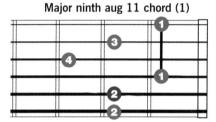

Major ninth aug 11 chord (2)
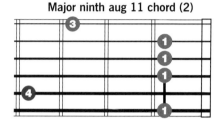

Major ninth aug 11 chord (3)

Thirteenth aug 9th chords (1st, 3rd, 5th, ♭7th, #9th, 11th, 13th)

Written example; A13+9 or A13#9

Thirteenth aug 9th chord (1)
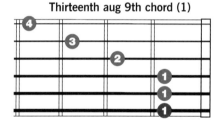

Thirteenth aug 9th chord (2)
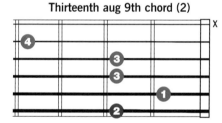

Thirteenth aug 9th chord (3)
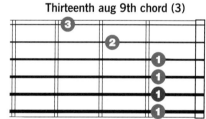

Thirteenth dim 9th chords (1st, 3rd, 5th, ♭7th, ♭9th, 11th, 13th)

Written example; A13-9 or A13♭9

Thirteenth dim 9th chords (1)
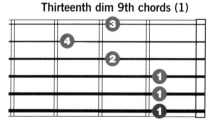

Thirteenth dim 9th chords (2)
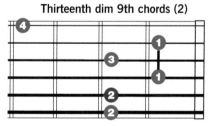

Thirteenth dim 9th chords (3)
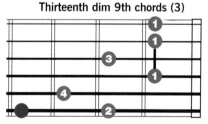

Note: Some of the more complex chords may not contain the 'root' (name) note (page 127). Where applicable, this note (although not played) is indicated in red, but without a fingering number.

Thirteenth aug 11th chords (1st, 3rd, 5th, ♭7th, 9th, #11th, 13th)

Written example; A13+11 or A13△#11

Thirteenth aug 11th chords (1)

Thirteenth aug 11th chords (2)
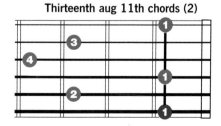

Thirteenth aug 11th chords (3)
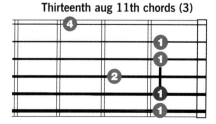

Index